C000075828

## Stop Press
==========
The lead times involved in producing a book of this ......  ...
necessarily quite long, and given the intention to publish soon after the
birth of the open gilt repo market on 2 January 1996 it has not been
possible to include developments occuring in late 1995, of which the 1995
Budget changes are the most significant. Accordingly we are providing
this insert listing the most recent developments and bringing the reader
up to date to 31 December 1995.

## Taxation of Gilts and Bonds (see Chapter 10).
====================================================

(1) In the Budget of 30 November 1995 the Chancellor of the Exchequer,
Kenneth Clarke, announced the abandonment of the attempt to bring larger
personal investors into the new (1996) tax regime, stating that all
private individuals and trusts, irrespective of the size of their
aggregated holdings of gilts and bonds, would continue to be taxed under
the existing rules (subject to some simplifications). This means that all
references in this book to the £200,000 aggregate nominal threshold and
to the tax treatment of investors above this threshold are now redundant.

(2) The 1995 Budget also assigned to the wastepaper basket the previous
Deep Discount, Deep Gain and Qualifying Indexed Securities legislation
relevant to private investors replacing it with a single set of rules for
what are now classified as "Discounted Securities". These are broadly
defined as securities issued at a discount to their redemption value of
more than 1/2% times the number of years to redemption, or if the term to
redemption is greater than 30 years, 15%. Discounted Securities however
specifically exclude, shares in a company, unstripped gilts, and two
newly defined categories, Excluded Convertible Securities and Excluded
Indexed Securities (both of which will fall into the capital gains tax
regime). The tax treatment of Discounted Securities is to treat realised
profits from the discount on such a security as chargeable to income tax
in the tax year in which disposal occurs.

(3) The 1995 Budget proposals also differed from those outlined in the
Inland Revenue's 10 July 1995 Press Release in respect of the tax
treatment of Gilts and Bonds held by Unit Trusts. The July proposals drew
a distinction between "authorised unit trusts dedicated to gilt and bond
investment" and "other (general) authorised unit trusts". The former
category were to be excluded from the new rules (though movements in the
value of such units were to be treated as if the units were bonds), but
the latter were to be subject to the new regime. However the 1995 Budget
Press release states that "Authorised unit trusts (without
differentiation) will remain subject to, essentially, the current rules,
so far as their own tax liabilities are concerned", and reiterates that
the tax position of private investors in unit trusts will be unaltered.
However where an authorised unit trust has more than 60% of its assets in
interest bearing assets, corporate holdings will effectively be taxed
under the new regime as if they were bonds.

The above changes have been incorporated into a revised Gilt and Bond tax
matrix distributed herewith, and which, it is suggested, should be
appended to the inside back cover pages of the book.

## Gilt-Edged Dividend Entitlement
==================================
The London Stock Exchange has also seen fit to instigate a change in the
criterion for establishing the entitlement for gilt-edged dividends. This
has been necessitated by the advent of the open gilt repo market and the
need for market practice regarding forward gilt bargains to harmonise
with other markets internationally. Up to the end of 1995 the dividend
status of a gilt was ex-dividend if the trade date concerned was on or
after the relevant ex-dividend date. From 2 January 1996 onwards a gilt
trade will be considered as ex-dividend if the SETTLEMENT DATE IS AFTER
THE EX-DIVIDEND DATE. Whilst this will make no difference to run of the
mill gilt-edged  bargains transacted for next business day settlement, it
will affect dividend entitlements for forward bargains spanning ex-
dividend dates.

# THE MERRILL LYNCH GUIDE TO THE GILT-EDGED AND STERLING BOND MARKET

**By the same author:**

*Inside the Gilt-Edged Market*, Woodhead-Faulkner Ltd, 1984

*Inside the New Gilt-Edged Market*, Woodhead-Faulkner Ltd, 1986

# THE MERRILL LYNCH GUIDE TO THE GILT-EDGED AND STERLING BOND MARKET

Patrick Phillips

The Book Guild Ltd
Sussex, England

The Book Guild Ltd.
25 High Street,
Lewes, Sussex

First published 1996
Copyright 1996 Merrill Lynch Gilts Limited, member of The Securities and Futures Authority Limited. The information herein was obtained from various sources; we do not guarantee its accuracy. Additional information available.

Set in Times
Typesetting by Poole Typesetting (Wessex) Ltd., Bournemouth

Printed in Great Britain by
Bookcraft (Bath) Ltd

A catalogue record for this book is
available from the British Library

ISBN 1 85776 070 0

# CONTENTS

**1    The origins of the gilt-edged market**                                        1
*1694-97, South Sea Bubble, Bank Charter Act, Consols, Goschen's Conversion, War Loan Conversion 1932, the post-war years, National Debt/PSBR/GDP 1945-94*

**2    The economic background to the gilt-edged market**                    9
*Inflation, monetary policy, fiscal policy, funding policy and the PSBR*

**3    The players in the game and the role of the 'authorities'**          34
*GEMMs, IDBs, SEMBs and the repo market, broker/dealers, role of the Bank of England, banks, discount houses, building societies, insurance companies, pension funds, international funds, retail gilt market, National Savings Stock Register*

**4    The fundamental characteristics of gilt-edged securities**          56
*Coupon rate, redemption, price conventions, accrued interest, partly paid stocks, ex-dividend status, special ex-dividend*

**5    The mathematics of the gilt-edged market**                              68
*Flat yield, redemption yield, compound interest theory, present value equations, accumulated returns, duration, convexity, performance yields, portfolio yields*

**6    Analytical methods for use with conventional gilt-edged securities**    100
*Price ratios, yield differences, weighted switches, balanced switches, switch profit projections, performance indices, balance-of-term yields, yield curve analysis, price model analysis*

**7    Index-linked gilts**                                                      138
*Origins of index-linked gilts, method of indexation, retail price index, money yields, real yields, discontinuities, evaluation of index-linked securities*

**8  Other non-conventional gilt-edged bonds**  154
*Convertible gilts, variable rate stocks, floating rate stocks*

**9  Gilt-edged futures and options**  162
*LIFFE, long gilt future, hedging operations, cash-and-carry operations and implied repo rates, short sterling interest rate future, options on gilt futures, negotiated options, volatility, option pricing theory and models*

**10  Taxation of gilt-edged securities and associated instruments**  192
*The change in the taxation of gilts and bonds announced in 1995, implications of the creation of an open gilt repo market, history of previous tax regimes, tax changes of 1986, accrued income scheme, withholding tax, FOTRA status, deep discount securities*

**11  Gilt-edged indices and performance measurement**  203
*FT Government Securities index, FT-Actuaries fixed interest price indices, calculation of performance yardsticks, internal rates of return, time-weighted rates of return, FT-Actuaries fixed interest yield indices*

**12  Gilt-edged settlement**  215
*Basic settlement arrangements, contingent bargains, role of the Central Gilt Office, settlement procedures and time deadlines, market maker settlement, investor settlement, stock registration*

**13  The sterling bond market**  226
*An historical overview of UK non-gilt fixed interest markets*

**14  Debentures and loan stocks**  232
*Status and security, dealing arrangements, price conventions, accrued interest, ex-dividend arrangements, settlement, custody, new issue procedures, evaluation criteria, taxation, covenants*

**15  Eurosterling bonds**  247
*Status and security, form and denomination, dealing arrangements, price conventions, accrued interest, ex-dividend arrangements, settlement, custody, new issue procedures, evaluation criteria, taxation*

**16  Bulldog bonds**  256
*Status and security, form and denomination, dealing arrangements, price conventions, accrued interest, ex-dividend arrangements, settlement, custody, new issue procedures, evaluation criteria, taxation*

**17  Preference shares** 268

*Net dividends, franked income, status of preference shares, dealing arrangements, price conventions, ex-dividend arrangements, settlement, new issue procedures, evaluation criteria, taxation*

**18  Permanent interest bearing shares (PIBS)** 278

*Origins of PIBS, status and security, dealing arrangements, price conventions, ex-dividend arrangements, settlement, new issue procedures, evaluation criteria, taxation.*

**Appendices** 287

*Sample prospectuses of various types of gilts, conventional, variable rate, floating rate, convertible, and index-linked*

# FOREWORD

Everyone with an interest in the working of the gilt-edged market will welcome the publication of Patrick Phillips' latest work, The Merrill Lynch Guide to the Gilt-Edged and Sterling Bond Markets.

Any work such as this which increases public knowledge of the gilt-edged market is always valuable. This book is especially well-timed, coming during a period of considerable market innovation. The start of open gilt repo trading and reform of the UK taxation of gilts and bonds mean that it is particularly timely to have a significant work of reference. As the Government Broker, with responsibility at the Bank of England for the government's borrowing operations, I greatly value the contribution this comprehensive and up-to-date book will make to better understanding of the way the market functions.

Additionally, I welcome the expansion of the book to cover the wider sterling bond markets, which form an increasingly important part of the overall United Kingdom securities market. Access to appropriate capital markets is essential for the successful development of UK companies and this book should promote a wider understanding of the various instruments, with beneficial results for both borrowers and investors.

Ian Plenderleith
Executive Director
Bank of England

# ACKNOWLEDGEMENTS

I would like to express my deepest thanks to everybody who has helped and encouraged me in writing, or perhaps I should say rewriting, this book – in particular Stephen Rumsey and the Merrill Lynch Gilts Ltd team in London. Stephen especially, because it was his idea that I should revisit my previous work on the Gilt-Edged market (*Inside the Gilt-Edged Market*, published by Woodhead Faulkner Ltd (1984) and *Inside the New Gilt-Edged Market* from the same publisher at the time of Big Bang in 1986) and update it to take into account all the changes that have occured in the intervening nine years, in particular those associated with the advent of the gilt repo market and the tax changes due to come into effect in April 1996. It was also his idea to expand the book's coverage to include the non-gilt sterling bond markets and I must give special thanks to Tony Moverley and John Holder for all the assistance they gave me in that area.

My thanks are also due to Carol Biss, Janet Wrench and the rest of the team at The Book Guild Ltd who have had the onerous task of dealing with not only some rather technical text but also a liberal helping of mathematical formulae and acturial notations, but somehow seem to have managed to emerge with their sanity and sense of humour intact.

# 1

## *The origins of the gilt-edged market*

What precisely is meant by the generic term 'the gilt-edged market'? To be specific, it is the market in securities issued by, or guaranteed by, Her Majesty's Government. Many people used to misuse the term, mostly to include local government issues (corporation stocks) and, in the very old days, Colonial and Commonwealth bonds as well. This was never, in fact, correct, since such issues never carried the explicit guarantee of the British Government; and for a long time between 1968 and 1985 the tax treatment of capital gains on these bonds differed from that on 'pure' gilts, so that it was not only incorrect but also inadvisable to include them in the same category.

Whilst gilt-edged bonds form a large part of the National Debt, they do not constitute the whole of it. Other than gilt-edged, there are National Savings, Treasury bills, short-term borrowings from the Bank of England and overseas borrowings, sometimes in the form of loans raised in other world markets, or other direct loans such as those from the International Monetary Fund.

It is generally accepted that the origin of the National Debt stems from the year 1694, when the Government of William III found it necessary to raise the sum of £1.2 million at 8% in perpetuity to help finance the cost of waging war against the French. Indeed the National Debt and the Bank of England both came into being at the same time, since the *quid pro quo* to the financiers who raised that initial sum for the Government was the granting to them of a charter to form a bank – that bank becoming the Bank of England. (This original loan remained on the Bank's balance sheet until on 27 July 1994, on the occasion of the Bank's tricentenary, it was announced that it was finally being repaid.)

Once the Government had experienced this method of raising finance and accepted the idea of issuing perpetual debt, similar loans followed and by 1697, when the war ended, the National Debt had grown to about £15 million.

In the early eighteenth century a rudimentary secondary market in Government debt evolved and was in existence at the time of the infamous 'South Sea Bubble' in 1720/21 which can be considered to be the UK's first financial market crash. It stemmed from a scheme under which the South Sea Company would issue shares in exchange for Government debt which it would then hold as an investment. To understand the background to this affair it must be realised that at that time nearly all Government debt was in the hands of companies incorporated by Royal Charter such as the Bank of England, the East India Company and the South Sea Company, so in principle this was not extraordinary. However, the Company's prospects excited an upward price spiral which caused the share price to multiply by about eight times in 1720. At somewhere close to the top of this price movement about half of the outstanding Government debt was exchanged for shares in the Company. In due course the 'bubble' burst, the price of the shares collapsed and many investors in the Company were ruined.

During the remainder of the eighteenth century the National Debt rose spasmodically mainly as a result of financing further wars against the French and the Spanish, and more latterly the American War of Independence. However, in the middle of this period, in 1751, a market milestone occurred in the form of the issue of 3% Consolidated Annuities into which many smaller issues were converted. Even then the market was very imperfect and access to it very restricted. It was not until 1783 when Pitt the Younger became Prime Minister that Government loans were, at his insistence, put out to public tender.

The next major milestone in the evolution of the market was the Bank Charter Act of 1844 which divided the Bank of England into two departments – the Issue Department responsible for all English note issuance, and the Banking Department.

In 1853 the Bank indulged in some financial innovation by bringing forward the first redeemable issue – previous issues had all been irredeemable. This had a forty-year life and a stepped-down coupon structure which was to become a feature of Government debt issues in the latter part of the nineteenth century. In this particular case the coupon rate for the first ten years was $2\frac{3}{4}$% reducing for the remainder of its life to $2\frac{1}{2}$%. A similar structure was adopted by G.J. Goschen who, as Chancellor of the Exchequer, in 1888 conducted 'Goschen's Conversion' of 3% Consols into what eventually became $2\frac{1}{2}$% Consolidated Stock 1923 or after. With this particular issue the coupon rate was set at 3% for its first year, 1888, $2\frac{3}{4}$% for the years 1889 to 1903, and $2\frac{1}{2}$% thereafter, which rate has persisted to the present day.

The other famous (or infamous) conversion operation without mention of which no history of the gilt-edged market would be complete is that of War Loan in 1932. The background to this event was the desire of the UK Government to reduce interest rates in order to alleviate the depressed economic conditions of the early 1930s and the chronic state of unemployment. The fact that by the end of the 1920s the annual debt servicing costs were absorbing as much as 40% of Government expenditure was an additional incentive to reduce rates. The solution decided upon by the Chancellor

2

of the Exchequer, Neville Chamberlain, was to announce, on 30 June 1932 that War 5% 1929/47 would be redeemed between then and December that year and that holders could, if they wished, convert into a new bond, War 3½% 1952/after. Although holders of War 5% 1929/47 were in no way debarred from accepting redemption at par, a great deal of moral suasion and calls to do one's patriotic duty abounded, and this led many holders, in later years, to feel that in some way or another they had been coerced into converting. Although in the light of all subsequent events such long-term investment in War 3½% 1952/after has proved to be disastrous, it should be realised that in the two years after conversion gilt-edged yields fell quite substantially, and the new War Loan traded above 109 in 1934, and as high as 110⅛ in 1935 so that those who converted had ample opportunity to take a profit had they wished to do so.

The importance historically of wars as a major factor in the inexorable increase in the size of the National Debt has already been mentioned and the twentieth century is no exception. In the present century the National Debt multiplied twelve times as a result of World War I, from £650 million in 1914, to £7,500 million in 1919; and whilst there was a small diminution during the inter-war years, it trebled again as a result of World War II, to stand at approximately £21,000 million by 1945.

Since 1945, however, the reasons for the continuing expansion in the National Debt have been completely different. The nationalisation of the coal, steel, gas, electricity and railway industries involved the issuance of government bonds in compensation, and whilst these industries theoretically represented assets offsetting this debt, in practice the nationalised industries taken *en bloc* tended to generate working deficits which in turn had to be financed by further borrowing. Additionally, the early post-war application of Keynesian economic principles – a long way removed from balanced budget philosophies – resulted in a budget deficit (as it used to be described) or Public Sector Borrowing Requirement (PSBR) in all but a handful of years between the end of World War II and the mid-1980s.

There followed a brief period in which it seemed that at last the UK's public finances had entered a virtuous circle, as buoyant tax revenues emanating from the 1986-1989 boom taken together with the proceeds from an aggressive privatisation programme, combined with a tighter policy towards Government expenditure under the Thatcher administration to produce substantial Public Sector surpluses. Indeed a major effect of this situation was to cause the authorities to embark upon a programme of buying in existing gilt-edged bonds through 1988, 1989 and into early 1990 at a rate which, had it been sustainabie (which it was not), would have extinguished the National Debt sometime early in the next century. But the inflationary pressures unleashed by the boom eventually had to be checked. Interest rates were raised progressively until base rates reached 15% in October 1989 where they remained for a year; and the economy started to slide into a long and painful recession marked by high levels of unemployment and increasingly heavy social costs. This, combined with the downturn in tax revenue that occurred as economic activity faltered, transformed the circle from virtuous to vicious in two short years.

Table 1.1 shows the way the value of the nominal National Debt has grown since 1946, together with similar figures for the nominal Gross Domestic Product (GDP) for the same period. From observation of the ratio between them one can see that the rate of growth of the National Debt has been markedly less than that of GDP. In the late 1940s the total nominal National Debt was over twice as great as annual GDP, but this ratio reduced steadily each year until 1980 since when it has fluctuated in the 35% to 46% range.

A great deal of the pre-World War II debt and early post-war debt was issued at low interest rate levels. As a result, the burden on the Exchequer of its debt servicing was fairly small, although, as Table 1.2 shows, debt servicing costs have, since the war, always represented a substantial part of the total Public Sector Borrowing Requirement (PSBR). But whereas debt servicing costs were growing at a modest rate up to about 1970, the advent of higher inflation caused interest rates to rise, which in turn increased the debt service costs each time maturing low-coupon issues had to be replaced with higher-coupon bonds. Additionally, the mid 1970s was a period in which British Governments of both political persuasions allowed public expenditure to rise very sharply, so that by 1980 debt service costs were over five and a half times what they had been ten years previously. Although debt interest continued to rise after that it did so at a more sedate pace and since 1985 has effectively plateaued just below the £19,000 million level. However, it is clear that debt servicing costs continue to be a major component of the PSBR.

The great problem associated with prolonged deficit financing, such as that conducted by British Governments in those years, is the compounding effect that occurs when further borrowing is incurred in order to meet interest payments on existing debt. What originates as a matter of simply paying interest on a loan, soon becomes one of paying interest on the interest, and before too long becomes one of paying interest on the interest on the interest. Whilst the problem is relatively mundane when interest rates are low, it becomes very significant in periods of double digit rates such as were experienced in the late 1970s and early 1980s. The political response to this has tended to be that interest payments are simply transfer payments from one sector of the economy to another; that, as they are taxable, the Government will claw back into its coffers some of this outflow anyway, and that as long as the total deficit (PSBR) does not get out of control in real terms (inflation adjusted) there need be no fundamental cause for concern.

4

**Table 1.1**   National Debt relative to Gross Domestic Product, 1946–1994

| Year | National Debt at 31 March (£ million) | GDP for calendar year (£ million) | Ratio |
|------|------------------|-------------------|-------|
| 1946 | 23,842 | 10,060 | 2.37 |
| 1947 | 25,834 | 10,765 | 2.40 |
| 1948 | 25,722 | 11,835 | 2.17 |
| 1949 | 25,267 | 12,565 | 2.01 |
| 1950 | 25,899 | 13,112 | 1.98 |
| 1951 | 26,017 | 14,612 | 1.78 |
| 1952 | 25,984 | 15,764 | 1.65 |
| 1953 | 26,051 | 16,906 | 1.54 |
| 1954 | 26,583 | 17,890 | 1.49 |
| 1955 | 26,934 | 19,304 | 1.40 |
| 1956 | 27,039 | 20,766 | 1.30 |
| 1957 | 27,007 | 21,920 | 1.23 |
| 1958 | 27,232 | 22,853 | 1.19 |
| 1959 | 27,376 | 24,213 | 1.13 |
| 1960 | 27,733 | 25,887 | 1.07 |
| 1961 | 28,252 | 27,432 | 1.03 |
| 1962 | 28,674 | 28,812 | 1.00 |
| 1963 | 29,848 | 30,586 | 0.98 |
| 1964 | 30,226 | 33,435 | 0.90 |
| 1965 | 30,441 | 36,035 | 0.84 |
| 1966 | 31,341 | 38,370 | 0.82 |
| 1967 | 31,936 | 40,400 | 0.79 |
| 1968 | 34,194 | 43,808 | 0.78 |
| 1969 | 33,984 | 47,153 | 0.72 |
| 1970 | 33,079 | 51,770 | 0.64 |
| 1971 | 33,442 | 57,748 | 0.58 |
| 1972 | 35,840 | 64,663 | 0.55 |
| 1973 | 37,156 | 74,257 | 0.50 |
| 1974 | 40,448 | 83,862 | 0.48 |
| 1975 | 46,404 | 105,852 | 0.44 |
| 1976 | 56,584 | 125,247 | 0.45 |
| 1977 | 67,166 | 145,983 | 0.46 |
| 1978 | 79,180 | 168,526 | 0.47 |
| 1979 | 86,885 | 198,221 | 0.44 |
| 1980 | 95,315 | 231,772 | 0.41 |
| 1981 | 113,037 | 254,927 | 0.44 |
| 1982 | 118,390 | 279,041 | 0.42 |
| 1983 | 127,927 | 304,456 | 0.42 |
| 1984 | 142,855 | 325,852 | 0.44 |
| 1985 | 158,252 | 357,344 | 0.44 |
| 1986 | 171,591 | 384,843 | 0.45 |
| 1987 | 185,741 | 423,381 | 0.44 |
| 1988 | 197,448 | 471,430 | 0.42 |
| 1989 | 197,323 | 515,957 | 0.38 |
| 1990 | 192,545 | 551,118 | 0.35 |
| 1991 | 198,695 | 575,321 | 0.35 |
| 1992 | 210,487 | 597,121 | 0.35 |
| 1993 | 248,781 | 630,807 | 0.39 |
| 1994 | 306,897 | 668,085 | 0.46 |

*Sources:* Central Statistical Office and Bank of England

**Table 1.2**  Debt Interest relative to PSBR, 1946–1994*

| Calendar year | Debt interest (£ million) | PSBR (£ million) | Excess of debt interest above PSBR (£ million) |
|---|---|---|---|
| 1946 | 532 | 646 | −114 |
| 1947 | 562 | 137 | 425 |
| 1948 | 551 | −270 | 821 |
| 1949 | 548 | −313 | 861 |
| 1950 | 549 | −352 | 901 |
| 1951 | 591 | 241 | 350 |
| 1952 | 652 | 552 | 100 |
| 1953 | 683 | 702 | −19 |
| 1954 | 689 | 435 | 254 |
| 1955 | 767 | 394 | 373 |
| 1956 | 799 | 547 | 252 |
| 1957 | 803 | 532 | 271 |
| 1958 | 893 | 448 | 445 |
| 1959 | 909 | 560 | 349 |
| 1960 | 1,021 | 707 | 314 |
| 1961 | 1,104 | 727 | 377 |
| 1962 | 1,114 | 511 | 603 |
| 1963 | 1,199 | 834 | 365 |
| 1964 | 1,257 | 980 | 277 |
| 1965 | 1,348 | 1,170 | 178 |
| 1966 | 1,465 | 949 | 516 |
| 1967 | 1,573 | 1,844 | −271 |
| 1968 | 1,794 | 1,252 | 542 |
| 1969 | 1,929 | −534 | 2,463 |
| 1970 | 2,025 | −51 | 2,076 |
| 1971 | 2,093 | 1,320 | 773 |
| 1972 | 2,277 | 1,950 | 327 |
| 1973 | 2,673 | 4,093 | −1,420 |
| 1974 | 3,490 | 6,451 | −2,961 |
| 1975 | 4,127 | 10,161 | −6,034 |
| 1976 | 5,293 | 8,899 | −3,606 |
| 1977 | 6,288 | 5,419 | 869 |
| 1978 | 7,097 | 8,340 | −1,243 |
| 1979 | 8,679 | 12,551 | -3,872 |
| 1980 | 10,888 | 11,786 | −898 |
| 1981 | 12,719 | 10,507 | 2,212 |
| 1982 | 13,952 | 4,868 | 9,084 |
| 1983 | 14,208 | 11,574 | 2,634 |
| 1984 | 15,670 | 10,300 | 5,370 |
| 1985 | 17,586 | 7,445 | 10,141 |
| 1986 | 17,151 | 2,499 | 14,652 |
| 1987 | 17,936 | −1,417 | 19,353 |
| 1988 | 18,197 | −11,868 | 30,065 |
| 1989 | 18,927 | −9,269 | 28,196 |
| 1990 | 18,746 | −2,124 | 20,870 |
| 1991 | 17,004 | 7,693 | 9,311 |
| 1992 | 17,138 | 28,650 | −11,512 |
| 1993 | 18,510 | 42,556 | −24,046 |
| 1994 | 22,169 | 37,094 | −14,925 |

*Source:* Central Statistical Office

*Note:* Prior to 1961 the figures relate to Central Government Debt interest (as a proxy for Total Debt Service Costs) and the public sector financial deficit (as a proxy for the PSBR).

**Table 1.3** The PSBR as a percentage of GDP, 1946–1994*

| Calendar year | PSBR (£ million) | GDP (£ million) | PSBR as % of GDP |
|---|---|---|---|
| 1946 | 646 | 10,060 | 6.42 |
| 1947 | 137 | 10,765 | 1.27 |
| 1948 | −270 | 11,835 | −2.28 |
| 1949 | −313 | 12,565 | −2.49 |
| 1950 | −352 | 13,112 | −2.68 |
| 1951 | 241 | 14,612 | 1.65 |
| 1952 | 552 | 15,764 | 3.50 |
| 1953 | 702 | 16,906 | 4.15 |
| 1954 | 435 | 17,890 | 2.43 |
| 1955 | 394 | 19,304 | 2.04 |
| 1956 | 547 | 20,766 | 2.63 |
| 1957 | 532 | 21,920 | 2.43 |
| 1958 | 448 | 22,853 | 1.96 |
| 1959 | 560 | 24,213 | 2.31 |
| 1960 | 707 | 25,887 | 2.73 |
| 1961 | 727 | 27,432 | 2.65 |
| 1962 | 511 | 28,812 | 1.77 |
| 1963 | 834 | 30,586 | 2.73 |
| 1964 | 980 | 33,435 | 2.93 |
| 1965 | 1,170 | 36,035 | 3.25 |
| 1966 | 949 | 38,370 | 2.47 |
| 1967 | 1,844 | 40,400 | 4.56 |
| 1968 | 1,252 | 43,808 | 2.86 |
| 1969 | −534 | 47,153 | −1.13 |
| 1970 | −51 | 51,770 | −0.10 |
| 1971 | 1,320 | 57,748 | 2.29 |
| 1972 | 1,950 | 64,663 | 3.02 |
| 1973 | 4,093 | 74,257 | 5.51 |
| 1974 | 6,451 | 83,862 | 7.69 |
| 1975 | 10,161 | 105,852 | 9.60 |
| 1976 | 8,899 | 125,247 | 7.11 |
| 1977 | 5,419 | 145,983 | 3.71 |
| 1978 | 8,340 | 168,526 | 4.95 |
| 1979 | 12,551 | 198,221 | 6.33 |
| 1980 | 11,786 | 231,772 | 5.09 |
| 1981 | 10,507 | 254,927 | 4.12 |
| 1982 | 4,868 | 279,041 | 1.74 |
| 1983 | 11,574 | 304,456 | 3.80 |
| 1984 | 10,300 | 325,852 | 3.16 |
| 1985 | 7,445 | 357,344 | 2.08 |
| 1986 | 2,499 | 384,843 | 0.65 |
| 1987 | −1,417 | 423,381 | −0.33 |
| 1988 | −11,868 | 471,430 | −2.52 |
| 1989 | −9,269 | 515,957 | −1.80 |
| 1990 | −2,124 | 551,118 | −0.39 |
| 1991 | 7,693 | 575,321 | 1.34 |
| 1992 | 28,650 | 597,121 | 4.80 |
| 1993 | 42,556 | 630,807 | 6.75 |
| 1994 | 37,094 | 668,085 | 5.55 |

*Source:* Central Statistical Office
*Note:* Prior to 1961 the Central Government Debt Interest is used as a proxy for the PSBR.

In this latter respect, the relationship between the PSBR and GDP is worthy of consideration. Table 1.3 is illustrative: column 3 shows the PSBR as a percentage of Gross Domestic Product year by year. The reader will note the quantum shift in the relationship in 1973 coinciding with the beginning of a period of higher inflation and widely fluctuating exchange-rate movements, the slow reversal of this trend under the Thatcher years culminating in the four years of Public Sector surplus (1987-1990) and the steep deterioration in the state of the public finances from there to 1993 and 1994. Expressed as a percentage of GDP the PSBRs for these years are close to the worst years of the mid-1970s and demonstrate the magnitude of the task faced by the Major Government in bringing public finances back to stability.

# 2

---

## *The economic background to the gilt-edged market*

There are a multitude of different factors which affect levels of prices and yields in the gilt-edged market. Some are economic, some are political, some are psychological, some are technical. A number are more or less permanent features of the gilt-edged scene whilst others are more transient. With the market reacting from day-to-day to such a wide variety of economic variables, both domestic and international, it is often far from clear which are the main driving forces of the market and how exactly they impact upon it. Many of these forces, however, are interrelated and the schematic diagram in Fig. 2.1 illustrates some of the main linkages. It can be seen that the chief determinants of market values are interest rates at the short end of the market, inflation (or, more correctly, inflationary expectations) at the long end, and the shape and slope of the yield curve in between.

The reasons for this are not hard to find. An investor such as a pension fund whose liabilities are essentially defined in 'real' terms must, of necessity, seek to invest in instruments whose prospective return will exceed (by whatever margin its actuary determines necessary) the rise in his liabilities brought about by inflation. Since this sort of investor tends to dominate the long end of the gilt-edged market, it follows that yields there will be affected by the broad consensus of opinion about prospective long-term inflation rates. The impact of inflation is very much less on deposit-taking investors who predominate at the short end of the market. With such investors inflation applies more or less equally on both sides of their balance sheets, i.e. on the real value of their deposit liabilities, and also on that of their invested assets. To these funds what really matters is the difference between the outward payments of deposit interest, and the realised rate of total return on their investments. This does not mean that inflation has no impact whatsoever on short-term rates – far from it, since interest rates are one of the main weapons available for economic management – but it does mean that it is normally less of a factor for investors whose natural habitat is at the short end of the market than for those at the long end.

To inflation and interest rates must be added two other major factors – the supply outlook, or more specifically the size of the Public Sector Borrowing

9

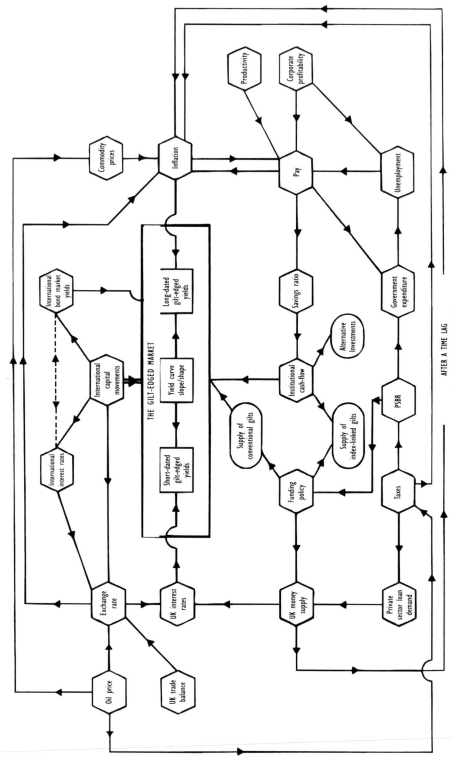

**Fig 2.1** The main determinants of values in the Gilt-edged market and their interrelationships

Requirement, and the increasing sensitivity of the gilt-edged market to movements in overseas bond markets that has developed as a result of the dismantling of capital controls and rapid advances in information technology. The main focus of this chapter will be on these issues.

At a practical level the gilt-edged analyst needs to be familiar with all key official data releases each month and have enough of an understanding of macroeconomic theory to be able to understand the dynamic forces in the economy and how they affect the outlook for inflation, monetary policy and the PSBR. Often, a given change in a particular economic fundamental can affect these three entities in different ways. For example, the market is likely to be sensitive to signs of faster growth in the economy, usually because it is concerned that this will in turn increase the outlook for inflation, and probably force the authorities to push up interest rates. However, faster growth could be viewed as good for gilts if the market revises down its forecast for the PSBR because it believes that such growth will result in an increase in tax revenues as profits rise and/or reduce social security payments as unemployment falls. What this demonstrates is that one of the prime skills required of a good gilt-edged analyst is the ability to assess correctly the likely net effect of a change in a given economic variable.

**Table 2.1**  Approximate release dates of UK monthly economic statistics

| Approximate date in the month | |
| --- | --- |
| 2nd | UK Official Reserves (M-1) |
| 5th | $M_0$ (provisional figures) (M-1) |
| | Full monetary statistics (M-2) |
| | Consumer credit figures (M-2) |
| | Housing starts and completions (M-2) |
| 6th | Industrial production (M-2) |
| 8th | Balance of global visible trade (M-3) |
| 12th | UK Producer Price Indices (M-1) |
| 14th | UK Retail Price Index (M-1) |
| | Average earnings (M-2) |
| | Unemployment and unfilled vacancies (M-1, prov.) |
| 15th | Retail sales (M-1) |
| 16th | Public Sector Borrowing Requirement (M-1) |
| 20th | Bank lending (M-1) |
| | Building Societies net inflow (M-1) |
| | Provisional estimates for $M_4$ and its components (M-1) |

*Note:* symbols in brackets denote the month to which the statistics relate. For example (M-1) indicates the previous month, (M-2) two months earlier.

## Inflation

What is inflation? Inflation can be defined as a sustained increase in the general level of prices. Clearly, it is impossible for the Central Statistical

11

Office (CSO), the main provider of economic data in the UK, to measure price changes for all of the millions of different products that exist in the economy at large. Instead the CSO compiles an index composed of a weighted basket of representative items, the prices of which it obtains monthly from retailers, known as the Retail Price Index (RPI); and the annual rate of change in this index, notwithstanding its imperfections, is the most usual definition of the inflation rate. Any measurement of this sort is necessarily retrospective, and as the RPI figures are released a month after the date to which they relate, the 'current' inflation rate so defined actually reflects price movements in the period thirteen months to one month in the past. No index of this sort can, however, be a perfect representation of the general level of prices and several commentators have suggested that in the US, for example, the equivalent consumer price index might be overstating inflation at the retail level by as much as 0.5%, firstly because it has not been adjusted rapidly enough to be properly representative of the full range of goods currently bought in that economy, and secondly because of the difficulty of taking into account changes in the quality of goods. Similar considerations may apply to the UK RPI, but whilst it may not be totally perfect it is seen to be free from bias, political or other, and as such, a fair and reasonable base for determining values in the index-linked market (see Chapter 7).

## Theories of inflation

Essentially, one can divide the wide range of theories about what determines inflation into two camps:

1. Demand-pull inflation.
2. Cost-push inflation.

*Demand-pull inflation and the 'output gap'*

This approach suggests that there will be accelerating upwards pressure on the general level of prices when aggregate demand in the economy exceeds aggregate supply. Conceptually, at the simplest level, it is not hard to accept that when there is more demand for a good than there is supply, sellers will be at an advantage and are likely to raise prices until either some of the buyers drop out of the market or supply is increased. A rise in prices is likely to affect both these factors to bring the market back into equilibrium. Extending this analysis to the economy as a whole, a rise in the level of demand is likely to push up the general level of prices as shown in Figure 2.2.

Assuming no change in supply, a shift in the aggregate demand curve from that represented by $D_1$ to that by $D_2$ (reflecting an increase in the total level of demand for goods and services in the economy as a whole), pushes prices up from $P_1$ to $P_2$.

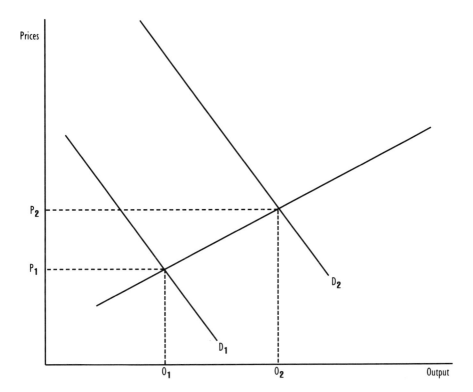

**Fig 2.2** Price/Output diagram (i)

Whilst this is an oversimplistic approach to the determination of inflation, it is the foundation for many of the more advanced theories of inflation. For example, a critical issue in discussions about inflation risk, not only in the UK but in several other countries, is the concept of the output gap. This is a measure of how far the current level of output is below its potential or 'full employment' level. Essentially, it is a measure of spare capacity in the economy. The assumption is that when there is a positive output gap, an expansion of demand will have only a limited impact on inflation. Since the economy has spare capacity, goods can be easily supplied.

Let us examine this using Fig. 2.3, a modified version of the earlier representation. In this diagram the aggregate supply curve has a relatively shallow gradient between points $A$ and $F$ so that a shift in the demand curve along this part of the supply curve imparts only limited upward pressure on prices. However, as growth continues and the economy moves into full employment, it becomes more difficult for producers to supply goods and reflecting this, from $F$ to $B$, the slope of the supply curve is much steeper and a given increase in the level of demand gives rise to a much stronger inflationary effect. Obviously, productivity and technological progress increase the

13

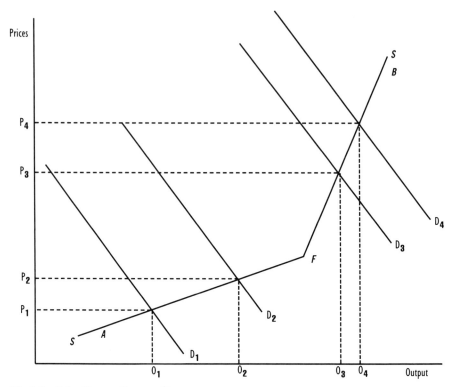

**Fig 2.3** Price/Output diagram (ii)

productive capacity of the economy over time and hence the key issue for the inflation watcher is whether the economy is growing above or below this trend level. During phases of strong economic recovery above-trend growth will move the economy along the aggregate supply curve towards $F$, and there will be a danger of being swept onto the $F$ to $B$ sector of the curve with its attendant inflationary risks.

On the other hand, during recessions, when the economy is growing below trend levels, spare capacity will be building up and the economy will be moving down the aggregate supply curve away from $F$ and towards $A$ suggesting that the inflation risk in such circumstances is minimal.

It is worth noting that when the economy is operating below its full employment level, i.e. along the $AF$ sector of the curve, a shift in aggregate demand from $D_1$ to $D_2$ results in a large increase in output (from $O_1$ to $O_2$) but only a small increase in prices ($P_1$ to $P_2$). But if the economy is operating beyond the full employment level with limited spare capacity, on the $FB$ sector of the curve the opposite result occurs. Here a demand shift from $D_3$ to $D_4$ produces only a small output rise ($O_3$ to $O_4$) but a swingeing increase in prices ($P_3$ to $P_4$).

14

Whilst this analysis is undoubtedly simplistic, it does provide an insight as to why the gilt-edged market is so sensitive to signs of accelerating growth. Moreover, since estimating how large the output gap is at any given point in the economic cycle is a very subjective issue (and one on which there has been a lot of disagreement amongst professional economists) it is not totally surprising that the market tends to err on the side of caution.

Professor Mervyn King, Executive Director and chief economist at the Bank of England has also noted that:

> 'it is the stickiness of prices and wages – the slowness of their response to changes in the balance between demand and supply – which is the source of the frustratingly long and variable time lags between changes in monetary policy and their impact on inflation.' (Mervyn King, 1994).

*Monetarist approach to inflation*

> 'Inflation is always and everywhere a monetary phenomenon.' (Milton Friedman, 1968)

The monetarist school of thought views inflation exclusively in terms of increases in the supply of money. They underline that in the past, the vast majority of inflationary periods were accompanied by an expansion in the money stock. A classic example of this was the inflation that swept through Europe in the sixteenth century as a result of the inflow of gold and silver following the Spanish conquest of the Americas. At a theoretical level, the monetarist case can be illustrated by considering the following equation pioneered by the economist Irving Fisher:

$$MV = PT$$

where,

$M$ = money supply
$V$ = velocity of circulation (basically the number of times a given money stock circulates around the economy within a given time period)
$P$ = price level, and
$T$ = the real income or output of the economy.

Monetarists assume that the velocity of circulation, $V$, is constant and that $T$, the output of the economy, is constrained by supply side factors such as the level of existing resources in the economy and the limits to gains in productivity. Hence, if the money supply, $M$, increases faster than these, so will the level of prices, $P$. Thus, for monetarists, inflation can only be controlled if the central bank restricts increases in the supply of money to within these limits.

Conceptually, monetarists see the effect of a change in the money supply on the economy in the following way. Firstly, it is assumed that an overall state of equilibrium exists in which individuals are content with the division of their wealth amongst various asset classes such as cash, bonds, equities and real assets such as housing and so on. Then following a rise in the money supply, individuals find themselves holding more cash as a proportion of their total wealth than they actually want to. As a result, they reduce their cash levels and increase their holdings of other assets, including real goods. If, however, the level of output in the economy ($T$ in Fisher's equation above) is constant or only capable of limited expansion, then this rise in demand will result in upwards pressure on prices. Viewed in this way, monetary theory can be seen to be a sub-set of the demand-pull approach to inflation discussed previously.

By contrast the Keynesian school of economic thought sees a change in the money supply affecting demand in the economy through a different route. Whilst subscribing to the view that individuals holding excess levels of cash will switch into other assets, they believe that when switches are made into assets such as short-term instruments and gilts this pushes down short- and long-term interest rates which in turn stimulates demand. But the end result, if aggregate supply in the economy is assumed to be constant, is the same.

*Cost-push approach to inflation*

There is another school of thought that rejects the previous two theories which attribute inflation to rises in aggregate demand beyond the supply capacity of the economy. At its most basic level, the cost-push school sees inflation being driven largely through increases in the costs of production and believes such rises can occur independently of any changes in the level of aggregate demand in the economy. As an example of this they could cite the two oil shocks in the 1970s which sharply increased the level of inflation in the world. Similarly, a depreciation of the currency which causes a rise in the prices of imported goods will put upwards pressure on inflation. But by far the most popular branch of the cost-push theory focuses on the labour market and wage settlements, highlighting the potential effect of aggressive bargaining by monopolistically powerful unions. Another linked concept is that of real wage resistance whereby workers, accustomed to high and rising real wages, can be expected to resist forces that adversely affect their real purchasing power.

Those theorists who support the cost-push approach do not disagree with monetarists that rising inflation is often accompanied by an expansion in money supply. However, they argue on the direction of causality and suggest that rising wages cause, or are accommodated by, an expansion in the money supply.

# Economic policy

> The overall objective of the Government's economic policy is to promote sustained economic growth and higher living standards... Economic growth is generated by businesses and their employees, not by Governments... The Government has the essential task of establishing a macroeconomic framework which provides the stability that businesses need to plan for the future. Volatile inflation, unsustainable public finances and sharp fluctuations in economic activity are all undesirable. (*Financial Statement and Budget Report 1994/95*)

At its most general level, the aim of economic policy can be seen as maximising the welfare of society over time subject to constraints such as the level of economic resources, the extent of technological development and (rather less obviously) the macroeconomic tools available. More specifically, policymakers need to specify and prioritise their objectives.

During the post-war period these have tended to include:

● full employment;
● price stability;
● a rising standard of living (economic growth);
● equilibrium in the balance of payments;
● and (more recently) attaining an exchange rate objective.

Both theoretically and empirically, these objectives often conflict. For example, when the economy is operating above the full employment level of output, the inflation risks may increase. In a free society it is the job of elected governments to decide on society's utility function, that is what combination of the above objectives best maximises overall welfare when (as is likely) one cannot achieve optimal results in all the objectives simultaneously.

A simple stylised model of conflicting objectives is illustrated in Fig. 2.4 (taken from A.W.M. Graham's paper 'Objectives and Instruments', to be found in Chapter 8 of the compendium volume *The economic system in the UK*, edited by D. Morris, 1990. Reproduced on page 18 by kind permission of Oxford University Press.)

The objective for the authorities is to achieve both internal equilibrium, that is full employment with stable prices, as well as external equilibrium characterised by the absence of either a balance of payments surplus or deficit. This position is represented in this diagram by the centrepoint, $O$. The vertical axis represents the foreign price of home production so that a depreciation of the currency moves us upwards and appreciation downwards. The horizontal axis represents the level of domestic demand (composed of consumption, investment and government spending). Such a model suggests that during periods of recession, the balance of payments improves (as

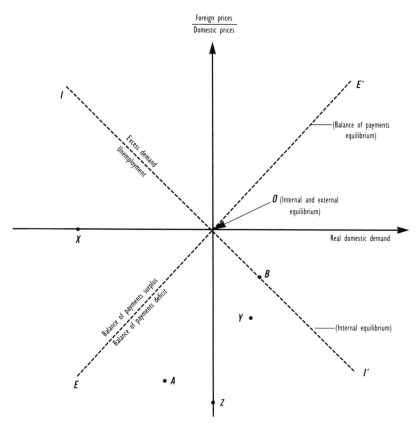

**Fig 2.4** Stylised model of conflicting economic objectives

import demand weakens) and the economy moves from $O$ to a point such as $X$ with higher unemployment. The authorities, would however, prefer to steer the economy back to point $O$ again via economic policy. Alternatively, during a period of boom, the economy may move above its potential level of output, generating excess demand, rising inflation and a balance of payments deficit. This is characterised by point $Y$ in the diagram. The authorities would then want to slow the economy down to move back to $O$ again. Whilst the model is undoubtedly over simplistic, it does illustrate some of the dilemmas facing policymakers with conflicting objectives.

Having established their priorities policymakers are then faced with deciding on the appropriate instruments to achieve their objectives. They have a wide range of instruments to choose from such as:

1.  *Monetary policy.* The Government, normally via the central bank, has a monopoly on the supply of cash into the economy. The central bank also can normally determine the short-term rate of interest either by setting an explicit target or through its operations in the money markets.

18

2. *Fiscal policy.* The Government has the ability to influence the overall economy through its power to levy taxes and control the level of public expenditure.
3. *Law creation.* This can either be in the form of setting up a legal framework within which the economy operates (such as anti-monopoly regulation) or alternatively affecting economic activity by creating laws that directly affect economic variables (such as direct quantitative controls on banks' ability to make loans).

During the post-World War II period, there has been a significant shift in objectives in economic policy. It is beyond the scope of this chapter to go into the economic history in detail, but it is worth highlighting the main periods briefly.

In the early period after the war, largely under the influence of the economist John Maynard Keynes, policymakers adopted a more active approach to demand management aiming to achieve full employment in the economy. However, this had to be done within the constraints imposed by the balance of payments and the effect of such policies on inflation. In the 1950s and 1960s economic policy was also considerably influenced by the perceived tradeoff between unemployment and inflation as reflected in the famous Phillips curve. With hindsight, one could argue that the period was characterised by over-optimism about the effectiveness and predictability of economic policy. Governments believed that the macroeconomic instruments available to them were sufficiently sophisticated to enable them to fine-tune the economy. By the 1970s, however, such optimism had begun to evaporate and the decade saw a gradual move away from active demand management as a means of achieving full employment. This reached its nadir in the early 1980s with the adoption by the new Conservative administration of Margaret Thatcher of the Medium-Term Financial Strategy (MTFS) whose objective was not full employment but rather the reduction of inflation and the achievement of price stability via targets on both the money supply and the PSBR.

## Monetary policy

While monetarists emphasise the need to control the growth of the money supply in order to maintain price stability, at a practical level, the authorities are faced with the far from simple question of which measure of money supply to seek to monitor and control. Before the development of a banking system and a credit based economy, the money supply was easily definable (and indeed tangible) normally being gold or silver coins. The introduction of paper money did not increase the difficulties of measuring money substantially, but the significant progress of financial innovation since World War II has made a precise definition of money supply much more difficult.

19

Money serves two main functions: it is a means of exchange and a store of value. The bulk of financial transactions these days are not conducted in cash but via cheques and credit cards. Hence a definition of money that only included cash would be a misleading indicator for the authorities. One could expand the definition to include bank current account deposits. But since it is now relatively straightforward to transfer funds from a savings to a current account, should not savings accounts be included also? In practice, the authorities monitor a whole range of indicators moving from the cash holdings, as the narrowest definition, to broad measures which include a wide range of bank and building society deposits. The main monetary aggregates currently (March 1995) being:

$M_O =$ notes and coins in circulation with the public
+ bankers' balances at the Bank of England.

$M_1 = M_O +$ non-interest bearing private sector Sterling sight deposits.

$M_2 = M_1 +$ private sector retail Sterling bank deposits
+ private sector holdings of retail building society shares and deposits
+ National Savings Bank ordinary accounts.

$M_4 = M_2 +$ private sector interest-bearing Sterling sight bank deposits
+ private sector time bank deposits
+ private sector Sterling bank certificates of deposit
+ private sector holdings of building society deposits and shares
– building society holdings of bank deposits and CDs and notes and coins.

$M_5 = M_4 +$ holdings by the private sector of money market instruments and National Savings instruments.

An alternative to monitoring several different monetary aggregates has more recently gained some favour – this is the Divisia measure of money supply. This approach gives weights to the different components of the monetary aggregates above according to their degree of 'moneyness'. Thus notes and coins in circulation have a high weighting because they are the most widely accepted means of payment, whilst at the other end of the spectrum, National Savings certificates are given only a small weight. In theory, divisia measures of money supply ought to be capable of providing a better and less confusing measure of developments in monetary conditions in the economy. In practice, given the problem of correctly assigning weights to the different components of money, the UK authorities are continuing to target narrow money, $M_O$, and broad money, $M_4$, whilst monitoring with some interest a divisia measure.

## Recent history of monetary policy

*The shift from direct controls to market mechanisms*

During the 1950s, direct controls on hire-purchase terms and central bank calls for restraint on bank lending were the dominant instruments of monetary policy. Changes in official interest rates were seen as an important means of signalling a tighter policy, but in the Keynesian spirit, were believed to act too slowly on the aggregate level of demand to be effective as the sole means of effecting changes in economic demand. This use of direct controls on credit growth was questioned by the Radcliffe Committee set up in 1957 which highlighted the efficiency losses from this inhibition of the free working of the market system, and the report stated that the authorities ought to 'regard the structure of interest rates ... as the centrepiece of the monetary mechanism'. However, direct controls continued to be used throughout the 1960s and it was not until the early 1970s that the authorities made the substantial shift away from direct controls on lending. Not only were there increasing concerns about the efficiency losses from such a policy, but there was also a feeling that direct control was becoming increasingly ineffective as a result of developments in financial markets. Specifically more and more lending business was being done by banks outside the traditional UK clearing banks which were under the control of the UK authorities. In 1971, a series of reforms were introduced. Known as Competition and Credit Control these dismantled many of the former quantitative controls and shifted the emphasis towards using market mechanisms as the main ways of executing monetary policy.

*Monetary targeting and the Medium Term Financial Strategy (MTFS)*

The Medium Term Financial Strategy introduced in the March 1980 Budget, set out to achieve a progressive reduction in the rate of money growth over a four-year period backed up by a decline in the ratio of the PSBR to GDP (see Table 1.3, Chapter 1). Intellectually, the strategy was based on the monetarist school of inflation led by Milton Friedman. In his March 1980 Budget the then Chancellor of the Exchequer, the Right Honourable Sir Geoffrey Howe (now Lord Howe) announced a target for the growth of the then widely accepted Sterling $M_3$ monetary aggregate of 7-11% for 1980/81, falling gradually by 1% per annum to 4-8% in 1983/84. The declining rate of monetary growth was to be matched by a parallel decline in the PSBR/GDP ratio which was projected to fall from 3.75% in 1980/81 to 3% in 1981/82 and 1.5% in 1983/84.

21

The intention to use fiscal policy as an additional means of reducing the growth of the money supply was a new approach and based on the monetary identity that a budget deficit not offset by equivalent sales of debt to the non-bank private sector would boost the money stock. One of the key elements in the MTFS was the announcement of a path for monetary growth well into the future which would serve to reinforce downwards pressure on inflationary expectations and more explicitly accepted the need for the authorities to build up their anti-inflation credibility with the private sector. The emphasis on medium-term objectives also represented a significant break from the Keynesian demand management principles of the 1950s and 1960s which were much more focused on the shorter-run objectives of maintaining full employment subject to the balance of payments constraint.

The operation of the MTFS in practice, however, proved to be problematic. Following the abolition of the supplementary special deposits scheme (colloquially known as the 'Corset'), Sterling $M_3$ growth accelerated and grew by 19.4% against the target range of 7-11% in the first year of its existence. In the next year, 1981/82, Sterling $M_3$ grew by 12.8%, again overshooting its target, but at least by less than the previous year. After the re-election of the Conservatives in 1983, the new Chancellor, Nigel Lawson, prompted by the unsatisfactory experience of Sterling $M_3$ targeting in 1980-83 introduced an additional monetary target, the narrow money measure, $M_0$. In both the 1984 and 1985 Budgets, $M_0$ and Sterling $M_3$ were assigned equal importance in the assessment of monetary conditions, but additionally in 1985 the authorities started to use the exchange rate as an indicator of the stance of monetary policy. Finally in the 1987 Budget, the authorities completely abandoned any explicit target for Sterling $M_3$ growth and concentrated on $M_0$ and the exchange rate.

*Exchange rate targeting 1987-88*

During 1987, the authorities attempted to hold sterling within a relatively narrow range centring around DM 3 to the £. This policy was in the spirit of the Louvre accord and could also be seen in the context of the then Chancellor's enthusiasm for early British entry to the European Exchange Rate Mechanism (ERM). By the spring of 1988, the authorities were finding it increasingly difficult to cap Sterling at this level. Foreign exchange intervention to this end was not proving particularly effective and the Treasury therefore decided to cut interest rates by $\frac{1}{2}$% on three separate occasions between mid-March and the middle of May, from 9% to $7\frac{1}{2}$%, despite the fact that initial signs of economic overheating had started to appear. As 1988 progressed, given a deteriorating current account and rapidly rising inflation the authorities reversed direction and raised interest rates which increased from 7.5% at the begining of June to 13% by the end of November. Further rises in base rates to a peak of 15% on 5 October 1989 were eventually required and laid the conditions for the long and painful recession which followed in the early 1990s.

The factors that accounted for the rapid monetary expansion in the second half of the 1980s are still not fully understood. But a major influence stems from financial deregulation which both increased the ability of individuals to borrow as well as raising the competition amongst lenders to facilitate credit demands. For example, banks entered the mortgage market and lent freely to the personal sector to buy houses. Whilst with hindsight, Nigel Lawson's policy of shadowing the DM and the resultant interest rate cuts of early 1988 can be seen as the springboard for the inflationary boom that followed, the amplitude of the stimulus was underestimated because of the widespread failure to appreciate fully the impact of financial deregulation.

*Monetary policy in the 1990s*

Economic policy in the early part of the 1990s has been dominated by the UK entry to and subsequent exit from the Exchange Rate Mechanism (ERM) of the European Monetary System. On 5 October 1990, the UK Government announced that it was going to enter the ERM at a central rate of DM 2.95 with 6% bands. Reasons for membership included the greater importance of the EC trade for the UK and also the desire to gain anti-inflation credibility. During the time of the UK's membership of the ERM, monetary policy was primarily aimed at ensuring that the pound stayed within its ERM target bands. Domestic objectives such as money supply growth or the level of economic growth became secondary. Since the DM is by far the most important ERM currency, this meant that the pace at which the UK could reduce interest rates was effectively going to be determined by the policy of the Bundesbank. Unfortunately for the UK and some other members of the ERM, the Bundesbank, in the aftermath of German reunification, had strong reasons of its own for maintaining high interest rates, and as a result UK rates, although not at their peak levels, remained high for much longer than would otherwise have been justified by domestic considerations alone.

In the end market forces proved to be the UK's, if not the Government's, salvation. On 16 September 1992, market forces pushed the pound down to its lower ERM band at DM 2.7780. At 11 a.m. it was announced that Minimum Lending Rate (MLR) had been set at 12% but when this proved ineffective in stemming the selling pressure it was raised again, at 2.15 p.m., this time to 15% to become effective the next day. Nevertheless sterling remained at its floor and just after 7.30 p.m. the Chancellor of the Exchequer, Mr Norman Lamont, announced sterling's suspension from the ERM and rescinded the decision to raise MLR to 15%.

Following the UK move back to floating exchange rates, monetary policy could once again be set with reference to UK domestic objectives (and interest rates started their long downward movement ending with the base rate cut to 5¼% in February 1994). The Treasury then moved to a more eclectic system of monetary policy in which they monitored a number of key variables such as money supply growth, the exchange rate and asset prices, but did not give precedence to any particular targeted variable. This move to a much more discretionary policy had the benefit of flexibility but left the Government vulnerable on the issue of policy credibility. In order to tackle this latter issue, the Chancellor made some moves towards increasing the independence of the Bank of England including allowing the Bank to publish its own quarterly *Inflation Report* and (perhaps most significantly) publishing the minutes of the monthly meetings on monetary policy that now take place between the Chancellor and the Governor of the Bank of England.

## Bank of England money market operations

To understand the implementation of monetary policy via short-term interest rates it is important to appreciate the operational relationship between the Bank of England and the UK money market. A key factor in this is that the Bank of England is the main banker to the Government so that any transfers of money from the private sector to the Government (or vice-versa) cause a net flow of cash between the banking system and the Bank of England. When this happens the banks will typically attempt to restore liquidity by drawing down some of the funds which they keep on deposit with the Discount Houses. The Discount Houses, in turn, attempt to restore their balances by either selling eligible bills to the Bank or borrowing from the Bank. Thus, the objective of the Bank of England when operating in the money market is primarily to offset the daily cash shortages or surpluses of the banking system by either injecting or withdrawing cash, at terms which it, the Bank, sets.

The Bank publishes its estimates of the cash position of the market three times a day. These can be accessed by market participants via various screen-based services. The Bank's initial forecast and the main factors are normally made known at 9.45 a.m. Subsequent revisions are usually announced at noon and then again at around 2.00 p.m.

The Bank has three main techniques to relieve money market shortages:

1.  *To make outright purchases of bills from the Discount Houses.* If the Bank announces that it is prepared to buy bills, the Discount Houses will generally offer bills to it, specifying a rate on each band. Bills are generally classified as falling into one of the following four maturity bands:

Band 1: 1-14 days
Band 2: 15-33 days
Band 3: 34-63 days
Band 4: 64-91 days.

By altering the rate it is prepared to re-discount bills, the Bank can send a signal to the markets that it wishes to see a change in the general level of interest rate and during times of interest rate uncertainty, the market pays especially close attention to its dealing rates (announced on Reuters' pages RTCA onwards, and on other information provider services).

2. *To make purchases of bills with accompanying re-sale agreements.* In this operation the Bank buys bills but agrees to sell them back to the market at an agreed price sometime in the future. This technique may be used to smooth out a known and possibly temporary market position. In addition, it may be used when the market is reluctant to sell bills outright because of uncertainty over the near-term outlook for interest rates.

3. *By lending directly to the market.* Discount Houses have borrowing facilities at the Bank with limits related to the capital base of each house. Direct lending has in the past proved a useful device for implementing changes in monetary policy. By refusing to relieve money market shortages by bill purchases, the Bank can force the Discount Houses to borrow from it. This technique may be used when the Bank is keen to signal a change in interest rates faster and more clearly than can be obtained by waiting for bill offers to respond to the initial rejection from the Bank. A variation of this technique which has been used by the Bank at times when it wishes to trigger an immediate change in interest rates is to announce a MLR which, for a short period ahead, will apply to its lending to the market.

## Fiscal Policy

*The Public Sector, the PSBR and the Gilt-Edged market*

The Government's role in the economy has increased significantly during the course of the twentieth century and in the UK government spending and taxation now account for approximately 40% of gross domestic product. As was demonstrated in the opening chapter of this book, in most of the years since World War II, government expenditure has exceeded receipts from taxation resulting in a public sector budget deficit. In order to finance this deficit, the authorities have a number of options:

1. Since the Government (through the Bank of England) is the monopoly supplier of cash, it can issue further notes and coin to the public.

2. To borrow from the Bank of England.
3. To sell National Savings instruments.
4. To sell tax instruments such as tax reserve certificates to people/companies with deferred tax liabilities.
5. To sell Treasury bills – mostly of 91 days' maturity.
6. To sell gilt-edged securities.

Additionally, they can borrow from abroad either directly from international markets or via a net change in the level of the UK official reserves of foreign currency. In practice, as Table 2.2 shows, sales of gilt-edged bonds are by far the most important means of financing the Budget deficit. The major reason for this is that financing the deficit by issuing further notes to the public or borrowing from the Bank of England (conceptually the same thing) has the effect of increasing the money supply and is potentially inflationary.

Since the budget deficit is the key determinant of the level of supply of gilts

**Table 2.2** The financing of the public sector borrowing requirement (PSBR)

|  | 1989/90 | 1990/91 | 1991/92 | 1992/93 | 1993/94 |
|---|---|---|---|---|---|
| Overall public deficit | –3,732 | 4,893 | 21,802 | 44,762 | 51,386 |
| Less privatisation proceeds | 4,219 | 5,345 | 7,923 | 8,184 | 5,420 |
| = Public sector borrowing requirement | –7,951 | –452 | 13,879 | 36,578 | 45,966 |
| – Local Authority borrowing requirement | 1,321 | 3,451 | 1,685 | –5,850 | –2,788 |
| + Local Authority borrowing from central Government | 2,262 | 1,472 | 639 | –7,267 | –659 |
| – Public corporations' borrowing requirement | –3,903 | –987 | 459 | 55 | 868 |
| + Public corporations' borrowing from central Government | –2,523 | –1,015 | 551 | 1,184 | 1,521 |
| = Central Government borrowing requirement (CGBR) | –5,630 | –2,459 | 12,925 | 36,290 | 48,748 |
| Financed by |  |  |  |  |  |
| Increase in notes and coin | 771 | 1,053 | –1,082 | 949 | 2,931 |
| Borrowing from Bank of England | 443 | –190 | 36 | –787 | 288 |
| Increase in National Savings | –1,720 | 1,387 | 3,136 | 4,353 | 4,089 |
| Sales of tax instruments | 268 | 149 | 22 | –329 | –252 |
| Net sales of Treasury bills | 5,733 | 1,029 | –1,683 | –4,374 | –2,014 |
| Net sales of gilt-edged bonds | –15,792 | –2,955 | 11,997 | 28,079 | 46,734 |
| Other public sector debt | 436 | –354 | –148 | 779 | 489 |
| Direct borrowing overseas | 797 | 1,812 | 621 | 6,882 | –1,730 |
| Net change in official reserves | 5,064 | –2,349 | –848 | 2,184 | –1,445 |
| Miscellaneous others | –1,630 | –2,041 | 874 | –1,446 | –342 |
| Central Government borrowing requirement | –5,630 | –2,459 | 12,925 | 36,290 | 48,748 |

*Source: Financial Statistics*

into the marketplace, it is clear why fiscal policy and the outlook for the PSBR is such an important focus for the gilt-edged analyst. The annual Budget is the occasion on which the Chancellor of the Exchequer outlines the Government's plans on taxation and public expenditure for the future and is the main economic event of the year for the gilt-edged market. Prior to 1993, the Budget (traditionally held in early March) concentrated on taxation issues while decisions on public expenditure were outlined separately in the Autumn Statement. However, it was argued that making decisions on taxation and expenditure at different times of the year was basically unsatisfactory and provided an insufficiently disciplined framework for Government ministers to frame their spending plans. Hence from 1993, the Budget, now switched to the end of November, covers both expenditure and taxation issues as well as detailing the Treasury forecasts upon which its proposals have been based. The Financial Statement and Budget Report (FSBR) which is released immediately after the Chancellor's speech to parliament on Budget day, apart from providing a thorough analysis of Budget detail, is extremely valuable to the gilt-edged analyst in providing an insight into official thinking on fiscal policy.

*Key issues in fiscal policy*

What is the optimal level of the budget deficit?

> The objective of Government fiscal policy is to bring the PSBR back towards balance over the medium term, and in particular to ensure that when the economy is on trend the public sector borrows no more than is required to finance its net capital spending. (*FSBR,* November 1993)

Three potential fiscal objectives are:

1.  *Maintaining a budget balance.* Advocates of the budget balance doctrine tend to extend the concept of 'good housekeeping' or 'not spending beyond one's means' from an individual level to that of the national government. In addition there is a perception that by increasing the National Debt one is passing some kind of burden to future generations. However, as long as the debt is held by domestic investors, the nation as a whole is neither better nor worse off. There has simply been a redistribution of the economic cake from taxpayers to debt holders who are recompensed by receiving a future stream of interest payments on the debt. A rather more convincing rationale for aiming for budget balance, favoured by classical economists, is that a reduced government participation in the economy will enhance efficiency and increase the potential for growth because the market is a more efficient allocator of resources than the state.

27

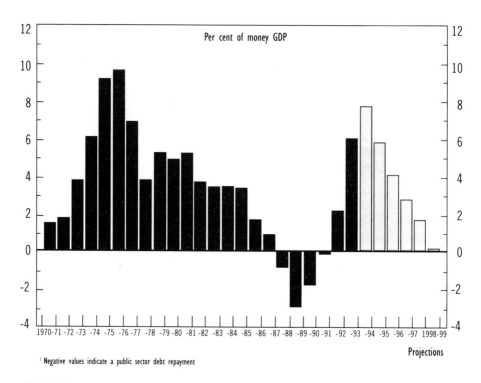

Per cent of money GDP

1970-71 -72 -73 -74 -75 -76 -77 -78 -79 -80 -81 -82 -83 -84 -85 -86 -87 -88 -89 -90 -91 -92 -93 -94 -95 -96 -97 1998-99

Projections

¹ Negative values indicate a public sector debt repayment

**Fig 2.5**   Public Sector Borrowing Requirement projections 1994–99
(Reproduced from Financial Statement and Budget Reports 1994/95)

2.  *Maintaining a stable debt to GDP relationship.* An alternative is to look at the sustainability of running a given deficit. The ultimate constraint on running a deficit is the ability to meet the costs of servicing that debt. Most of these costs are interest payments which, for a given level of interest rates, will tend to rise as a proportion of GDP when the debt stock is rising as a proportion of GDP. Hence fiscal optimality may alternatively be defined as the level of borrowing that would produce a stable debt/GDP ratio. Moreover, an unsustainable level of interest payments may increase markets fears that the Government will be tempted to monetise the deficit, which action involves substantial inflationary risks.

3.  *Maintaining a stable Capital Stock to Debt ratio.* This would happen if the Government was able to keep the PSBR equal to its net investment. The capital assets of the public sector provide services over a number of years and there is nothing inappropriate about the public sector borrowing in order to finance such public projects provided that the utility or revenue from such projects at least meets the cost of servicing that debt. However, the difficulties in consistently defining all public sector capital projects, let alone measuring the benefits flowing from them, makes this approach impractical.

In conclusion, there is no clear cut formula for determining the optimal level for the budget deficit, even if there is broad agreement that the 1993/94 and (projected) 1994/95 levels are too high. Achieving budget balance by the end of this decade looks like wishful thinking given current (1994) levels. Even if there was the political will to accept the extreme fiscal squeeze such a target would require, which is doubtful, it is far from clear that it is a wholly desirable objective. A more convincing approach may be to attempt to contain the PSBR/GDP ratio within the level of trend growth, say, below 3%.

*Structural versus cyclical budget deficits*

Even when the authorities have decided the level of budget deficit they wish to attain over the medium-term, a further issue lies in assessing how much the current deficit is the result of temporary or cyclical factors and how much is long-term and structural. If, for example, a large proportion of the deficit is due to a cyclical downturn, then there may well be a strong economic case (as well as the obvious political one) for taking no discretionary fiscal action on the view that as the economy moves back to productive potential the fiscal balance will be self-correcting.

Various economic models have split the changes in the budget balance into cyclical and non-cyclical, or structural, components. This, however, is a very subjective business. Assessments vary substantially between forecasters depending on their individual views of how far the economy is operating below potential output, whilst estimates of what constitutes potential output are in turn model-specific. Another important factor to be taken into account is how sensitive one assumes changes in the deficit are to changes in the rate of economic growth. Recent work by the Treasury has suggested that the relationship between the PSBR and the cycle is probably stronger than used to be assumed to be the case.

## Funding policy and the relationship between the PSBR and the money supply

The Government's full-funding rule refers to the means by which the authorities finance the PSBR. Its objective has generally been to neutralise the stimulatory effect of the Government's budget deficit on money supply given the assumption that a faster money supply growth is inflationary in the long-run. Under the present (1995/96) definition, the net total of maturing debt, the PSBR and any underlying increase in foreign exchange reserves have to be met by sales of National Savings products and gilts of three years or longer maturity to the private sector (though changes to the rule will be made beginning in 1996/97 – see later in this chapter).

It is important to understand why the absence of offsetting sales of gilts to the private sector for a given PSBR would boost money supply growth. Consider the following basic illustration:

> Social security payments contribute towards the PSBR. If the Government pays an unemployed worker a £30 benefit and he then deposits the cheque at bank A, this causes the operational deposits of bank A at the Bank of England to increase by £30 thus increasing the cash in the overall banking system by the same amount. However the money supply may be expected to increase by more than this £30 given the ability of bank A to make bank loans backed up by the new cash. But, if at the same time, the Bank of England sells £30 worth of gilts to the non-bank private sector, and this is paid for by drawing £30 out of the banking system then the impact on the money supply is neutralised.

Whilst this example is trivial, the theory is exactly the same for any area of deficit spending and is the underlying principle behind the full-fund rule. Indeed the link between the PSBR and money supply was most visibly illustrated by the Medium-Term Monetary Policy adopted in the early 1980s when the policy of reducing the PSBR was linked to explicit monetary targets.

It is however, worth noting that the authorities have rarely been able to follow the full-fund rule precisely in any given fiscal year and most recently, the policy objective has been to achieve a full-fund over the medium-term, so that an under-fund in any given fiscal year would be permissible as long as it could be offset by an equivalent over-fund in subsequent years.

The current (1995/96) funding rule was outlined in the March 1993 Budget when the Chancellor announced that sales of gilts to banks and building societies would no longer need to be accompanied by offsetting sales of gilts to the non-bank private sector. The authorities justified that change by stating that the previous policy was 'not appropriate when demand for credit is weak and the growth of the private sector's liquidity is subdued' and argued that over a period of years 'this will not change the total amount of debt sales, except to the extent that there is a long-term trend in bank and building society holdings'.(*FSBR* 1993/94.) It is likely that the weakness of broad money growth at the time made the authorities less concerned about the potential positive boost to money supply enabled by this change in the funding rule. But a more important factor is likely to have been that with the PSBR expected to rise to a record £50 billion in 1993/94, the authorities wished to minimise the amount of gilts required to be absorbed by the non-bank sector.

Then, in July 1995, the funding rule was further amended and restated in the *Report of the Debt Management Review* as follows:

> Beginning in 1996/97, the Government has decided to introduce a new framework for financing, which will continue to provide the necessary

discipline to ensure a prudent maturity structure for debt issuance. The Government will aim to sell sufficient gilts, of any maturity, Treasury bills and National Savings products to finance the Central Government Borrowing Requirement (plus maturing debt and any net increase in the foreign exchange reserves). All such debt issuance will take place within a set maturity structure to be determined every year. This maturity structure will be published in the *Debt Management Report* before the beginning of each financial year. The Government has no current plans to make significantly greater use than at present of short-term debt issuance.

The significant elements here are the change in the funding target from the PSBR to the CGBR and the inclusion within the funding definition of Treasury bills sales for the first time.

## The impact of rising international capital mobility on the gilt-edged market

The dramatic rise in international capital mobility over the past few years has contributed to a greater integration of international capital markets. As a result, the influence upon the gilt-edged market of overseas bond markets and economic developments outside the UK has increased significantly. Since the early 1980s, Governments around the world have increasingly acknowledged the benefits of allowing greater international capital mobility and followed a substantial policy of dismantling capital controls. Specifically, there has been a significant rise in the extent and scope of currency convertibility, and nowadays residents in almost all the major industrialised countries enjoy widespread freedom to acquire and dispose of capital. As well as a more accommodating legal and regulatory framework, the huge advances in information technology over the last decade have made investing in overseas financial markets easier to effect and monitor (and thus less risky), and the rapid development of derivatives markets has generally enhanced the process. As a result international capital movements have increased substantially over the last decade with the pace of growth accelerating in the 1990s. Relative to GDP, capital mobility has not been seen at current levels since the pre-1914 gold standard period when countries running large current account surpluses, most notably Britain, recycled funds back to developing countries to finance investment there.

However, one major difference between the most recent phase of capital mobility and that in the 1880-1914 period is the much greater importance of institutional investors. During the 1980s, the gradual relaxation of legal restrictions on overseas investment saw the demand for overseas assets from Japanese insurance companies increase significantly as these funds attempted to diversify their portfolios. But in the 1990s Japanese investors' appetite for

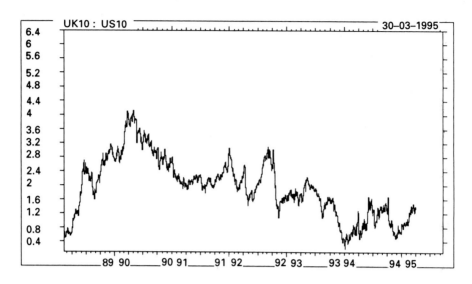

**Fig 2.6** Yield Difference between ten-year bonds in the U.K. and U.S. government markets

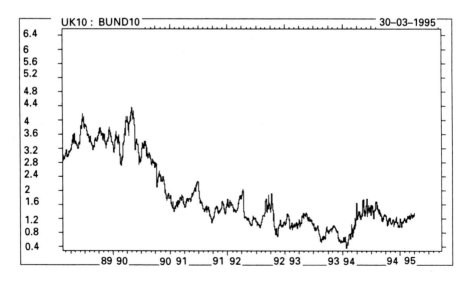

**Fig 2.7** Yield Difference between ten-year bonds in the U.K. and German government markets

32

overseas investments has diminished and US institutional investors have taken over as the driving force for international capital flows, though the motivation for such activity, the diversification of risk, has remained the same.

Gross capital flows from the main industrial countries (excluding official and short-term banking transactions) came to about $850 billion in 1993. Such flows averaged around $500 billion per year during the 1985-93 period and only $100 billion per year in the first half of the 1980s. The Bank for International Settlements (BIS) has suggested that by the second half of 1993, the total international securities transactions for the G7 countries amounted to around $6 trillion per quarter, which is about five or six times the value of international trade. One result of this has been the significant increase in the proportion of financial assets held by non-residents. The BIS has suggested that as much as 20-25% of total outstanding government bonds in the Group of Ten countries (excluding Japan) are now held by non-residents.

The effect of all this has been to cause a much closer correlation between the major bond markets of the world, and in the case of the UK the relationships between the gilt-edged market and the US Treasury market and the German Government market are particularly important.

# 3

---

## *The players in the game and the role of the 'authorities'*

In the last chapter it was shown how the gilt-edged market provides a means by which a large part of the public sector deficit can be funded. It is clear that within the gilt-edged arena the Government itself is thus a major, if not the major player in the 'game'. Whilst for all sorts of tactical and strategic reasons the government 'authorities' may at some times be a seller of bonds and at other times a buyer, over most periods they can be expected to be net sellers of debt for funding purposes.

On the other side of the coin are the investors, the wide range of individuals, corporations, financial institutions, etc. who need to invest and for whom gilts represent a potential investment medium.

Between them is interposed the gilt-edged market itself where business is conducted and where bonds and money change hands. It is sometimes difficult to appreciate the enormity of the change in the gilt-edged market brought about by the 1986 deregulation. Apart from the fact that the dealings in the new market are now very largely conducted via telephone and telescreen networks instead of face to face on the market floor, the roles to be played by market participants have been radically altered by the change from single- to dual-capacity trading.

Under the pre-1986 single-capacity system a Stock Exchange firm was required to opt to act in either a jobbing or a broking role, but was not permitted to perform both functions. This distinct separation of capacity produced a clear demarcation of interests. The jobbers were the 'stallkeepers' of the market. They traded their 'book' for profit and stood in the market quoting two-way (bid and offer) prices in the full range of gilt-edged bonds. Brokers, on the other hand, acted solely as the agents for the investing public. They had a prime responsibility to effect their clients' orders to the client's best advantage, and for carrying out such bargains brokers charged their clients commission.

One of the main criticisms of the old market was that there were not enough jobbing firms with large enough capital resources to provide the market with the level of liquidity it really required. By 1985 there were only

34

eight jobbing firms operating in gilts. Two of these were large: Wedd Durlacher Mordaunt and Akroyd & Smithers PLC. Next in size came Pinchin Denny followed by three smaller firms, Wilson & Watford, Charlesworth, and Giles & Cresswell, and then the small regional firms Moulsdale (Liverpool) and Aitken Campbell (Glasgow). Thus it was hardly surprising that when revolutionary change appeared on the horizon and the end of single capacity became inevitable, the Bank of England should decide to replace the old gilt-edged market with a new system in which there would be a greater number of market-making firms and substantially increased amounts of dedicated capital. Rather than 'redesign the wheel' the Bank chose to model the new gilt-edged market very closely on the United States Treasury bond market.

## Gilt-edged market-makers (GEMMs)

In the post-1986 market the old separation between jobber and broker has been done away with and it has become permissible to combine principal and agency functions within the same firm, though not all firms have wished to do so. At the core of the market are a number of registered market-making firms with obligations to make on demand and in any trading conditions – continuous and effective two-way prices at which they stand committed to deal, in appropriate size as discussed in advance with the Bank of England, thereby providing continuous liquidity for the investing public. The sizes of positions that these market-makers can take are constrained by the need for each firm's aggregated position risk to be contained within certain prudential limits which are determined and monitored by the Bank. Each market-maker is required to commit an amount of dedicated capital to his gilt-edged operation and the greater this is the wider are his prudential limits.

In return for the obligations to make prices without favour 'in fair weather and in foul' and submit to the prudential control of the Bank, market-makers are able to avail themselves of certain privileges which are not open to other participants in the market. These are as follows:

1. To have a direct dealing relationship with the Bank in gilt-edged securities.
2. To have, subject to the agreement of the Government, exemption from Section 472(1) of the Income and Corporation Taxes Act 1970, which enables them to claim relief against tax for the full trading loss made by buying bonds cum-dividend and selling them ex-dividend in the ordinary course of business, regardless of the time interval between purchase and sale.
3. To be able to offset, for tax purposes, dividends paid by them on bonds they have sold against dividends received on bonds they have purchased.

4. To be able both to lend and borrow bonds through approved Stock Exchange money-brokers (though the exclusivety of this privilege will cease with the emergence of the open gilt repo market in January 1996 – see later in this chapter).
5. To have borrowing facilities at the Bank of England against approved security up to maximum amounts related to the market-maker's capital and reserves.
6. To have access to the inter-dealer broker (IDB) mechanism (see later in this chapter).

On top of all this there was one further stipulation to the effect that all GEMMs would be required to become members of The Stock Exchange for regulatory purposes and for the maintenance of professional standards. In the first half of 1985 the Bank of England invited applications from investment houses prepared to operate under these conditions as market-makers. There then followed a period when each prospective market-maker's candidature was thoroughly scrutinised before the Bank issued a list of twenty-nine firms to whom it was prepared to award a 'franchise'. Of those original applicants only thirteen have stayed in the business all the time since then. Some seeing the extent of the potential competition withdrew before even 'coming under starter's orders' at the time of Big Bang, some pulled out in the light of their experiences in the market in the period 1987-89, two other GEMMs merged as a result of takeover activities involving their parent companies, another retired from the market in April 1994, and one other has informed the authorities that it will cease to operate as a market-maker in January 1996 when the repo market comes into being.

But it has not all been one-way traffic. There have also been new entrants to the market. The big four Japanese houses, Nomura, Nikko, Daiwa and Yamaichi have joined the ranks of the GEMMs as have Deutsche Bank also; whilst in the first half of 1994 Merrill Lynch and Hoare Govett returned to the market after absences of five and six years respectively. In mid-August 1994 a completely new entrant, Winterflood Gilts Limited, whose specialisation is in the retail end of the market, commenced operations as well. This means that at the end of July 1995 the full list of GEMMs consisted of the twenty-two firms shown here below:

ABN AMRO Hoare Govett Sterling Bonds Limited
Aitken Campbell (Gilts) Limited
BT Gilts Limited
Barclays de Zoete Wedd Gilts Limited
Baring Sterling Bonds Limited
C.S. First Boston (Gilts) Limited

Daiwa Europe (Gilts) Limited
Deutsche Bank Gilts Limited
Goldman Sachs Government Securities (UK)
HSBC Greenwell Limited
Kleinwort Benson Gilts Limited
Lehman Brothers Gilts Limited
Merrill Lynch Gilts Limited
J.P. Morgan Sterling Securities Limited
Nomura Gilts Limited
NatWest Gilts Limited
Nikko Gilts Limited
Salomon Brothers UK Limited
UBS Gilts Limited
S.B.C. Warburg (Gilt-Edged) Limited
Winterflood Gilts Limited
Yamaichi Gilts Limited

One thing should be made clear here. Despite being described as 'gilt-edged market-makers' – a generic title chosen for them by the Bank of England in preference to the American term 'primary dealers' – these firms do not necessarily limit their operations to market-making and transacting other firms' orders. Most of them have trained sales teams backed up by economic and technical research, each working to bring high-quality order-flow to its own market-makers. It can be seen that there is a very high level of inter-dependence between the three essential elements of such firms. The salesmen need their market-makers' prices to be competitive in width and size, the market-makers need the salesmen to understand and, if possible, anticipate investor demands and the flow of business, and the whole operation needs a strong capital base and fine credit lines in order to maximise its profitability.

## Inter-dealer brokers

The change to a more US-style market in 1986 also brought into existence here a new type of intermediary: the inter-dealer broker (IDB). IDBs exist to provide a means by which market-making firms can trade with each other whilst maintaining anonymity. They form an inner ring to the market, matching one market-maker's bid with another's offer and vice versa. They only deal with registered GEMMs. They do not deal with the public.

Just as the Bank of England vetted the applications of prospective market-makers for the new market, so they also vetted the firms wishing to set up as IDBs. In this case, however, the Bank required applicants to demonstrate that there was a demand for their individual services from the (then) twenty-nine

GEMMs. This caused a certain amount of difficulty because the general consensus of opinion amongst the GEMMs was that the optimum number of IDBs to combine choice without undue fragmentation of the inner market was either three or four, whilst there were six similar candidates all planning to do much the same thing. In the end the Bank decided to authorise all six to operate and that is how this new market began its life at the time of Big Bang. But over the intervening years these numbers have been slimmed down by market forces and today (end-July 1995) only three gilt-edged IDBs are operating, namely:

Cantor Fitzgerald Gilts
Garban Gilts Limited
Williams, Cooke, Lott and Kissack Limited.

Since 15 May 1995 a competitive alternative service for GEMMs has been provided on a voice-broking basis by Liberty EurAsia Limited, but here anonymity is sacrificed and, unlike the three IDBs mentioned above, Liberty are not members of the London Stock Exchange.

## Securities borrowing and lending and the gilt repo market

There is another vitally important activity that occurs daily at the heart of the gilt-edged market, without which it would be unable to function efficiently, and which is virtually invisible to most investors. This is the business of borrowing and lending gilts. Whilst most people can easily identify with the concept of borrowing or lending money, the idea of doing the same with bonds is often found to be confusing. Why, the question goes, should anybody need or want to borrow securities? The answer to this is quite simple: dealers borrow securities (in this case, gilts) in order to be able to deliver them to somebody to whom they have sold them, in order to obtain cash payment. The most usual case is that of a market-maker who has a bear position in a certain bond, but still makes a two-way market in that issue. If he then satisfies further buying orders in that bond, he will be unable to demand payment unless he can deliver bonds to the buyer. This will mean that he will be out of the cash which could be earning interest for him. If, however, he borrows the bonds and delivers them, he will receive payment, and at some later time when his position in that bond turns round he can unwind his borrowing. This ability of market-makers to lend and borrow bonds readily is an essential ingredient in maintaining the high level of liquidity and the general fluidity of the gilt-edged market day by day.

In the past this whole sphere of activity has been tightly controlled and operated through a set of specialised intermediaries known as 'stock exchange money brokers' (SEMBs) whose principal business is the provision of services to market-makers. Only GEMMs and discount houses (in the cases of bonds up to seven years to maturity) have been permitted to borrow bonds, all transactions have had to be conducted through SEMBs and lenders have had to be authorised by the Inland Revenue. To date there has been no open 'repo' market for government bonds in the UK of the sort that exists, for example, in the United States, Germany and France. But that situation is now set to change and from 2 January 1996 an open gilt repo market will exist in the UK.

At this juncture it is necessary to explain exactly what is meant by a repo. The expression is used in its broadest sense to describe a pair of transactions under which a sale of a given security by one party to another is linked to a subsequent repurchase from the same counterparty at some later date on terms agreed at the outset which reflect the interest rate implicit in the transaction. By using this device the original buyer effectively 'borrows' the security in question for the time specified in return for making a short-term loan of cash to his counterparty for the same period. This shows the essential two-way nature of a repo both as a securities borrowing mechanism allowing any market participant to run short positions in the respective security on the one hand, and as a high quality fully colaterallised short-term instrument for cash rich investors on the other.

Gilt repos will be governed by a standard Legal Agreement and a Code of Best Practice which will require (at least) daily mark-to-market valuations of the security concerned, the provision for making margin payments when colateral values decline below the repo's cash value (including interest earned), and netting in the case of a default. As such they will be differentiated from other similar but less formal (and thus more risky) devices such as undocumented buy/sellbacks.

In an economic sense there is no effective difference between the older stock borrowing and lending regime and the repo market, and the UK authorities have taken great care to create a 'level playing field' so that the two systems can operate freely side by side. In particular SEMBs will be able to act, if they wish, as intermediaries in both repo and stockborrowing, though just how their individual businesses will develop is not necessarily clear. Currently there are eight such firms, namely:

Cazenove Money Brokers
King & Shaxson Money Brokers Limited
Lazard Money Broking Limited
Lehman Brothers Money Brokers Limited
L.M. (Moneybrokers) Limited
Prudential-Bache Capital Funding (Money Brokers) Limited
Rowe & Pitman Money Broking Limited
Sheppards Moneybrokers Limited.

One area where the introduction of a repo market will cause significant change is in regard to tax. As is explained in more detail in Chapter 10, the basic tax regime under which the market has previously functioned has been the payment of periodic interest payments net of tax at the standard rate of income tax. A continuation of those arrangements would have caused acute difficulties for any repo spanning the respective security's ex-dividend date. In order to accommodate this problem, arrangements have been made for professional market participants to receive such interest payments gross as from 2 January 1996. In order to redress the negative impact on the Inland Revenue of this change, those participants receiving interest gross will, in future, be required to settle their tax accounts with the Inland Revenue on a quarterly rather than an annual basis.

## Broker/dealers

So far the focus of this chapter has been directed to the activities of market-making firms and those closely related to them. Whilst it is through these firms that the bulk of institutional and international business passes, it is important not to lose sight of the independent broker/dealers. They act as agents for the public to achieve best execution for their bargains. They carry out very much the same function that pure stockbrokers did in the pre-1986 market, but in one specific regard their role has changed. Whereas in the old days they were not allowed to take principal positions, since 1986, and subject to London Stock Exchange rules they have been permitted to transact their clients' business with their own book. There is also the question of commission. Most bargains transacted direct with market-makers are not subject to a commission charge, but when dealing through a broker/dealer one can expect a commission to be charged to remunerate them for establishing the most advantageous place in which to deal and processing the necessary paperwork.

## The role of the 'Authorities'

In the old market before Big Bang there was one broker that was quite different from all the others and that was the Government Broker (or the GB, as he was colloquially known in the market). By tradition the Government Broker was the senior partner of the firm of Mullens & Co. and was responsible for carrying out the day-to-day market activities of the 'authorities' acting through the Bank of England. This function was a long way removed from ordinary stockbroking and the operations of the Government Broker were strictly separated from Mullens' non-government business. The GB had his own team usually consisting of himself, his deputy (another partner in Mullens) plus market-dealing staff. His team had no dealings with any other brokers (including the other part of Mullens), but dealt solely with the jobbing system. This particular system was well suited to the needs and requirements of the old jobbing system but was obviously inappropriate for the new market with its far greater number of market-makers. So tradition gave way to practical reality and the Government Broker and his team gave up their lives as stockbrokers and moved inside the Bank of England to become members of its gilt-edged division. From there a team of half a dozen staff keep in routine daily communication (between 9.00 a.m. and 5.00 p.m.) with the GEMMs dealing with them over the telephone. There are also special occasions when the Bank and market operate outside normal hours. For example, at the last two General Elections in June 1987 and April 1992 many market-makers decided to trade through the night as the voting results were declared, and on both occasions the Bank's dealing room was in operation as well. In fact history was made on 10 April 1992 when the Bank created and sold to the market some £800 million bonds at about 2.30 a.m when it became clear that against most expectations the Conservative party were going to win that election.

To understand how they operate it is important to comprehend the ways in which Government bonds are sold in the United Kingdom. There are a number of different methods available to the authorities but the one which has become predominant is the gilt-edged auction. Like many other of the post-1986 developments in the market the structure of the auction has its roots in the US Treasury market.

Up to the end of March 1995 market practice had seen gilt-edged auctions operate to the following type of schedule. On the relevant Friday at 3.30 p.m. the Bank of England would make a preliminary announcement of its intention to hold a forthcoming auction, and indicate approximately the maturity area of the bonds to be auctioned. On the Tuesday of the next week, again at 3.30 p.m., the Bank would release specific details of the auction such as:

Quantity of bonds to be issued;
Name, coupon rate, maturity, interest payment dates, etc;
Date of the auction.

Normally the date of the auction would be on the Wednesday eight days later, i.e. twelve days after the preliminary announcement, and during that intervening period the bonds could be traded on a 'when-issued' basis – starting immediately after the Tuesday 3.30 p.m. announcement.

Though this procedure worked reasonably well over the years since Big Bang in 1986, a significant body of market opinion felt that the market would be better served by having a fixed calendar of auctions and a more generous period of notice regarding the maturity area for future auctions. On 30 March

1995 the UK Treasury announced in their *Debt Management Report 1995/96* their intention to meet substantially these requirements.

From April 1995 onwards a calendar of auction dates for the forthcoming financial year will be announced in advance. At the beginning of each calendar quarter the approximate maturity areas of bonds to be sold at auction in the coming quarter will also be announced together with a progress report on the funding programme for the financial year to date. The initial announcement under these arrangements stated that 1995/96 auctions would be held on:

Wednesday 26 April 1995
Wednesday 28 June 1995 (subsequently revised to 29 June 1995)
Wednesday 26 July 1995
Wednesday 27 September 1995
Wednesday 25 October 1995
a Wednesday in late November or early December (depending on the timing of the UK Budget)
Wednesday 31 January 1996
Wednesday 27 March 1996

The procedure for announcing full details at 3.30 p.m. on the Tuesday prior to each auction will continue as in the past. Interestingly the new arrangements make provision, for the first time, for the possibility of an auction being split between more than one gilt, in which case separate auctions may be held on successive days.

Bids in a gilt-edged auction can be made on either a competitive or a non-competitive basis, and must be made on the official application forms published with the issue prospectus. The only exception to this rule being that GEMMs may make competitive bids by telephone to the Bank of England up to 10.00 a.m. on the date of the auction. These bids can be for their own account or for those of their clients wishing to keep their options open until the last possible moment, and most often are a combination of the two. Competitive bids must be for one amount and at one price expressed as a multiple of 1/32nd of £1. Under current arrangements they are required to be for a minimum of £500,000 nominal, above that in round multiples of £100,000 for applications for between £500,000 and £1,000,000 of bonds, and above that level in multiples of £1,000,000 nominal. Once those bids have been accepted by the Bank – and it is important to appreciate that the Bank has reserved for itself the right to reject any bid or part of a bid – they are ranked in descending order of price and bonds are sold to those whose competitive bids are at or above the lowest price the Bank is prepared to accept. In this system (and unlike the old 'tender' system – discussed later) the price paid by applicants whose competitive bids are accepted is the price which they individually bid, with the result that not all bonds are sold at the same price. Successful competitive bids made at prices above the lowest accepted price are alloted in full, but those made at the lowest accepted price may only be partially satisfied.

Non-competitive bids are available for investors wishing to bid for smaller amounts and who are not able or willing to commit themselves to the auction pricing mechanism. These bids must be for not less than £1,000 nominal and not more than £500,000 nominal, and must be in multiples of £1,000 nominal. Again the Bank of England reserves the right to reject any non-competitive bid, but subject to that contingency not occurring a non-competitive bid will be accepted in full at the weighted average price at which competitive bids have been accepted rounded down to the nearest 1/32. The auction process does not take a great deal of time to complete after the final bids are made just before 10.00 a.m. One can normally expect the Bank to announce the result soon after 10.45 a.m. that morning.

There are two principal criteria by which to judge the success or otherwise of an auction. The first is the number of times the amount of bonds on offer is covered by the totality of bids. Auctions covered by a factor of two or more will be regarded as very successful, but in cases where the cover is not much above one, the market will have cause for concern. The other is the length of the auction's 'tail'. The tail is defined as the difference in price between the average price paid and the lowest price accepted in the auction. A long tail is generally regarded as a sign of potential market weakness.

Of course, there is one possible scenario in which even these criteria may be useless, and that is in the event of an auction not being fully covered or, more likely, only covered by taking into account bids at prices so low as to be unacceptable to the Bank of England. In such cases the Bank has the option to sell less than the full amount originally offered and ignore the unacceptably low bids.

Before the auction system became so dominant the more usual method of making an offer for sale of gilt-edged bonds to the general public was the tender-price method. Under this system would-be buyers were invited to submit tenders for an amount of bonds and the price they were prepared to pay for that amount. Sometimes the Bank of England would stipulate a minimum tender price below which applications would not be considered; at other times there would be no formal minimum tender price. Basically bonds were allotted to those applicants tendering the highest prices, but the actual issue price was fixed as the lowest price at which any bond was allotted, and was the same for all successful applicants. (This contrasts with the bid-price auction system where bonds are allotted at the actual price bid in respect of each application.)

The following example illustrates how the tender-price system worked.

Imagine an issue of £1,000 million bonds with a minimum tender price of 96. When the applications are collected and analysed it is found that:

> £5 million bonds have been applied for at $97\frac{1}{4}$
> £25 million bonds have been applied for at 97
> £670 million bonds have been applied for at $96\frac{3}{4}$
> £1,200 million bonds have been applied for at $96\frac{1}{2}$
> £1,000 million bonds have been applied for at $96\frac{1}{4}$
> £1,000 million bonds have been applied for at 96

The bonds applied for at $97\frac{1}{4}$, 97 and $96\frac{3}{4}$ total £700 million and will be allotted in full. This leaves £300 million further bonds to be allotted to applicants for £1,200 million applied for at $96\frac{1}{2}$. These are proportionately scaled down, each applicant at this price receiving 25% of his requirement. The issue price, however, is the lowest price at which applications are successful (even if only in part), in this case $96\frac{1}{2}$, and all bonds are allotted at this price.

The last time this method was used was for the issue of £800 million Treasury 9% 2008 C on 11 April 1991. Since then the Bank has favoured using the bid-price auction system which has proved its efficiency and is well understood by the international investing community (though in the 1995 *Debt Management Review* several favourable references are made to 'uniform-price auctions', which may presage some future change in this direction).

Historically, the tender-price system had evolved out of an earlier fixed-price system largely as the result of an (in)famous occasion in February 1979 when Treasury $13\frac{3}{4}$% 2000/03 was issued. With the old fixed-price system there was a basic timetable which normally allowed at least three business days to elapse between the announcement of an issue (on this occasion at 3.30 p.m. on Friday 16 February) and the actual issue date which in this case was fixed for the following Thursday, 22 February 1979. Also, the issue price would be fixed at the time of the announcement, and if the market moved down substantially in these intervening days this could jeopardise the success of an issue. If, on the other hand prices rose this would make the bonds to be issued very cheap in relation to the rest of the market and create excess demand for them. This is precisely what happened with Treasury $13\frac{3}{4}$% 2000/03. Between the Friday evening announcement and the following Thursday morning the long end of the gilt-edged market rose by about four points. The resulting demand for the new bonds was so large that in the half-hour between 9.30 a.m. and 10.00 a.m. when the application list closed, the Bank of England's new issue department in Watling Street was besieged with brokers' and banks' messengers, all trying to lodge applications for their clients, and what were later politely described as 'disorderly scenes' took place. The affair has subsequently become enshrined in gilt-edged folklore as the 'Battle of Watling Street' and since then the Bank has not used the fixed-price system for an open offer for sale to the public.

A variant of the fixed-price system has still been used in recent years. It has tended to come into play when, sensing a sudden build up of demand in the market, the authorities have wished to create, in the shortest possible time, a reasonably large amount of additional bonds to have available for sale. This has been done by the authorities issuing new bonds at a fixed price directly to the Bank of England, from whose portfolio they can be sold into the secondary market as soon as the next business day. This particular method was especially suitable for bringing forward issues of about £1,000 million in size, as compared with a typical auction size of nearer £3,000 million.

However, these are not the only ways new gilt-edged bonds have been created and brought to the market. It has also been open to the authorities to create small additional tranches of existing issues (referred to in the market as 'taps') and sell these directly to the Bank of England, which in turn can 'tap' them out to the market as demand dictates. This is a convenient and quick method, particularly well suited for bringing out modest quantities of bonds when a full-blooded new issue might be less than easily digested. Alternatively a clutch of three or four taps, say £200 million each of a short-dated, a medium-dated, a long-dated and an index-linked issue, could be fed into the market to take advantage of strong market conditions. The flexibility of this system made it a very well-used weapon in the authorities' issuing armoury and as recently as 1992/93 57% of conventional gilts sold during that year were issued in that way. Since then this percentage has diminished as the emphasis has swung increasingly towards the auction system. In the 1995 *Report of the Debt Management Review* it was announced that in future taps will only be used as a market management mechanism, and that the proportion of conventional gilts to be issued in that way will not normally exceed 10% of total issuance. Index-linked gilts will, however, continue to be sold primarily through the tap system. Nowadays the creation of a tap is announced at 10.15 a.m. for bids from GEMMs at a tender half an hour later at 10.45. The Bank publishes details of the result of this and any subsequent tenders so that all market participants can be aware of the supply situation.

Lastly there are what are rather charmingly described as 'unofficial sales'. These are occasional sales of gilts from official portfolios made by the Bank in response to specific bids by GEMMs. The range of gilts available for sale is constantly updated and published via information vendor screens. The essential difference between this and the tap system is that here the Bank only responds to bids, it does not actively offer stock to the market.

In all the foregoing, the emphasis has been placed on the authorities' part in selling debt. But they can operate on the buying tack also. One of their functions is to smooth out the redemption of maturing issues by gradually buying in bonds over the last few months of their lives. This action helps spread the period of cash outflow caused by redemption, and also improves the liquidity of the very short end of the market, as it is known that any such bonds offered for sale will be readily bought in by the Bank of England. Apart from this, there are a number of Government or Bank of England funds whose investments may include gilts, of which the National Insurance fund is a good example, and the Bank will deal for them, either as a buyer or seller according to their needs.

There are other times when, for tactical reasons, the authorities may be buyers of bonds. In extenuating circumstances they have the option to stabilise a falling market by coming in and buying bonds, but these occasions are relatively rare – a recent occasion being during the 'global bond sell-off' of February 1994. In the past they have also been known to facilitate switch business by being prepared to buy in shorter issues in exchange for longer 'tap' issues. Bonds taken in in this way then become available for sale back to the market through the 'unofficial sales' route.

Finally there has been the recent development by the Bank of England of permanent repo and secured loan facilities under which it is prepared to add liquidity to the money market on a temporary basis by buying gilts from certain types of financial institutions subject to their agreement to repurchase them subsequently. This capability, which came on stream in January 1994, replaced a temporary arrangement that had been in operation since September 1992. Under the new arrangement UK banks, discount houses, GEMMs and building societies are able to participate in regular repos, conducted twice a month (on the Wednesdays following the first and third Mondays of each month). The period of the repo can be until the next or next-but-one rollover date and the effective rate of interest involved is the yield equivalent to the Bank of England's discount rate for 15- to 33-day commercial bills. All these operations are now legally covered by a Master Agreement signed by each counterparty which includes margin arrangements, and which came into effect on 20 April 1994. This form of specialised repo should not be confused with the more general open gilt repo market planned to come into operation on 2 January 1996 which is open to all-comers and in which the Bank of England does not expect to be a direct participant.

## The financial institutions

Reference has been made to the financial institutions as investors in gilts. These institutions fall broadly into two main categories: those with deposit liabilities, and those with longer-term liabilities, such as life assurance funds and pension funds. There are, however, other classes of investor which do not readily fit into these convenient compartments, of which unit trusts, investment trusts, the trustee departments of the banks, and the private investor in general, are particular examples. All of these have differing investment requirements, some of which may be met by the gilt-edged market. In order to understand the market, it is thus necessary to understand the needs of those whose actions will tend to have the greatest impact on the supply and demand for bonds. As we have already seen, the Bank of England, acting for the authorities, is (usually) the largest player on the supply side. It is now necessary to look at the institutions, and examine their impact on the demand side.

## Commercial banks

The prime function of the commercial banks is to take in deposits and make loans to all sections of the general public. Although in the UK the London clearing banks and the Scottish clearing banks – both having extensive branch banking systems – dominate the scene, they are only a part of a much wider banking system, all of which comes under the regulation of the Bank of England for the purposes of monetary control. Over and above their formal liquidity requirements, the banks are also subject to a degree of prudential control as to their lending and investment policy. The attitude of the Bank of England is generally to leave these matters to individual banks' best judgements, but it does monitor their books and it will in certain circumstances 'suggest' that a bank changes the stance of its portfolio. As regards tax there is no differentiation between interest payments and capital gains (or losses), they are all aggregated with a bank's mainstream profits and taxed accordingly.

## Trustee savings banks

The trustee savings banks (TSBs) have very much the same prudential limitations acting upon them as the clearing banks. They obtained their name because their activities were controlled by local groups of trustees to protect the savings of the poor. For that reason historically they were precluded from making loan advances, and so a much higher proportion of their assets needed to be invested in securities. In recent years, however, they have developed into commercial banks, and since 1979 have offered cheque books, loan facilities and credit card facilities to their customers. There has also been a process of rationalisation in this part of the banking sector since that time. In

1981 sixteen separate TSBs existed, but their activities have now mainly been concentrated into three units, TSB Bank, TSB Scotland and TSB Channel Islands whilst the Trustee Savings Bank of Northern Ireland was sold to Allied Irish Banks in 1988. Their taxation basis is similar to that of the commercial banks.

## Discount houses

There are seven discount houses – Union Discount, Gerrard & National, Alexanders Discount (incorporating Jessel Toynbee), Cater Allen, Clive Discount, King & Shaxson (incorporating Smith St Aubyn), and Seccombe Marshall which, together with a subsidiary of the investment bank H.S.B.C. Greenwell, form the London Discount Market Association (LMDA). The main difference between these two classes of LMDA members is that seven older houses are authorised under the 1987 Banking Act to take unsecured deposits from outside the banking system, whilst investment banking subsidiaries are not.

Pre-1985 the discount houses were all British and completely independent. Nowhere else in the world were similar entities to be found. Their strength and importance sprang from the pivotal position they occupied in the UK banking system, and the fact that it is through the discount market that the Bank of England conducts its operations in the money market. But the wind of change that blew through the City in the wake of The Stock Exchange's 'revolution' caused alliances of money market and gilt-edged market operations to be forged so as to be able to offer clients dealing capability right down the maturity spectrum, from the shortest dates to the irredeemables, and many of these alliances involved overseas interests. Traditionally, the discount houses would borrow the day-to-day surpluses of the commercial banks and invest this money, together with their own capital, in other short-term instruments, such as Treasury bills, commercial bills, gilt-edged bonds, certificates of deposit, etc. By the reverse token, they would undertake to repay the banks their funds when required. Such demands from the banks would often leave the discount market short, and these situations would be alleviated by the access the market has to the Bank of England. Under this arrangement a discount house has two opportunities (one in the morning and the other before 2.30 p.m.) to offer parts of its bill portfolio within four prescribed maturity bands, for the Bank of England to purchase. The rates at which the Bank of England is prepared to buy such bills are some of the most critical money market interest rates. Through its activity in this field the Bank can exert great influence over the whole range of short-term interest rates– if the Bank of England is not satisfied with the rate at which bills are offered it can decline to take them and force the discount house to borrow directly at a rate of the Bank's choosing at 2.30 p.m.

Another feature of the discount market is its agreement to underwrite the weekly Treasury bill issue by submitting tenders that collectively total not less than the amount of bills to be issued. Many years ago this commitment, *inter alia*, caused there to be a preponderance of Treasury bills in the portfolios of the houses, but when the size of the Treasury bill issue was reduced in the early 1980s their commercial bill book grew to be much larger than that of their Treasury bills. More recently, however, the nature of the money market has changed again as the major banks have tended to manage their liquidity by holding many more bills directly, and the discount houses' function has become rather more that of market-making intermediaries through which the banks deal in bills, either between themselves, or with the Bank of England.

The investment policies of discount houses are largely influenced by the existence of multipliers which are applied to their capital and reserves to limit the size and risk profiles of their assets. Under this system various classes of assets suitable for discount house investment are accorded risk coefficients on a scale in which the risk factor (broadly speaking) increases as maturities increase. The size of a discount house's book is thus not only related to that of its capital and reserves, but also to the type of assets it chooses to hold. Thus, if a discount house wishes to take an aggressive stance in a relatively high-risk area this will have a restrictive effect on the size of their permissible operations in other areas.

## Building societies

As their name suggests, the main *raison d'etre* of the building societies has been the provision of mortgage finance for house purchase. The societies are not companies but non-profit-making friendly societies regulated by the Building Societies Commission. Despite a considerable incidence of mergers in recent years, there are still a large number of individual building societies though the top six or seven account for about 85% of overall building society assets. Much of this concentration has come about as a result of the Building Societies Act 1986 which allowed the larger societies to undertake a whole new range of commercial activities such as owning and developing land, lending on an unsecured basis and for non-housing purposes, and opened the door towards incorporation and public flotation – a route taken some time ago by the Abbey National and, more latterly, the Halifax and Leeds Permanent – before transforming themselves into banks. However, these new freedoms have not significantly interfered with their traditional business. Basically the societies take in deposits from the general public (augmented by wholesale funds from the money and capital markets), and lend on house mortgages. Since their borrowing is potentially short-term, and their lending essentially long-term, they need considerable protection against adverse

49

events. One protection they have is that for the majority of their mortgage lending the rate is not fixed permanently, but can be moved upwards and downwards in line with interest rates in general and their own deposit rates in particular. Even where they offer fixed-rate mortgages the period during which the rate is fixed is normally limited to five years or thereabouts. Furthermore, building societies are required to operate within the constraints of an agreed solvency ratio and for prudential reasons many prefer to run liquidity ratios in the region of 15%-20%. Short and medium-dated gilt-edged bonds are major investment classes for such purposes, and with regard to tax their position is very similar to that of the banks in so far as their investment income and capital gains are all treated as part of their basic trade and business and taxed accordingly.

## Corporate funds

Although their presence was always dwarfed by the size of the financial institutions, a significant number of industrial and commercial companies have in the past made use of the gilt-edged market as a place in which to deploy some part of their surplus funds. The main attraction for doing so was the tax-free nature of capital gains on gilts that existed prior to the 1996 taxation changes, which meant that for corporate funds, lower coupon short-dated gilts could often produce higher net-of-tax returns than could be obtained from the money market. Under the new (1996) tax regime capital gains on gilts (other than Funding $3\frac{1}{2}$% 99/04 and Treasury $5\frac{1}{2}$% 08/12) and bonds are treated as income items and this opportunity is effectively no longer open to them. Some cash rich companies, however, may continue to hold some of their liquidity in gilts, but if they do it will probably be more for reasons of convenience or credit standing rather than obtaining enhanced net-of-tax returns.

## General insurance companies

The term 'general' is used to distinguish those companies whose trade and business is to write insurance against general risks – motor insurance, fire, marine, property, etc. – from those which deal with life insurance business. In the course of business, general insurance companies receive premiums, which are investable. The nature of the business is such that investments need to be reasonably liquid, and the short and medium sectors of the gilt-edged market provide these companies with a suitable form of investment. Their tax position is that both interest payments and capital gains are treated as income items and on this consideration alone there should normally be no preference between them, but where in recent years physical underwriting operations have produced losses, such companies have often found it more valuable to have the certainty of immediate investment income flow to offset these losses, rather than the prospect of an eventual capital gain.

## Life assurance companies

Nowadays, life companies do more than simply write pure life assurance business, they have annuity funds, they write pension business, and have a plethora of marketing devices that have taken them into unit-linked savings schemes also. However, in the main their liabilities are essentially long term, and in many cases their major investment concern is to produce real rates of return (i.e. after allowing for the ravages of inflation) on the various contracts and policies they write. Life funds will thus be invested in equities, property and overseas securities, as well as bonds. Within the gilt-edged market their natural habitat is at the longer end of the market, thus roughly matching the nature of their liabilities, though their investments often include short- and medium-dated bonds for tactical purposes.

Historically, tax has played a very important part in the fund management of a life office. In particular, the fact that until the advent of the 1996 tax changes life offices qualified for freedom from capital gains tax on gilts and qualifying corporate bonds significantly influenced their investment strategies. Under the new tax regime, however, capital gains from their gilts (other than Funding $3\frac{1}{2}\%$ 99/04 and Treasury $5\frac{1}{2}\%$ 08/12) and bonds will be treated as income and taxed as such.

Broadly speaking, life companies are subject to corporation tax on the balance of their income minus expenditure, the so-called I-E, at a 'policyholder' rate limited to the basic rate of income tax (currently 25%). However, that part of I-E which, based on a notional case I computation, can be seen as attributable to 'shareholder' rather than 'policyholder' is liable to tax at the full corporation tax rate. In practice many life offices offset their management expenses against their gilt-edged investment income. If these expenses exceed their total gilt income (interest payments plus capital gains) then, to all intents and purposes, the effective tax rate on their gilt-edged portfolio is zero.

## Pension funds

These are perhaps the institutions which can have the longest-term liabilities. A pension fund accepting a new entrant aged twenty now may still be paying benefits in sixty years time; and even a closed fund with no new entrants can still face the prospect of having outflows for some years forward. Since in most schemes benefits are linked to final (or final-average) salaries, and salaries are in turn influenced by inflation, it can be appreciated that inflation is the major long-term concern of the pension fund managers. Accordingly, pension funds have been much larger investors in real assets such as equities and property, which (it is hoped) offer longer-term protection against inflation, rather than in fixed-interest bonds. Some funds have gone so far as to have zero gilt-edged or fixed-interest exposure, but a figure of 5% to 10% of assets is a more usual proportion; though this may tend to rise in future in the wake of the UK Government's 1994 review of occupational pension schemes and the future impact of the solvency provisions proposed therein.

Most funded schemes need to produce real rates of return (i.e. in excess of inflation) of between 2% and 3% per annum to meet their actuarial requirements, and this has not always been easy to achieve, especially during the 1970s, when inflationary pressures were at their height. Their task has been made somewhat easier by the advent of index-linked gilts with long-dated maturities and benefits linked to the RPI, and significant amounts of these securities have found their way into pension fund portfolios, often at the expense of 'conventional' gilts.

The majority of pension funds are 'approved' schemes, by which it is meant that they have been given exemption from tax on their investment activities by the Inland Revenue. This applies to both investment income and capital gains tax, and as such they are known as 'gross' funds.

## Merchant banks and fund management companies

A great deal of pension fund investment is carried out by external fund managers, especially when the funds in question are insufficiently large to warrant the expense of setting up an independent fund management operation. This business has very largely been captured by the merchant banks, fund management groups such as the investment and unit trust managers, and the investment departments of the life offices. It is a fiercely competitive business, where investment performance is closely monitored, and where league tables abound.

Another activity of the fund management groups that grew rapidly in the early 1980s was the gilt-edged unit trust. Before the 1980 Finance Act, the taxation climate was impropitious for unit trusts investing in gilts. Legislative changes introduced at that date made these trusts liable only to basic rate tax on interest payments (and, after 1986, on accrued income) and exempted capital gains made by these trusts from capital gains tax.

Under the 1996 taxation arrangements, capital gains on most gilts and bonds are normally considered as income and lumped together with dividends and interest payments for tax purposes. But applying this principle to these unit trusts would have caused considerable difficulties since these funds are basically required to distribute to unit holders each year the totality of their net income. If this income were to include unrealised capital gains this would obviously give rise to cash flow problems.

Therefore it was decided that authorised unit trusts dedicated to gilt-edged and bond investment would themselves be excluded from the new arrangements and continue to be taxed as before, but that movements in the value of units in such trusts would be treated as if the units were bonds.

## Higher rate taxpayers

Althouth it is an obvious misnomer to describe such individuals as an institution, historically they had a dominant effect on the low-coupon sector of the market, especially at the short end where bonds standing at substantial discounts to par maximised guaranteed tax-free capital appreciation and minimised highly taxed income. In the more distant past both Conservative and Labour Governments saw fit to issue low-coupon gilts in order to tap demand from this class of investor. But with the progressive reduction in the highest rates of taxation on investment income from 98% to 40%, and the advent in 1989 of deep-discount legislation, the authorities have ceased this practice and this sector of the market has steadily diminished as previously existing low-coupon bonds have been redeemed and not replaced.

Two of the longest outstanding issues, Funding $3\frac{1}{2}$% 99/04 (originally issued as far back as 1954) and Treasury $5\frac{1}{2}$% 08/12 (1960) have been specifically exempted from the 1996 taxation changes on the grounds that they are widely held by private investors, and assurances on their tax treatment were given by the then Chancellor of the Exchequer in Parliament in 1965. Holdings of these gilts, irrespective of size, will continue to be exempt from tax on movements in their capital value.

## International funds

Perhaps one of the greatest changes to have occurred in the gilt-edged arena over the past few years is the huge impact on the market of non-domestic investors. Although the influence of international investors had grown steadily through the early 1980s and was not insignificant at the time of Big Bang in 1986, few at that time would have envisaged how the global bond market would develop, and how the gilt-edged market would change from being primarily a domestically orientated market to being just as much a constituent member of that wider market.

There are a number of factors behind this development, including the fact that the greater openness and liquidity in the gilt-edged market that has come about as a result of its redesign has made it more attractive to overseas investors. Secondly, similar improvements in other European Government bond markets and a tendency towards yield convergence in those markets, has created conditions conducive to switching between them. Historically the main categories of overseas investors were central monetary institutions such as central banks, international organisations such as the World Bank and

United Nations agencies and other generally conservative institutions ranging from Japanese insurance companies to Swiss banks. To those can be added the proprietary trading units of global investment banks, highly active and hugely leveraged hedge funds making aggressive currency and interest-rate-related plays across the world's bond markets, and the more internationally orientated investment strategies being pursued by the world's leading fund managers.

However, the activities of these international funds in the gilt-edged market are often concentrated at the shorter end of the maturity spectrum up to about the ten-year maturity point, at which point most of the world's main Government bond markets have highly liquid benchmark issues, and which for some of them is the effective extent of their maturity range. This has tended to create a break point or hinge in the gilt-edged yield curve at about that maturity, and in normal conditions the longer one goes beyond that point the greater is the domestic influence on the market.

## Private investors, the retail gilt market and the National Savings Stock Register (NSSR)

Whilst professional wholesale business dominates the gilt-edged market by value, one must not lose sight of the existence of the retail sector of the market mainly serving the private investor where the number of bargains can often exceed those of professionals.

Most of this business comes to the market in the ordinary way through agency stockbrokers, but an alternative route exists via the activities of the National Savings Stock Register (NSSR). This allows investors to buy or sell any gilt-edged security by completing a form obtainable from most post offices and sending it (with payment where applicable) to the Department of National Savings in Blackpool. Obviously such bargains are done without the investor having knowledge of the dealing price involved – the NSSR transacts bargains (normally) on the day they receive them – but by way of compensation for this, commission rates on small bargains are very cheap compared with most stockbrokers' minimum rates. Additionally dividends from securities held on the NSSR are paid without deduction of tax at source, but obviously must be declared to the Inland Revenue at some later date. There is no upper limit to the size of investments that someone can hold on the register nor to the amount that can be sold at any given time (subject to all those bonds being held on the register and not elsewhere), but there is a £25,000 limit on the amount that can be invested by this route in any particular issue on any single day. One further significant difference between dealing on the NSSR or through a stockbroker, bank or independent financial adviser is that the NSSR is unable to provide any advice to the would-be investor whereas this can be expected to be readily available from the others.

This is often an important consideration for private investors especially those not particularly experienced in the ways of the gilt-edged or other fixed-interest markets.

Over recent years retail gilt-edged business has tended to become concentrated upon a small number of market-makers who have developed it as a high-volume low-margin business with specialised computer systems to handle this sort of turnover. These include Aitken Campbell (Gilts) Limited, H.S.B.C. Greenwell Limited, NatWest Gilts Limited, U.B.S. Gilts Limited, and Winterflood Gilts Limited.

# 4

---

## *The fundamental characteristics of gilt-edged securities*

If asked to give a simple description of what represented a gilt-edged bond, the average investor might reply by saying that it was a redeemable fixed interest security issued by or guaranteed by Her Majesty's Government on which interest would be paid every half-year. Whilst this description covers most of them, it by no means covers all of the bonds that comprise the gilt-edged market.

### General features of conventional gilts

In its simplest form the standard gilt-edged bond has a name, a nominal interest rate (known as the 'coupon' rate), and a redemption date.

*Name*

To all intents and purposes, the name of the bond is of no special significance, except as a matter of identification. There is no difference in the market standing of bonds with different names, such as Treasury, Exchequer, Funding, Conversion, Consols, War and so forth, on account of their name. It may be that certain issues with a given name may be less marketable than others, but this will be for other reasons, such as perhaps the size of the issues outstanding, rather than simply because of their name.

If, however, the official title of a gilt-edged security contains the word 'Loan' instead of the more usual 'Stock' this indicates that the security is available in bearer as well as registered form.

For example:
$8\frac{1}{2}\%$ Treasury Loan 2007 can be held in bearer form
but,
9% Treasury Stock 2012 is not available in bearer form.

(The use of the word 'Stock' here may cause some confusion to readers outside the UK. In the UK equities have historically been referred to as 'shares' and fixed-interest securities as 'stocks', whilst in the United States equities are known as 'stocks' and fixed-income securities 'bonds'. In this book we have adopted the US tradition and used the 'bonds' nomenclature as far as possible, but where the word 'Stock' appears in an official sense, as it does above, its occurrence is unavoidable.)

*Nominal rate of interest (or 'coupon' rate)*

For the standard gilt, this represents the annual amount of interest paid per £100 nominal of that particular issue. In most cases this is paid semi-annually, on fixed days six months apart, e.g. 15 January and 15 July, or 10 March and 10 September, etc. Two issues break this rule: Consolidated $2\frac{1}{2}\%$ Stock, the oldest existing gilt which for historical reasons pays four coupons of $\frac{5}{8}\%$ each year, on 5 January, April, July and October, and a relative newcomer to the market, Floating Rate Treasury Stock 1999 issued on 31 March 1994 which also pays quarterly (see Chapter 8). For those who worry about jargon, the word 'coupon' derives from the use of bearer bonds, where, in order to claim one's dividend when it fell due, it was necessary to clip the requisite coupon from one's bond, and present this coupon to a paying agent, usually a bank, in order to obtain one's interest. Since the great majority of gilts nowadays are securities registered at the Bank of England, whence dividends are paid directly to their holders, coupon clipping has become largely a thing of the past. Thankfully, however, the terms 'coupon' and 'coupon rate' have survived in this context – since the phrase 'nominal rate of interest per cent per annum' is, to say the least, somewhat cumbersome.

Most gross coupon payments amount to half the respective bond's coupon rate, but there are exceptions to this rule, notably in cases where the coupon to be paid reflects interest for a period other than a simple half-year. This happens frequently with new issues when the date of issue does not happen to be precisely six months before the first interest payment date, and/or when the new issue is partly paid. In such cases, an adjusted interest payment is made that takes into account both these factors.

The other non-standard interest payments are those related to variable-rate bonds, floating-rate bonds or index-linked bonds, all of which are specialist subjects dealt with in detail later on in this book, but are distinguished from normal gilts by the simple fact that their half-yearly interest payments are tied to Treasury bill rates in the case of the 'variables', money market rates in the case of the 'floaters', and to the progress of the RPI in the case of the index-linked issues.

*Redemption date*

The standard gilt-edged issue will have a specified date on which it is due to be redeemed (repaid) by the Government. Some have two dates between which they must be redeemed. The Government has the option of redeeming such bonds at any time after the first redemption date, and must redeem them at the very latest on the last redemption date. For most bonds, redemption is at par, i.e. £100 per £100 nominal stock, but this is not so in the case of index-linked stocks, where not only are interest payments linked to the RPI, but redemption values also. One older issue, Conversion 3½% 1961/after, has a sinking fund which accelerates redemption by applying a sum of not less than 1% of the amount outstanding at the end of any half-year in which the daily average price is below 90, to buying in such bonds for cancellation during the following half-year.

*Size of issue*

Although not part of any formal title or identification, an important item is the size of any particular issue. There is, however, no such thing as a standard size of issue; the nominal amount being brought into existence at the time of each new issue being tailored to meet the circumstances of the moment, but recent practice has been to gravitate towards larger liquid issues of around £3,000 million; and certainly those gilts with much smaller amounts outstanding tend to suffer from lesser marketability.

The size of a particular issue is one item which can change during its life-time. In recent years it has become increasingly commonplace for additional tranches of existing issues to be created and fed to the market when the Government needs to fund, rather than continually creating completely new issues. This has been beneficial in two ways. Firstly, it has facilitated the formation of a number of very large and highly liquid issues which are preferred by international investors, and secondly it has avoided expanding the gilt-edged list to the point at which it would become unwieldy. This process was also enhanced by the fact that between November 1989 and January 1991 the authorities conducted a series of conversion operations specifically aimed at consolidating some of the many smaller issues in the gilt-edged list into these bigger and more liquid issues. Treasury 9% 2008 is a good example of the result of these activities as it has been the result of two minimum price tenders, one auction, four taps, a conversion offer to holders of Conversion 9¾% 2006 and a fixed price tranche issued directly to the Bank as illustrated in Table 4.1.

## Benchmark issues

The creation, as described above, of large 'pools of liquidity' in the form of issues with a total size of £5,000 million and greater has facilitated the estab-lishment of a series of *de facto* benchmark issues along the maturity spectrum which are widely used by the interest-rate swap market as bases for swap pricing. This is a relatively new feature of the gilt-edged market which had a previous history of treating all issues equally as far as possible. Benchmark issues not only need to be large and liquid they also need to carry coupon

58

**Table 4.1**

| | | | | | |
|---|---|---|---|---|---|
| 11.02.1987 | £1,000m | ! | Treasury 9% 2008 | | issued by minimum price tender |
| 23.09.1987 | £800m | | Treasury 9% 2008 | A | issued by auction |
| 15.11.1989 | £721m | | Treasury 9% 2008 | B | to replace Conversion 9¾% 2006 |
| 11.04.1991 | £1,000m | ! | Treasury 9% 2008 | C | issued by minimum price tender |
| 15.05.1992 | £350m | | Treasury 9% 2008 | | tap |
| 03.07.1992 | £200m | | Treasury 9% 2008 | | tap |
| 11.12.1992 | £250m | | Treasury 9% 2008 | | tap |
| 30.06.1993 | £1,000m | ! | Treasury 9% 2008 | D | fixed price – direct to the Bank |
| 21.11.1994 | £300m | ! | Treasury 9% 2008 | | tap |
| | | | | | |
| Total | £5,621m | | | | |

*Note:* ! indicates that on each of these occasions a proportion of the issue was reserved for the Commissioners for the Reduction of the National Debt.

rates as close as possible to current gross yield levels, and for that reason are most often recently issued bonds.

## 'Free of tax to residents abroad' (FOTRA) status

There are also a significant number of gilts which are exempt from all UK taxation to non-residents of the United Kingdom, on application to the Inland Revenue. A major advantage of these is the payment to non-residents of the UK of gross dividends which would otherwise have tax at basic income tax rate deducted at source. The importance of this concession to overseas investors has diminished slightly since the introduction of CGO 'Star' accounts which allow, amongst others, corporates not resident in the UK to receive gross dividend payments, but for overseas personal investors it is still significant.

One of these bonds is War 3½% 1952/after, the (in)famous 'War Loan', which differs from virtually every other bond in the gilt-edged list in that its dividends are automatically paid gross (without tax deduction) to all holders, wherever they are resident. This is not to say that dividends from War Loan are not subject to tax in the hands of a UK investor – they are. It is simply that, for historical reasons, the Bank of England does not deduct tax at source, but leaves that pleasure to the subsequent actions of the Inland Revenue. The only other bond currently paying interest gross to allcomers is Floating Rate Treasury Stock 1999, though any others of that type that may appear in due course can reasonably be expected to follow suit.

## Gross accrued interest, taxation of income and price conventions

There have been two major watersheds for the gilt-edged market in the past ten years.

More recently, in early 1996, there has been the introduction of the gilt-repo market and the change in the tax treatment (for non-personal UK investors) of capital gains on (most) gilts and bonds so that from now onwards such gains will be considered to be income items and taxed accordingly.

The previous watershed was in 1986 when capital gains tax on gilts and qualifying corporate bonds (QCBs) was removed and the accrued income scheme was introduced. These events, *inter alia*, shaped the way for certain market practices and conventions, and an appreciation of their history should enhance one's understanding of the market.

It is easiest to consider these events in chronological order.

Prior to 28 February 1986 the whole of the consideration (including gross accrued interest) of any gilt-edged or corporate bond bargain was considered to be a capital item, and only actual dividends received were treated as income for tax purposes.

On 28 February 1986 the accrued income scheme (AIS) came into force under which income was assessed as accruing on a day-to-day basis, and only the 'clean price' element of a bargain's total value was considered to be capital. Under the AIS income tax was levied on the sum of the dividends received plus the gross accrued interest at the time of sale less the gross accrued interest at the time of purchase. The effect of this was to ensure that the amount of taxable income was proportional to the period of time a bond was held. This removed the profitability from the practice hitherto widely adopted by net funds of converting income into capital by selling bonds full of accrued interest shortly before their ex-dividend dates. This in turn opened up the way for the abolition of capital gains tax on gilts (and most other fixed-interest bonds) on 2 July 1986.

A major repercussion of all this was to cause a change in the way prices of gilts are quoted separating the capital and income components, so that since 28 February 1986 prices of all gilts have been quoted as a basic price plus or minus so many days' gross accrued interest.

In contrast, the changes in the taxation of bonds to be brought into effect in April 1996, whilst radically affecting the behaviour of many investors, has not caused there to be any change in the market's pricing conventions, which together with certain mathematical relationships are summarised below.

*Market price (MP).*   This is the market price quoted by the market-makers, published in the press, etc., and at which bargains are struck. This is the price which will be shown as the bargain price on any contract note.

*Gross accrued interest (GAI).*   This is an amount per £100 nominal that represents the interest that has accrued on the bond in question in respect of the time period between the most recently paid interest payment date and the current settlement date. In cases where a bond is quoted ex-dividend (XD) in respect of a coupon payment still to be received, the accrued interest relates to the number of days from the settlement date to the date of this forthcoming dividend, and is a negative quantity. Where the bond in question is a new issue which has not yet paid its first interest payment, accrued interest is counted from the day of issue, i.e. the day on which cash payments are made in return for the issue of bonds. If, as is often the case, such bonds are issued partly paid, accrued interest is computed on a proportionate basis (see later examples).

*Total price (TP).* This is a bond's total cash value per £100 nominal. It is the total amount of money (excluding dealing expenses) that would change hands between buyer and seller, should a bargain be struck at a given market price.

*Settlement date.* Unless specific arrangements have been made for special settlement, gilt-edged bargains are settled on the first business day following the bargain date.

Having defined these items let us now examine the relationships between them. Under the post-28 February 1986 regime the following relationship applies to all gilts:

Total price (TP) = Market price (MP) + Gross accrued interest (GAI).

*Clean price (CP).* This is the total price (TP) plus (in the case of partly-paid bond) any outstanding calls minus accrued interest. In normal usage, 'clean price' is deemed to mean total price less gross accrued interest, however where funds are subject to tax on income but not on capital gains, the phraseology 'net clean price' is often encountered. In such cases the net clean price is simply the total price minus the net accrued interest after deduction of tax on the accrued interest at the relevant rate.

It is thus clear that post-28 February 1986 (gross) clean prices are identical with market prices, i.e.

Clean price (CP) = Market price (MP)

but before 28 February 1986 the following price relationships ruled:

For short-dated bonds (i.e. those with lives to final maturity of five years or less):

Total price (TP) = Market price (MP) + Gross accrued interest (GAI)
Clean price (CP) = Total price (TP) – Gross accrued interest (GAI)
= (MP + GAI) – (GAI)
= Market price (MP).

For bonds with lives to final maturity longer than five years:

Total price (TP) = Market price (MP)
Clean price (CP) = Total price (TP) – Gross accrued interest (GAI)
= (MP) – (GAI)
= Market price – Gross accrued interest.

Consider now some examples relating to certain bonds as they stood in the market on Tuesday, 1 February 1994 (settlement day: Wednesday 2 February 1994):

1. *Treasury 9% 13.10.2008 with a quoted price 123 12/32 cum dividend.*
   To find the gross accrued interest (GAI), adopt the following procedure:

   (a) Establish the date of the most recently-paid interest payment = 13.10.1993.
   (b) Calculate the number of days between this date and the settlement date (2.2.1994) = 112 days.
   (c) (GAI) = $9 \times 112/365 = 2.762$.

   Thus the total price (TP) = (MP) + (GAI)
   $$= 123.375 + 2.762$$
   $$= 126.137.$$

   The clean price is found by subtracting the accrued interest from the total price. For a gross fund (or a fund taxed equally on income and capital gains), the (gross) clean price will thus equate to the market price, but for a fund subject to tax on income only at, say, 25%, the net (@ 25% tax) clean price (NCP) is found as:

   (NCP) (@ 25% tax) = (TP) – $(1 - 0.25) \times$ (GAI)
   $$= 126.137 - (0.75 \times 2.762)$$
   $$= 124.065.$$

   Next, let us have a look at a second bond on the same day, 1 February 1994.

62

2.  *Treasury 8¾% 25.8.2017 with a quoted price 127 16/32 ex-dividend.*
    The first thing to realise here is this bond is quoted in an ex-dividend
    form. This means that a buyer would be acquiring it without the rights
    to the forthcoming interest payment, i.e. 4⅜% on 25.2.1994. The gross
    accrued interest inherent in the bond on this date reflects the time period
    between this date and the settlement date (2.2.1994) and, since these
    dates are in reverse order, the accrued interest is negative, viz. number
    of days between the 'last' interest date and the settlement date =
    −23 days.

    Thus, gross accrued interest (GAI) = 8.75 × (− 23)/365
    $$= -0.551.$$

    Once again the total price (TP)= (MP) + (GAI), but in this case the
    accrued interest is negative, so that

    $$(TP) = 127.5 + (-0.551)$$
    $$= 126.949.$$

## Dividends and accrued interest on partly paid gilts

In recent years, it has become increasingly common for new gilts to be
issued in a partly-paid form, whereby the issue price is paid in instalments
spread over a number of months ahead. This has often given rise to confusion as to how calculation of accrued interest on such issues should be done
correctly. The situation is complicated by the fact that there are three
possible forms of new issue – fixed price, minimum tender price and auction
– and the process is marginally different in each of these. The basic
principle is, however, quite straightforward. The accrued interest for any
period is equal to the coupon rate times the number of days elapsed, divided
by 365, and multiplied by a factor representing the partly-paid nature of the
gilt for that period. The numerator of these factors is simply the sum of the
part payments already made. The denominator is the fully paid issue price,
and that is where the problem lies because this is defined differently in each
of the three cases.

1.  For *fixed price* issues the denominator is the fixed price (i.e the sum of
    the partly-paid issue price plus all subsequent calls).
2.  For *minimum tender price* issues the denominator is the minimum tender
    price irrespective of the actual issue price determined by the tender.
3.  For *auctions* the denominator is 100.

The following three examples demonstrate how the system varies.

*Example 1. Fixed price issue: Treasury 8½% 2007 C.*
This bond was issued on 6 August 1993, at an issue price of 108 1/2 spread
as follows:

| | | | |
|---|---|---|---|
| At issue: | 25 | on | 6 August 1993 |
| First call: | 35 | on | 13 September 1993 |
| Second call: | 48½ | on | 8 November 1993 |

Issue price   $\underline{108\frac{1}{2}}$

*Problem:* calculate the relevant gross accrued interest for bargains done on
15 November 1993 (for settlement 16 November 1993).

For the thirty-eight days between 6 August and 13 September 1993, the bond
'earns' accrued interest at 25/108.5 of the full rate, i.e.

$$8.5 \times 38 \times (25/108.5)/365 = 0.203901.$$

For the fifty-six days between 13 September and 8 November 1993, the bond
'earns' accrued interest at 60/108.5 of the full rate, i.e.

$$8.5 \times 56 \times (60/108.5)/365 = 0.721167.$$

Between 8 November and settlement day 16 November, it 'earns' accrued
interest at the full rate for the eight days involved, i.e.

$$8.5 \times 8/365 = 0.186301$$

making the total gross accrued interest for that day 1.111369.
  In exactly the same way the Bank of England calculates the value of the
reduced first interest payment only substituting the date of that interest
payment in place of the settlement date in the above process. In this particular case the first interest is due to be paid on 16 January 1994, and the third
element (reflecting now the sixty-nine days between the second call and that
date) becomes,

$$8.5 \times 69/365 = 1.606849$$

so that the value of the first interest payment due on 16 January is,

$$0.203901 + 0.721167 + 1.606849 = 2.531917$$

which the Bank rounds upwards to four decimal places to 2.5320.

*Example 2. Minimum tender price: Treasury 10% Convertible 1990.*
This bond was issued on 18 January 1984 subject to a minimum tender price of 95¾. The issue was made £20 paid, with a call of £45 due on 13 February and the balance of the issue price to be paid on 12 March. The issue price determined by the tender was 96, so that the actual payment spread was as follows:

> At issue:      20  on  18 January 1984
> First call:     45  on  13 February 1984
> Balance due: 31  on  12 March 1984
>
> Issue price    96  compared with minimum tender price of 95¾

The process for calculating accrued interest and the reduced first interest payment is basically the same as above but the denominator in the partly-paid factors here is 95.75 (the minimum tender price) and *not* 96 (the actual issue price).

If we restrict ourselves to calculating the value of the first interest payment due on 25 October 1984 we find it to be:

$10 \times 26 \times (20/95.75)/365 = 0.148789$ for the 26 days whilst £20 paid.
$+ 10 \times 28 \times (65/95.75)/365 = 0.520763$ for the 28 days whilst £65 paid.
$+ 10 \times 227 /365 \quad\quad\quad = 6.219178$ for the 227 days fully paid.

$\overline{6.888730}$ rounded up by the Bank to 6.8888

*Example 3. Auction: Treasury 7% 2001.*
This was issued on 29 July 1993, partly-paid, with a call of £40 to be paid on 6 September, a final call of £40 on 11 October, and a first interest payment on 6 May 1994. Under the auction system each 'parcel' of bonds issued is done so at the individual price bid for it and so there is no singly defined issue price. For accrued interest and first interest payment calculation purposes the issue is 'deemed' to have been made at par, with the period to the first call being considered, in this case, to £20 paid. The denominator in the partly-paid factor is thus 100. If, once again, we restrict ourselves to calculating the value of the first interest payment, here due on 6 May 1994, we find it to be:

$7 \times 39 \times (20/100)/365 = 0.149589$ for the 39 days whilst £20 paid.
$+ 7 \times 35 \times (60/100)/365 = 0.402740$ for the 35 days whilst £65 paid.
$+ 7 \times 207 /365 \quad\quad\quad = 3.969863$ for the 227 days fully paid.

$\overline{4.522192}$ rounded up by the Bank to 4.5222.

## Ex-dividend status

The great proportion of gilt-edged debt is in the form of bonds registered at the Bank of England, and dividends are paid by the Bank directly to the beneficial owners. The administrative logistics of this process require a certain amount of time to prepare the dividend warrants and arrange for their despatch to their respective bond owners. To enable this to be done, gilt-edged bonds are made 'ex-dividend' seven working days (or in the case of War $3\frac{1}{2}$% 1952/after ten working days) before the interest payment is due, and dividend warrants are sent to the holders whose names are on the Bank of England's register at that date. After a bond has become 'ex-dividend' or 'XD', a buyer will purchase it without the right to receive the next (pending) interest payment, and the market, allowing for this factor, will adjust the total price down accordingly. The amount by which the ex-dividend total price is lower than the cum-dividend total price is approximately equal to the discounted value of the pending dividend and thus varies according to market conditions and short-term interest rates. The effect of this on market (quoted) prices is normally to make the ex-dividend quoted price fractionally higher than the previous day's cum-dividend quoted price.

The seven working days (ten working days for War Loan) ex-dividend period is, however, a relatively new arrangement. Before 1 January 1996 the ex-dividend period was about five times longer and was determined by the following set of 'rules' an understanding of which may be useful to practitioners examining pre-1996 gilt-edged prices.

1. The basic rule was that the ex-dividend date was five weeks and two days (thirty-seven days) before the relevant interest payment date. If this date was a weekend date or public holiday, then the ex-dividend date was the first business day following it.

2. The basic rule above did not apply to Consol $2\frac{1}{2}$% 1923/after, which pays interest four times a year on 5 January, April, July and October. Historically this stock was always made ex-dividend on the first day of the previous month, i.e. 1 December, 1 March, 1 June, 1 September, or the next business day if this was a holiday or weekend date. This rule also extended to any other issue which had dividend payment dates in common with Consol $2\frac{1}{2}$%, e.g. Funding $5\frac{3}{4}$% 87/91 (since redeemed), Treasury 8% 02/06, and Treasury 3% 1966/after.

3. These two rules used (it was thought) to cover all possible eventualities, until the authorities managed to issue Exchequer $10\frac{1}{2}$% 1987 with dividend dates 6 April, 6 October. This created the anomaly that applying 'Rule (1)', above, would normally assign this bond ex-dividend dates 28 February (29 February in leap years) and 30 August, both of which

66

pre-date the ex-dividend dates of Consol 2½%, etc., despite the fact that the dividends are to be paid a day later. To avoid this juxtapositioning, the Bank of England decided to make the bond go ex-dividend on the same basis as Consol 2½% 1923/after, and indicated that this principle would be extended to any other issues where a similar problem might occur.

## Special ex-dividend status

In addition to the ex-dividend period defined above, there has for many years been a three-week period immediately prior to the ex-dividend date in which gilts can be traded either cum-dividend in the ordinary way, or specially ex-dividend (Sp. XD). The effect of this facility is to create an overlap between the market in a gilt cum-dividend and ex-dividend, thus allowing market-makers to match buyers and sellers in either mode over a three-week period, rather than experience unnecessary congestion in business over the official ex-dividend date.

It used to be that this facility was denied to 'shorts' (of less than five years' life to final maturity) and War 3½% 1952/after, but this restriction was removed on 24 May 1993.

It has been suggested that in view of the shortening of the official ex-dividend period described in the foregoing section, some change to the special ex-dividend arrangements may follow, perhaps reducing its timespan, or even abolishing it, but as of end-July 1995 no decisions had been announced.

## Non-standard gilt-edged bonds

At the beginning of this chapter we outlined the basic features of conventional gilts. The use of the word 'conventional' in this context implies that there are, or have been in the past, other gilts with differing characteristics, and these have fallen into four categories:

1. Index-linked Gilts.
2. Convertible Gilts.
3. Variable-rate Gilts.
4. Floating-rate Gilts.

These are dealt with in detail in later chapters of this book – index-linked gilts in Chapter 7 and the others in Chapter 8.

# 5

## The mathematics of the gilt-edged market. Redemption yields, compound interest, and all that

Most people who invest money normally have two main considerations to take into account when choosing where it should be placed: security and rate of return. The security aspect of gilts has been treated elsewhere in this book; this chapter deals with rates of return and yield.

### Flat yield and redemption yield

To the layman, the concept of yield is a simple one, normally being thought of as the dividend, rental or interest rate, divided by price. Whilst this definition may suffice for equities and property, it is far from satisfactory for gauging the returns from redeemable securities where allowance has to be made for capital gains or losses to redemption, as well as income flow. It is thus timely at this point to describe and define 'flat yield' and 'redemption yield'.

*Flat yield* (alternatively called 'interest yield', or 'income yield') is the gross coupon rate divided by the *clean price* of a given bond:

$$f = \frac{g}{P - a} \tag{5.1}$$

where,
$g$ represents the bond's coupon rate
$P$ represents the bond's total price
$a$ represents the bond's accrued interest.

As an example, consider a bond with a 6% coupon, priced at $92\frac{1}{8}$, with forty-three days' accrued interest included in the price. In this case the flat yield is:

$$f = \frac{6}{92.125 - (6 \times 43 / 365)} \tag{5.2}$$

$$= 0.65632$$

i.e. 6.563% gross.

Under the provisions of the 1996 changes in the tax treatment of gilts and bonds, for UK corporate investors and personal investors whose aggregate bond holdings exceed £200,000 nominal, capital gains are subject to income tax and thus for major investors there is no longer any basic differentiation between the income and capital elements in a bond's total return. As such, flat yields are most frequently considered in gross terms. However, for investors not subject to these arrangements but operating under a tax regime whereby income only is taxed, the concept of a *net flat yield* is still valid, and can be calculated as shown below.

Using the same example as previously, but applying tax at a rate of 25% on income, produces a net flat yield:

$$= \frac{6 \times (1 - 0.25)}{92.125 - [6 \times (1 - 0.25) \times 43 / 365]}$$

$$= 0.049129$$

i.e. 4.913% net of tax at 25% on income.

It is important to note that, because the accrued interest quantity is 'netted' as well as the coupon rate, the *net flat yield* is not equal to the net of the gross flat yield (except when the accrued interest is zero).

*Redemption yield* is a measure of value which combines the benefits to the investor of both the income flow and the eventual capital profit (or loss) to its redemption value (not always necessarily at par) in a single figure, expressed as a rate of return per cent per annum.

There is a convention concerning gilt-edged yields which it is important to understand. Because (most) gilt-edged and (most) other fixed-interest stocks in the United Kingdom make interest payments every half-year, redemption yields are computed as rates of return per half-year, and then doubled. Thus, when one speaks of a redemption yield of, say, 6.56% per annum, the true rate being used is actually 3.28% per half-year. For those people who may not at first sight appreciate the significance of this, it is worth considering the difference between the compounded values of:

(a) 6.56% compounded over ten years, and
(b) 3.28% compounded over twenty half-years.

(a) $= 1.0656^{10} = 1.88774$
(b) $= 1.0328^{20} = 1.90689$

a difference of over 1%, and this difference increases significantly at higher rates and for longer periods.

The foregoing introduces the reader to an elementary facet of compound interest theory, on which all redemption yield analysis is based. Because it is fundamental to the whole of this subject, the following section is included at this juncture, before going on to a formal definition of a redemption yield.

## Compound interest theory

Imagine that it is possible to invest only in an investment that gives a constant return of $y\%$ per annum paid half-yearly. An initial investment of 1 would, after the first half-year, produce interest of $y/200$. (For the sake of convenience and also because it concurs with actuarial notation, this value of $y/200$ is denoted by the symbol $i$.) After being credited with interest of $i$, the total value of the investment has thus grown to $(1 + i)$. If this amount is left invested for a further six months, it will produce a second interest payment, this time equal to $i(1 + i)$.

Adding in this, the total value of the investment now becomes

$$1 + i + i(1 + i)$$

$$= 1 + 2i + i^2$$

$$= (1 + i)^2.$$

This procedure can be repeated *ad nauseam*, but the essential feature of compound interest theory now becomes patently clear – that the future compounded value of 1 invested for $n$ half-years at a rate of $y\%$ per annum

$$= (1 + i)^n, \quad \text{where } i = y/200.$$

Conversely, the present (discounted) value of 1 receivable in $n$ half-years' time

$$= \frac{1}{(1+i)^n}$$

Again, following actuarial notation, this value is written $v^n$

$$\text{where } v = \frac{1}{(1+i)}$$

We have now established the basis for calculating the present value ($PV$) of any future payment of either capital or dividend given a particular interest rate at which to discount them. For instance, the $PV$ of a series of payments of 6, 8, 10, 15, 20, 23, at the end of 1, 2, 3, 4, 5, 6 half-years respectively, is the expression

$$PV = 6v + 8v^2 + 10v^3 + 15v^4 + 20v^5 + 23v^6.$$

If the rate of interest to be used in this discounting process is, say, $y = 5\%$ per annum:

$$v = \frac{1}{(1 + y/200)} = \frac{1}{1.025}$$

$$\text{and } PV = \frac{6}{1.025} + \frac{8}{1.025^2} + \frac{10}{1.025^3} + \frac{15}{1.025^4} + \frac{20}{1.025^5} + \frac{23}{1.025^6}$$

$$= 5.854 + 7.615 + 9.286 + 13.589 + 17.677 + 19.833$$

$$= 73.854.$$

Taking another example, where the benefits to be received are half-yearly interest payments of 3 over the next three years, followed by capital repayment of 100 at the end of that time, the present value can be written as:

$$PV = 3v + 3v^2 + 3v^3 + 3v^4 + 3v^5 + 3v^6 + 100v^6$$

$$\text{where } v = \frac{1}{(1 + i)}$$

$$\text{and } i = y/200.$$

We have thus established from first principles the formula for calculating the present value or price of the investment producing such a series of benefits – i.e. a 6% coupon rate three-year fixed-interest bond, redeemable at 100.

Table 5.1 shows the relationship between price (present value) and yield in this example, using three different yield bases, 5%, 6% and 7%.

## Redemption yield: definition and equations

Once an understanding of the method of constructing a bond's value has been grasped, it is now possible to make the following formal definition:

**A redemption yield is that rate of interest at which the total discounted values of future payments of income and capital equate to the current total price.**

**Table 5.1** Relationship between present value and yield (using yield bases of 5%, 6% and 7%)

| Yield % p.a. = y | 5% | 6% | 7% |
|---|---|---|---|
| $i = y/200$ | 0.025 | 0.030 | 0.035 |
| $1 + i$ | 1.025 | 1.030 | 1.035 |
| $v = 1/(1 + i)$ | 0.97561 | 0.97087 | 0.96618 |
| $3v$ | 2.9268 | 2.9126 | 2.8986 |
| $3v^2$ | 2.8554 | 2.8278 | 2.8005 |
| $3v^3$ | 2.7858 | 2.7454 | 2.7058 |
| $3v^4$ | 2.7179 | 2.6655 | 2.6143 |
| $3v^5$ | 2.6516 | 2.5878 | 2.5259 |
| $3v^6$ | 2.5869 | 2.5125 | 2.4405 |
| Present value of income flow | 16.5244 | 16.2516 | 15.9857 |
| PV of capital repayment = $100v^6$ | 86.2297 | 83.7484 | 81.3501 |
| Total present value = price | 102.7541 | 100.0000 | 97.3357 |

It has to be realised that, whereas given a particular yield it is possible to compute the corresponding price of a bond, there is no explicit formula for the reverse operation – i.e. given price, compute yield. Instead it is necessary to use some form of iterative process to solve the problem, and computer programs used for this purpose do just that. But for those people who ask the perennial question 'What is the formula for yield?', the answer is that there isn't one – there is only a formula for price.

In the simple case where a bond is standing at a dividend payment date (and is quoted without the right to receive that dividend, i.e. ex-dividend), the following formula applies:

$$P = \frac{g}{2}v + \frac{g}{2}v^2 + \frac{g}{2}v^3 + \ldots + \frac{g}{2}v^n + 100v^n \qquad (5.3)$$

where,

$g$ denotes the coupon rate

$n$ denotes the period to maturity in half-years

$v = 1/(1 + \text{yield}/200)$ and $P$ represents the *total price* of the bond inclusive of accrued interest.

This can be rewritten as

$$P = \frac{g}{2}(v + v^2 + v^3 + \ldots + v^n) + 100v^n \qquad (5.4)$$

The expression within brackets is known actuarially as an 'annuity certain', and is denoted by the symbol ($a_{\overline{n}}$). The components of ($a_{\overline{n}}$), i.e. $v$, $v^2$, $v^3 \ldots v^n$ form a geometric series, whose sum can be found by this (neat) method:

$$a_{\overline{n}|} = v + v^2 + v^3 + \ldots + v^n$$

$$\text{Therefore } (v\,a_{\overline{n}|}) = v^2 + v^3 + \ldots + v^n + v^{n+1}$$

$$\text{Thus } (1-v)(a_{\overline{n}|}) = v + 0 + 0 + \ldots + 0 \; - v^{n+1}$$

$$\text{leading to } (a_{\overline{n}|}) = \frac{(v - v^{n+1})}{(1-v)} = \frac{(1 - v^n)}{i}$$

a formula frequently found in actuarial work. Equations (5.3) and (5.4), however, are specific to the case of a bond being valued on a dividend payment date; in the more general case the basic equation of value is

$$P = \frac{g}{2}(v^q + v^{q+1} + \ldots + v^{q+n}) + Rv^{q+n} \tag{5.5}$$

where
$g$ denotes the annual coupon rate,
$R$ denotes the redemption value
$q$ denotes the time (measured in half-years) between the current settlement date and the actual business day on which the next interest or dividend payment will be received (after allowing for the incidence of weekends and bank holidays) and
$n$ denotes the time (in half-years) from the next receivable interest date to redemption.

For convenience again, this can be written as:

$$P = \frac{g}{2}[v^q(1 + v + v^2 + \ldots v^n)] + Rv^{q+n}$$

$$= v^q\left[\frac{g}{2}(1 + a_{\overline{n}|}) + Rv^n\right] \tag{5.6}$$

Given the *total price P*, solving this equation for $v$ and using the relationship

$$y = 200\,[(1/v) - 1]$$

enables yields to be determined.

Where bonds are partly paid the outstanding calls due form part of the 'price side' of the equation, e.g.

73

$$P + C_1 v^{m1} + C_2 v^{m2} + \ldots$$

where $P$     denotes the total partly paid price
and $C_1, C_2$   denote the calls due
and $m_1, m_2$   denote the time periods (in half-years) between the current
            settlement date and the dates of payment of those calls.

(With partly paid bonds there is likely to be a further complication: because the bond is partly paid, the first interest payment will most often be non-standard, i.e. not equal to half the coupon rate. In the following examples such non-standard coupon payments are represented by the symbol $g^*$).

One cannot emphasise too strongly that the item $P$ used throughout this analysis is the *total price* of the bond and (since February 1986) is composed of its quoted price, $Q$, plus gross accrued interest, $a$.

If one chooses to write $P = Q + a$ and take into account the calls due and the non-standard first coupon payment the above equation transforms to:

$$Q + a + C_1 v^{m_1} + C_2 v^{m_2} + \ldots = v^q\left[\left(g^* + \frac{g}{2}a_{\overline{n}}\right) + Rv^n\right]$$

leading to

$$Q = v^q\left[\left(g^* + \frac{g}{2}a_{\overline{n}}\right) + Rv^n\right] - a - \left[C_1 v^{m_1} + C_2 v^{m_2} + \ldots\right] \qquad (5.7)$$

*Net redemption yields.*    Exactly the same compound interest principles can be applied to net of tax values in order to obtain net redemption yields.

    Under the pre-1996 tax regime when capital gains made on bonds were tax-free this was not a particularly complex exercise even though in most cases it involved taking into account the operation of the accrued income scheme.

    Under the accrued income scheme (which came into operation on 28 February 1986) an investor was additionally liable to income tax on the gross accrued interest at the time of sale, with a similar offsetting tax credit relating to the gross accrued interest at the time of purchase. According to the terms of the 1985 Finance Act these tax payments were deemed to be payable (or receivable) on the next actual dividend date following disposal or acquisition. Thus in order to compute net redemption yields under these arrangements it is necessary to know the size of these items, let us say, $= a$ at purchase and $= b$ at sale; and the time periods between acquisition and the next following dividend date, say, $= s$; and between sale and its next following dividend date, say, $= z$.

Given all these quantities the basic equation of value for net redemption yields becomes:

$$P - tav^s = v^q(1-t)\frac{g}{2}(1+a_{\overline{n}}) + Rv^{q+n} - tbv^{q+n+z}$$

The final term in this equation is usually redundant since in most cases redemption takes place on a scheduled dividend date. In such cases $b = 0$ and the relationship simplifies to:

$$P = Q + a = tav^s + v^q(1-t)\frac{g}{2}(1+a_{\overline{n}}) + Rv^{q+n}$$

or,

$$Q = v^q(1-t)\frac{g}{2}(1+a_{\overline{n}}) + Rv^{q+n} - a(1-tv^s) \tag{5.8}$$

and when partly paid bonds are involved:

$$Q = v^q(1-t)\left(g* + \frac{g}{2}a_{\overline{n}}\right) + Rv^{q+n} - a(1-tv^s) - (C_1 v^{m_1} + C_1 v^{m_2} + ...) \tag{5.9}$$

However, as mentioned in Chapter 3, there are many other market participants for whom gilt-edged transactions form part of their trade or business (as opposed to being considered investments), and in such cases both dividends and capital gains were treated as components of their overall profits and subjected to corporation tax, and the accrued interest scheme did not apply. If the capital gain in question was based on dirty prices and deemed to be taxable at redemption then general net redemption yield took the form:

$$P = Q + a = v^q(1-c)\frac{g}{2}(1+a_{\overline{n}}) + [R - c(R - Q - a)]v^{q+n}$$

leading to,

$$Q = \frac{v^q(1-c)\frac{g}{2}(1+a_{\overline{n}}) + Rv^{q+n}(1-c) - a(1-cv^{q+n})}{1 - cv^{q+n}} \tag{5.10}$$

where c = the rate of corporation tax/100.

And when partly-paid bonds were involved:

$$Q = \frac{\left\{ v^q(1-c)\left(g * + \frac{g}{2}a_{\overline{n}}\right) + Rv^{q+n}(1-c) - a(1 - cv^{q+n}) \right.}{1 - cv^{q+n}} \left. \frac{- [C_1(v^{m_1} - cv^{q+n}) + C_2(v^{m_2} - cv^{q+n}) + \ldots]}{} \right\}$$ (5.11)

Under the post-April 1996 bond taxation arrangements the situation is rather more complex. There are now three main classes of taxed investors and the methods of computation of net redemption yields varies accordingly:

*Class 1: UK personal investors whose aggregated gilt-edged and other bond nominal holdings are £200,000 or below*

These investors are taxed on interest payments and are subject to the accrued income scheme. Capital gains continue to be tax-free.

The relevant equations of value for determining net redemption yields for this class are (5.8) and (5.9) above.

(*Note*: This regime also applies to all UK holdings of Funding $3\frac{1}{2}$% 99/04 and Treasury $5\frac{1}{2}$% 08/12 irrespective of size.)

*Class 2: UK personal investors whose aggregated gilt-edged and other bond holdings exceed £200,000 nominal*

These investors are taxed as to income tax on both interest payments as they occur and capital gains at sale or redemption. The accrued income scheme does not apply.

For such investors net redemption yields can be obtained from equations (5.10) and (5.11) above substituting the investor's partic-ular tax rate for $c$ (the rate of corporation tax) in each case.

*Class 3: UK corporate investors*

For this class of investors interest payments will continue to be taxed in the normal way, but the accrued income scheme will no longer apply. Changes in a bond's capital value are now considered as income items and are assessable to tax at each accounting year-end rather than only at disposal or redemption. Such taxation of unrealised gains requires end-year valuations to be made each year and for tax to be levied on the difference in value over each tax

76

year. Investors have the choice of using either a strict mark-to-market valuation basis under which tax payments reflect the actual performance of the bond during the year in question, or an accrual basis under which roughly equal tax payments are due each year. Clearly net redemption yields assuming a mark-to-market valuation basis are impossible to compute since to do so would require prior knowledge of future end-year values, but net redemption yields based on an accruals basis can be calculated. The following (over-simplified) example illustrates how:

Imagine an investor subject to 25% tax buying a 6% coupon five-year bond at a price of 90 at the end of his tax year.

If the investor were to use a 'straight-line' accrual basis of valuation for tax purposes his bond will be deemed to be valued at

92 at the end of the first year
94 at the end of the second year
96 at the end of the third year
98 at the end of the fourth year, and
100 at redemption at the end of the fifth year

This will give rise to a tax liability of $0.50 = (2 \times 0.25)$ each year in relation to the potential capital gain as well as the usual tax of $0.75 = (3 \times 0.25)$ on each semi-annual coupon payment. It is next necessary to determine the timing of the respective tax payments because these will not necessarily be made at the same time as coupon payments are made. For the purpose of this example let us assume they are made three months after the end of the tax year. The equation of value then becomes

$$
\begin{aligned}
90 = {} & 3(v + v^2 + v^3 + \ldots + v^{10}) + 100v^{10} \\
& - 0.75(v^{1.5} + v^{2.5} + v^{3.5} + \ldots + v^{10.5}) \\
& - 0.50(v^{2.5} + v^{4.5} + v^{6.5} + v^{8.5} + v^{10.5})
\end{aligned}
\tag{5.12}
$$

This is found to give a value for $v$ of 0.968955 which corresponds to a net redemption yield of 6.408% per annum semi-annually compounded.

*Net cash flow yields*

The net redemption yield example shown above (equation 5.12) illustrates some of the complexities involved when net-of-tax returns are required to be calculated. In this particular example an assumption was made that the tax payments would be made three months after the interest payments were received, but in practice this will vary. For some investors basic rate tax will be deducted at source and higher rate tax paid some time later, and for those using quarterly tax accounting the time lag between receiving a gross interest payment and paying tax on it will vary depending on the individual bond's interest payment dates.

Another potential variable is the rate of tax involved. There is normally an implicit assumption that this will remain constant during the life of the investment. But this is not always the case. For example, the progressive reduction in corporation tax between 1982/83 and 1986/87 gave rise to five different rates ranging from 52% down to 35% during this period. The hard facts of the matter are that in order to make truly meaningful net present value assessments of a specific bond's benefits to a taxed investor or trader it is really necessary to build a model involving all the prospective net cash flows and the dates on which they are expected to occur, and discount them individually rather than use generalised formulae. Performing this task has been greatly facilitated by the widespread availability of computer spreadsheets and the rates of return so obtained can best be described as 'net cash flow yields'.

### The 'exact days' method of yield calculation

The formulae in equations (5.3) to (5.11) inclusive above are based on the term to maturity being divided into two components $q$ and $n$ (half years) as described in equation (5.5) and this convention or minor variations of it have been used in UK fixed interest markets for many years. There is, however, another convention which has latterly come into use internationally in which the value of each individual receipt of income or capital repayment is discounted by a factor representing the exact number of days between expected receipt and the value date in question. Such calculations take into account delays that can be expected to occur if payment dates fall at weekends or on public holidays and proponents of the method often describe yields computed in this way as 'true yields' or 'exact days yields'. The method has a number of advantages not least the avoidance of discontinuities over ex-dividend dates; but suffers from the practical disadvantage of requiring access to some form of computer capability and possession of a schedule of public holidays, such as Easter, in future years in order to function, whereas the traditional method of calculation can, if necessary, be performed by hand. Differences between yields calculated using these different conventions are normally only significant when the term to maturity is relatively short, but at all times practitioners should take care to make yield comparisons on a like for like basis only.

## Redemption yield and total return

It will not have escaped notice that in the foregoing section there has been a welter of mathematical formulae, and whilst these are essential in a book such as this, they may have tended to obscure the scene for the less mathematical of readers who may wish to have a more qualitative answer to the question 'What exactly is a redemption yield?'.

To help in this respect Table 5.2 details the prices of three different bonds, with coupon rates of 3%, 6% and 9% respectively, valued on a constant gross redemption yield (GRY) basis of 7%, using the formulae established earlier. To get an idea of how a redemption yield combines both the income and capital components of total return, it is instructive to look at the return produced from holding any of these bonds over some sample six-month periods.

Firstly, consider the total return brought about by holding the 6% coupon bond over the time when its maturity reduces from ten years to nine-and-a-half years. At the end of this time a gross coupon of 3 will be received. From the table above it can be seen that, whilst the bond stays on a 7% gross redemption yield basis, its price will move over this period from 92.8938 to 93.1451 – a capital gain of 0.2513. Combining these two elements produces a total return of 3.2513 on an initial value of 92.8938. The percentage return over the six months is therefore $100 \times 3.2513 / 92.8938 = 3.50\%$, equivalent to 7% per annum compounded semi-annually.

**TABLE 5.2** Prices of three sample bonds valued on a 7% gross redemption yield (compounded semi-annually) for maturities ranging from 0 to 10 years

| Term (years) | Coupon 3.00 | Coupon 6.00 | Coupon 9.00 |
| --- | --- | --- | --- |
| 0.0 | 100.0000 | 100.0000 | 100.0000 |
| 0.5 | 98.0676 | 99.5169 | 100.9662 |
| 1.0 | 96.2006 | 99.0502 | 101.8997 |
| 1.5 | 94.3967 | 98.5992 | 102.8016 |
| 2.0 | 92.6538 | 98.1635 | 103.6731 |
| 2.5 | 90.9699 | 97.7425 | 104.5151 |
| 3.0 | 89.3429 | 97.3357 | 105.3286 |
| 3.5 | 87.7709 | 96.9427 | 106.1145 |
| 4.0 | 86.2521 | 96.5630 | 106.8740 |
| 4.5 | 84.7846 | 96.1962 | 107.6077 |
| 5.0 | 83.3668 | 95.8417 | 108.3166 |
| 5.5 | 81.9969 | 95.4992 | 109.0016 |
| 6.0 | 80.6733 | 95.1683 | 109.6633 |
| 6.5 | 79.3945 | 94.8486 | 110.3027 |
| 7.0 | 78.1590 | 94.5397 | 110.9205 |
| 7.5 | 76.9652 | 94.2413 | 111.5174 |
| 8.0 | 75.8118 | 93.9529 | 112.0941 |
| 8.5 | 74.6974 | 93.6743 | 112.6513 |
| 9.0 | 73.6206 | 93.4052 | 113.1897 |
| 9.5 | 72.5803 | 93.1451 | 113.7098 |
| 10.0 | 71.5752 | 92.8938 | 114.2124 |

It can be shown that the same result will be obtained from any other pair of adjacent values in the above table, even when a bond is above par and the capital element is negative.

This approach can now be expanded further by the following logical approach. Since the total return over each separate six-monthly period, using this price progression, is equal to 3.5%, then the total compound interest rate of return over the whole period will be 3.5% per half-year i.e. 7% per annum using the standard convention.

However, the important words in the last paragraph are 'using this price progression', for the above result will not occur in any other circumstances, except perhaps by chance. Once this is fully appreciated it becomes easier to understand what a redemption yield is, and equally importantly what it is not. A redemption yield is, as stated earlier, the rate of interest at which the sum of all discounted future benefits to be obtained from an investment equate to its current price. It is not a guaranteed compound rate of return to be earned from making an investment at that price. For that to happen would require all further coupon payments to be investable on precisely that same yield basis also, which in practice is highly unlikely.

This brings us to the next important concept – that of the 'roll-up' rate. The roll-up rate of interest is the rate at which (it is assumed that) forthcoming coupon or interest payments can be invested – or 'rolled-up' – in future. If the roll-up rate is greater than the initial redemption yield then the realised rate of return will exceed the redemption yield, and vice versa. The importance of roll-up rate considerations is greatest when dealing with high coupon bonds and long maturities, but the fixed interest analyst should remember the existence of this factor at all times, especially when making comparisons between bonds with significantly different coupon rates. As an example of this factor, it is worth looking at Tables 5.3 and 5.4 which show the results of investing £100,000 by purchasing a holding of our 9% ten-year bond on a 7% gross redemption yield, and compounding the dividend flows by reinvesting in the same bond on one of the two following bases:

1. Using a roll-up rate of 7%, by assuming the price stays on a constant 7% gross redemption yield (as shown in Table 5.2).
2. Using a roll-up rate of 9%, by assuming the bond moves immediately to par and remains there until maturity.

Summarising the examples in Tables 5.3 and 5.4 we can see that using a 7% roll-up rate, £100,000 accumulates to £198,978.89 over the ten years and the realised compound rate of return is (not surprisingly) 7% per annum; but with a 9% roll-up rate the accumulated value is some £12,181 more, at £211,160.44, and the realised return significantly greater at 7.616%.

Whilst the two schedules shown in Tables 5.3 and 5.4 are instructive in

**Table 5.3** Compound accumulation of a 9% ten-year bond on a constant 7% reinvestment basis

| Investable cash at the start of the half-year | Term to maturity | Gross red yield | Price on this GRY | Nominal bonds purchased | Total nominal bonds | Coupon payment at end of the half-year |
|---|---|---|---|---|---|---|
| 100,000.00 | 10.0 | 7.00 | 114.21 | 87,556.17 | 87,556.17 | 3,940.03 |
| 3,940.03 | 9.5 | 7.00 | 113.71 | 3,464.99 | 91,021.15 | 4,095.95 |
| 4,095.95 | 9.0 | 7.00 | 113.19 | 3,618.66 | 94,639.81 | 4,258.79 |
| 4,258.79 | 8.5 | 7.00 | 112.65 | 3,780.51 | 98,420.32 | 4,428.91 |
| 4,428.91 | 8.0 | 7.00 | 112.09 | 3,951.07 | 102,371.39 | 4,606.71 |
| 4,606.71 | 7.5 | 7.00 | 111.52 | 4,130.94 | 106,502.33 | 4,792.60 |
| 4,792.60 | 7.0 | 7.00 | 110.92 | 4,320.76 | 110,823.08 | 4,987.04 |
| 4,987.04 | 6.5 | 7.00 | 110.30 | 4,521.23 | 115,344.31 | 5,190.49 |
| 5,190.49 | 6.0 | 7.00 | 109.66 | 4,733.12 | 120,077.43 | 5,403.48 |
| 5,403.48 | 5.5 | 7.00 | 109.00 | 4,957.25 | 125,034.68 | 5,626.56 |
| 5,626.56 | 5.0 | 7.00 | 108.32 | 5,194.55 | 130,229.23 | 5,860.32 |
| 5,860.32 | 4.5 | 7.00 | 107.61 | 5,446.00 | 135,675.23 | 6,105.39 |
| 6,105.39 | 4.0 | 7.00 | 106.87 | 5,712.69 | 141,387.93 | 6,362.46 |
| 6,362.46 | 3.5 | 7.00 | 106.11 | 5,995.84 | 147,383.77 | 6,632.27 |
| 6,632.27 | 3.0 | 7.00 | 105.33 | 6,296.74 | 153,680.51 | 6,915.62 |
| 6,915.62 | 2.5 | 7.00 | 104.52 | 6,616.86 | 160,297.38 | 7,213.38 |
| 7,213.38 | 2.0 | 7.00 | 103.67 | 6,957.81 | 167,255.19 | 7,526.48 |
| 7,526.48 | 1.5 | 7.00 | 102.80 | 7,321.37 | 174,576.56 | 7,855.95 |
| 7,855.95 | 1.0 | 7.00 | 101.90 | 7,709.49 | 182,286.05 | 8,202.87 |
| 8,202.87 | 0.5 | 7.00 | 100.97 | 8,124.37 | 190,410.42 | 8,568.47 |

| | |
|---|---|
| Redemption capital value | 190,410.42 |
| Final coupon payment | 8,568.47 |

| | |
|---|---|
| Total accumulated value (reinvesting at 7%) | 198,978.89 |

Since $(198,978.89/100,000)^{1/20}=1.035$ precisely, the realised semi-annually compounded rate of return on this basis is 7.00% per annum.

showing how the compounding effect can work, they are a trifle cumbersome, and the figures quoted above can be derived more elegantly. Let us take a general example of a bond with coupon rate $= g$ per annum, term to maturity $= n$ half-years and current price $= P$. If it is only possible to reinvest coupons as they occur at $Z\%$, i.e. using a roll-up rate of $Z\%$, then for every 100 nominal of bonds the accumulated value at maturity will consist of the sum of the following:

(i) Capital repayment at redemption         $= 100$

(ii) The final coupon payment         $= g/2$

(iii) The compounded value of the coupon 6 months from maturity         $= (g/2)(1 + Z/200)$

(iv) The compounded value of the coupon 1 year from maturity         $= (g/2)(1 + Z/200)^2$

... and so on, until ...

(xxi) The compounded value of the coupon $(n - 1)$ half-years from maturity         $= (g/2)(1 + Z/200)^{(n-1)}$

**Table 5.4** Compound accumulation of a 9% ten-year bond initially priced on a 7% gross redemption yield basis, but accumulating dividends at a 9% reinvestment rate

| Investable cash at the start of the half-year | Term to maturity | Gross red yield | Price on this GRY | Nominal bonds purchased | Total nominal bonds | Coupon payment at end of the half-year |
|---|---|---|---|---|---|---|
| 100,000.00 | 10.0 | 7.00 | 114.21 | 87,556.17 | 87,556.17 | 3,940.03 |
| 3,940.03 | 9.5 | 9.00 | 100.00 | 3,940.03 | 91,496.19 | 4,117.33 |
| 4,117.33 | 9.0 | 9.00 | 100.00 | 4,117.33 | 95,613.52 | 4,302.61 |
| 4,302.61 | 8.5 | 9.00 | 100.00 | 4,302.61 | 99,916.13 | 4,496.23 |
| 4,496.23 | 8.0 | 9.00 | 100.00 | 4,496.23 | 104,412.36 | 4,698.56 |
| 4,698.56 | 7.5 | 9.00 | 100.00 | 4,698.56 | 109,110.91 | 4,909.99 |
| 4,909.99 | 7.0 | 9.00 | 100.00 | 4,909.99 | 114,020.91 | 5,130.94 |
| 5,130.94 | 6.5 | 9.00 | 100.00 | 5,130.94 | 119,151.85 | 5,361.83 |
| 5,361.83 | 6.0 | 9.00 | 100.00 | 5,361.83 | 124,513.68 | 5,603.12 |
| 5,603.12 | 5.5 | 9.00 | 100.00 | 5,603.12 | 130,116.79 | 5,855.26 |
| 5,855.26 | 5.0 | 9.00 | 100.00 | 5,855.26 | 135,972.05 | 6,118.74 |
| 6,118.74 | 4.5 | 9.00 | 100.00 | 6,118.74 | 142,090.79 | 6,394.09 |
| 6,394.09 | 4.0 | 9.00 | 100.00 | 6,394.09 | 148,484.88 | 6,681.82 |
| 6,681.82 | 3.5 | 9.00 | 100.00 | 6,681.82 | 155,166.70 | 6,982.50 |
| 6,982.50 | 3.0 | 9.00 | 100.00 | 6,982.50 | 162,149.20 | 7,296.71 |
| 7,296.71 | 2.5 | 9.00 | 100.00 | 7,296.71 | 169,445.91 | 7,625.07 |
| 7,625.07 | 2.0 | 9.00 | 100.00 | 7,625.07 | 177,070.98 | 7,968.19 |
| 7,968.19 | 1.5 | 9.00 | 100.00 | 7,968.19 | 185,039.17 | 8,326.76 |
| 8,326.76 | 1.0 | 9.00 | 100.00 | 8,326.76 | 193,365.94 | 8,701.47 |
| 8,701.47 | 0.5 | 9.00 | 100.00 | 8,701.47 | 202,067.40 | 9,093.03 |

| | |
|---|---|
| Redemption capital value | 202,067.40 |
| Final coupon payment | 9,093.03 |

| | |
|---|---|
| Total accumulated value (reinvesting at 9%) | 211,160.44 |

Since $(211,160.40/100,000)^{1/20} = 1.0380795$, the realised semi-annually compounded rate of return on this basis is 7.616% per annum.

Summing these items produces a total accumulated value of

$$100 + \frac{g}{2}\left[1 + (1 + \frac{Z}{200}) + (1 + \frac{Z}{200})^2 \ldots + (1 + \frac{Z}{200})^{n-1}\right]$$

$$= 100 + \frac{\frac{g}{2}[(1+j)^n - 1]}{j}$$

where $j$ represents $Z/200$

The item $[(1 + j)^n - 1]/j$ is another actuarial function and is often written as $s_{\overline{n}|}{}^j$.

In the second of our previous examples the term to maturity was ten years, so that $n = 20$. The coupon rate was 9%, so $g = 9$, $g/2 = 4.5$ and the reinvestment rate for dividends was 9%, i.e. $Z = 4.5, j = 0.045$. Applying this formula gives the following results:

For every £100 nominal of bonds the accumulated value at maturity

$$= £100 + 4.5 \, (1.045^{20} - 1) / 0.045$$
$$= £100 + 141.1714$$
$$= £241.1714.$$

At the outset the price of £100 nominal of bonds (on a 7% gross yield basis) was £114.2124. To find the compound rate of return over the ten years represented by these values it is necessary to solve the simple equation:

$$114.2124 \, (1 + r)^{20} \; = \; 241.1714$$
$$(1 + r)^{20} \; = \; 241.1714/114.2124$$
$$= \; 2.1116044$$

$$\text{Thus} \quad (1 + r) \; = \; 1.0380795$$

$$\text{and } r \; = \; 0.0380795$$

equivalent to a compound rate of $0.0380795 \times 200 = 7.616\%$, as previously calculated.

The use of the functions $a_{\overline{n}}$, $v^n$, $s_{\overline{n}}$, are basic to a whole range of compound interest calculations, and any aspiring gilt-edged analyst should aim to be proficient in their application.

## Accumulated returns

There is no widely accepted name used to describe the compound rates of return found by assuming varying 'roll-up' rates for dividend accumulation, but the expression 'accumulated returns' is broadly descriptive, and this nomenclature will be used in this book for that purpose.

Whilst it has already been demonstrated that if the roll-up rate is higher than the redemption yield, the accumulated return will also be higher, and vice versa, what has not yet been shown is how great the differential effect can prove to be between bonds of widely differing coupons.

Let us now compare the prospective accumulated returns yields of two twenty-year bonds, priced on a 8% gross redemption yield basis, the first having a coupon rate of 3%, and the second a coupon rate of 9%, if, say, a 7% roll-up rate is assumed.

Bond A 3% 20-year GRY = 8%   Price =  50.5181
Bond B 9% 20-year GRY = 8%   Price = 109.8963

Using a 5% roll-up rate the accumulated values of £100,000 invested in the two bonds can be found thus:

An initial investment of £100,000 produces:

a holding of £197,949 nominal of Bond A or
a holding of  £90,995 nominal of Bond B.

The accumulated values of these holdings over twenty years to maturity using a roll-up rate of 7% are:

Bond A: $(1.5\, s_{\overline{40}|} + 100) \times 197,949/100$

$$= \left(1.5 \times \frac{1.025^{40} - 1}{0.025} + 100\right) \times 1979.49$$

$$= £398,083.$$

Bond B: $(4.5\, s_{\overline{40}|} + 100) \times 90,995/100$

$$= \left(4.5 \times \frac{1.025^{40} - 1}{0.025} + 100\right) \times 909.95$$

$$= £366,993.$$

If $A_{5\%}$ and $B_{5\%}$ are used to denote the respective accumulated returns using a 5% roll-up rate, then:

(i)   $(1 + A_{5\%}/200)^{40} = 398083/100000$
(ii)  $(1 + B_{5\%}/200)^{40} = 366993/100000$

from which it can be found that

$$A_{5\%} = 7.028\%$$
$$B_{5\%} = 6.608\%$$

The difference between these two accumulated returns shows clearly the importance of making correct assessments as to the likely course of future (roll-up) interest rates when choosing long-term fixed interest investments. Simply picking the highest redemption yield (on an equal-risk basis) is no guarantee of best accumulation performance if that involves buying the very high-coupon bond at a time when interest rates are set to fall.

## Modified duration (volatility)

All of the foregoing has looked at fixed-interest investment from the longer-term standpoint, e.g. to redemption. In practice, very few investments run to maturity, the vast majority being for intermediate periods ranging from a number of years to a few days, hours or even minutes. Since the gilt-edged market is a very liquid one, and one where dealing expenses are small, it attracts its fair share of short-term activity, some of which may emanate from private investors, but the majority of which is professional in nature. To the short-term operator the long-term yield (redemption or accumulation) attractions of gilts are largely academic. To them a redemption yield represents more a convenient form of rating, by which they can make price relativity judgements, rather than a measure of intrinsic value. What matters more to the short-term trader is not so much the redemption yield itself, but prospective short-term changes in the yield structure that will produce beneficial price actions. However, because bonds have differing physical characteristics (coupon rate, term to maturity, etc.) there are potentially wide differences in the price movements of individual gilts that can result from applying the same change in yield to all of them.

For example, a 6% bond with six months to run to maturity would be priced at 100 to yield 6% gross, and at 100.4878 to yield 5%, whereas a $3\frac{1}{2}$% undated bond would be priced at 58.3333 and 70.0000 on a similar basis. The percentage price movement brought about by an instantaneous (i.e. for the same settlement date) 1% reduction in yield from 6% to 5% would therefore be 0.4878% on the former and 20.0000% on the latter. This gearing factor which relates instantaneous price movement to the corresponding yield movement was known for many years in the gilt-edged market as 'volatility', but the widespread use of that word to mean something rather different in option pricing theory has required a change in nomenclature to avoid confusion. In a later section of this chapter we shall show that 'volatility' as we used to call it is closely related to Macaulay duration and as so is now generally referred to as 'modified duration'. It is formally defined by the differential calculus relationship:

$$\text{modified duration} = -\frac{1}{P}\frac{dP}{dy}$$

where $P$ and $y$ represent price and yield respectively.

The modified duration of a bond is a function of three variables:

(i) *Its term to maturity.* Normally modified duration rises as maturity lengthens, but there are some instances of very low-coupon long-dated bonds having modified durations greater than that of the undateds.
(ii) *Its coupon rate.* Normally lower-coupon bonds have higher modified durations than higher-coupon bonds of the same maturity.
(iii) *Its yield.* If all other variables remain constant, modified duration rises as the yield level falls. This is easily seen in the case of the undateds, since the percentage change in price for a 1% change in yield from, say, 6% to 5% is obviously much greater than one from 16% to 15%. In the former case prices rise by 20%, and in the latter by 6.67%. (For further analysis of the relationship between modified duration and the level of yields see the section on Convexity later in this chapter.)

It should be noted that in (iii) above the price changes have been related to finite differences in the yield basis, in this case − 1%, whereas the formal definition is couched in notation of differential calculus where such changes are infinitesimal. Certain investors prefer to express modified duration in terms of finite yield changes, but this presents problems as the absolute size of a percentage change in price of a bond can be different for a rise in yield from that produced by a fall in yield of the same amount. Whilst this may, at first sight, seem surprising a further example (Table 5.5) using the undateds is instructive. Consider a $3\frac{1}{2}$% undated bond:

**Table 5.5**

| Gross yield | Clean price | Change in price from 6% gross yield | |
|---|---|---|---|
| | | in absolute | as % of price to yield 6% |
| 5% | 70.000 | | |
| | | 11.667 | 20.00% |
| 6% | 58.333 | | |
| | | 8.333 | 14.29% |
| 7% | 50.000 | | |

This shows that the modified duration produced by considering a 1% finite difference in yield would either be 20.00% or 14.29%, depending on which of the two alternative definitions was chosen. By contrast, the figure derived from the calculus definition taking an 6% yield basis turns out to be 16.67% as demonstrated here:

$$\text{modified duration} = w = -\frac{1}{P}\frac{dP}{dy}$$

86

In the case of an undated bond (and using clean prices):

$$P = 100\frac{g}{y}$$

where $g$ denotes the coupon rate and $y$ the yield.

Differentiating with respect to $y$,

$$\frac{\mathrm{d}P}{\mathrm{d}y} = -100\frac{g}{y^2}$$

$$\text{so that } w = \frac{-y}{100g} \times \frac{-100g}{y^2} = \frac{1}{y}$$

i.e. the modified duration of an undated bond is the reciprocal of its yield.

The modified duration figure for a given bond provides the gilt-edged analyst with a useful approximate ready reckoner for translating instantaneous yield changes into equivalent price variations. The word 'approximate' is used because, as mentioned above, the modified duration figure itself varies with the yield level and is not a constant, but for most practical purposes where the change in yield is small, the percentage price variation approximates to the bond's modified duration multiplied by the change in yield. (Where large changes in yield are concerned consideration has to be given to an entity known as 'convexity' which is explained a little later in this chapter.) This follows from the definition of modified duration ($w$):

$$w = -\frac{1}{P}\frac{\mathrm{d}P}{\mathrm{d}y}, \text{ so that } \frac{\Delta P}{P} \simeq -w\Delta y$$

where $\Delta P$ and $\Delta y$ represent relatively small finite changes in price and yield respectively.

The left-hand side of this equation is the proportionate change in value relating to an absolute change in price of $\Delta P$. This expression can take differing values depending on the value of the denominator $P$.

If for any reason an investor bases his investment calculations on *clean prices*, then by using a *clean price P* as denominator he will obtain a *clean modified duration*. Conversely, if total market prices (sometimes referred to

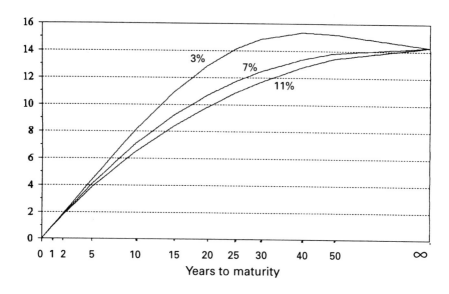

**Fig 5.1** Modified Duration of 3%, 7% and 11% coupon bonds of varying maturities (all valued on a 7% G.R.Y.)

as *dirty prices*) are used, the ensuing figure will be that of *dirty modified duration*.

When the term of the bond is an integral number of half-years, the mathematical formula for modified duration can be derived as follows:

$$P = \frac{g}{2}[v + v^2 + v^3 + \ldots + v^n] + 100v^n$$

Since $\dfrac{dP}{dy} = \dfrac{dP}{dv} \times \dfrac{dv}{dy}$ it follows that modified duration $= -\dfrac{1}{P}\dfrac{dP}{dv} \times \dfrac{dv}{dy}$

Now $\dfrac{dP}{dv} = \dfrac{g}{2}[1 + 2v + 3v^2 + \ldots + nv^{n-1}] + 100nv^{n-1}$

Also since $v = \dfrac{1}{(1 + y/200)}$ we obtain $\dfrac{dv}{dy} = -\dfrac{v^2}{200}$

The expression within square brackets in the equation for $dP/dv$ can be summed thus:

$$S = 1 + 2v + 3v^2 + \ldots + nv^{n-1}$$

88

Therefore $vS = \qquad v + 2v^2 + \ldots + (n-1)v^{n-1} - nv^n$

Subtracting $(1-v)S = 1 + \;\; v + \;\; v^2 + \ldots + v^{n-1} - nv^n$

so that $S = \dfrac{1-v^n}{(1-v)^2} - \dfrac{nv^n}{1-v}$

and modified duration $(w)$ is thus defined by the expression:

$$w = \frac{1}{P}\left(\frac{g}{2}S + 100nv^{n-1}\right)\frac{v^2}{200}$$

As an example, consider a 6% bond, with a term of 15 years standing on a gross redemption yield of 7%, i.e. $g = 6$, $n = 30$, $y = 7$:

here $\qquad v = 1/1.035 = 0.966184$

$\qquad (1 - v^{30}) = 0.643722$

$\qquad (1 - v)^2 = 0.001144$

so that $\qquad \dfrac{(1-v^{30})}{(1-v)^2} = 562.9148$

$\qquad 30v^{30} = 10.68835$

$\qquad (1 - v) = 0.033816$

so that $\qquad \dfrac{30v^{30}}{(1-v)} = 316.0698$

and thus $\qquad S = 246.8450$

also $\qquad 100 \times 30v^{29} = 1106.244$

$\qquad v^2/200 = 0.004668$

thus $\qquad \dfrac{dp}{dy} \equiv = -\left(\dfrac{6}{2} \times 246.845 + 1106.244\right) \times 0.004668 = -8.6199$

and as $\qquad P = \quad 90.804$

modified duration in this case is found to be $= 9.493$

## Convexity

At the beginning of the foregoing section reference was made to the fact that the modified duration of a bond at any instant in time is not a constant but varies with the level of yields. The following chart seeks to illustrate this point. It shows the modified durations of bonds all with a coupon of 7%, over a range of maturities from six months to thirty years together with the undateds, at a variety of different yield levels.

It can be seen from Fig. 5.2 that modified duration varies only a little with respect to the level of yields at the short end of the market, but as maturities lengthen there is considerable variation as represented both by the slope and the curvature of the chart's 'contours'. This is a manifestation of the entity known as convexity.

The relationship between modified duration and convexity is best illustrated mathematically. Using Taylor's expansion it is possible to express the change in price ($\Delta P$) caused by a corresponding change in yield ($\Delta y$) as follows.

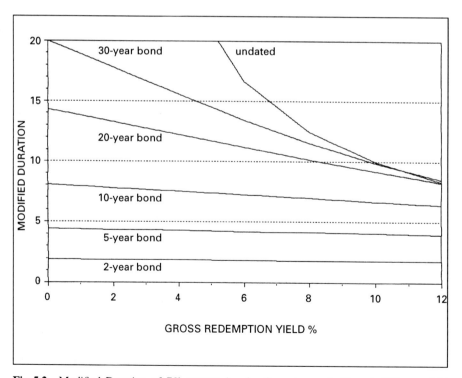

**Fig 5.2** Modified Duration of 7% coupon bonds of varying maturities at different yield levels

90

$$P + \Delta P = P + \frac{dP}{dy} \cdot \Delta y + \frac{1}{2} \cdot \frac{d_2 P}{dy^2} \cdot (\Delta y)^2 + \frac{1}{2} \cdot \frac{1}{3} \cdot \frac{d_3 P}{dy^3} \cdot (\Delta y)^3 + \ldots$$

This means that the proportionate change in price $\Delta P/P$ for a given change in yield, $dy$, may be written thus,

$$\frac{\Delta P}{P} = \frac{1}{P} \cdot \frac{dP}{dy} \cdot \Delta y + \frac{1}{2} \cdot \frac{1}{P} \cdot \frac{d_2 P}{dy^2} \cdot (\Delta y)^2 + \frac{1}{6} \cdot \frac{1}{P} \cdot \frac{d_3 P}{dy^3} \cdot (\Delta y)^3 + \ldots$$

and when $\Delta y$ is small terms after the first two are relatively insignificant.

Now whereas the value of the first term on the right hand side of this equation is proportional to the modified duration of the bond, the second term reflects its convexity which is defined as,

$$\text{Convexity} = \frac{1}{P} \cdot \frac{d_2 P}{dy^2}$$

**Table 5.6**  Convexity at varying maturities and yield levels for a 7% coupon bond

| Yield % | 1 year | 2 years | 5 years | Term 10 years | 20 years | 30 years | Undateds |
|---|---|---|---|---|---|---|---|
| 12.00 | 0.013 | 0.041 | 0.194 | 0.551 | 1.123 | 1.350 | 1.389 |
| 10.00 | 0.013 | 0.042 | 0.200 | 0.587 | 1.327 | 1.737 | 2.000 |
| 8.00 | 0.014 | 0.043 | 0.206 | 0.624 | 1.540 | 2.226 | 3.125 |
| 6.00 | 0.014 | 0.044 | 0.213 | 0.662 | 1.777 | 2.822 | 5.556 |
| 4.00 | 0.014 | 0.045 | 0.219 | 0.700 | 2.027 | 3.516 | 12.500 |
| 2.00 | 0.014 | 0.046 | 0.226 | 0.738 | 2.285 | 4.282 | 50.000 |

From Table 5.6 one can see that convexity basically increases with term to maturity, and decreases as yield levels rise. It is also the case that the convexity of lower coupon bonds is greater than that of those with higher coupons. Long-dated zero coupon bonds, in particular, have significantly greater convexity than full coupon bonds.

The broad message is that, all other things being equal, convexity is good for you. In Table 5.7 we can compare two hypothetical bonds both standing on the same yield basis and having identical modified durations. From this one can clearly see that for identical changes in yield the bond with the greater convexity will rise in value more quickly than the other if yields fall, and fall more slowly if yields rise.

**Table 5.7**

|  | Bond A | Bond B |  |
|---|---|---|---|
| Coupon rate | 7 | 0 |  |
| Term (years) | 20 | 11.05 |  |
| Redemption yield % | 7.00 | 7.00 |  |
| Modified duration | 10.68 | 10.68 |  |
| Convexity | 1.66 | 1.19 |  |
| Yield | Total price | Total price | Price ratio % A/B |
| 4.00 | 141.0332 | 64.5559 | 218.47 |
| 5.00 | 125.1028 | 57.9432 | 215.91 |
| 6.00 | 111.5574 | 52.0352 | 214.39 |
| **7.00** | 100.0000 | 46.7539 | **213.89** |
| 8.00 | 90.1036 | 42.0304 | 214.38 |
| 9.00 | 81.5984 | 37.8033 | 215.85 |
| 10.00 | 74.2614 | 34.0186 | 218.30 |

## (Macaulay) duration

In an earlier section we mentioned a link between modified duration and duration pure and simple, often referred to as 'Macaulay duration' after Frederick Macaulay who identified its properties as far back as 1938.

*(Macaulay) duration* is the weighted average length of time between purchase of a bond and receipt of the benefits of its component parts (interest payments, capital repayments, etc.) where the weightings applied are the present values of the benefits involved. It produces a figure that is conceptually something like an average life of a bond and (as the following analysis will show) is closely mathematically related to modified duration. Applying the notations previously used in this chapter, and assuming again the term is an integral number of half-years, the weighted average time period to receipt of benefit is

$$\frac{v\frac{g}{2}+2v^2\frac{g}{2}+3v^3\frac{g}{2}+\ldots+nv^n\frac{g}{2}+100nv^n}{v\frac{g}{2}+v^2\frac{g}{2}+v^3\frac{g}{2}+\ldots+v^n\frac{g}{2}+100v^n}\text{ half years}$$

The denominator of this expression is quite simply the bond's price, $P$, and the numerator can be recognised from an earlier equation as being equal to:

$$v\times\frac{dP}{dv}$$

Duration (measured in whole years) can thus be expressed as:

$$h = \frac{1}{2} \cdot \frac{v}{P} \cdot \frac{dP}{dv}$$

Now, since modified duration

$$w = -\frac{1}{P}\frac{dP}{dy} \text{ and } \frac{dv}{dy} = -\frac{v^2}{200}$$

it is possible to relate (Macaulay) duration ($h$) to modified duration ($w$) thus:

$$h = \frac{1}{2} \cdot \frac{v}{P} \cdot \frac{dP}{dv}$$

$$= \frac{1}{2} \cdot \frac{v}{P} \cdot \frac{dP}{dy} \cdot \frac{dy}{dv}$$

$$= \frac{1}{2} v(-w)\left\{-200/v^2\right\}$$

$$= 100\frac{w}{v}$$

$$= 100\,w\,(1+i)$$

That is duration (in years) = 100 × modified duration × [1 + (yield/200)].

Applying this formula to the previous example of a 6% fifteen-year bond yielding 7%, whose modified duration was 9.493%, we obtain a (Macaulay) duration equal to

$$100 \times \frac{9.493}{100} \times [1+7/200] = 9.83\,\text{years}$$

## The significance of duration and its place in immunisation theory

Over the years past a considerable amount of work has been done developing portfolio immunisation techniques to deal with the problem of the uncertainty of realised rates of return caused by roll-up rates in practice almost always varying from the redemption yield on which the bond was purchased.

It is instructive to consider the prospective compounded rates of return obtained from holding a bond where the roll-up rate differs from the redemption yield on which it was bought, over a variety of holding periods.

Table 5.4 earlier in this chapter charts the progress of the accumulated value of a 9% ten-year bond in the hypothetical case of it having been bought on a 7% gross redemption yield, but where a fall in its price soon after purchase to 100 (at which it then remains) allows the reinvestment of all its dividend payments subsequently at 9%. The effect of being able to roll-up dividends at a higher rate (9%) than the purchase yield (7%) is clearly beneficial if the bond is held to redemption. The example in Table 5.4 shows that the realised compound rate of interest obtained from that strategy would be 7.616%.

What, however, would the comparable rates of return be from other strategies involving shorter holding periods?

**Table 5.8**  Realised rates of return from holding a bond as described in Table 5.4 for different time periods

| Holding period (years) | Accumulated value (£) | Realised compound rate of return % p.a. |
|---|---|---|
| 0.5 | 91,496.19 | -17.008 |
| 1.0 | 95,613.52 | -4.436 |
| 1.5 | 99,916.13 | -0.056 |
| 2.0 | 104,412.36 | 2.171 |
| 2.5 | 109,110.91 | 3.518 |
| 3.0 | 114,020.91 | 4.422 |
| 3.5 | 119,151.85 | 5.070 |
| 4.0 | 124,513.68 | 5.557 |
| 4.5 | 130,116.79 | 5.937 |
| 5.0 | 135,972.05 | 6.241 |
| 5.5 | 142,090.79 | 6.490 |
| 6.0 | 148,484.88 | 6.698 |
| 6.5 | 155,166.70 | 6.874 |
| 7.0 | 162,149.20 | 7.026 |
| 7.5 | 169,445.91 | 7.157 |
| 8.0 | 177,070.98 | 7.271 |
| 8.5 | 185,039.17 | 7.373 |
| 9.0 | 193,365.94 | 7.463 |
| 9.5 | 202,067.40 | 7.543 |
| 10.0 | 211,160.44 | 7.616 |

What this shows is that for shorter holding periods the effect of the initial fall in price to a 9% yield level has a greater (and negative) impact than the benefits derived from having a higher roll-up rate, but for longer holding periods the reverse is the case.

From the values in Table 5.8 we can see that in order to obtain a realised yield of 7%, i.e the same as the purchase yield, an investor would need to hold the bond for a little short of seven years (to be precise 6.91 years). Similar exercises using roll-up rates of 8%, 6% and 5% result in holding periods of 6.97, 7.08 and 7.13 years respectively. The central value of these four values which have been derived from using roll-up rates spaced symmetrically either side of the initial purchase yield is 7.02 years. It so happens that this is precisely the (Macaulay) duration of a 9% ten-year bond standing on a 7% yield basis. This is not a coincidence as the following analysis will demonstrate.

Consider a bond purchased at a price of $P_0$ to give a redemption yield of $y_0$. Next let us assume it moves immediately to a price of $P_1$ and a corresponding yield of $y_1$, and that it subsequently remains on that redemption yield basis as time progresses. Let the critical holding period be $n$ half-years.

To meet the investor's demand for a rate of return equal to the purchase redemption yield requires there to be a gross performance over this period of $(1 + y_0/200)^n$.

The actual performance produced by this hypothesis can be considered as the product of $P_1/P_0$ (caused by the initial change in the yield basis) and $(1 + y_1/200)^n$, the subsequent accumulation for $n$ half-years at the roll-up rate of $y_1$. Equating these two entities one obtains:

$$(1 + y_0/200)^n = (P_1/P_0) \times (1 + y_1/200)^n$$

If one now takes logarithms,

$$n = \frac{\log P_1 - \log P_0}{\log(1 + y_0/200) - \log(1 + y_1/200)}$$

which tends to a central value of

$$-\frac{d(\log P)}{d[\log(1 + y/200)]}$$

$$= -200\frac{(1 + y/200)}{P}\frac{dP}{dy}$$

$$= 100 \times \text{modified duration} \times [1 + (\text{yield}/200)] \text{ in whole years,}$$

which is identical to the formula for (Macaulay) duration established earlier.

We can now see the place of duration in immunisation theory as the expected holding period necessary to ensure a realised rate of return equal to the purchase yield. The word 'expected' is used here to reflect the fact that, as we have seen in the practical example earlier, there is a singly defined holding period meeting this criterion, but this value is the central one based on the probability that roll-up rates are likely to vary equally either side of the purchase yield.

## Performance yields

So far, consideration has been given to two main sets of circumstances: holding bonds to redemption or looking at instantaneous price and yield changes. The vast majority of investments fall into neither of these categories, but are of an intermediate nature.

Again, there is no formally accepted terminology to describe the total return, or return per cent, from a fixed-interest security held over such a period, but the words 'performance' and 'performance yield' have been used by many people in this context for some years and are acceptable for this purpose.

Performance yields can be computed on exactly the same principle as redemption yields, with the simple variation that the redemption value is replaced by the value of the sale proceeds, and the time period is that between purchase and sale.

Imagine a 6%, fifteen-year bond, bought on a 9% gross redemption yield basis (at a price of 75.567) and subsequently sold five years later on a 7% yield (at a price of 92.894). The performance yield for this bond over the five years is found by solving the following equation of value:

$$75.567 = 3\,a_{\overline{10}|} + 92.894v^{10}$$

to give an answer of 11.463%.

Performance yields can either be retrospective, such as above, or prospective. In the latter case, a postulated value has to be put on the bond at the forward point in time, and this forecasting process introduces a further variable into the game, one which did not exist with redemption yields, where the forward value is fixed and known. In such instances, analysts will most likely arrive at their idea of forward price by 'guesstimating' a future (gross redemption) yield basis for the bond, and then translating that yield into a price.

If the assumed future gross yield basis is lower than the current one, then they will be taking a bullish view of the market; if it is higher they will be bearish. The neutral view is to assume (however rightly or wrongly this turns out to be) that the future yield basis is the same as that pertaining at the outset.

Gross performance yields resulting from a neutral view turn out to be exactly equal to the gross redemption yield involved. This is hardly surprising when one remembers the progression of bond prices shown in the tables in the early part of this chapter, and how, when a bond stays on a given yield 'contour', its returns over successive periods each equate to that particular yield. This often unappreciated truism is best summed up as 'If you buy a bond to yield $y\%$, and sell it when it still yields $y\%$, your rate of return will also be $y\%$.'

## Portfolio yields

One aspect of fixed-income mathematics that has proved bothersome to many practitioners over the years has been the problem of combining redemption yields. Most usually this would occur when it was necessary to express the characteristics of a portfolio of bonds in terms of averages, e.g average coupon rate, average life, average modified duration etc. Whilst the foregoing can be obtained by forming value-weighted arithmetic averages of the entities concerned, the same process produces incorrect and potentially dangerously misleading results if applied to redemption yields. An example using a simple two-bond portfolio illustrates this fact.

Consider this portfolio to be composed of equal holdings of two bonds, Bond A being a 9% one-year issue and Bond B a 7% 20-year one. Let us also assume (for the purpose of further simplicity) that both bonds are priced at par so that their yields are also 9% and 7% respectively.

The overall redemption yield of the portfolio (the 'portfolio yield') is that rate of interest at which the present discounted values of all the portfolio's future payments of interest and capital when summed equate to the total portfolio value. However, to obtain this yield it is not totally necessary to break down the portfolio into all these individual components; there is a way in which one can work with the constituent bonds.

If the portfolio yield is, say, $y\%$ then the corresponding value of the portfolio will be the sum of the value of Bond A to yield $y\%$ and that of Bond B to yield $y\%$ likewise. Working on that basis let us study Table 5.9 to examine the portfolio values at a range of yields between 7% and 9% to get an idea of where the portfolio yield lies.

**Table 5.9**

| Yield % | Price of Bond A | Price of Bond B | Portfolio value |
|---|---|---|---|
| 7.0 | 101.89969 | 100.00000 | 201.89969 |
| 7.5 | 101.41965 | 94.86225 | 196.28190 |
| 8.0 | 100.94305 | 90.10361 | 191.04666 |
| 8.5 | 100.46984 | 85.69204 | 186.16188 |
| 9.0 | 100.00000 | 81.59841 | 181.59841 |

Since the portfolio consists of equal nominal amounts of the two bonds we need to look in this table to see what sort of yield corresponds to a portfolio

97

value of 200. Clearly this is not 8% – the arithmetic average of the two bonds' yields – for at this yield the portfolio would only be worth 191.04666. On the contrary it is somewhere between 7% and 7.5% and can actually be shown by more precise calculations to be 7.165%.

What this indicates is that the contribution of the yield of the shorter-dated bond in forming the overall portfolio yield is far less than that of the longer bond. In fact if the yields of the components of a portfolio are weighted both by value and by modified duration the resultant weighted average yield will be found to be an extremely close approximation to the actual portfolio yield.

In the case above the modified duration of the one-year bond was 0.93633 and that of the twenty-year bond 10.67754. The weighted average yield on this basis is,

$$\frac{(100 \times 0.93633 \times 9.000) + (100 \times 10.67754 \times 7.000)}{(100 \times 0.93633) + (100 \times 10.67754)}$$

= 7.161% (compared with the true yield of 7.165%).
The rationale for this can be explained thus:

Let a portfolio be composed of a number of bonds, Bond 1, Bond 2, ... whose prices are denoted by $P_1(y_1)$, $P_2(y_2)$ ..., where their respective yields are $y_1$, $y_2$, ..., and where the sizes of the nominal holdings are $N_1$, $N_2$, ... etc. Let the portfolio yield be designated by $y_0$.

By definition the value of the portfolio at the portfolio yield must equate to the sum of the values of its constituent parts each valued on their own individual yield basis. Thus we can form the following equation of value,

$$N_1 \cdot P_1(y_0) + N_2 \cdot P_2(y_0) + \ldots = N_1 \cdot P_1(y_1) + N_2 \cdot P_2(y_2) + \ldots$$

$$N_1 \cdot [P_1(y_0) - P_1(y_1)] + N_2 \cdot [P_2(y_0) - P_2(y_2)] + \ldots = 0$$

If we now introduce the approximation that,

$$[P_1(y_0) - P_1(y_1)] = P_1(y_1) \times (y_0 - y_1) \times W_1 \text{ (modified duration of Bond 1)},$$

and so on for all the bonds, the equation of value transforms into,

$$N_1 \cdot P_1 \cdot W_1 \cdot (y_0 - y_1) + N_2 \cdot P_2 \cdot W_2 \cdot (y_0 - y_2) + \ldots = 0$$

leading to,
$$y_0 = \frac{N_1 \cdot P_1 \cdot W_1 \cdot y_1 + N_2 \cdot P_2 \cdot W_2 \cdot y_2 + \ldots}{N_1 \cdot P_1 \cdot W_1 + N_2 \cdot P_2 \cdot W_2 + \ldots}$$

which is the average of the constituent yields ($y_1$, $y_2$, etc.) when weighted both by value ($N_1 \cdot P_1$, $N_2 \cdot P_2$, etc.) and by modified duration ($W_1$, $W_2$, etc.) as described earlier.

The value to practitioners of this device is considerable since it simplifies many calculative routines used in portfolio analysis, but it is important always to remember that results obtained from it will be close, often extremely close, approximations to actual portfolio yields but not necessarily precisely accurate figures.

# 6

## Analytical methods for use with conventional gilt-edged securities

Successful gilt-edged investing is essentially a combination of good timing and good security selection. Of these two factors, good timing is undoubtedly the more difficult to achieve, but, by the same token, it is probably the factor from which the greatest profitability emanates. In the gilt-edged market, even a cheap bond bought just before a major market decline can hardly be expected to perform positively whilst a dear bond bought at the onset of a bull market can hardly fail to do well in absolute terms. This is because the size of relative price fluctuations in the gilt-edged market are generally much smaller than the amplitudes of the market's overall price movements. This is in sharp contrast to the situation pertaining in the equity market, where the benefits from inspired stock selection can often easily outweigh those of an adverse general market movement.

Accordingly, investors, after assessing the risk profile they are prepared to adopt, should address the following questions before embarking on an investment strategy in the gilt-edged market:

1. What is the overall market outlook?
2. What are the relative attractions of the differing sectors of the market: shorts, mediums, longs?
3. Within the most favoured sector(s), which bonds are cheap and which bonds are dear.

The first question is essentially about interest rates and yield levels in general, and relates particularly to timing. It will most probably require the investor to make some form of economic assessment before arriving at a conclusion, and this may well be augmented by some form of technical (chart) analysis depending on the particular investor's attitude to that subject.

The second question will also involve the investor in making judgements regarding potential changes in both the level and shape of the yield curve over some medium-term time horizon – typically a six-month or one-year view. Again technical analysis can be useful, even if only in allowing current inter-sector relativities to be viewed in some form of historical perspective.

The third of these three basic questions is all to do with individual bond selection, and a welter of complex and sophisticated forms of analysis have evolved over the years for dealing with it. This is the part of gilt-edged analysis where the mathematical approach is at its strongest, and the following section of this book will deal in detail with the techniques in general usage.

In this particular area there are basically two forms of comparative analysis, which comprise a variety of techniques.

1. Methods comparing one bond against another:
   (a) Price differences.
   (b) Price ratios.
   (c) Yield differences and ratios.
   (d) Switch profit projections.
   (e) Performance indices.
   (f) Balance-of-term yields.

2. Methods comparing a single bond against the market in general:
   (a) Yield curve analysis.
   (b) Price model analysis.

For reasons of historical precedence, we shall begin by looking at comparisons of one bond against another.

## Price differences

This was probably the very first analytical method ever used for making regular inter-bond comparisons and was very simple and totally unsophisticated. It dates from a time long before the advent of electronic calculators and computers when calculating a ratio involved long division or the use of logarithmic tables and when the resultant statistics were recorded manually. In this system the differences in price between pairs of bonds were calculated and recorded regularly (e.g. daily). This price difference history would then be used as a yardstick against which to judge whether the current price difference was 'normal', by lying somewhere in the middle of the historical range, or was 'anomalous' by being at or close to one extremity or the other of that range. In the latter case, a price 'anomaly' was considered to exist which, it was hoped, could be turned to advantage by selling the dearer bond and switching into the cheaper of the pair. Switching of this sort between bonds of broadly similar coupon and maturity characteristics became known as 'anomaly switching' – terminology that has persisted through to the present day.

The use of price differences had many shortcomings, notably the fact that they could not reflect relative proportionate changes in values between two bonds (unless their prices were roughly equal), and that, when dirty prices were being used, as was often the case, discontinuities would occur every time one of the bonds went ex-dividend. This made them fundamentally unsuitable as a tool for use in serious gilt-edged analysis, and as soon as mechanical aids to calculation arrived on the scene they were superseded by price ratios.

## Price ratios

This method gets over the afore-mentioned problems by considering the ratio of the two bonds' clean prices – i.e. their total prices minus accrued interest net of tax at the relevant rate; and the fact that the method can be tailored to suit gross and net funds alike gives it wide appeal. Furthermore, by operating on clean prices, the price discontinuities at ex-dividend dates are removed, and the fact that one is dealing with a ratio rather than a difference means that proportionate changes in the price of one bond relative to the other are accurately reflected in the relevant statistic. To get an idea of how the method works and the apparent ease with which it can be applied let us look at a potential switch between two reasonably similar long-dated gilts, Conversion 9% 2011 and Treasury 9% 2008, in mid-July 1994. On the day in question they were priced as shown in Table 6.1.

**Table 6.1**

|  | Quoted (clean price) | Gross accrued interest | Total price | Flat yield | Gross redemption yield |
|---|---|---|---|---|---|
| Conversion 9% 2011 | 105 21/32 | 0.025 | 105.681 | 8.518 | 8.366 |
| Treasury 9% 2008 | 104 25/32 | 2.244 | 107.025 | 8.589 | 8.414 |

The gross price ratio at these relative prices is found by dividing the two clean prices, one by the other, and is normally expressed in percentage terms. Here it is,

$$\frac{(105\frac{21}{32})}{(104\frac{25}{32})} \times 100 = 100.835$$

Fig. 6.1 shows how this ratio has varied over the past two and a half years, and provides a form of perspective against which to judge current relative valuations. It shows that the ratio has recently swung from a low of about 99 to a high of about 101.80, and that the current ratio of 100.835 does not represent particularly attractive terms for switching between these bonds in either direction.

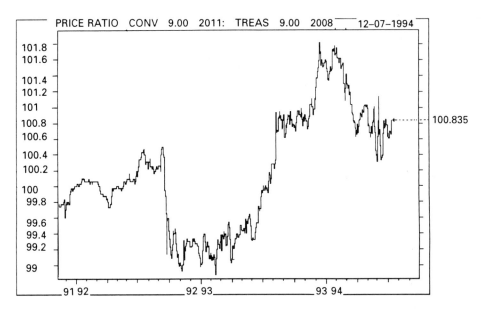

**Fig 6.1** Price Ratio of Conversion 9% 2011 v Treasury 9% 2008 (as at 12th July 1994)

The reader will notice that this example involves the use of a gross price ratio, i.e. one applicable to an investor not subject to income tax on dividends. Since February 1986 prices of all gilt-edged securities have been quoted in the clean form plus or minus gross accrued interest so that in order to form a gross price ratio it is normally only necessary to divide one quoted price by the other. This short-cut only applies to gross ratios, but since these are relevant to both gross funds and funds taxed under the accrued interest scheme these are the most widely used. However, if one is dealing with a fund subject to a different rate of tax on income than on capital gains, price ratio comparisons need to be made using net clean prices. In these circumstances it is safest first to construct total prices by adding the gross accrued interest applicable to each quoted price, and then deduct from those total prices the net accrued interest in each case to form the relevant net clean prices. Price ratios are a commonly used analytical tool in the gilt-edged market, but certain caveats about their use need to be made.

Firstly, a general caveat, applicable to all forms of what may be termed 'retrospective analysis'. By making judgements about current valuations in this way, one is essentially using past history as a guide to future normality. Before so doing the investor should question whether such an assumption is justifiable, whether there have been, or are in the pipeline, any fundamental changes in, say, taxation, market structure, etc., which might make past relationships a bad guide as to the future.

The second caveat concerning the use of price ratios is that they do not take into account differences in the income flows from the two bonds.

103

A simple example makes this clear. Let us consider two bonds, A and B, both with lives of exactly five years. Let A be a 9% bond priced at 100 and let B be a 3% bond priced at 80. The gross price ratio (clean price A divided by clean price B) × 100 is thus (100/80) × 100 = 125.00.

Let us further assume that over the course of the next six months Bond A moves to a price of 105, whilst Bond B moves up to 84. The price ratio will thus be (105/84) x 100 = 125.00, the same as before, but the total performances of the two bonds will be far from equal, for Bond A will have disbursed a half-yearly dividend payment of $4\frac{1}{2}$, whilst the equivalent dividend from Bond B will only have been $1\frac{1}{2}$.

The total performance of A is equal to the change in price over the period (105-100), plus dividends received (4.5), divided by the initial total price (100) = 9.5%. Likewise, the total performance of B = [(84 - 80) + 1.50]/80 = 6.875%. Thus, whilst the price ratio has remained constant, Bond A has outperformed Bond B by 2.625%.

It will therefore be seen that, when using price ratios as an analytical tool, great care must be taken to compensate for dividend flow differences.

The following formula provides a way of computing the necessary adjustments. In symbolic terms the price ratio, $R$, can be expressed as:

$$R = \frac{P_a - G_a \cdot T_a}{P_b - G_b \cdot T_b}$$

where $P_a$ and $P_b$ represent the total prices of Bonds A and B, $G_a$ and $G_b$ the coupons of Bonds A and B, and where $T_a$ and $T_b$ denote the time elapsed since the last coupon payment dates respectively.

The above equation can be rewritten by taking logarithms of both sides:

$$\log R = \log(P_a - G_a \cdot T_a) - \log(P_b - G_b \cdot T_b)$$

Now differentiate both sides with respect to time:

$$\frac{1}{R} \cdot \frac{dR}{dT} = \frac{-G_a}{(P_a - G_a \cdot T_a)} - \frac{-G_b}{(P_b - G_b \cdot T_b)}$$

= (− flat yield of Bond A) − (− flat yield of Bond B)

= $(F_b - F_a)$

where $F_a$ and $F_b$ denote the two bonds' flat yields.

This leads to the approximation $\Delta R \simeq (F_b - F_a) \cdot R \cdot \Delta T$

Put in words, this states that the simple passage of time will bring about a change in the price ratio ($\Delta R$) equal to (minus) the difference in the two flat yields multiplied by the ratio itself, multiplied by the extent of the time period in years. Let us now see how this applies to our earlier example.

Here the initial flat yield of Bond A, $F_a = 9.00\%$,
and the initial flat yield of Bond B, $F_b = 3.75\%$.

Thus, $F_b - F_a = 3.75 - 9.00 = -5.25$
The initial ratio $= 125.00$.
The time period was a half-year.

Using the approximation above, the requisite adjustment to the 125 price ratio figure can be established as

$$= \frac{-5.25}{100} \times 125 \times \frac{1}{2} = -3.28125$$

This adjustment expressed as a percentage of the price ratio of 125 is 2.625%, the same as the difference in total performance between the two bonds established earlier. Thus, whenever using price ratio as a basis of comparison between two bonds, the investor/analyst should first calculate the size of the underlying natural trend in the ratio figure and, where charts are being used, should superimpose the trend upon the graph before making his judgements.

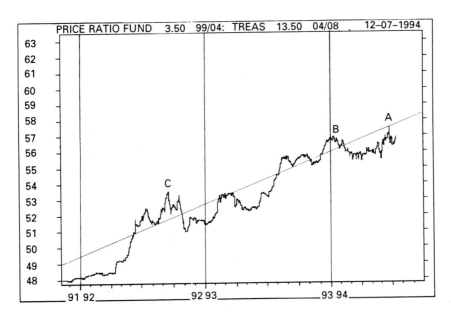

**Fig 6.2**  Price Ratio of Funding 3½% 99/04 v Treasury 13½% 04/08 (as at 12th July 1994)

105

In Fig 6.2 we show the relationship between two bonds of similar assumed (2004) maturities, but vastly different coupon rates, and as a result significantly different flat yields. On 12 July 1994 they were priced as shown in Table 6.2.

**Table 6.2**

| | | Quoted (clean) price | Gross accrued interest | Total price | Flat yield | Gross redemption yield |
|---|---|---|---|---|---|---|
| Funding | 3½% 99/04 | 73 14/32 | −0.010 | 73.428 | 4.766 | 7.282 |
| Treasury | 13½% 04/08 | 129 7/32 | 4.032 | 133.250 | 10.447 | 8.923 |

Difference in flat yield = 5.681

The trend line representing this flat yield difference has been drawn on this chart through the recent high point, (A), from which it can be seen that better terms for making the switch occurred in early January 1994,(B), and even better again in September 1992, (C).

## Yield differences and ratios

It is probably fair to say that yield differences ('spreads') are the most widely used analytical device for making relative value assessments in fixed-income markets around the world, and the gilt-edged market is no exception to the rule. For a start, the concept of a gain in yield being obtained by selling a low-yielding bond and buying a higher yielding one is easily grasped by even the least sophisticated of investors, as is the fact that switching terms of a gain of, say, 0.75% in redemption yield are better than those of a gain of only 0.65%.

Furthermore, yield differences as an analytical tool do not suffer from the problems associated with price ratios, since the values of both the income flows and capital repayments are taken into account in calculating each individual redemption yield. Yield ratios, which purists might be expected to prefer to yield differences, are however, only rarely encountered, although it is the view of the author that they may on occasions give better indications of anomalies, especially when the absolute level of yields changes substantially over the time period under review.

A typical yield difference chart looks like the one in Fig. 6.3 between Conversion 10¼% 1999 and Treasury 9½% 1999. From this chart it can be observed that the yield difference has fluctuated pretty regularly between 0.11% and 0.24% over the last two-and-a-half years. There would therefore appear to be a reasonably good case for preferring to invest in Conversion 10¼% 1999 when the yield difference is greater than 0.175, and Treasury 9½% 1999 when it is below this figure. There would also appear to be a *prima facie* case for switching out of Treasury 9½% 1999 and into Conversion 10¼% 1999

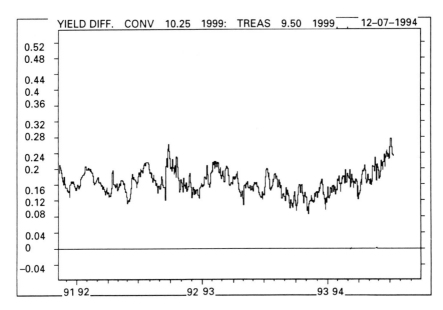

**Fig 6.3** Yield Difference between Conversion 10¼% 1999 and Treasury 9½% 1999 (as at 12th July 1994)

if and when the yield margin exceeds 0.24%, or the other way if the yield difference drops below 0.11%. So, if such a golden opportunity arises, why should not the investor grasp it in both hands? What could go wrong?

Firstly, it is possible that some new factor may appear on the scene which could cause the yield difference between these two bonds to move into a different range. Secondly, the investor should examine the amplitude of the yield difference to ensure that even if he opened his switch on the very best terms, and subsequently closed the operation towards the lower end of the range, there would be sufficient profit for him after allowing for dealing and administrative expenses. Sometimes apparently attractive switches between similar bonds turn out, on further inspection of this sort, to have only limited profit potential.

However, by far and away the greatest caveat that must be applied to the use of yield differences is that they cannot take into account differences in durations of the two bonds, i.e. that a given change in the yield of one bond may well produce a change in its value that is markedly different to that produced in the other by precisely the same change in yield. If the two bonds have very similar durations, then yield differences are a very satisfactory and simple analytical device for measuring relative values between them. The further apart their durations are, the greater the danger that their relative total performances will not correlate closely with fluctuations in the corresponding yield difference. Where large differences in duration exist, and when the market's general yield levels change substantially, it is quite possible to open a switch for a gain in yield, and close it at a later time for a further gain in yield, but end up making an overall loss in money terms as a result.

The deliberately exaggerated example in Table 6.3 demonstrates.

**Table 6.3**

| 15 January | Sell 8%  5-year Bond A: Price = 113 4/32 | GRY = 5.00 |
|---|---|---|
|  | Buy 8% 25-year Bond B: Price = 118 | GRY = 6.53 |
|  | Opening gain in gross redemption yield | = 1.53 |
| 15 July same year | Sell 8% 25-year Bond B: Price = 95 | GRY = 8.49 |
|  | Buy 8%  5-year Bond A: Price = 96 12/32 | GRY = 9.00 |
|  | Closing gain in gross redemption yield | = 0.51 |

*Switch accounting*

|  | Bond A | | Bond B | | Net cash flow |
|---|---|---|---|---|---|
| 15 January | −1,000,000 Bond A @ 113.125 | £1,131,250 | +£958,686 Bond B @ 118.000 | £1,131,250 | nil |
| 15 July | Dividend foregone (4.0) | £40,000 | Dividend received (4.0) | £38,347 | −£1,653 |
| 15 July | +£1,000,000 Bond A @ 96.375 | £963,750 | −£958,686 Bond B @ 95.000 | £910,752 | −£52,998 |
|  |  |  |  | Gross switch profit/loss | −£54,651 |

Summary of the operation: a gain in yield of 1.53% on the opening of the switch and futher gain in yield of 0.51% at the closing of the switch contrives to produce a loss of over 4.8% in money terms. Thus, just as the inability to make allowance for differing income flow is the Achilles' heel for price ratios, so the duration factor is the drawback associated with yield differences.

## Weighted switches

One way in which this drawback can be overcome is by transacting switches where the money values of the holdings sold and bought are not equal but are weighted in inverse proportion to the two bonds' modified durations. By so doing the investor establishes a degree of protection from a parallel shift in the yield structure, thus allowing the profitability of the strategy to reflect changes in the yield difference only. An additional finesse will exist if the bond to be purchased has a greater convexity than that being sold. Weighted switches are useful devices for taking advantage of excessively sloping yield curves in a relatively riskless manner, but for some reason are far less frequently executed than standard money-for-money switches.

## Balanced switches

Perhaps one reason for the reticence of investors to undertake weighted switches is the matter of accounting for the cash imbalances that they involve. This problem can be avoided if the weighting effect is provided not by the injection or extraction of cash, but by structuring composite switches using more than two bonds so that the overall money-weighted modified duration of the unit to be sold matches that of the bond (or bonds) to be bought. For such a balance to be obtained at least one of the bonds comprising the composite unit must have a modified duration greater than that of the single bond, and at least one other must have a modified duration less than that value.

In practice most balanced switches consist of three bonds, either selling two bonds to buy the central bond or vice versa, and for fairly obvious reasons switches of this ilk have become known as butterfly switches. Their very nature means that they are particularly well suited to exploit humps or (less frequently) dips in the yield curve's shape which arise from time to time. As an example let us consider the yield structure of 12 July 1994 which priced the bonds as shown in Table 6.4.

**Table 6.4**   Example of a (modified) duration balanced switch

|      | Nominal holding (N) | | | Total price (P) | GRY (Y) | Modified duration (W) | Risk units (N) × (P) × (W) |
| --- | --- | --- | --- | --- | --- | --- | --- |
| Sell | 7,066,450 | Treasury 9½% | 1999 | 104.792 | 8.184 | 3.644 | −26,984,090 |
| Buy | 10,000,000 | Treasury 9¾% | 2002 | 109.820 | 8.676 | 5.438 | 59,720,116 |
| Sell | 3,395,407 | Treasury 9% | 2012 | 105.346 | 8.355 | 9.152 | −32,736,026 |
|  |  |  |  |  |  |  | 0 |

The general formula for calculating the requisite nominal holdings to achieve the dual balance of money and risk comes from solving the simultaneous equations,

$$N_1 \cdot P_1 \cdot W_1 + N_2 \cdot P_2 \cdot W_2 = N_0 \cdot P_0 \cdot W_0$$

$$N_1 \cdot P_1 + N_2 \cdot P_2 = N_0 \cdot P_0$$

where suffixes $_0$, $_1$ and $_2$ refer to Treasury 9¾% 2002, Treasury 9½% 1999 and Treasury 9% 2012 respectively.

These yield the following expressions for $N_1$ and $N_2$,

$$N_1 = N_0 \cdot \frac{P_0 \cdot (W_2 - W_0)}{P_1 \cdot (W_2 - W_1)} \text{ and } N_2 = N_0 \cdot \frac{P_0 \cdot (W_0 - W_1)}{P_2 \cdot (W_2 - W_1)}$$

The yield of the composite unit comprised by the two bonds to be sold can be determined using the formula developed for portfolio yields in Chapter 5. Algebraically it can be written as:

$$\frac{N_1 \cdot P_1 \cdot W_1 \cdot Y_1 + N_2 \cdot P_2 \cdot W_2 \cdot Y_2}{N_1 \cdot P_1 \cdot W_1 + N_2 \cdot P_2 \cdot W_2}$$

In this case it gives a value of,

$$\frac{26984090 \times 8.184 + 32736026 \times 8.355}{59720116} = 8.278\%$$

which means that this strategy results in a gain in yield of 39.8 basis points with minimal market directional risk.

## Switch profit projections

One useful method which allows the analyst to use yield difference considerations when considering money-for-money switches where differences in durations exist is the switch profit projection. The basis of this system is to make a series of forward switch projections, each made at a different overall market yield level, but all based on a common assumption as to the future yield difference; and observe how the potential profits or losses relate to market levels. Any such method requires the user to make a realistic 'guesstimate' of the future 'normal' yield difference between the two bonds, and this is usually done after consulting charts of their recent yield history.

The projection shown in Table 6.5 is a good example of this approach. Here the investor has already examined the yield difference history of Treasury 9% 2008 against Treasury $9\frac{3}{4}\%$ 2002 and observed that between January 1992 and June 1994 this figure swung from $-0.60\%$ to $+0.37\%$ and has averaged $-0.11\%$.

Let us assume that on 20 June 1994 he was considering making the switch from Treasury 9% 2008 into Treasury $9\frac{3}{4}\%$ 2002 at prices of 101 25/32 : 103 26/32, terms which represented a gain in gross redemption yield of 0.307%, and was looking to reverse it on a yield difference of $-0.11\%$ (the recent

**Table 6.5** Example of switch profit projections

| | Sell Treasury 9% 2008 | | | Buy Treasury 9 3/4% 2002 | | | |
|---|---|---|---|---|---|---|---|
| 20.06.94 | Price 101.78 | GRY 8.775 | | Price 103.81 | GRY 9.082 | | Yield gain 0.307 |
| Projections 20.06.95 | Price | GRY | Projected return % | Price | GRY | Projected return % | Projected profit % |
| Y-2 | 117.20 | 6.984 | 21.79 | 116.06 | 6.874 | 19.30 | −2.49 |
| Y-1 | 108.14 | 7.984 | 13.82 | 110.11 | 7.874 | 14.17 | 0.35 |
| Y | 100.02 | 8.984 | 6.42 | 104.54 | 8.874 | 9.26 | 2.84 |
| Y+1 | 92.73 | 9.984 | −0.46 | 99.33 | 9.874 | 4.56 | 5.02 |
| Y+2 | 86.18 | 10.984 | −6.85 | 94.44 | 10.874 | 0.06 | 6.91 |

*Note:* In this example projected returns have been calculated assuming that dividends on both bonds are reinvested at the average yield, 8.984%

average) a year later. Table 6.5 shows how the profitability of such a switch varies with the future market level.

The central projection is based on the neutral view that the average of the two bonds' yields ($Y$, in this case 8.984) will be the same at the forward date as it was at the outset, whilst the two projections above and below assume that the average yield will be 1% and 2% higher and lower respectively. It can be seen that the projected profits range from 6.91% (if yields rise 2%) to −2.49% (if yields fall 2%) and the switch breaks even if yields fall about 1.12%.

This form of analysis permits the investor to see the essential nature of the trade-off between the yield anomaly and the duration effect of an overall market movement, and allows him to decide whether to make the switch or not, fully knowing the risk-reward relationship involved.

Now let us take a look at an alternative to price ratios.

## Performance indices

These are indices which are reasonably simple to construct and which are designed to measure the total performance – capital movements plus income receipts of each bond. The concept behind the system is to envisage how the value of a fund would fluctuate if it were invested in a single bond, and reinvested the dividends received from that investment by buying more of that bond at the market price on the first day ex-dividend.

Thus, for a given bond the performance index so formed is basically a product of two items:

1.  The bond's total market price (inclusive of gross accrued interest).
2.  The nominal amount of the bond in question which rises proportionately each time a dividend is received.

**Table 6.6** Construction of a performance index for an 8% bond

| Day | | Nominal holding (N) | Quoted price (Q) | Gross accrued interest (A) | Total value (Q) + (A) = (V) | Gross performance index (N) × (V)/100 |
|---|---|---|---|---|---|---|
| 0 | Int. pay date | 105.2389 | 95.000 | 0.022 | 95.022 | 100.000 |
| 1 | | 105.2389 | 95.250 | 0.044 | 95.294 | 100.286 |
| 2 | | 105.2389 | 96.500 | 0.066 | 96.566 | 101.625 |
| 3 | | 105.2389 | 96.375 | 0.088 | 96.463 | 101.516 |
| ... | | ... | ... | ... | ... | ... |
| ... | | ... | ... | ... | ... | ... |
| ... | | ... | ... | ... | ... | ... |
| ... | | ... | ... | ... | ... | ... |
| 168 | | 105.2389 | 98.875 cd | 3.704 | 102.579 | 107.953 |
| 169 | | 105.2389 | 98.500 cd | 3.726 | 102.226 | 107.582 |
| 170 | | 105.2389 | 98.250 cd | 3.748 | 101.998 | 107.341 |
| | weekend | | | | | |
| 173 | last day cum | 105.2389 | 98.125 cd | 3.814 | 101.939 | 107.279 |
| 174 | first day ex | 109.5420 | 98.000 xd | −0.175 | 97.825 | 107.159 |
| 175 | | 109.5420 | 97.375 xd | −0.153 | 97.222 | 106.498 |
| 176 | | 109.5420 | 99.000 xd | −0.132 | 98.868 | 108.303 |
| 177 | | 109.5420 | 98.875 xd | −0.066 | 98.809 | 108.238 |
| | weekend | | | | | |
| 180 | | 109.5420 | 97.500 xd | −0.044 | 97.456 | 106.755 |
| 181 | | 109.5420 | 97.375 xd | −0.022 | 97.353 | 106.643 |
| 182 | | 109.5420 | 98.000 xd | 0.000 | 98.000 | 107.351 |
| 183 | last day cum | 109.5420 | 98.125 | 0.022 | 98.147 | 107.512 |
| ... | | ... | ... | ... | ... | ... |
| ... | | ... | ... | ... | ... | ... |

As an example, take the case of an 8% bond which at the outset of this analysis (chosen for convenience to be a dividend date for this bond) is priced at, say, £95. An investment of £100 at this time in this bond would therefore have produced an initial holding of £105.2389 nominal. The gross performance index for this bond is defined simply as the total value of this holding. Table 6.6 shows the progress of such an index through a complete dividend cycle.

The compounding of income is demonstrated by the action of this index when the bond goes ex-dividend on day 174 (seven working days before the first coupon payment is due). This dividend is worth 4% gross and this amount is then used to purchase (notionally) further amounts of this bond at the first day ex-dividend all-in price of 97.825. The additional nominal amount of bonds thus purchased is:

$$105.2389 \times 4.000 / 97.825 = £4.3031 \text{ nominal,}$$

which when added to the initial holding increases it to £109.5420.

After this time the system continues as before but using this larger nominal holding until the next ex-dividend date when the process is repeated in like fashion. Purists could argue that since the dividend would not actually be received by a holder until seven working days after the ex-dividend date, the correct amount of value to be applied to the notional reinvestment process should not be simply the gross value of the relevant coupon, but that value discounted at short-term money rates for the length of the ex-dividend period. Whilst this argument is indeed technically correct, for most practical purposes it can be ignored.

This system provides a framework for making price and performance comparisons between bonds of all sorts including index-linked bonds for whom this approach is particularly well suited. This can be done by simply forming the ratio of the two relevant performance indices and comparing the current figure with its historic series. The main merits of this approach are the neat way it overcomes the drawback associated with price ratios, namely the problem of accounting for dividend income flow, and the fact that it allows for the compounding effect of income reinvestment. The method can also be easily adapted to form composite indices of performance for groups of bonds and even whole portfolios, but, like so many other similar analytical devices, it is wholly retrospective in nature.

## Balance-of-term yields

In contrast to performance indices, balance-of-term yields (often referred to as 'reinvestment rates') are a method which produces a critical statistic which can be viewed prospectively as well as retrospectively. To understand what balance-of-term yields are, and how they can be applied to make inter-bond selection judgements, consider the following train of thought.

Take firstly the shorter-dated of the two bonds and make a prospective assessment of its performance to redemption. This will depend on the rate of tax applicable (if any) to dividend income and/or capital gains, and, just as importantly, the 'roll-up' rate (see Chapter 5) at which dividends can be expected to be reinvested as they occur. But because one is making a projection to a redemption date the forward capital value of the bond is known. The next stage is to calculate, using the same assumptions as to tax and roll-up rates, the price that the longer-dated of the two bonds would need to stand on at the date of redemption of the shorter, so as to make the two bonds' performances over that period identical. From this price can be calculated the corresponding redemption yield for the 'balance of the term' of the longer bond. In essence, the analyst is looking at two ways of investing for the full term of the longer bond:

1. To invest outright by buying the longer bond.
2. To buy the shorter bond and at the time of its redemption to reinvest in the longer bond for the balance of the term.

The choice of which of these will be most profitable can be gauged by the value of the implied balance-of-term yield. If this is abnormally high, then there will be a *prima facie* case for buying the longer-dated bond outright, whilst if it is very low this would indicate that an investor should prefer to invest initially in the shorter of the two bonds and switch longer later. The following example illustrates this.

Let Bond A be a 7% ten-year bond priced at 94 and giving a gross redemption yield of 7.878%. Let Bond B be an 8% twenty-five-year bond, with a price of 96 and a gross redemption yield of 8.385%. For the purpose of simplicity, let us assume that there is no question of tax on either income or capital gains, and that in the investor's judgement 8% is a suitable roll-up rate for compounding dividend payments. On these assumptions, the performance to redemption of the shorter Bond A is calculated as the accumulated value of a holding of this bond, divided by its current price, i.e.

$$\frac{(g/2) \cdot s_{\overline{n}} + 100}{P_a}$$

$$= \frac{3.5 \times [(1.04^{20} - 1)/0.04] + 100}{94} = 2.172588$$

It is now necessary to calculate the price of Bond B ($P_b$) on the same date to give the same performance. This is done by solving the equation

$$\frac{4.0 \times [(1.04^{20} - 1)/0.04] + P_b}{96} = 2.172588$$

leading to, $\qquad\qquad P_b = 89.456$

To judge whether this price is likely to be within the bounds of possibility, it is necessary to calculate the gross redemption yield that it represents at this

Table 6.7  Balance of term yields at varying roll-up rates

| Roll-up rate (% p.a.) | Breakeven price | Balance of term yield % |
|---|---|---|
| 4 | 91.788 | 9.009 |
| 5 | 91.258 | 9.078 |
| 6 | 90.693 | 9.153 |
| 7 | 90.094 | 9.233 |
| 8 | 89.456 | 9.319 |
| 9 | 88.778 | 9.411 |
| 10 | 88.057 | 9.511 |
| 11 | 87.290 | 9.618 |
| 12 | 86.474 | 9.733 |

future date, i.e. when Bond B will have a remaining life of fifteen years. This is the 'balance-of-term yield', and in this particular case turns out to be 9.319%.

It is interesting to see how much the balance-of-term yield is affected by changes in either the assumed roll-up rate, or the rates of tax applicable to the investor.

Table 6.7 shows that balance-of-term yields are highly dependent upon the choice of roll-up rate assumed, and thus it is important to choose roll-up rates carefully. Frequently used assumptions for roll-up rates include the following:

1.  The redemption yield of the shorter bond.
2.  The redemption yield of the longer bond.
3.  The average of (1) and (2).
4.  A constant mid-range figure, say 6%.
5.  A rate so chosen that the balance-of-term yield it produces and the roll-up rate equate.

None of these is ideal, but the use of a constant figure (4) has the advantage that a time series based on daily balance-of-term yields computed on this basis will serve as a neat form of dividend-adjusted price comparator.

Turning now to the effect of tax on balance-of-term yields, let us observe what variations are required to allow the method to be applied by an investor subject to income tax on dividends but for whom capital gains are tax-free.

In our previous example we first chose a suitable roll-up rate of 8% gross. If now the income tax rate applicable is, say, 25% a net roll-up rate of, say, 6% may be more appropriate. Furthermore, the net dividends to be accumulated will now be 2.625% and 3% per half-year for the 7% and 8% bonds respectively. Under these conditions the net performance of the shorter Bond A will be:

$$= \frac{2.625 \times [(1.03^{20} - 1)/0.03] + 100}{94} = 1.814199$$

The projected price of Bond B to give level performance with this is found by solving the equation:

$$\frac{3.0 \times [(1.03^{20} - 1)/0.03] + P_b}{96} = 1.814199$$

giving rise to a price $P_b = 93.552$, which, when translated into a GROSS redemption yield, produces a *net balance-of-term yield* of 8.782%.

This is a very much lower figure than that produced earlier for a gross fund, which indicates that the switch longer from Bond A (7%; ten-year term) to

Bond B (8%; twenty-five-year term) on these terms is less advantageous to the net fund than to a gross one.

There is often some confusion associated with the practice of quoting net of tax balance-of-term break-even levels by reference to gross redemption yields, as in the example above. Why is this done? The basic reason is that in balance-of-term analysis one is essentially trying to make a judgement based on the level of the break-even price of the longer bond, and it is in gross yield terms that market levels are most usually gauged. Some people, especially those new to this form of analysis, have difficulty in making the correct interpretation of the figures once they have been calculated. The rule of thumb that can be safely applied is simple: the higher the balance-of-term yield is, the better are the terms for switching longer. Calculating balance-of-term yields by this classic method is often onerous and time-consuming. An alternative approach exists which centres on two points of logic.

Firstly, if two bonds have the same yield then that yield is also their balance-of-term yield; secondly, if two bonds perform equally over a period of time their balance-of-term yield will remain the same. Thus the balance-of-term yield can be considered as that level of yield at which if both bonds were to stand, their resulting total price ratio would equate with that of the actual situation.

In Table 6.8 we show the prices that the two bonds used in our earlier example would be valued at if they were to stand on level yields at varying levels between 9% and 10%.

**Table 6.8** Equivalent level yield method for determining balance-of-term yields

|  |  | Bond A | Bond B | Ratio % |
|---|---|---|---|---|
| Coupon rate % |  | 7% | 8% |  |
| Term to maturity |  | 10 years | 25 years |  |
| Price |  | 94 | 96 | 97.917 |
| Gross redemption yield |  | 7.878 | 8.385 |  |
| Price to yield | 9.00 | 86.992 | 90.119 | 96.530 |
|  | 9.10 | 86.401 | 89.219 | 96.841 |
|  | 9.20 | 85.814 | 88.333 | 97.149 |
|  | 9.30 | 85.233 | 87.462 | 97.452 |
|  | 9.40 | 84.658 | 86.605 | 97.751 |
|  | **9.456** | 84.337 | 86.131 | **97.917** |
|  | 9.50 | 84.087 | 85.762 | 98.047 |
|  | 9.60 | 83.521 | 84.932 | 98.338 |
|  | 9.70 | 82.960 | 84.116 | 98.626 |
|  | 9.80 | 82.404 | 83.313 | 98.910 |
|  | 9.90 | 81.853 | 82.522 | 99.189 |
|  | 10.00 | 81.307 | 81.744 | 99.465 |

From Table 6.8 we can see that their actual relative valuation is equivalent to both bonds being valued on a 9.456% yield, and thus that 9.456% is established as the balance-of-term yield derived from this approach. Why does this differ from that of 9.319% computed by the classic method in our earlier example? The answer lies in the roll-up rate assumption implied by the method. In the equivalent level yields method the implicit roll-up rate is that of the balance-of-term yield itself, in this case 9.456%, whereas in the classic example an 8% roll-up rate was pre-chosen.

However, inspection of Table 6.7, which shows how balance-of-term yields calculated by the classic method vary with different roll-up rate assumptions, demonstrates that the two different methods are wholly consistent with one another.

So far all the analytical methods considered have been for comparing one bond with a single alternative. We shall now switch our attention to two methods of a more global nature which compare individual bonds against the market as a whole: 'yield curve analysis' and 'price model analysis'.

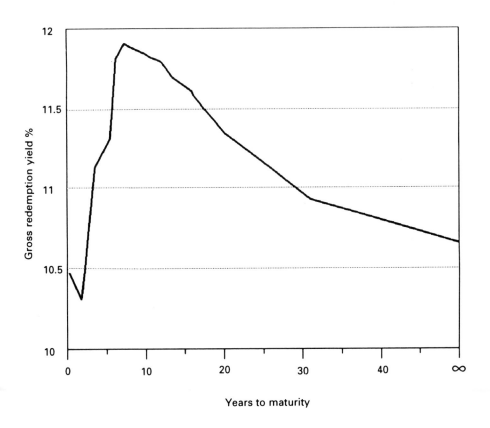

**Fig 6.4**  Basic Gilt-Edged Yield Structure at 30th November 1982

117

## Yield curve analysis

The concept of a yield curve has been around for many years. Essentially it is the shape or curve formed by plotting a graph of yields (nearly always gross redemption yields) on a graph's *y*-axis against some function of life to maturity on its *x*-axis. Traditionally it was normal for liquidity preference considerations to keep short-dated yields low, for the curve to rise towards the medium sector of the market before flattening out in the longs and approaching the irredeemables almost horizontally. However the diversity of economic circumstances experienced by the UK over the past twenty or thirty years has given rise to yield curves of a wide variety, and some of the more extreme are illustrated below.

Fig. 6.4 shows the yield curve at the end of November 1982. Its main feature is the hump in the yield structure centered just short of the ten-year maturity point. This is an unusual yield curve shape and it is interesting to examine the causes of it. In this case the prime reason for the hump was the persistent policy of the authorities of refusing to issue long-dated bonds at what were then considered to be very high nominal rates of interest. The

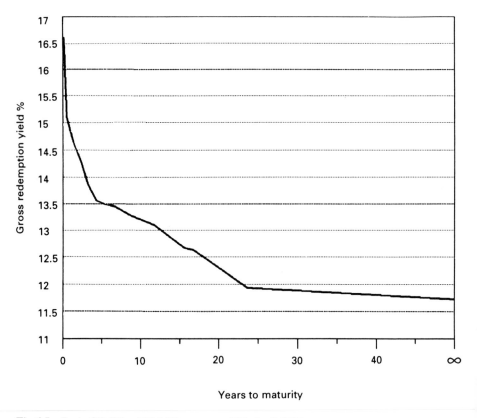

**Fig 6.5**   Basic Gilt-Edged Yield Structure at 30th April 1990

rationale for this was that, in the Government's view, inflation was about to come under control. When this happened much lower gilt-edged yields would be the order of the day and it would thus be bad housekeeping to saddle future generations with the burden of servicing long-dated debt carrying the then 'excessive' coupon rates. Whilst the Government was substantially correct in its inflation assessment on that occasion, the practical effect of this funding policy was that all the bonds that would normally have been issued into the long-medium and long-dated sectors of the conventional market were redirected to the short and short-medium maturity area instead. The hump in the yield curve was the result of the glut of issues in the shorter dated sector and the virtual famine at the long end.

Fig. 6.5 is a good example of a steeply inverted yield curve resulting from the very high short-term interest rates imposed upon the UK economy as part of the anti-inflationary strategy of 1989-1992.

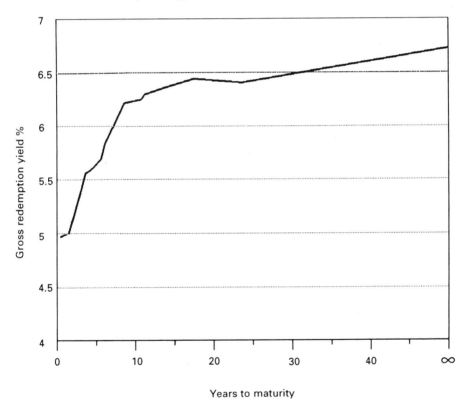

**Fig 6.6** Basic Gilt-Edged Yield Structure at 31st December 1993

Finally Fig. 6.6 portrays the yield structure at the end of the 1990-93 bull market when short-term rates had been progressively reduced to help stimulate the economy and when long-term yields, although reflecting the lower levels of inflation then pertaining, had not fallen so far or so fast.

But whilst observation of yield curve shapes and levels in this mode neatly complements economic analysis, it is as a central measure of value that the yield curve is probably most valuable to the gilt-edged analyst. Prior to the advent of readily accessible computer power, the yield curve could not really be used for this purpose. It was just possible to fit a curve to the points representing bonds' yields and lives to maturity, using mechanical hand calculators and/or seven-figure logarithms, but the sheer volume of the arithmetical calculations involved and the time taken to complete them made this an infrequently performed task. However, by the late 1950s and early 1960s computer power was starting to become available to the investment analyst, and this obstacle to progress started to disappear. The method was first brought into public prominence as a result of a paper delivered by G.T. Pepper to the Institute of Actuaries in 1963. Today there are many different forms of yield curve each with its own particular *modus operandi* but all basically doing the same thing – providing a measure of the central market yield level at any specified maturity, against which yields of individual bonds can be measured. This value is normally called the 'yield curve value', and the difference between the yield of an actual bond and the yield curve value for the same maturity is normally referred to as the bond's 'yield curve deviation'.

The yield curve is said to be 'positively sloped' when yields rise as maturities lengthen; but if yields fall as maturities lengthen the yield curve is said to be 'reverse sloped', or 'negatively sloped'. If, over a period of time, shorter-dated yields fall faster than longer-dated ones, the yield curve is said to 'steepen'; but if the reverse happens, it is said to 'flatten'. If medium-dated yields exceed the average of short and long yields the maturity area coinciding with the highest yields is called the 'hump' of the yield curve.

When first introduced in the early 1960s, yield curve analysis appeared to be manna from heaven. Instead of having to keep a multitude of records of yield differences between innumerable pairs of bonds, all that seemed necessary was to record the daily yield curve deviations of each bond against the yield curve.

But things weren't quite that simple. Fund managers who had grown up with, and had cut their teeth on, price ratios and yield differences were loath to give up using those tools of their trade, which they themselves could calculate, for the new statistics which, of necessity, they had to take on trust from an outside source. Furthermore, rival gilt-edged brokers using different curve-fitting techniques might possibly produce different assessments of cheapness and dearness, and as a result in the early days it was felt that, whilst yield curve analysis was extremely convenient and allowed one to spot potential anomalies quickly, one should use the traditional methods to double-check its recommendations before embarking on a switch. Additionally it has to be realised that at this time most UK financial institutions were not subject to capital gains tax and also were very risk averse, so that a large proportion of gilt-edged business then was anomaly-switching between bonds of similar date and coupon. Futhermore, at that time the range of coupons on gilt-edged issues was very narrow. For example, on 1 January 1964 there was just one gilt with a coupon of 6% (Conversion 6% 1972), whilst at the other end of the range the lowest coupon rate was $2\frac{1}{2}\%$ (Savings $2\frac{1}{2}\%$ 1964/67, Treasury $2\frac{1}{2}\%$ 1975/after, and Consol $2\frac{1}{2}\%$). With only a limited coupon range in existence, the spread between the highest and lowest yields in any particular segment of the market was also tight, and as a result it was not particularly difficult, even without computers, to construct curves which fitted the market structure quite closely.

Problems with yield curve analysis started to occur in the latter part of the 1960s and early 1970s, as interest rates and yields rose and bonds with steadily increasing coupon rates were issued. As a result of the taxation system that applied to gilts at this time (and right up until the announcement of the 1996 changes) generally favouring capital gains rather than income, gilt-edged market values tended to have a distinct yield to coupon rate correlation, with high-coupon bonds normally yielding rather more than lower-coupon issues of the same maturity. Thus the continual creation of successively higher coupon issues resulted in computed yield curve values rising faster than the general level of actual yields. This tended to invalidate the system, since current deviations could not be compared with their past histories on a like-for-like basis. By the end of 1976 the spread of coupons of gilt-edged bonds had widened to 13% – from $15\frac{1}{2}\%$ (Treasury $15\frac{1}{2}\%$ 1998) to $2\frac{1}{2}\%$ (Treasury $2\frac{1}{2}\%$ 1975/after and Consol $2\frac{1}{2}\%$) – a range almost four times as wide as had existed thirteen years earlier; and research was started to find a further form of market analysis that would compensate for coupon variations as well as maturity differences when determining central market values. This led to the development of a number of three-dimensional price models (discussed in the next section). However, despite its difficulties, the yield curve continues to be popular due mainly to its ease of comprehension and the fact that its general methodology can be applied to many different bond markets around the world.

How, then, if one wished to construct a yield curve should one go about it? The first step would be to define which issues should contribute to the process. Since it is normally the current coupon bonds at any given time that set the going rates, it is advisable to restrict 'contributor' bonds to a homogeneous group of similar bonds in a fairly narrow coupon band centred on these rates. Ideally these should include bonds both above and below par in all maturity sectors of the market, but this is not always possible. At the same time one needs to put down a marker that if at some future time the yield structure of the market alters so much that the bonds chosen now are no longer representative of the then going rates, a new selection will have to be made and the whole process (including the re-working of historical values) done all over again.

The next step is to decide the scales of the x-axis and y-axis for the curve. It is usual for the y-axis scale to be bonds' gross redemption yield, though there are certain variants on this which will be discussed later. The choice of x-axis scale is not so obvious. Simply using the term to maturity as x-axis scale presents the impossibility of dealing with irredeemables. This can be overcome relatively easily by the adoption of a transformation of the form:

$$x = 1 - e^{-k.n.}$$

where $k$ is a constant
and $n$ is the term to maturity measured in half-years.

This transformation assigns an irredeemable bond an x-value of 1, and a bond at redemption an x-value of 0 whatever value is chosen for '$k$'.

The choice of the constant '$k$' determines how bonds other than those at the extremities of the market are spread along the x-axis. Since the seven-year maturity point is considered by many to be a 'half-way' point across the maturity spectrum, it is reasonable to assign '$k$' a value that produces an x-value of 0.5 when $n = 14$, (but the choice is up to the individual user). The value of '$k$' that meets this criterion is $k = 0.0495105$.

Other key values produced in this transformation are,

| Years = | 0 | 1 | 2 | 3 | 4 | 5 | 7 | 10 | 15 | 20 | 30 |
|---|---|---|---|---|---|---|---|---|---|---|---|
| $x =$ | 0.000 | 0.094 | 0.180 | 0.257 | 0.327 | 0.390 | 0.500 | 0.629 | 0.774 | 0.862 | 0.949 |

Third and last comes the task of fitting a curve to the scatter of $(x, y)$ points representing the contributor bonds. The simplest method is to use a polynomial of the form:

$$y = a_0 + a_1 \cdot x + a_2 \cdot x^2 + a_3 \cdot x^3 + \dots + a_m \cdot x^m$$

(once again the choice of '$m$', the degree of the polynomial is up to the user) and apply a statistical process known as 'least squares' to it.

This process obtains values for the curve's coefficients $a_0, a_1, a_2, a_3, \dots a_m$ which minimize the sum of the squares of the differences between the actual y-values of the bonds and the equivalent curve values. Once these coefficients have been established they can be fed back into the equation above and the value of the yield curve at any point along its length can be determined.

122

In principle all that looks pretty easy. In practice it is quite difficult to find the exact form of polynomial that produces a fitted curve that replicates closely enough the curve that an analyst would instinctively draw by hand. If the polynomial has too few coefficients, for example if it were linear ($m = 1$) or quadratic ($m = 2$), it will not fit humps and dips in the yield structure when they occur, and if there are too many coefficients it will become unstable and will fit so closely that measuring deviations from the curve becomes pointless. Some users, therefore, have fitted different curves to different sectors of the market and spliced them together where the sectors meet or overlap. But this is not the only approach.

J.M. Brew in an article entitled 'Gilt-Edged Yield Curves' published in *The Investment Analyst* No. 16, December 1966 took a rather different line. He started by querying the use of conventional redemption yields as a criterion for comparing the relative valuation of bonds, on the grounds that in each redemption yield calculation a different roll-up rate assumption was being made. He therefore sought to find a set of alternative 'yields' that reflected relative value but were all based on a common premise. To do so he went back to an even earlier (1961) paper of F.S. Jamieson (*Faculty of Actuaries, T.F.A.*, **27**, 93) whose thinking was as follows.

If we write the basic compound interest equation of value for a fixed interest bond (for simplicity having a term to maturity of an integral number of half-years, $n$) as:

$$P = \frac{g}{2} \cdot a_{\overline{n}|} + 100 \cdot v^n$$

where $v = 1/(1 + i)$ and $i = y/200$ and as per Chapter 5.

Multiplying throughout by $(1 + i)^n$ this becomes,

$$P \cdot (1+i)^n = \frac{g}{2} \cdot s_{\overline{n}|} + 100$$

$$P \cdot [(1+i)^n - 1] = \frac{g}{2} \cdot s_{\overline{n}|} + (100 - P)$$

Now since 
$$s_{\overline{n}|} = \frac{(1+i)^n - 1}{i}$$

this equation can be further rearranged,

$$P \cdot i \cdot s_{\overline{n}|} = \frac{g}{2} \cdot s_{\overline{n}|} + (100 - P)$$

or,

$$\frac{y}{200} = i = \frac{g}{2 \cdot P} + \frac{(100 - P)}{P \cdot s_{\overline{n}|}}$$

$$y = 200 \cdot i = \frac{100 \cdot g}{P} + \frac{(100 - P)}{P} \cdot \frac{200}{s_{\overline{n}|}}$$

This shows how the conventional redemption yield can be considered to be the sum of the flat yield and the proportional capital gain to maturity scaled down by the factor $200/s_{\overline{n}|}$, where the rate of interest used in calculating $s_{\overline{n}|}$ is the redemption yield itself.

The Jamieson/Brew school of thought felt it illogical to use implicitly different interest rates in calculating $s_{\overline{n}|}$ for each different bond in the market and sought instead to use a single accumulation function $S(n)$ which would apply to all bonds and which would vary only in relation to the term to maturity, $n$. It could be that $S(n)$ might be assigned values equal to the compound interest function $s_{\overline{n}|}$ at some constant rate if one chose so, but it was not necessary for $S(n)$ to take that form. If, however, $S(n)$ was constructed in that way, the rate of interest used in its construction was called the 'reproductive rate'.

This opened the way for the creation of an alternative measure of value which we shall here call 'return' (in order to distinguish it from 'yield' which will be taken to signify a value derived from conventional compound interest procedures).

'Return' is defined as,

$$r(n) = \frac{100 \cdot g}{P} + \frac{(100 - P)}{P} \cdot \frac{200}{S(n)}$$

Using this method Brew started by looking at pairs of bonds and established a formula for what we have previously referred to as the 'balance-of-term yield', and which he called the 'reinvestment rate', between two bonds having terms to maturity $n$, $m$, and returns $r(n)$, $r(m)$ respectively. Expressed in 'return' terms this was,

$$r(n, m) = \frac{r(n) \cdot A(n) - r(m) \cdot A(m)}{A(n) - A(m)}$$

where $A(n)$ and $A(m)$ are present value equivalents of the accumulation functions $S(n)$ and $S(m)$, linked by the relationship:

124

$$A(n) = \frac{S(n)}{1 + [r(n)/200] \cdot S(n)} \text{ and similarly for } A(m).$$

Brew saw that if one constructed a scatter chart plotting bonds' values of $r(n) \cdot A(n)$ against the y-axis, and their corresponding values of $A(n)$ against the x-axis, the reinvestment rate between any two bonds was equal to the gradient of the line joining their respective plots on that chart. This chart he called the Reinvestment Chart.

To get an idea of how this method works in practice we have created in Table 6.9 below a hypothetical set of bonds spread across the maturity range from 2 years ($n = 4$) to 30 years ($n = 60$).

Table 6.9   Reproductive rate = 8.000

| Coupon = g | Price = P | n | S(n) | Return r(n) | x A(n) | y r(n)·A(n) |
|---|---|---|---|---|---|---|
| 5.50 | 99.75 | 4 | 4.24646 | 5.632 | 3.7929 | 21.3611 |
| 11.00 | 111.50 | 6 | 6.63298 | 6.756 | 5.4189 | 36.6077 |
| 6.75 | 97.25 | 8 | 9.21423 | 7.555 | 6.8352 | 51.6377 |
| 9.00 | 107.00 | 10 | 12.00611 | 7.321 | 8.3404 | 61.0638 |
| 7.50 | 95.75 | 14 | 18.29191 | 8.318 | 10.3885 | 86.4140 |
| 10.00 | 110.00 | 20 | 29.77808 | 8.480 | 13.1608 | 111.6077 |
| 8.00 | 93.00 | 30 | 56.08494 | 8.871 | 16.0816 | 142.6527 |
| 9.00 | 101.00 | 40 | 95.02552 | 8.890 | 18.1905 | 161.7145 |
| 8.50 | 95.00 | 60 | 237.99069 | 8.992 | 20.3418 | 182.9054 |

As can be seen from Fig. 6.7 the points on this chart are fairly close to being in a straight line. If they were exactly in line then the reinvestment rate between every pair of these bonds would be the same, and a form of market equilibrium could be considered to exist. Brew was thus drawn to the idea that the most logical form for the yield curve to take was that of the regression line of $r(n) \cdot A(n)$ on $A(n)$ drawn on a reinvestment chart.

Practitioners not familiar with the use of 'curvilinear coordinates', $r(n) \cdot A(n)$ and $r(n)$, have sometimes found this concept difficult to grasp, and it is thus worth looking at a variation of this method in which return, $r(n)$, is plotted against the reciprocal of $A(n)$, $1/A(n)$. Let us now consider the line joining two points, $[1/A(n), r(n)]$ and $[1/A(m), r(m)]$, representing bonds of maturities $n$ and $m$ in this alternative representation.

This line has an equation,

$$\frac{y - r(n)}{r(n) - r(m)} = \frac{x - 1/A(n)}{1/A(n) - 1/A(m)}$$

125

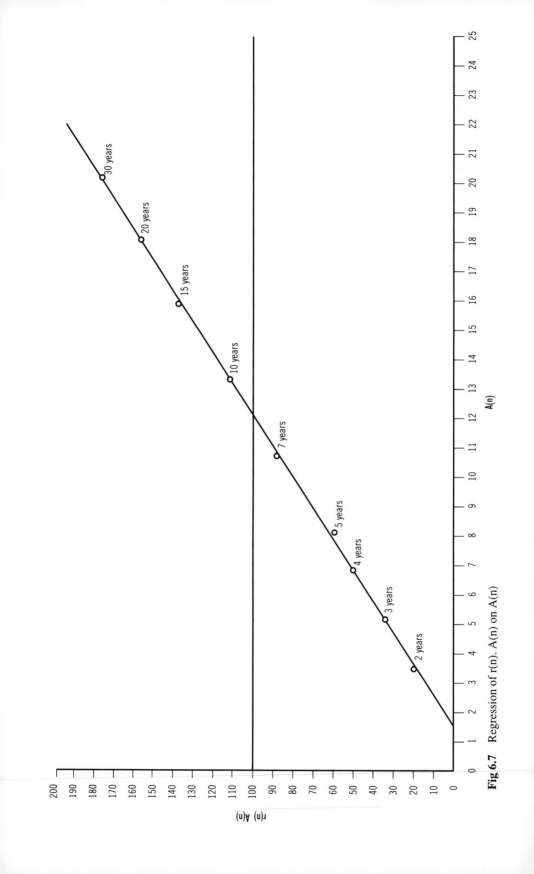

**Fig 6.7** Regression of r(n). A(n) on A(n)

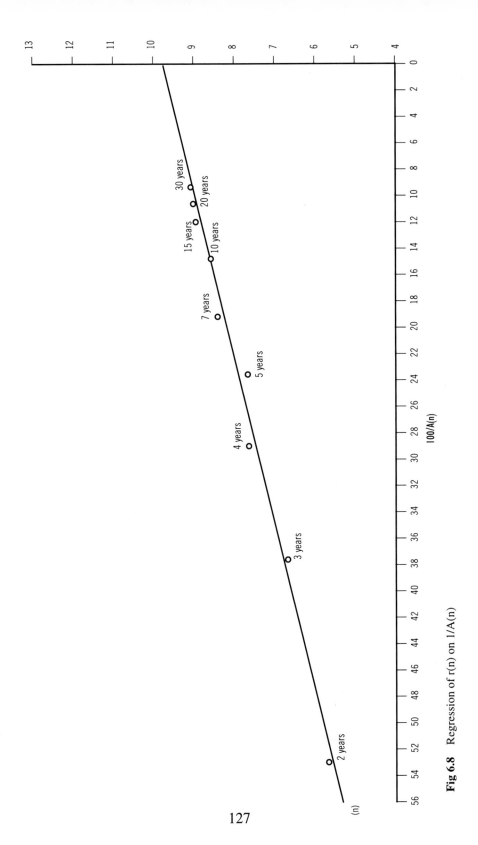

**Fig 6.8**  Regression of r(n) on 1/A(n)

127

which can be rearranged as,

$$y = \frac{r(n) - r(m)}{1/A(n) - 1/A(m)} \cdot x + \frac{r(n) \cdot A(n) - r(m) \cdot A(m)}{A(n) - A(m)}$$

The second term on the right hand side of this equation is the value of the intercept on the y-axis made by this line. Its formula is precisely that of the reinvestment rate between these two bonds that we established earlier in this section.

Thus whilst under the Brew system families of parallel lines represent sets of equivalent market values, under this alternative system such equivalence is achieved by the family of lines that ali pass through the same point on the y-axis. This suggests that the line of regression of $r(n)$ on $1/A(n)$ is also a natural form of yield curve worthy of consideration.

It is interesting to note that both these types of regression lines transform into classic yield curve shapes when their values are replotted onto charts drawn using term to maturity as their x-axis scale, but by their very nature such yield curves will be either monotonic increasing or monotonic decreas-

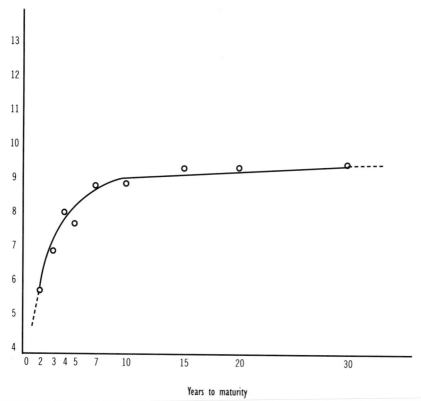

Years to maturity

**Fig 6.9**   Transformation of regression of r(n) on 1/A to linear maturity scale

128

ing or totally flat. They will not fit either humps or dips in the yield structure and the valuation of bonds in such areas will be made to appear anomalous in this sort of system when that may not always be the case.

Another form of yield curve favoured by some gilt-edged practitioners is that found by plotting redemption yield against the reciprocal of modified duration. The thinking behind this choice of scale for the $x$-axis runs as follows.

Given two bonds, A and B, with redemption yields $y_A$, $y_B$, and modified durations $w_A$, $w_B$, respectively, it is possible to construct a series of synthetic bonds whose modified durations lie between that of A and B by holding weighted combinations of those two bonds.

Let us consider a synthetic of this sort designed to have a modified duration of $w$.

This can be acheived by holding amounts of Bond A and Bond B whose money values are proportionate to:

$$\frac{w - w_B}{w_A - w_B} \text{ and } \frac{w_A - w}{w_A - w_B} \text{ respectively.}$$

In Chapter 5 we showed how the yield of a combination of bonds approximates extremely closely to (and for many practical purposes can be taken to equate to) the money weighted and modified duration weighted average yield of its constituent parts. Using this relationship we obtain a yield for this synthetic of,

$$y = \frac{(w - w_B) \cdot w_A \cdot y_A + (w_A - w) \cdot w_B \cdot y_B}{(w - w_B) \cdot w_A + (w_A - w) \cdot w_B}$$

It can be shown that this expression is the same as the equation of the line joining points whose coordinates are $(1/w_A, y_A)$ and $(1/w_B, y_B)$, and thus that the yields of synthetics made from these bonds lie on the line joining the Bonds A and B on a chart plotting their yields against the reciprocal of their modified duration. Straight lines drawn on charts using this scale are therefore natural candidates for an intrinsic form of yield curve and results derived from this type of analysis are often quite similar to those produced by the Brew method.

Another way in which it is possible to make use of the 'yield to inverse (modified) duration' relationship is to fit an envelope of straight lines joining the highest of the yields along the range of values to produce an efficient frontier of value for the market. Whilst this is not a yield curve in the accepted sense it can provide users with a set of base yield values against which to compare yields of individual bonds with the same modified duration. The big difference is that here comparisons are being made with the cheapest values (highest yields) provided by the market rather than central values as is the case with more traditional yield curve methods. This system does, however, have a considerable practical advantage. Because the envelope consists simply of a small number of straight lines joining consecutive high points it does not require heavy computer power to produce and can if necessary be drawn by hand.

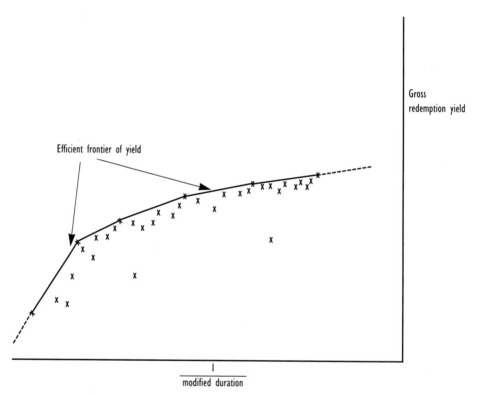

**Fig 6.10**   The Efficient Frontier of a market's yield structure

Yet another approach was that of Professor Stephen Schaefer of the London Business School whose paper 'Tax-induced clientele effects in the market for British Government securities' was published in *The Journal of Financial Economics* **10** (1982). The essence of the Schaefer method was to examine the cash flows generated by individual gilt-edged securities and see if they could be bettered by a portfolio (with non-negative holdings) of alternative gilts. He used a series of monotonic decreasing discount functions to enable this analysis to be performed not just as it applied to gross investors, but at a wide variety of rates of tax on income also. In this sort of analysis an individual gilt was considered to be dear if it could be bettered by an alternative portfolio, and fairly (neutrally) valued if it could not. In the latter case the optimum portfolio would consist entirely of the gilt under comparison and there is thus no way in the Schaefer system that individual gilts could be 'cheap' – they could only be dear or neutral. In fact because this analysis was done for every relevant tax rate (in 1982 Schaefer used tax rates ranging from 0% to 100%), a gilt was optimal if, and only if, it was neutrally valued at all tax rates; and only dear if there was no rate of tax at which it could be valued neutrally. When this was the case the gilt's absolute margin of 'dearness' against 'the market' was taken to be the minimum 'dearness' figure resulting from the various analyses at all those different tax rates.

## Price model analysis

As outlined in the previous section, price model analysis came about as a result of the need to find an analytical system that would relate bonds' valuations, not simply as a function of maturity (as in the two-dimensional yield-maturity yield curve method), but to take into account coupon variations as well. Essentially it was to find a form of equation:

$$P = P(g,n)$$

where $g$ represents coupon and $n$ term to maturity.

There have been a number of varying approaches to solving this problem, some of which are well documented by virtue of having been the subject of public discussion in actuarial or Bank of England papers. Other work has been performed by stockbrokers and GEMMs for more private circulation and application.

The approach of R.S. Clarkson, BSc, FFA, to this question provoked widespread interest in the whole subject of three-dimensional price modelling when his paper, 'A mathematical model for the gilt-edged market', was read first to the Faculty of Actuaries in Edinburgh in February 1978, and subsequently to the Institute of Actuaries in London in January 1979. Clarkson used a curvilinear model in which he eschewed the normal compound interest functions such as $a_{\overline{n}|}$ and $v^n$, and concentrated instead on relationship between the flat yield, $g/P$, and the proportionate capital gain to redemption, $100/P$, for the bonds under consideration.

In order to understand the thinking behind this method it may be helpful to look at the chart below (Fig. 6.11). At first sight it looks horrifyingly complicated but if we explain it step by step the basic simplicity of Clarkson's approach will soon become apparent. The first things to explain about the chart are the choice of axes and the scales used. Here the $y$-axis value is 100 divided by clean price, $100/P$, and the $x$-axis value is the flat yield, $g/P$, so that if the clean price of a bond in question is 80 and the coupon is 8%, then $y$ is equal to 1.25 and $x = 0.10$.

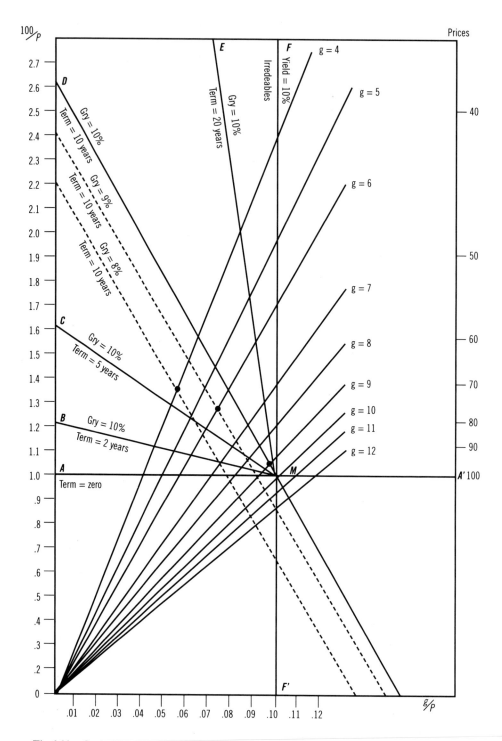

**Fig 6.11**  Capital/Income diagram for the Clarkson model

132

The next feature to look at is the fan of lines all emanating from the origin of the chart, point O. Each of these lines corresponds to a coupon rate ranging from 4% to 12%, and it is a simple consequence of the choice of axes that a bond with a given coupon will remain on the relevant line for the whole of its life until maturity. For the purpose of simplicity this example has initially been constructed to look at a hypothetical situation where all bonds are valued on a 10% gross (redemption) yield. On this basis the irredeemable bonds all have plots sitting on the vertical straight line FF′ whose equation is $x = 0.10$.

Next let us consider the other extremity of the maturity scale, the moment of redemption. At this time the price of any bond, irrespective of coupon, will be 100 so that they all lie on the horizontal straight line AA′, $y = 1$. Plots of sets of bonds with maturities between these two extremes lie in shapes that slant basically from top-left to bottom-right on this chart. It is an interesting (but not always appreciated) fact that bonds of varying coupon rates but the same maturity and the same redemption yield lie on straight lines that pass through the point on line AA′ whose $x$-value is equal to the redemption yield in question. In this case the yield is 10%, i.e $x = 0.10$, and this point is labelled M on the diagram.

As examples of this phenomenon the lines MB, MC, MD, and ME represent bonds of two years, five years, ten years, and twenty years to maturity all valued on a 10% yield basis, and the points where these lines intersect with the $y$ axis, e.g. B, C, and D represent zero coupon bonds of these respective maturities valued similarly.

Finally let us look at the effect of changing the yield basis of our ten-year bonds to 9% and then 8%. The lines of these alternative scenarios are the dotted ones that run nearly parallel to MD, just below and to the left of it. We can use these to observe the pattern generated by the sort of yield structure often encountered in the gilt-edged market in the past where gross yields basically increase with coupon. If, for example, our 4% coupon ten-year-bond yielded 8%, our 6% coupon bond yielded 9% and our 9% coupon bond yielded 10% (as marked by heavy dots on the chart), the relationship between these on the chart is not a straight line but a gentle convex curve instead.

Once one grasps the basic concept of Clarkson's 'capital-flat yield' diagram it is not too difficult to envisage his three-dimensional market structure. Clarkson saw that for any particular maturity the model values for bonds with that maturity would lie on a slanted line (or gentle curve) of the sort discussed above, and that if you stacked an infinite number of these (relating to every maturity from redemption to eternity) one behind the other, you would obtain a surface reflecting model market values for all combinations of coupon and maturity. Its shape has often been likened to

133

that of a twisted rope ladder with each rung (sometimes slightly bent) relating to a different maturity.

Clarkson's basic model price equation takes the form

$$\frac{1}{P} = 1 + h(n) + f(n) \int_0^{i_0 - g/P} l(n,t)\, dt$$

where $n$ is the term to maturity

$i_0$ is a positive constant (representing irredeemable yields)

$h(n)$ is a continuously differentiable function of $n$

$f(n)$ is a positive continuously differentiable function of $n$

and $l(n,t)$ is a positive smooth function of $n$ and $t$ with:

$$l(n,0) = 1$$

$$\text{and } \frac{d}{dt} l(n,t) <= 0$$

If one relates this equation to the capital-flat yield diagram as described earlier one can see that the first two terms, $1 + h(n)$, equate to the value of the intercept on the $y$-axis made by the model's line/curve for bonds with term to maturity equal to $n$. As we have already demonstrated this point represents the valuation of a zero coupon bond of this maturity, i.e. the capital constituent of the price. This leaves the final term to account for the remaining income content.

The formal theory, a description of the functions $h(n)$, $f(n)$ and $l(n)$, and an explanation of the calculative process by which Clarkson determined the parameters of his surface, and how he put the system to practical use is set out in great detail in the *Journal of the Institute of Actuaries* (**106**, II, September 1979), together with transcripts of a fascinating verbal discussion which followed it, and any analyst wishing to delve further into this method of analysis will find it rewards close study.

An earlier approach to three-dimensional market building was introduced in a paper by Dr K.S. Feldman, BSc, PhD, FIA, entitled 'The Gilt-edged Market Reformulated', published in the *Journal of the Institute of Actuaries* (**104**, II, dated September 1977). The essence of the Feldman approach (and also that behind a similar model built sometime later by R.T. Eddleston, MA, FIA) was that, at any particular time, there exist implicitly two discounting functions $A(n)$ and $V(n)$ (both functions of term to maturity measured in half-years, $n$, the former for discounting a series of equal income items, and the latter for discounting single capital payments. At any particular time the coefficients of these two functions are found by applying a 'least-squares' fit to the observed prices of bonds in the market, and from these coefficients hypothetical model prices can be deduced. Both the Feldman and Eddleston models were fundamentally linear in coupon (though Eddleston made some special adjustments for low-coupon issues), the Feldman version taking on a basic form of equation

$$P(g,n) = \frac{g}{2} A(n) + 100\,V(n),$$

whilst Eddleston replaced the annuity function $A(n)$ by its component parts using a factor $U(n)$ to discount each individual coupon payment thus,

$$P(g,n) = \frac{g}{2}[U(1) + U(2) + \ldots + U(n)] + 100\,V(n),$$

There was considerable intellectual purity in this approach, but it suffered from the drawback that in practice the market tended to place price premiums on bonds with sizeable run-ups to par thus introducing an element of curvilinearity into the price to coupon relationship.

However there were ways in which this facet of the problem could be taken into account. One was to differentiate between the capital value of the gain/loss to maturity and the part of the eventual redemption value represented by the current price. If this was done the equation of price changed to involve three separate discounting functions $U(n)$, $V(n)$ and $W(n)$ as follows,

$$P = \frac{g}{2}\{U(1) + U(2) + \ldots + U(n)\} + PV(n) + (100 - P)W(n).$$

These discounting functions were clearly the key elements in this type of model. They all needed to take the value of 1 when $n = 0$ and tend to zero as $n$ tended to infinity. Not surprisingly this suggested a basic exponential form such as:

$$U(n) = e^{-(a_1 n + a_2 n^2 + a_3 n^3 + \ldots)}$$

but there are practical difficulties in applying curve fitting devices such as 'least squares' to expressions of this type. An alternative was to follow the approach described earlier in this chapter when considering yield curves, and make the transformation

$$x = 1 - e^{-kn}$$

and then consider $U(n)$, $V(n)$, and $W(n)$ to be polynomials of the form

$$U(n) = a_0 + a_1\,x + a_2\,x^2 + a_3\,x^3 + \ldots$$

$$V(n) = b_0 + b_1 x + b_2 x^2 + b_3 x^3 + \ldots$$

and
$$W(n) = c_0 + c_1 x + c_2 x^2 + c_3 x^3 + \ldots$$

The number of coefficients in each of these polynomials was not fixed (and some of the coefficients are interrelated by virtue of the functions' boundary conditions); nor was it necessarily the case that all the polynomials had the same number of terms. These were choices left for individual model-builders to make in order to meet their own particular requirements, but just as was the case with yield curve fitting, using too few coefficients would produce too rigid a price structure, using too many would produce an unstable model. Given these complexities and bearing in mind the enduring popularity of the yield curve to which we referred earlier, the question may be asked as to why one bothered to construct three-dimensional price models as complex as this. Although the most usual application of a price model was in calculating theoretical values against which actual prices of bonds in the market could be compared and assessed, one of their most valuable attributes was their ability to produce accurate hypothetical values in areas of the market where no physical bonds existed. Apart from the obvious advantage this provided in pricing new issues in virgin areas it also greatly facilitated making historic studies of market values and structures unhindered by the analyst's usual bugbear – the fact that the characteristics of whichever bond he has chosen as representative of the market will change as time progresses and maturities shorten. Given a database derived from a three-dimensional model it was perfectly simple to take a cross-section of its values on a regular, say daily, basis to produce, for example, a time series of 'the market's' price or yield for a constant coupon rate and a constant term to maturity. This proved to be a better base for making, say, computations of historic option volatility for instruments of that precise coupon and maturity than values derived from an individual bond used as a proxy. Again, taking the relevant cross-sections of this sort of model gave the user easy access to constant coupon price values and thus to constant coupon yield curves, par yield curves, zero-coupon yield curves and spot rates.

The basic change in the gilt-edged market's price and yield structure, brought about by the 1996 taxation changes which tax capital gains on bonds as income, has to a very large extent removed the need for three-dimensionality in such model-building. This is not to say that models of the type mentioned above do not fit the market, but rather that in the new circumstances the three discounting functions become more similiar and a single function applied to both income and capital items equally may suffice.

One such device which has been developed by the Fixed Income Analytics Group at Merrill Lynch in New York is the Merrill Lynch exponential spline model. Basically this model uses a single discount function such as $U(n)$ described earlier, and applies it to the values of a selected series of current-coupon benchmark bonds at a given moment to produce spot discount factors for any required maturity at that particular time. The present value at that time of each individual coupon payment or capital repayment of a bond can then be determined by multiplying the value of the payment by its respective discount factor, and the sum of all such present values forms the model value of that bond against which its actual value can be compared and judgements as to its relative cheapness or dearness made.

To date the model has been applied to the US Treasury market, the French and Canadian government bond markets and, latterly, the gilt-edged market as well. All the evidence to date confirms the view that such discount-factor-based models are intrinsically stable and economically efficient, and represent a major advance in bond market analysis from more traditional yield curve fitting methods.

But perhaps it is in the field of projective analysis that the greatest value of market modelling lies. A well-designed model gives the gilt-edged analyst a structure into which to input his own forecasts about future market levels, yield patterns and relative bond valuations and produce prospective rates of return to a specified time horizon for all issues in the market. In turn these can be used as feedstock for portfolio management and optimisation programmes allowing portfolios to be managed in a consistent and efficient way. Obviously the success or otherwise of such management is mainly dependent on the accuracy of the forecasts made, but without the modelling capability the process cannot be conducted other than in a piecemeal fashion.

# 7

## Index-linked gilts

### Basics

Index-linked gilts are obligations of the UK Government.

The Government guarantees to pay the respective interest payments on index-linked gilts on their due dates, and redeem them on the date stated in its prospectus in just the same way as it does with conventional gilts.

The big difference is that whereas conventional gilts have fixed coupon rates and are redeemed at par (100), index-linked gilts have coupons and redemption values which are linked to the UK General Index of Retail Prices (RPI), which is an official consumer price index determined monthly.

### Origins of the index-linked market

Index-linked gilts first saw the light of day following the 1981 Budget speech on 10 March 1981 when the then Chancellor of the Exchequer, the Rt Hon. Sir Geoffrey Howe (now Lord Howe) announced the issue of £1,000 million 2% Index-Linked Stock 1996. The issue was made by tender on 27 March 1981 and was restricted to pension funds or similar institutions writing pension business. Between then and the Budget of 1982 two further issues were made, namely,

£1,000 million 2% Index-Linked Stock 2006;
£750 million 2½% Index-Linked Stock 2011.

Whilst there were certainly some sound reasons for restricting ownership of these bonds to pension funds and the like, this did not enhance their marketability. This factor requires the existence of a body of willing buyers and willing sellers at any given price and time, which one-class ownership tends to preclude. Since it seemed to be the Government's intention to do a fair part of its future funding by selling index-linked debt, this was unfortunate. Finally, after (it is suspected) much agonising in the Treasury and the Bank of England, it was announced in the 1982 Budget speech that henceforth ownership restrictions were to be removed, and index-linked gilts were to be made available to all and sundry, non-residents included; and at the same time a medium-dated issue, £750 million 2% Index-linked Stock 1988, was created. Over the years since then fourteen further issues have been created, four of which have run their course to redemption, and one which carried an option to be converted into a conventional gilt was thus transformed.

At the end of March 1995 there were thirteen outstanding index-linked gilts which are listed below together with the then nominal amount of each issue.

£1,200 million Index-Linked  2% 1996
  £800 million Index-Linked $4\frac{5}{8}$% 1998
£1,600 million Index-Linked $2\frac{1}{2}$% 2001
£1,450 million Index-Linked $2\frac{1}{2}$% 2003
£1,000 million Index-Linked $4\frac{3}{8}$% 2004
£1,750 million Index-Linked  2% 2006
£1,750 million Index-Linked $2\frac{1}{2}$% 2009
£2,100 million Index-Linked $2\frac{1}{2}$% 2011
£2,450 million Index-Linked $2\frac{1}{2}$% 2013
£2,800 million Index-Linked $2\frac{1}{2}$% 2016
£2,750 million Index-Linked $2\frac{1}{2}$% 2020
£2,450 million Index-Linked $2\frac{1}{2}$% 2024
£1,300 million Index-Linked $4\frac{1}{8}$% 2030

As at 31 March 1995 these had a total market capitalisation of £33.7 billion and represented 14.8% of the total gilt-edged market by value.

## Market liquidity of index-linked gilts

Because of its size relative to the larger conventional market questions have been asked at times as to the nature of market liquidity in index-linked gilts. In its early days the market in these bonds was all too often one-way, i.e. all buyers, no sellers or vice-versa. This made for a volatile and illiquid market. The Bank of England, however, recognised that this was in nobody's best interest and has, over the years, helped to add liquidity to the index-linked sector through its secondary market operations. In normal market conditions market makers will tend to quote prices with a 6/32 bid-offer spread for sizes of £2.5 million to £5 million nominal. Much larger bargains than this can be effected and are facilitated by the confidence market makers have in the Bank's attitude to the market.

. Basically the Bank of England will meet a build-up of demand for index-linked gilts by creating further tranches of existing issues if it feels that circumstances warrant it. Likewise it will respond to offers of index-linked gilts from market makers active in the sector by bidding in size at a level of their choosing (which tends to be dependent on the size of the sale and the market conditions prevailing at the time) provided that the issue in question is not one where the Bank has a tap in current operation.

This practice of bidding for index-linked gilts by the Bank of England is specifically related to the index-linked sector and does not apply to conventional gilts. It contrasts with a general unwillingness of most other global index-linked issuers to bid back for their own bonds, and this feature has played an important part in making this market the most liquid of its kind in the world today.

## Form of indexation used

Each index-linked payment, either of interest or capital, is related to the RPI for the month eight months prior to that in which it is received.

Values are adjusted by the ratio of this RPI to a 'base RPI' which is that pertaining to the month eight months before the month of issue.

The following example illustrates the *modus operandi*:

*2% Index-Linked Stock 2006 was issued in July 1981.*
Counting back eight months from this date brings one to November 1980 as the base month for this bond.

The RPI for November 1980 was 274.1, and this is established as the base RPI for this bond.

The bond is due to be redeemed on 19 July 2006. Again, counting back eight months, one arrives at November 2005. The capital repayment to be made on redemption will be,

$$100 \times \frac{\text{RPI for November 2005}}{\text{RPI for November 1980}}$$

Coupon payments are computed in an identical fashion. The nominal coupon rate is here 2% per annum, i.e. 1% per half-year, index-linked. Since May 1999 is eight months before January 1999, the coupon payment to be made on 19 January 2000 will therefore be,

$$1 \times \frac{\text{RPI for } May \text{ 1999}}{\text{RPI for November 1980}}$$

and similarly for other coupons.

The accuracy to which both the repayment of capital and interest payments are calculated is not the same for all index-linked gilts. For the first three issues, namely, Index-Linked 2% 1996, Index-Linked 2% 2006 and Index-Linked 2½% 2011 the authorities chose to round down to two decimal places. For all subsequent issues values have been rounded down to four places of decimals.

## Why does the UK Government use a lagged form of indexation?

One main reason for choosing this form of eight-month-lagged indexation was to ensure that the next receivable coupon could be determined well in advance of the time period to which it related. Since gilt-edged securities used to become quoted 'ex-dividend' about thirty-seven days before the due interest payment date, and since the RPI for each month is announced in the middle of the following month, it is clear that eight months was the minimum practical lag period.

## Side effects of using lagged indexation

It does, however, have the somewhat unusual effect of adjusting values for inflation in the eight months preceeding the date of issue, and giving no compensation for inflation in the last eight months of an index-linked gilt's life. For many index-linked issues with long periods to maturity this feature may not be particularly significant, but it is a critical factor for bonds where the last eight months to maturity represents a large proportion of their remaining life; and once an index-linked gilt moves into its last eight months' life, it becomes a fixed-interest instrument pure and simple.

## The general index of retail prices – (RPI)

The RPI is a non-seasonally adjusted index, calculated monthly and published by the Central Statistical Office towards the middle of the sub-sequent month. It is not (unlike many other official statistics) normally subject to revision, and for years it was generally assumed that if extenuating circumstances ever required it to be retrospectively adjusted index-linked values would not be revised, but would continue to be based on the index figures originally published. This assumption was proved to be false when on 13 July 1995 HM Treasury and the Central Statistical Office announced that an error had been identified in the calculation process affecting the RPI values for March and May 1995. The Bank of England then issued revised values for coupon payments linked to those months' RPIs, and ruled that accrued interest amounts on bargains in the affected bonds transacted before the day of the announcement should stand, but that for bargains struck post-announcement should be based on the revised coupon rates.

The progress of the RPI since index-linked gilts were introduced to the market is shown in table 7.1.

141

**Table 7.1**

|       | Jan   | Feb   | March | April | May   | June  | July  | Aug   | Sept  | Oct   | Nov   | Dec   |
|-------|-------|-------|-------|-------|-------|-------|-------|-------|-------|-------|-------|-------|
| 1980: | 245.3 | 248.8 | 252.2 | 260.8 | 263.2 | 265.7 | 267.9 | 268.5 | 270.2 | 271.9 | 274.1 | 275.6 |
| 1981: | 277.3 | 279.8 | 284.0 | 292.2 | 294.1 | 295.8 | 297.1 | 299.3 | 301.0 | 303.7 | 306.9 | 308.8 |
| 1982: | 310.6 | 310.7 | 313.4 | 319.7 | 322.0 | 322.9 | 323.0 | 323.1 | 322.9 | 324.5 | 326.1 | 325.5 |
| 1983: | 325.9 | 327.3 | 327.9 | 332.5 | 333.9 | 334.7 | 336.5 | 338.0 | 339.5 | 340.7 | 341.9 | 342.8 |
| 1984: | 342.6 | 344.0 | 345.1 | 349.7 | 351.0 | 351.9 | 351.5 | 354.8 | 355.5 | 357.7 | 358.8 | 358.5 |
| 1985: | 359.8 | 362.7 | 366.1 | 373.9 | 375.6 | 376.4 | 375.7 | 376.7 | 376.5 | 377.1 | 378.4 | 378.9 |
| 1986: | 379.7 | 381.1 | 381.6 | 385.3 | 386.0 | 385.8 | 384.7 | 385.9 | 387.8 | 388.4 | 391.7 | 393.0 |
| 1987: | 394.5 |       |       |       |       |       |       |       |       |       |       |       |
| 1987: | 100.0 | 100.4 | 100.6 | 101.8 | 101.9 | 101.9 | 101.8 | 102.1 | 102.4 | 102.9 | 103.4 | 103.3 |
| 1988: | 103.3 | 103.7 | 104.1 | 105.8 | 106.2 | 106.6 | 106.7 | 107.9 | 108.4 | 109.5 | 110.0 | 110.3 |
| 1989: | 111.0 | 111.8 | 112.3 | 114.3 | 115.0 | 115.4 | 115.5 | 115.8 | 116.6 | 117.5 | 118.5 | 118.8 |
| 1990: | 119.5 | 120.2 | 121.4 | 125.1 | 126.2 | 126.7 | 126.8 | 128.1 | 129.3 | 130.3 | 130.0 | 129.9 |
| 1991: | 130.2 | 130.9 | 131.4 | 133.1 | 133.5 | 134.1 | 133.8 | 134.1 | 134.6 | 135.1 | 135.6 | 135.7 |
| 1992: | 135.6 | 136.3 | 136.7 | 138.8 | 139.3 | 139.3 | 138.8 | 138.9 | 139.4 | 139.9 | 139.7 | 139.2 |
| 1993: | 137.9 | 138.8 | 139.3 | 140.6 | 141.1 | 141.0 | 140.7 | 141.3 | 141.9 | 141.8 | 141.6 | 141.9 |
| 1994: | 141.3 | 142.1 | 142.5 | 144.2 | 144.7 | 144.7 | 144.0 | 144.7 | 145.0 | 145.2 | 145.3 | 146.0 |
| 1995: | 146.0 | 146.9 | 147.5 | 149.0 | 149.6 | 149.8 | 149.1 | 149.9 | 150.6 |       |       |       |

The RPI is periodically rebased to a value of 100. The figures shown in the upper part of the table above had a base of January 1974=100. Those in the lower part are based on January 1987=100. The RPI for January 1987 on the 'old' basis was 394.5, so it can be seen that the two series are linked by a factor of 3.945.

As a measure of price inflation the RPI is far from perfect. It was stated a little earlier that it is not seasonally adjusted but it is subject to certain seasonal influences, notably a sharper than normal upward movement after the Budget when increases in indirect taxation and excise duties normally take place, to be followed over the summer months by an easing as the prices of seasonal foods fall back. The index also contains a weighting reflecting mortgage interest costs, and this has the rather bizarre effect that when interest rates are raised to dampen inflation pressures this very measure acts to push up the RPI even further. However despite its imperfections the RPI is an index whose integrity is trusted by the public and this has been a major factor in establishing confidence in index-linked securities.

## Accrued interest on index-linked gilts

The basic priciples for calculating accrued interest on conventional bonds which were outlined in detail in Chapter 4 also apply to index-linked bonds. However the coupon rate used when calculating index-linked accrued interest is not constant but is indexed up to the date of the next interest payment date to occur in the calendar. It is important to draw the distinction here between:

(a)  the next interest payment date to occur in the calendar, and

(b)  the date of the next interest payment receivable.

It is (a) that determines the coupon rate to be used in accrued interest calculations.

When a bond is cum-dividend these two entities are the same, but when a bond is ex-dividend (b) will normally be six months later than (a).

For example let us consider Index-Linked $2\frac{1}{2}\%$ 2016 in December 1993.

This bond has interest payment dates 26 January, 26 July. It was issued on 19 January 1983 so its base month for indexation is May 1982, and its base RPI is 322.0 on the 'old' basis, which is equivalent to,

$$322/3.945 \ (= 81.6223067) \text{ on the present RPI basis.}$$

On Friday 17 December 1993 the bond was 147 days cum-dividend in respect of the payment due on 26 January 1994. The coupon for this half-yearly payment is linked to the RPI for May 1993 (141.1) and was thus:

$$2.50 \times \frac{141.1}{(322/3.945)} = 2.1608 \quad \text{when rounded down to four decimal places,}$$

and the gross accrued interest for this date was,

$$2.1608 \times 147/182.5 = 1.74048 \text{ (cum-dividend).}$$

By the following Monday, 20 December 1993, the bond had become ex-dividend, and carried −36 days accrued interest. Despite the fact that the next interest payment receivable by a buyer on this basis will now not be until 26 July 1994, the accrued interest was still calculated with regard to the coupon to be paid on 26 January 1994 and was thus,

$$2.1608 \times (-36)/182.5 = -0.42624 \text{ (ex-dividend).}$$

Only after the 26 January 1994 had passed did interest on this stock start to accrue at the rate relevant to the payment due on 26 July.

## Evaluation of index-linked gilts.

In common with conventional gilts the most frequently used tool for evaluation purposes is that of redemption yield. However in contrast to the situation with conventionals where the values of all future payments of interest and repayments of capital are fixed and known, and such yields can be computed precisely, with index-linked gilts yield calculations have to be based on expectations of future inflation in the form of 'guesstimates' of future values of the RPI for the period between evaluation and eight months before redemption.

In cases of index-linked gilts in, say, the last fifteen months of their life it is not unreasonable to take an economic view and try to make specific forecasts of the RPI figures that will determine the penultimate and final coupons and the capital repayment amount. However, beyond that sort of time horizon, forecasting of this nature is not really a practical proposition and a rather less subjective method for projecting future values is required.

## Money yields

A method frequently used is to assume a constant future annual inflation rate which is applied to the most recently published monthly RPI figure to produce forecasts for the RPI out into the future. From these forecast RPI figures the money value of future coupon payments and redemption values can be projected and redemption yields computed using the same compound interest principles explained in Chapter 5. Yields formed in this way are termed 'money yields' (as opposed to 'real yields' which will be dealt with later) and as such can be compared directly with redemption yields on conventional gilts. In Table 7.2 we can see the prospective benefits resulting from a variety of different assumptions regarding inflation. The money yield in each case is that particular rate of interest at which the sum of the discounted values of these projected benefits equals the current total price. As Table 7.2 illustrates the assumed future inflation rate is a major determinant of money yields, and if the figure assumed proves to be unrealistic so will the money yield values that result from it.

In the example in Table 7.2 only the first receivable coupon was definitely known on the bargain date. All the others had to be obtained by making projections from the latest known RPI figure, i.e that for April 1994, 141.2. Whilst this is the way of things in the majority of cases it is not always thus. Where a bond has dividends paid close to the end of the months in question, it is possible for the RPI value which will determine the second receivable coupon to be announced before the bond goes ex-dividend for the first time. In such cases the first two coupons are certain and the projected figures start with the third coupon.

The general equation of value relating Total Price (including gross accrued interest) and gross money yields for index-linked bonds is,

$$P = v^q \cdot \left[ G_1 + \frac{g}{2} \cdot K \cdot \frac{\{v - v^{n+1} \cdot (1+j)^{n/2}\}}{\{1 - v\sqrt{1+j}\}} + v^n \cdot 100 \cdot K \cdot (1+j)^{(n-1)/2} \right]$$

**Table 7.2** Money yields produced by different future inflation assumptions index-linked 2% 1996 on 1 June 1994

| | | | | | | |
|---|---|---|---|---|---|---|
| Quoted price | | 198.312 | for settlement on 02.06.94 | | | |
| Gross accrued interest | | 0.889 | | | | |
| Total price | | 199.201 | 199.201 | 199.201 | 199.201 | 199.201 |
| Last known RPI | April 1994 | 144.2 | | | | |
| Assumed annual inflation rate % | | 3.00 | 4.00 | 5.00 | 6.00 | 7.00 |
| | Date | | | | | |
| Known coupon | 16.09.94 | 2.08 | 2.08 | 2.08 | 2.08 | 2.08 |
| Projected coupon | 16.03.95 | 2.13 | 2.14 | 2.14 | 2.15 | 2.15 |
| Projected coupon | 16.09.95 | 2.17 | 2.18 | 2.20 | 2.21 | 2.23 |
| Projected coupon | 16.03.96 | 2.20 | 2.23 | 2.25 | 2.28 | 2.31 |
| Projected coupon | 16.09.96 | 2.23 | 2.27 | 2.31 | 2.35 | 2.39 |
| Projected capital repayment | 16.09.96 | 223.61 | 227.43 | 231.27 | 235.13 | 239.03 |
| Money yield % p.a. | | 7.384 | 8.148 | 8.904 | 9.656 | 10.406 |
| Sum of discounted present values of future payments | | 199.201 | 199.201 | 199.201 | 199.201 | 199.201 |

where:

$G_1$  denotes the first receivable coupon (e.g. 2.08 in the above example),

$g$  denotes the nominal annual coupon rate (e.g. 2.00 above),

$j$  denotes the assumed annual inflation rate divided by 100,

$q$  denotes the time (measured in half-years) between the relevant settlement date and the actual business day on which the next interest payment will be received,

$n$  denotes the time (in half-years) from the next receivable interest date to redemption,

$$v = \frac{1}{(1 + \text{money yield} / 200)}$$

and

$$K = \frac{\text{latest RPI}}{\text{the bond's base RPI}} \times (1 + j)^{(m-8)/12}$$

where $m$ equals the number of months between that of the latest published RPI and that in which the second receivable coupon will occur.

## Real yields

If one were to follow classic compound interest methods to calculate real yields one would first need to project the prospective money values of a bond's coupons and capital repayment on a suitable inflation assumption, then deflate them to real values as at the relevant settlement date, and finally find a 'real yield' at which these discounted real values add up to the present price. In practice, however, there is a straightforward mathematical relationship between money yields, real yields and the assumed rate of inflation which allows one to do most of the work in money terms and transform the yield into real terms at the end of the process. This can be expressed thus,

$$1+\frac{Y}{200}=\left(1+\frac{R}{200}\right)\cdot\sqrt{1+\frac{J}{100}}$$

or,

$$R=200\times\left[\frac{(1+Y/200)}{\sqrt{(1+J/100)}}-1\right]$$

where $Y$ and $R$ are semi-annually compounded money yields and real yields respectively, and $J$ is the assumed annual rate of inflation.

If we apply this formula to the money yields in the example above we can observe the relationship between real yields and the inflation assumption more closely (Table 7.3).

**Table 7.3**   Money yields and Real yields: Index-Linked 2% Stock 1996

| Assumed inflation rate (annual) | Money yield % (semi-annual) | Real yield % (semi-annual) | Money yield minus real yield % |
|---|---|---|---|
| 3.00 | 7.384 | 4.342 | 3.042 |
| 4.00 | 8.148 | 4.106 | 4.042 |
| 5.00 | 8.904 | 3.869 | 5.035 |
| 6.00 | 9.656 | 3.636 | 6.020 |
| 7.00 | 10.406 | 3.407 | 6.999 |

Table 7.3 illustrates three important facts about real yields:

1. That there is no uniquely defined real yield for a given price.
2. That real yields are not simply money yields minus the rate of inflation.
3. That for a given price, but varying inflation assumptions, the derived real yield values decrease as the assumed inflation rate rises.

Because of this last point it is clear that for meaningful comparisons of real yields to be made, whether they be between different bonds at the same time or of the same bond at different times, they must be based on a consistent inflation assumption. For anybody compiling statistical records of index-linked yields, money or real, this means choosing a rate that can survive the passage of time. The rate used by many practitioners for this purpose for many years has been 5% per annum, though, in the more recent lower inflation climate there has been a growing school of thought that favours 3%.

## Yield discontinuities

Even with such a consistent approach discontinuities in the time series of real yields can and do occur. These happen on the days when the monthly RPIs are announced, if the actual rate of change in the RPIs of successive months is other than at this constant assumed rate. If the actual monthly increase of the RPI is less than the assumed rate for one month, then the real yield (calculated on the basis of the newly updated RPI figure) will be less than the comparable figure calculated on the previous basis, and vice-versa.

A good example of this happened on 15 December 1993 when the RPI for November was released. On that day Index-Linked 2½% Stock 2016 was priced at 154 25/32. Up to the time of this announcement the most recent RPI figure was that of 141.8 for October 1993. Using this as a base for forward projections of the RPI at an annual inflation rate of 5% leads to a real yield for this bond of 3.0256%. When the November figure was released, far from rising in line with 5% inflation, it actually showed a small fall to 141.6. Valuing the bond on the same real yield basis but using the November figure as the new base results in a price of 153 15/16, some 27/32 lower than before. This effect was, of course, not restricted to just this one bond, Index-Linked 2½% 2016. The valuation of all index-linked issues will have been affected in a similar fashion.

## Duration of index-linked bonds

Another feature of index-linked bonds is the fact that their durations (whether related to money yields or real yields) are considerably higher than those of conventional gilts of similar maturities. Table 7.4 illustrates this.

**Table 7.4**  Modified durations of index-linked bonds of varying maturities compared with those of conventional bonds on the same money yield

|  |  | 1 year | 2 years | 5 years | 10 years | 20 years | 30 years |
|---|---|---|---|---|---|---|---|
| Index-Linked | 2½% | 0.95 | 1.88 | 4.53 | 8.49 | 14.83 | 19.39 |
| Index-Linked | 4% | 0.95 | 1.86 | 4.40 | 8.04 | 13.61 | 17.57 |
| Conventional | 8½% | 0.94 | 1.80 | 4.01 | 6.65 | 9.54 | 10.80 |

These figures in Table 7.4 relate to index-linked bonds valued on a real yield of 3.475% assuming future inflation of 5%, which equates to a money yield of 8.5%, and conventional bonds also on an 8.5% redemption yield basis.

## Tax considerations

The next main point to cover is that the relative attractions of index-linked gilts have to date been much greater for high-rate taxpayers than for the gross

147

funds to whom they were originally restricted. This is because the (taxable) interest component of the total return from an index-linked gilt is small in comparison with the (up to now tax-free) capital component, and in this respect these issues, especially the shorter-dated ones, have had a considerable amount in common with conventional low-coupon gilts. This effect has been more marked in the case of those index-linked gilts carrying the lower type of nominal coupons (e.g. 2% or $2\frac{1}{2}$%) as opposed to some of the more recently created (1992) issues with nominal coupon rates in the range $4\frac{1}{8}$% to $4\frac{5}{8}$%.

Fig. 7.1 shows a series of broken parallel lines each representing the net money yields (at rates of income tax from 0% to 40%) of Index-Linked $2\frac{1}{2}$% 2001 on 1 June 1994 based on a given future inflation assumption; whilst the solid line represents the equivalent net redemption yields on the nearest comparable conventional bond, Treasury 7% 2001.

What this chart demonstrates is that given a prospective inflation assumption of, say, 4%, gross funds and taxed funds whose rate of tax on income was less than about 15% (and whose capital gains were not taxed) would at that time have done better in the conventional bond, but that taxpayers paying more than 15%, in particular basic rate (25%) and top-rate (40%) taxpayers should have preferred the index-linked bond. If on the other hand future inflation was then felt likely to be above 4.8% the index-linked bond should have been preferred by all these classes of investors.

Such considerations will continue to apply to private investors whose aggregate bond holdings do not exceed £200,000 nominal after 6 April 1996 when the 1996 taxation changes come into effect, as for them capital gains on gilts (including index-linked gilts) will still be tax-free.

For corporate investors and private investors above the '£200,000 nominal threshold' the situation (as at the end of July 1995) is not yet totally clear, but still looks relatively favourable for index-linked gilts. When details of the new tax regime were announced on 10 July 1995 it was stated: 'The element in the return on indexed gilts due to indexation of the principal repayment will remain tax-free. The precise method of achieving this will be announced as soon as possible'. Whichever form this takes, some part of these investors' capital gains on index-linked gilts will remain tax-free as long as the RPI continues to rise.

It is important, however, to realise that these considerations are restricted to index-linked *gilts* and do not extend to index-linked corporate bonds where, as stated by the Inland Revenue press release, 'investors will be taxable on their full profits, with no exemption for the indexation element'.

## Relative evaluations of index-linked bonds

Given all the complexities of this sector of the market many investors are unsure whether the analytical methods used for making comparisons

148

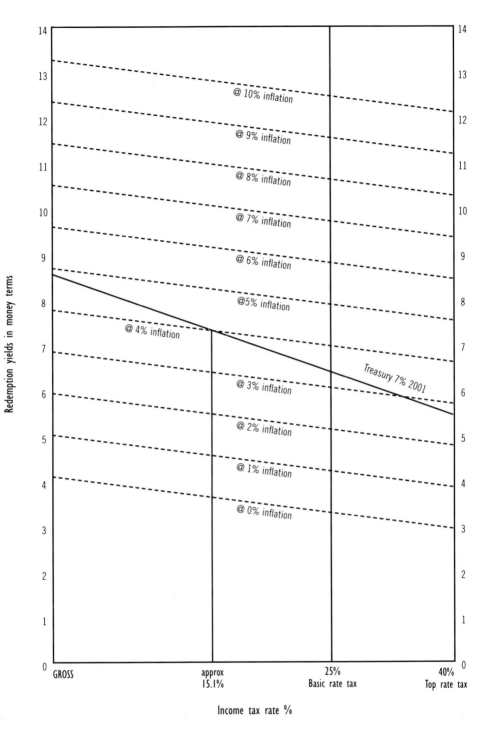

**Fig 7.1**  Comparative net yields obtainable from Index-Linked 2½% 2001 and Treasury 7% 2001 at varying tax rates and inflation assumptions

between conventional bonds can also be applied to index-linked bonds. Subject to certain provisos, see below, many of them can.

*Clean price ratios*

As highlighted earlier in this book a fundamental problem exists with clean price ratios in that the time series of any given ratio has an inbuilt trend caused by the difference between the flat yields of the two bonds under comparison. Where two index-linked bonds are being compared this problem is compounded by virtue of the fact that their flat yield difference will have discontinuities each time one of the bonds passes a dividend payment date. However, because many index-linked bonds have similar coupons the size of the flat yield difference is often small, and where this is the case, and where the time period over which the price ratio is being observed is short, the method can be used, but it is not totally precise. Obversely, clean price ratios are quite unsuitable for making long-term comparisons between bonds with markedly different flat yields, such as between index-linked bonds and their high-coupon counterparts in the conventional sector of the market.

*Real yield differences*

These are reasonably satisfactory for measuring relativities between index-linked bonds of broadly similar maturities, even if the underlying inflation assumption varies from time to time, as long as both yields are based on the same assumption at any particular time. This comes about by consideration of the basic equation linking money and real yields, thus:

$$1 + \frac{Y}{200} = \left(1 + \frac{R}{200}\right) \times \sqrt{1 + \frac{J}{100}}$$

If we substitute $\quad 1 + \dfrac{Q}{200} \text{ for } \sqrt{1 + \dfrac{J}{100}}$

i.e. using a semi-annual compounding equivalent inflation rate $Q$ in place of the annual compounding rate $J$, then this equation becomes,

$$1 + \frac{Y}{200} = \left(1 + \frac{R}{200}\right) \times \left(1 + \frac{Q}{200}\right)$$

which leads to, $\quad R = \dfrac{Y - Q}{(1 + Q/200)}$

150

Thus given two index-linked bonds, A and B, with money yields $Y_a$ and $Y_b$, their real yield difference is,

$$(R_a - R_b) = \frac{(Y_a - Q)}{(1 + Q/200)} - \frac{(Y_b - Q)}{(1 + Q/200)}$$

$$= \frac{(Y_a - Y_b)}{\sqrt{1 + J/100}}$$

Thus if the money yield difference $(Y_a - Y_b)$ remains constant at, say, 0.20, and the annual assumed inflation rate is varied from, say, 10% to 3%, the real yield difference will only be altered from,

$$\frac{0.20}{\sqrt{1.10}} \text{ to } \frac{0.20}{\sqrt{1.03}}$$

i.e. from 0.1907 to 0.1971, less than one basis point. Discrepancies of this small order of magnitude are hardly grounds for invalidating the general use of this most frequently used analytical method.

Differences between real yields on index-linked bonds and redemption yields on conventional bonds are meaningful only if the inflation rate assumption used in the computation of the real yields is constant over the period of history being considered. Differences of this sort compiled using real yield time series where the inflation assumption is taken to be the most recent (at the time of computation) year-on-year percentage change in the RPI, as is the case in some databases, must be treated with some caution.

*Real balance-of-term yields*

These can be used to give good indications of the relative valuations of two index-linked bonds whose maturities are significantly different, but once again any time series using this statistic requires the use of a constant inflation rate assumption. The basic method involves using money values to form a money balance-of-term yield and then transforming that into real terms.

## Breakeven inflation rates

This is a method for comparing index-linked bond values with those of similarly dated conventional bonds. In essence it turns the problem around and calculates the future rate of inflation required to make the money yield on the particular index-linked bond equate to the redemption yield of the conventional gilt. Computations of this sort can be done allowing for any specific incidence of tax, and if the resulting figure is lower than the perceived future rate of inflation then the index-linked bond should be favoured, and vice versa. Care needs to be taken, however, in choosing a suitable conventional bond in such exercises. If, for example, the investor is a top-rate (40%) taxpayer the conventional gilt to be used as a comparator needs to be the issue with the best net (@40% tax) redemption yield in that maturity area. Likewise for gross funds the comparison needs to be made between the index-linked bond and the highest yielding similarly-dated current coupon conventional gilt.

## Index-linked yields as a determinant of equity valuations

Since index-linked bonds and equities are both classes of real assets it follows that the valuations put on one of them will affect, even if only indirectly, the valuations of the other. In this case it is more usual for index-linked real yields to form the base against which equity yields can be judged rather than the other way around.

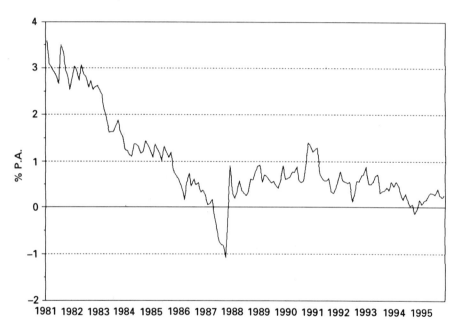

**Fig 7.2**  Equity dividend yield minus index-linked gilt real yields

Fig. 7.2 shows the difference between sample long-dated real yields and that of the FT–SE Actuaries All-Share Index dividend yield since the introduction of index-linked gilts in 1981. This shows that over the last ten years – from the end of 1983 through to 1994 – the yield spread between equities and index-linked stocks has seldom fluctuated outside the range 0 to 1.50%. The only time that this relationship has been severely breached was in 1987 when equity yields were driven down to a full 1% below those of index-linked gilts prior to the equity market 'crash' in October that year. There would thus seem to be reasonable grounds for considering equities to be fairly fully valued whenever the "All-Share" dividend yield declines to a level close to that of real yields on long-dated index-linked gilts.

# 8

## Other non-conventional gilt-edged bonds

### Convertible Gilts

These are similar in most regards to the standard conventional gilt, except that they carry an option for the owner to convert his or her holding into predefined amounts of a different gilt-edged bond at some time or times in the future. They usually take the form of a short or short-medium bond that can be converted into a longer issue. The conversion terms are normally arranged so as to make this a more expensive way of acquiring the longer bond than purchasing it in the market at the outset – the difference in price being the value to the investor of having the option to convert or not.

The first convertible was issued in 1973, and was Treasury 9% Convertible 1980. Each £100 nominal of the bond was convertible into £110 nominal of Treasury 9% 2000 as an alternative to redemption on 3 March 1980. As things turned out, market values on that day were such that a holding of this new bond would have been worth rather less than the straightforward redemption value of the Treasury 9% 1980, and as a result the conversion opportunity was exercised only by a handful of people (presumably) in the search for some form of esoteric wallpaper! Of the £1,000 million Treasury 9% Convertible 1980, only £577,364.59 was converted into Conversion 9% 2000, making this bond at that time one of the smallest ever gilt-edged issues; and one which only rarely traded in the market until the first of three further tranches was created in March 1986.

After this first issue in 1973 the market had to wait eight years until February 1981 before the authorities ventured into this field again. Possibly because of the experience of the earlier bond, this time they used a different format offering holders the option of converting into varying amounts of a longer issue at a number of different dates in the future. This format (which is described more fully later) has basically remained unchanged since then.

The incidence of convertible issuance has, however, been patchy. After the long gap between 1973 and 1981, there were then thirteen convertible issues between the first of the new breed, Exchequer 12% Convertible 1985 on 27 March 1981, and Treasury 8% Convertible 1990 on 16 December 1987, and then another long gap until the emergence of Treasury 7% Convertible 1997 in May 1994. This latest bond is a good example of how latter-day convertibles are structured. The conversion terms of Treasury 7% Convertible 1997 permit the holder to convert into Treasury 9% 2012 (an already existing issue) on various terms during the life of the bond, not simply at redemption. These are as follows:

On 6 August   1994   £89 nominal of Treasury 9% 2012 for each £100 nominal of Treasury 7% Convertible 1997.
On 6 February 1995   £88 ditto.
On 6 August   1995   £87 ditto.
On 6 February 1996   £86 ditto.

If not converted on any of these occasions the bond will be redeemed in the ordinary way on 6 August 1997.

Thus, it can be seen that on an 'if converted' basis there are four different possible valuations for this bond, depending on which conversion is likely to be exercised. In this case the conversion terms deteriorate as time progresses and the nearest conversion would appear to be the most attractive judging by their relative redemption yields.

Calculation of yields in these circumstances is simply a matter of establishing which dividends and capital repayments will be obtained from each

**Table 8.1**  Gross dividends and capital repayments for various conversion options *re* Treasury 7% Convertible 1997

| Payment dates | Not converted | Converted 6 August 1994 | Converted 6 February 1995 | Converted 6 August 1995 | Converted 6 February 1996 |
|---|---|---|---|---|---|
| 6 August   1994 | 1.3809 | 1.3809 | 1.3809 | 1.3809 | 1.3809 |
| 6 February 1995 | 3.5000 | 4.0050 | 3.5000 | 3.5000 | 3.5000 |
| 6 August   1995 | 3.5000 | 4.0050 | 3.9600 | 3.5000 | 3.5000 |
| 6 February 1996 | 3.5000 | 4.0050 | 3.9600 | 3.9150 | 3.5000 |
| 6 August   1996 | 3.5000 | 4.0050 | 3.9600 | 3.9150 | 3.8700 |
| 6 February 1997 | 3.5000 | 4.0050 | 3.9600 | 3.9150 | 3.8700 |
| 6 August   1997 | 3.5000 | 4.0050 | 3.9600 | 3.9150 | 3.8700 |
| Redemption | 100.0000 | ... | ... | ... | ... |
|  |  | ... | ... | ... | ... |
| 6 February 1998 |  | 4.0050 | 3.9600 | 3.9150 | 3.8700 |
| 6 August   1998 |  | 4.0050 | 3.9600 | 3.9150 | 3.8700 |
| ... |  | ... | ... | ... | ... |
| ... |  | ... | ... | ... | ... |
| ... |  | ... | ... | ... | ... |
| 6 August   2011 |  | 4.0050 | 3.9600 | 3.9150 | 3.8700 |
| 6 February 2011 |  | 4.0050 | 3.9600 | 3.9150 | 3.8700 |
| 6 August   2012 | Dividend | 4.0050 | 3.9600 | 3.9150 | 3.8700 |
| 6 August   2012 | Redemption | 89.0000 | 88.0000 | 87.0000 | 86.0000 |

*Note:* The figure of 1.3809 as the dividend for payment on 6 August 1994 is in no way connected with the conversion options. It is simply a non-standard first interest payment of the sort described in Chapter 5.

option, and then applying the compound interest techniques of Chapter 5 to each of them in turn. The schedule in Table 8.1 shows how the cash flows vary with the different options.

Table 8.2 shows the range of gross redemption yields of the bonds, based on a market price of 98 29/32 ( + 0.134 gross accrued interest) on 1 June 1994.

**Table 8.2**   Gross redemption yields as at 1 June 1994 for Treasury 7% Convertible 1997. Price = 98 29/32

| If unconverted | Redeemable 6 August 1997 | 7.390% |
|---|---|---|
| If converted on 6 August 1994 | Redeemable 6 August 2012 | 7.816% |
| If converted on 6 February 1995 | Redeemable 6 August 2012 | 7.651% |
| If converted on 6 August1995 | Redeemable 6 August 2012 | 7.496% |
| If converted on 6 February 1996 | Redeemable 6 August 2012 | 7.350% |

Having calculated these yields, the potential investor is then faced with the problem of seeing how they compare with those of conventional bonds in the market. This is normally done by making assessments of what the 'correct' yields of the bond should be, either as a short-dated bond (without a conversion option), or as a pure long-dated bond. Such yields are normally found by reference to existing bonds with similar coupon rates and maturities, but where the 'convert-into' bond is one which is already quoted in the market, comparisons are even simpler.

In the example above the investor would need to estimate the gross yields upon which a non-convertible 7% 1997 bond and a conventional 9% 2012 bond would be neutrally valued relative to existing bonds in the market at that time (in this case 7.88% and 8.71% respectively). Once such values have been determined it is then possible to calculate the premium being paid for the conversion option and assess whether it is justifiable or not.

The question of establishing the value of conversion options like these is quite complex. Since the development of general option pricing models it has become usual for problems of this sort to be attacked using option theory. Here one can start breaking the problem down by valuing each of the conversion options separately. The minimum value of the composite of all these must logically be the maximum of their individual values as European style options, but there can also be a further element of value reflecting the ability of the holder, at each conversion date except the last, to allow the investment to run on to the next exercise opportunity. It is also the case that valuing conversion options is more complex than straightforward options exerciseable at a given price. With conversion options it is the price relationship between two bonds that determines whether or not it is advantageous to convert at any given opportunity rather than just a single price. This involves

156

judgements as to the future volatilities of prices/yields of both the short- and long-end of the market. A number of investment banks and securities houses have developed models to cope with these problems but their output is normally fairly restricted and there is often quite a wide disparity in their results.

A less state-of-the-art way (but one that is available to investors without access to option pricing models) of performing some analysis is to create a graph plotting the convertible bond's gross redemption yield if converted to a 'long' against its 'unconverted' yield as a 'short'. In Fig. 8.1, showing the position as at 1 June 1994, the slanted lines represent the relationships between these two yields for each of the conversion options available, whilst the horizontal line, OL, and the vertical line OS, represent the estimated 'correct' yield levels for 7% 1997 and 9% 2012 bonds respectively. (Note that the axes have been inverted so that the price of the bond rises as one moves along the slanted lines from bottom-left to top-right.) Logic dictates that the convertible should not yield more than these levels, since if it did, switching into it from comparably dated non-convertible bonds could be expected to occur. It therefore follows that the point P representing the market value of the convertible should, theoretically, always be in the upper right-hand segment of such diagrams.

The conversion premium is the amount by which the market price is within the area bounded by the lines OL and OS. In this particular example the convertible's price is about $1\frac{1}{4}$ points above its intrinsic value as a 'short' (represented on the graph by the point M) and some $7\frac{3}{4}$ greater than its alternative value as a 'long' (represented by the point N).

The flexibility of this graphical approach can be illustrated by considering a hypothetical example in which there is now a sudden parallel shift downwards in yield of say, 1.50%, across all sectors of the market. This would move the horizontal and vertical lines OL and OS to new positions on the graph represented by the dotted right-angle at the top-right of the diagram, and one can see at a glance that in these circumstances the price of the convertible would then be determined more by considerations of long-dated yields rather than those of the shorts.

This form of analysis illustrates the alternative nature of a convertible bond's valuation and the size of the premium element involved. What it does not do is assess whether the premium is worth paying or not. As has been mentioned earlier calculating the fair value for the premium in cases such as these involving more than a single conversion option is a highly complex business for even the best option pricing models. However, the fact that OL and OS are limiting axes for the price P supports the case for considering that a convertible's fair value should lie on some form of hyperbolic curve tangential to the lines OL and OS like that drawn in Fig. 8.1. If so, the

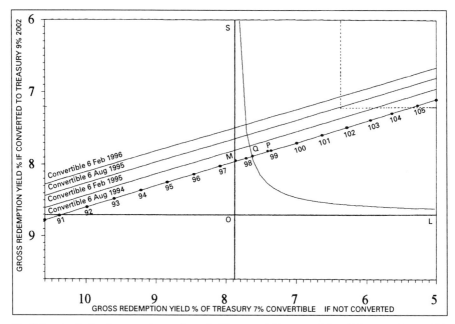

**Fig 8.1**  Analysis of conversion options for Treasury 7% convertible 1997 as at 1 June 1994

convertible's fair value price will be represented by the point $Q$ where the hyperbola intersects the relevant slanted line, and its current over- or under-valuation by the difference in price $PQ$.

The exact form of this curve will very much depend on the individual analyst's view of the prospective volatility of short- and long-term yields, but is also a function of the length of time to the date of conversion. The longer the option period the further away the curve will pass from the point $O$. Conversely, as a bond approaches a conversion date the hyperbola will progressively resemble the lines $OL$ and $OS$ themselves.

The diminishing nature of the conversion premium is not always fully appreciated and investors should be wary of propositions based solely on the fact that 'the premium is at a historically low level', and of comparisons made between convertibles with differing conversion terms and periods by reference to the relative size of their conversion premiums alone. Furthermore, it may be necessary to look beyond the most immediate conversion date to observe the full value to an investor of all a bond's conversion options, especially if a bond's conversion terms deteriorate only very gradually at each consecutive conversion date or not at all. This would cause the family of slanted lines representing the various conversion options to be bunched closely together, and the hyperbola for some forward conversion date may well intersect the relevant slanted line at a higher implied price than those corresponding to nearer conversion dates.

## Variable-rate gilts

Back in the mid-1970s, the UK authorities started to place an increasing amount of importance in the month-by-month management of the monetary aggregates – in particular, Domestic Credit Expansion, M3 and Sterling M3. In order to neutralise the excess money supply in the system, they sought to make sales of gilts to the non-bank public. This seemingly simple plan often proved rather less easy to implement in practice, as a result of the essential 'Catch 22' element involved. UK domestic investors, especially the financial institutions (who were then pretty well awash with gilts anyway), needed to have the prospect of falling interest rates, and some confidence that the money supply was in control, if they were to invest further in gilts; and, since at that time precisely the opposite conditions pertained, these potential buyers were conspicuously absent from the market. So, just when the authorities most urgently needed to sell gilts, the buyers were unwilling, and vice versa.

In order to overcome this impasse the search was joined for some form of capital protective instrument that would be saleable at times when interest rates were already high but not necessarily expected to fall. The preferred solution to this problem was the issuance of a number of variable-rate gilts, whose main characteristics were similar to today's floating-rate notes. There was, however, one very distinct difference between these variable-rate gilts and 'orthodox floaters'. Whereas it is customary for floating rate notes to have each coupon determined at the beginning of the period for which interest is to be paid, the UK authorities decided that the (variable) coupon rate should be linked to the average Treasury bill rate over the period involved. This turned out to be counter-productive. Apart from anything else, it made day-by-day calculations of such key items as accrued interest, extremely cumbersome. Furthermore, the fact that these bonds were issued with lives of less than five years to maturity (i.e. they were shorts), meant that they were really much more suitable for the banking system than for the non-bank public, at which they were primarily targeted.

The precise details of the method used to determine both the coupon payments and the day-to-day accrued interest of variable-rate gilts are shown in the appendix at the back of this book. However, it is probably sufficient to state that for those variable-rate bonds dated 1981, 1982 and 1983 the coupon rate was set as the average Treasury Bill tender rate over the relevant period, plus $\frac{1}{2}\%$.

## Floating-rate gilts

In late March 1994 the Bank of England surprised the gilt-edged market by producing a new form of bond for its auction on 30 March. Eleven years after redemption of the last variable-rate gilt (see above) it saw fit to resurrect the basic concept of a floating-rate issue as a relatively safe haven for investors at a time of volatile and turbulent markets. The lessons of the variables had been well learned and for Floating Rate Treasury Stock 1999 coupons are set by reference to the London Inter-Bank three-month Deposit Bid Rate (LIBID) at the beginning of each interest payment period minus $\frac{1}{8}$%.

However, the security is unusual for a gilt in that it pays interest four times a year instead of semi-annually, and these interest payments are made without deduction of any UK tax at source. The methods used for the exact determination of its coupons and their precise payment dates look slightly unusual to the eyes of gilt-edged practitioners as they follow floating rate note (FRN) market conventions rather than those of the gilt-edged market. For this issue, interest is scheduled to be paid on 9 June 1994 and thereafter on the first business day falling three months after the preceeding interest date. If, however, application of this formula would cause an interest payment date to fall in the next month, the interest date is taken to be the immediately preceeding business day, and all subsequent payment dates will be the last business days of the third month in this three-monthly cycle. The precise coupon amount is calculated by multiplying the coupon rate (as determined above) by the actual number of days in the relevant interest period and dividing by 365, and the Bank's practice is to publish both the rate and the amount as soon as possible after 11 a.m. on each interest determination day.

The launch of £2,500 million of this particular instrument was well received by the market, and encouraged by this, three months later the Bank augmented it by creating a further £2,000 million tranche of the same issue on a fully fungible basis. More recently, in February 1995, a smaller tranchette of £600 million was created and fed into the market direct from the Bank, making this issue's total size £5,100 million as at the end of March 1995. Most of this issue has found its way into the hands of banks, building societies and similar financial institutions for whom it is particularly suitable since it carries a low (10%) risk asset ratio weight and counts as a primary liquid asset for liquidity purposes.

Assessment of value of floating rate instruments cannot be undertaken by conventional gilt-edged methods because, by their very nature, not all future coupon payments are known at the time of evaluation. However, a process not dissimilar to that used in calculating real yields for index-linked bonds can be applied to 'floaters'. It involves making an assumption about the future rate of LIBID (or whatever other base interest rate is relevant for the bond in question), further assuming that this will remain constant over the life of the bond, and calculating a yield on this basis. This is the equivalent of computing a 'money yield' for an index-linked bond. From this 'money' value the assumed base interest rate can then be extracted leaving as a residual item a yield margin over the relevant base rate.

Such analysis allows floating rate instruments to be compared with each other but does not greatly assist when absolute values are required or when it is wished to assess floating rate values against those of conventional gilts. In these cases it is often useful to assume that the 'floater' will stand at, or close to, par at the date of the next coupon reset and treat it as being redeemed at that assumed price on that date. This is reasonable if the credit standing of the borrower is of the highest order, as it is with the British Government, but may not be realistic with lesser credits.

# 9

## Gilt-edged futures and options

In the autumn of 1982, trading commenced on the London International Financial Futures Exchange, known colloquially as LIFFE (pronounced 'life') and one of the initial contracts established, together with currencies, short-term interest rate futures, and three-month Eurodollar deposit futures, was a long-dated gilt-edged contract. Because of their existence and the fact that market-makers, brokers/dealers, banks, and various other players in the game, have seats on LIFFE, and are active participants in this parallel market, there is a need in this book to cover at least the basic aspects of this subject and its interplay with the gilt-edged market proper (known to futures operators as the 'cash' market).

### What exactly are financial futures?

In its broadest sense, a futures contract is an obligation to buy or sell a particular commodity at a specified price on a specified future date. If and when a market is made to deal in these specified futures contracts, instead of the actual commodity itself, this becomes a futures market. Where the underlying commodity to be traded is a physical entity, such as gold, copper, zinc, grain, pork bellies, or even potatoes, it is not too difficult to envisage the concept. With financial futures, the underlying commodity is less tangible, being perhaps a foreign currency exchange rate, an interest rate, or, in the case in which this book is most interested, the price of some gilt-edged bond.

### How the gilt futures market works

Obviously, there has to be some link between values in the 'cash' market and the prices in the equivalent future. The mechanism that links the two is the process of delivery by which, at the end of the time period specified for the particular futures contract, the sellers have the option either to close their position by buying back their contracts, or to deliver the given commodity (through some form of clearing mechanism) to those with open bought positions. In practice, most positions are closed out prior to delivery, but the fact that the seller has the delivery option means that the relative prices in the two markets have to converge as the contracts mature.

The long gilt-edged contract is currently specified as the price of £50,000 nominal of a notional 9% long-dated British Government bond, but the terms of the contract actually permit the seller to deliver any gilts (subject to certain specific provisos, see later) with maturities in the ten-year to fifteen-year range. Obviously, the seller, unless he is either insane or has some special reason of his own, will choose to deliver whichever of these eligible bonds conveys the least value. Thus, the futures price will normally 'track' the 'cheapest deliverable instrument'.

At present the Long Gilt Future is the only gilt future traded on LIFFE. Back in the 1980s there were at various times a short-dated and a medium-dated gilt contract as well. Unlike the long-dated contract neither of these managed to attract enough transaction volume to justify their existence and they were finally taken out of service on 17 January 1990.

In the LIFFE market there are a number of separate contracts traded for each 'commodity', each relating to different delivery months, each spaced three months apart running on a March, June, September, December cycle. The contract month nearest to the current date is usually referred to as the 'nearby' month, though once that contract month has begun it is known as the 'spot' month. Experience so far in London has been that the vast majority of business transacted is done in the 'nearby' contract.

In complete contrast with the gilt-edged market, the dealing method is by 'open outcry', whereby traders meet in recessed octagonal 'pits' and shout out their bids or offers in order to match buyer with seller. Once transactions have been made, they are recorded in writing by both parties and reported to the market officials, and quickly fed into the market's computer. This computer in turn links with the futures market price display system, and those of commercial information providers such as Bloomberg, ICV, Knight Ridder, Reuters, Telekurs, and Telerate, and it is no exaggeration to say that the price at which a trade is done will be public knowledge across the world a matter of seconds after it is transacted. Prices of futures contracts are quoted by reference to discrete minimum price movements called 'ticks', the size of which varies between contracts. For the long gilt-edged contract the tick size is $\frac{1}{32}$nd of a point.

The major dissimilarity between futures and the 'cash' gilt market is that futures are always dealt in on margin, by which it is meant that initially only a small proportion of the quoted futures price needs to be paid by the futures trader. There are two forms of margin, known as 'initial' (or 'original') margin and 'variation' margin, both of which are settled with London Clearing House (LCH), which is the clearing house for LIFFE contracts. The clearing house acts as guarantor of the contracts, and, once a trade has been registered, each party then has an open position with the clearing house rather than with its original counterparty.

Initial margin, which varies according to the volatility of the individual contract, is the amount required to be paid when an investor originally takes out a futures contract, whether buying or selling. The purpose of initial margin is to provide a performance bond against potential loss.

The concept of variation margin becomes clear when one realises the mechanism by which futures bargains are settled. Unlike securities markets, in which profits and losses only crystallize when positions are finally closed out, in the futures markets all positions are valued daily on the basis of the exchanges' closing official settlement price, a process known as 'marking to market'; and profits or losses resulting from the day's change in prices are credited or debited to the investor's account. In an adverse trading situation, an investor will be called upon to put up further 'variation' margin in order to preserve a solvent account. This *modus operandi* means that an investor with a continuing adverse trading position has a continuing day-by-day negative cash flow, and as such is forced to face the reality of his loss-making situation very quickly. This feature, combined with the cushion provided by initial margins, is singularly effective in preventing overstretched debt positions from arising.

In order to get an idea of the cash flows involved, consider the progress of a single transaction in the long gilt future.

Date:   4 July 1994
Action: Buy one September 1994 Long Gilt contract @ 100-16
        (Note: in this case prices are quoted as integers + $\frac{1}{32}$nd, i.e. 100-16
        denotes $100 \frac{16}{32}$, i.e. $100\frac{1}{2}$)
Valuation of this contract = £50,250
Initial margin paid to clearing house, say 3% = £1,500.

Date:   4 July 1994
Closing settlement price = 100-09 (down $\frac{7}{32}$ on the day)
Valuation of this contract = £50,140.62, therefore variation margin required to be paid to clearing house = £109.38

Date:   5 July 1994
Closing settlement price = 100-05
Valuation of contract = £50,078.12
Change on the day = –£62.50, to be settled with clearing house, and so on.

Now let us look at the situation when the contract runs through to delivery, because it is the possibility of this happening that links prices in the cash and futures markets together.

For the gilt-edged futures contracts there is no unique settlement day. The seller can choose to deliver bonds on any business day in the required delivery month. The choice of date and the choice of gilt (from within the eligible list) belong to the seller, who is required to give notice of his intention to deliver prior to the close of business on LIFFE two business days before his chosen delivery date. The amount to be paid to the seller for the bonds delivered is determined by the 'exchange delivery settlement price' (EDSP) which is struck at 11 a.m. on notification day. The cash sum due to change hands obviously varies, depending on which issue the seller has opted to deliver, and is based on a bond price factor system which is explained below.

In the case of the long gilt future the notional contract specifies a 9% coupon rate, and thus the bond price factors of each (deliverable) bond are determined as the clean prices of those bonds to give a gross redemption yield of 9% on the first calendar day of the delivery month. Bonds eligible for delivery are those whose lives to maturity on the first day of the delivery month lie between ten and fifteen years, and exclude convertible, variable-rate, index-linked issues, any bond not paying interest semi-annually, or capable of being called for early redemption. In addition, partly-paid issues are ineligible for delivery if they are partly paid at any time in the delivery month, and otherwise eligible bonds may not be delivered during their special ex-dividend periods or on the business day either side of this period.

Table 9.1 shows the list of deliverable gilts in existence on 1 May 1994, and their price factors for each of the three futures contracts, June through to December 1994. It should be noticed that individual bonds' price factors vary for the different contracts, and that not all the bonds shown are deliverable for all of the three contract months.

**Table 9.1**  Bond price factors for long gilt contracts at 1 May 1994

|  |  | June 1994 | September 1994 | December 1994 |
| --- | --- | --- | --- | --- |
| Conversion 9½% | 2004 | 1.0330202 | 1.0332141 | n/d |
| Treasury 6¾% | 2004 | 0.8490094 | 0.8510702 | n/d |
| Conversion 9½% | 2005 | 1.0339194 | 1.0340951 | 1.0332121 |
| Treasury 7¾% | 2006 | 0.9077338 | 0.9093555 | 0.9105157 |
| Treasury 8½% | 2007 | 0.9622269 | 0.9618049 | 0.9630175 |
| Treasury 9% | 2008 | 0.9996841 | 1.0002774 | 0.9999282 |
| Treasury 8% | 2009 | n/d | n/d | 0.9191725 |

*Note:* n/d signifies that the bond is not eligible for delivery against the contract in question.

The invoice price for settlement by delivery of a single contract is calculated thus:

$$[(bond\ price\ factor$$

multiplied by

*exchange delivery settlement price on notification day)*

plus

*gross accrued interest to delivery day]*

multiplied by

*500*

Let us assume that, in this case, the seller wished to complete a strategy, in September 1994, by delivering £50,000 nominal of Conversion 9½% 2004. The first thing he would discover is that this bond would be in its special ex-dividend period from 29 August until its official ex-dividend date on 19 September 1994. This means that the first eligible delivery day will be Tuesday 20 September. If he wished to make delivery on that day he would have to give notice two business days earlier, on Friday 16 September. The LIFFE exchange delivery settlement price for that day was 99-25 (99.78125). This, multiplied by the price factor of 1.0332141, comes to 103.0953944, and to this is added the gross accrued interest relating to delivery day (20 September) of –0.9109589 to make an all-in price of 102.1844355. Since the contract relates to £50,000 nominal stock, this total is multiplied by 500 to produce a contract invoice value of £51,092.22.

The choice of which bond to deliver is crucial in these matters. Individual price anomalies and the shape of the yield curve over the range of deliverable gilts can cause significant discrepancies between the 'cash' market price and the equivalent futures delivery value of a gilt to occur, and a seller choosing to settle by delivery should take particular care not to give away value by delivering the wrong bond.

Once again, it may be instructive to examine a table of values taken towards the end of the delivery month. Table 9.2 shows that the futures price has converged to within 0.129 of that of Conversion 9½% 2004, which is

**Table 9.2** Comparison of futures delivery values with cash market prices for September 1994 long gilt contract.
(Exchange delivery settlement price (EDSP) 11 a.m. 16 September 1994 = 99.78125

| For delivery on second succeeding business day i.e. 20 September 1994 | | Price factor (September 1994 contract) | Gross accrued interest 20 September | Exchange delivery invoice price | Cash gilt total market price including GAI 11 a.m. 16 September | Relative dearness of cash gilts |
|---|---|---|---|---|---|---|
| Conversion 9½% | 2004 | 1.0332141 | –0.91096 | 102.184 | 102.313 | 0.129 |
| Treasury 6¾% | 2004 | 0.8510702 | 2.163699 | 87.085 | 88.207 | 1.123 |
| Conversion 9½% | 2005 | 1.0340951 | –0.72877 | 102.455 | 102.839 | 0.384 |
| Treasury 7¾% | 2006 | 0.9093555 | 0.254795 | 90.991 | 92.078 | 1.086 |
| Treasury 8½% | 2007 | 0.9618049 | 1.536986 | 97.507 | 98.826 | 1.319 |
| Treasury 9% | 2008 | 1.0002774 | –0.56712 | 99.242 | 100.721 | 1.479 |

therefore perfectly suitable for delivery, but it also shows that most of the other gilts are dear in relation to the futures market, and just how much value would be thrown away if they were delivered instead.

## Uses of the gilt-edged futures market

What are the uses to which gilt-edged futures can be put that cannot be found in the 'cash' market? These divide broadly into two categories: speculative or trading activities on the one hand, and hedging operations on the other. Because futures are dealt in on margin they can be highly geared and because of this they are an attractive vehicle for use by speculators and market traders should they wish to operate in this way. But it should be remembered that if prices subsequently move against them they will experience immediate variation margin calls, and bearing this in mind it would be imprudent to commit themselves to too high a level of gearing.

The next point to make is that futures markets allow one to back a view that the market may move downwards as well as upwards. In the gilt-edged market itself it is difficult for traders to open outright bear positions, unless they have access to some stock borrowing or repo facility. No such problem exists with futures.

Futures can also be used advantageously to anticipate an investment fund's cash flows. Take the case where a fund manager knows that he has new money due to arrive in the coming months, but is fully invested at the current moment. If he feels that the market is going to rise substantially before his new money arrives he can, for a modest outlay, take up a bull position in the futures market, which – if his view is correct – will produce a profit roughly equivalent to that which he would have obtained by early investment in the cash market.

## Hedging operations

Hedging is the name used to describe taking a position in futures contrary to that of a (roughly) equal position in another market (in this case, the 'cash' gilt market). Hedging is often a matter of taking out some form of insurance against a feared market movement, when, for some reason or other, the investor does not want to liquidate, or is precluded from selling, his principal investment. A good example might be that of a holder of a gilt who needs to retain his holding in order to obtain a specific dividend payment but fears the market may collapse. Futures give him the opportunity to insure his position now, by selling an equivalent number of futures contracts. If the market reverse that he fears comes about, it will affect the value of his gilt-edged holding adversely, but he will make a compensating profit from his bear position in the futures market.

Most hedging operations, however, are professional in nature resulting from the use made by investment banks, securities houses and gilt-edged market makers of the gilt contract as a highly liquid alternative to actual gilts. For example, an investment bank launching a sterling fixed interest issue will normally hedge its inventory by going short of an equivalent risk position in either gilts or the gilt-edged future. Or a gilt-edged market maker wishing to change his book at short notice will often buy or sell gilt contracts in the LIFFE 'pit' rather than use the IDB network or wait for suitable customer business to materialise. The fact that the LIFFE long-gilt future contract is highly liquid enhances its attractions in this respect.

## 'Cash-and-carry' operations

This delightful phraseology is used to describe a combined futures and cash market arbitrage strategy, whereby an investor runs a matched position holding gilts and at the same time being short of an equal nominal amount of futures. Even when this involves a long gilt-edged bond and long-dated futures, it is still essentially a short-term money operation, the overall return of which is the balance of the profits/losses on the two offsetting positions taken between instigation and the chosen delivery date. This is generally known as the 'implied repurchase rate', or 'implied repo-rate'.

When implied repo-rates are all markedly below money market rates for the period to delivery, the opposite operation can be considered. This can be termed a 'reverse cash-and-carry', as it involves selling the relevant gilt-edged bond and buying futures. This releases cheap cash to the investor which he can place in money markets at the higher rate. A certain element of danger is involved in this strategy, since the investor is no longer the seller of the futures, and therefore does not control the timing or the choice of bond to be delivered. If, however, there is only a single clearly distinguishable cheapest deliverable bond that the futures market is 'tracking' and if the implied repos on this bond to all possible delivery dates are still below money market rates, it should, in theory, be possible to profit from this type of operation, but opportunities are rare.

One has to be very careful when talking about 'implied repo-rates'. There is a popular misconception that there is a unique 'implied repo-rate' associated with a given pair of gilt and futures prices, and that the operation is insulated from variations in the level of the market at delivery, or the choice of delivery date during the delivery month. This is a very dangerous fallacy, as the next few examples will show.

Table 9.3 shows the implied repo-rates existing on 3 June 1994 for cash-and-carry strategies against September 1994 futures, based on the (neutral) view that the futures price at delivery would be the same as that ruling at that date. Two main facts are quickly apparent. Firstly, the implied repo-rates

**Table 9.3** Implied repurchase rates on cash-and-carry strategies. September 1994 long gilt contract (neutral assumption).

| | | Price 3 June 1994 | First delivery day, 1 September 1994 | | Last delivery day, 30 September 1994 | |
|---|---|---|---|---|---|---|
| September 1994 future | | 102 | 102 | | 102 | |
| | | Clean price | Delivery value | Repos % | Delivery value | Repos % |
| Conversion 9½% | 2004 | 106.9375 | 108.7454* | 2.70 | 104.7372 | 4.13 |
| Treasury 6¾% | 2004 | 89.3750 | 88.6215 | −4.34 | 89.1578* | −1.43 |
| Conversion 9½% | 2005 | 107.2813 | 109.0174* | 1.73 | 105.0092 | 3.39 |
| Treasury 7¾% | 2006 | 95.2500 | 92.6056 | −2.85 | 93.2214 | −0.20 |
| Treasury 8½% | 2007 | 101.0625 | 99.1986 | −3.51 | 99.8740 | −0.65 |
| Treasury 9% | 2008 | 105.3750 | 105.5050* | −4.59 | 101.7077 | −1.43 |

*Note:* The figures in the above table marked by * are shown in order to illustrate the progression of the implied repo rates with time, but in reality the bonds marked are not deliverable on the days in question as they are specially ex-dividend on that day.

increase as the delivery date extends to the end of the month, and secondly, the only practical strategies of this kind would be those involving either Conversion 9½% 2004 or its sister issue, Conversion 9½% 2005. A less obvious fact that shows up in the table is that four out of the six eligible bonds are not deliverable at some time or another during the month because of the timing of their special ex-dividend periods.

Next, let us compare the values in Table 9.3 with those in Table 9.4, in which similar calculations are made, but based this time on an assumption that September 1994 futures prices will be rather higher (110) at delivery.

It can be seen quite clearly that in this case implied repo-rates of bonds with factors in excess of unity are increased, whilst those on bonds with factors below one are diminished. This is hardly surprising when one thinks about it

**Table 9.4** Implied repurchase rates on cash-and-carry strategies. September 1994 long gilt contract (bullish assumption).

| | | Price 3 June 1994 | First delivery day, 1 September 1994 | | Last delivery day, 30 September 1994 | |
|---|---|---|---|---|---|---|
| September 1994 future | | 102 | 110 | | 110 | |
| | | Clean price | Delivery value | Repos % | Delivery value | Repos % |
| Conversion 9½% | 2004 | 106.9375 | 117.0111* | 3.70 | 113.0029 | 4.88 |
| Treasury 6¾% | 2004 | 89.3750 | 95.4301 | −9.74 | 95.9664* | −5.48 |
| Conversion 9½% | 2005 | 107.2813 | 117.2902* | 2.76 | 113.2820 | 4.16 |
| Treasury 7¾% | 2006 | 95.2500 | 99.8805 | −5.89 | 100.4962 | −2.48 |
| Treasury 8½% | 2007 | 101.0625 | 106.8931 | −4.70 | 107.5684 | −1.55 |
| Treasury 9% | 2008 | 105.3750 | 113.5072* | −4.59 | 109.7100 | −1.42 |

*Note*: The figures in the above table marked by * are shown in order to illustrate the progression of the implied repo rates with time, but in reality the bonds marked are not deliverable on the days in question as they are specially ex-dividend on that day.

since a cash-and-carry strategy involves equal nominal amounts of bond and futures, which will favour higher priced bonds in a rising market, and vice versa.

The relationships between all the various parameters can be put into focus by the following analysis of a cash-and-carry operation subsequently closed by delivery through LIFFE.

Let,

$S$    represent the price factor of the gilt for this contract

$g$    represent the gilt's coupon rate

$P_0$    represent the initial total purchase price of the gilt

$P_1$    represent the disposal total price of the gilt

$F_0$    represent the initial futures price

$F_1$    represent the final futures price

$t_0$    represent the time period between the last coupon payment and the purchase date

$t_1$    represent the time period from the last coupon payment to delivery

$m$    represent the initial margin on the future

The profit from the operation has two components:

(i)   the profit from holding the gilt $= P_1 - P_0$
(ii)  the profit from the bear operation in futures $= F_0 - F_1$.

The initial outlay is $P_0$ plus the initial margin on the futures contract of $m$. The simple interest return derived from the operation, $r$, can thus be defined as:

$$r = \frac{(P_1 - P_0) + (F_0 - F_1)}{P_0 + m} \times \frac{100}{t_1 - t_0} \qquad (9.1)$$

Now the invoice price $P_1$ is related to the delivery future price $F_1$ by the relationship:

$$P_1 = (F_1 \times S) + g \cdot t_1$$

thus,
$$r = \frac{F_1 \cdot S + g \cdot t_1 - P_0 + F_0 - F_1}{P_0 + m} \times \frac{100}{t_1 - t_0}$$

$$= \frac{[F_1 \cdot (S-1) + g \cdot t_1] - (P_0 - F_0)}{P_0 + m} \times \frac{100}{t_1 - t_0} \qquad (9.2)$$

170

If we now use $C_0$ to denote the initial clean price of the bond, so that

$$P_0 = C_0 + g \cdot t_0$$

then we can write,

$$r = \frac{[F_1 \cdot (S_1 - 1) + g \cdot (t_1 - t_0) - (C_0 - F_0)]}{P_0 + m} \times \frac{100}{t_1 - t_0} \qquad (9.3)$$

It is worth looking at the numerator between the square brackets and examining its three components.

(i)   Final futures price, $F_1$, multiplied by the price factor minus 1;

(ii)   The accrued interest, $g.(t_1 - t_0)$, over the period of the operation;

(iii)   The difference between the initial clean price of the bond, $C_0$, and the initial futures price, $F_0$.

The most usual cash-and-carry assumption is the neutral one that the delivery futures price $F_1$ will be the same as the initial one, i.e. $F_1 = F_0$, so that deviations from that assumption in reality will cause the *realised* cash-and-carry rate to exceed the *assumed* cash-and-carry rate by an amount

$$= \frac{(F_1 - F_0) \cdot (S - 1)}{P_0 + m} \times \frac{100}{t_1 - t_0}$$

When a bond has a coupon rate equal to the notional coupon rate of the relevant future, its price factor will be 1 (or so close to 1 as not to matter) and this divergence will be equal to zero. But for all other bonds this potential divergence is an important factor to be taken into account.

The second point that can be appreciated from looking at equation (9.3) is that the realised simple interest rate of return is equal to:

$$\frac{100 \cdot g}{P_0 + m} \text{ (approximately the flat yield of the bond)}$$

$$\text{plus,} \quad \frac{F_1 \cdot (S - 1) - (C_0 - F_0)}{P_0 + m} \times \frac{100}{t_1 - t_0}$$

For any given value of $F_1$ (the projected futures price) the absolute value of

171

the second element diminishes as the time period $(t_1 - t_0)$ lengthens. Thus, when this factor is positive, the best delivery option is the earliest date, and if it is negative a cash-and-carry operation will show the highest return by being left open until the last possible opportunity.

If we apply this theorem to repos based on neutral assumptions, i.e assuming $F_1 = F_0$, then the criterion for establishing the optimal delivery date is:

If $C_0 < F_0 \cdot S$ then the earliest delivery date gives the highest repo.
If $C_0 > F_0 \cdot S$ then the latest delivery date gives the highest repo.

In all of the above theory one factor has been omitted in order to keep the mathematics as straightforward as possible, which in real life cannot be ignored, and that is the cost or gain to the investor of the variation margin cash flows during the life of a cash-and-carry operation. If the general market rises, his futures position will go into a loss situation and his total outlay will increase, thus diminishing the eventual overall return. If markets fall, this effect will work to his advantage. It also makes a difference when these movements occur, since the investor may, in theory, obtain (pay) interest on the positive (negative) variation margin flows, and these amounts will be greater or lesser, depending on when these price movements occur. The assumption generally used is that the price movement from $F_0$ to $F_1$ takes place evenly over the time period concerned.

## Other hedging activities

An important element in the cash-and-carry operations discussed above was that the total position could be closed by making delivery. This meant that a holding of a gilt-edged bond would be matched by an equal and opposite nominal exposure in the futures market. But this would most often mean that in value terms the position would be under-hedged if the clean price, $C_0$, of the bond was greater than the futures price, $F_0$, or over-hedged if $C_0$ was less than $F_0$.

If, therefore, an investor were to use the futures market to hedge a position in the gilt market itself without expecting to use the delivery mechanism, how should he gear his hedge? If he uses the following procedure, he should not go far wrong; though it cannot be stated too forcibly that there is no such thing as the perfect hedge.

First of all, he should quantify the extent of the bond price movement against which he wishes to seek protection, and time period in which it is expected to occur.

Secondly, he must make an assessment of which of the eligible bonds is likely to be the cheapest deliverable bond at the future date, and through this bond estimate the likely prospective futures price should the anticipated market movement take place.

Finally, he should calculate the ratio of the change in value of the bond (allowing, if necessary, for the receipt of dividends en route) to the change in the futures price. This is called the 'hedge ratio' and should be applied to the size of his gilt-holding to determine the number of futures contracts that will best 'insure' him against that particular eventuality. For this method to be effective there needs to be a close correlation between movements in the prices of the bond to be hedged and the cheapest deliverable gilt. Where the characteristics of the bond and the future diverge, such close correlation will be unlikely, and the reader is warned against being tempted to think that, say, short-dated gilts can be accurately hedged by a combination of the short sterling interest rate futures and (longer) gilt-edged futures contracts. If the shape or slope of the yield curve alters significantly, hedges, even those mathematically balanced on a weighted average duration basis, will be unlikely to track the underlying bond precisely.

### The LIFFE three-month sterling interest rate future

Reference was made in the previous paragraph to this contract, often referred to as the 'short-sterling' contract, which is a futures contract linked to three-month LIBOR (London inter-bank offered rate) at various future dates. Although not strictly a gilt-edged derivative, its very nature and the overlap of activities in the money market and the very short end of the gilt-edged market justify some mention of it here.

There are several ways in which this contract differs from the long gilt contract. One is its size. The short-sterling contract has a unit of trading of £500,000, ten times that of the nominal size of the long gilt future. Secondly, the liquidity of this instrument extends to as many as twelve forward contracts whereas that of the long gilt future is very much concentrated in the spot and nearby contracts. Thirdly, the method of price quotation is different. Because price movements of short-term instruments are opposite in direction to the interest rate movements that cause them, short-sterling futures prices are quoted in the form 100 minus the relevant interest rate and expressed in decimal form. Thus a December futures price of 92.17 is reflecting expectations that three-month interest rates will be in the region of 7.83% in the coming December.

Just as with the long gilt most short-sterling transactions are closed out before delivery, but unlike the long gilt there is no physical delivery mechanism and bargains not previously closed out are completed by a cash settlement determined by the exchange delivery settlement price (EDSP) on the last trading day – the third Wednesday of the delivery month. The important thing to realise about short-sterling contracts is that they reflect views of future levels of three-month interest rates and not current three-month rates. Their fair price thus represents the forward-forward rate required to produce level performance from the following two strategies.

1.  Invest for the period, $n_1$ days, between now and the delivery date at the currently obtainable rate of interest for that period, say, $y_1$; and then reinvest for three months (let us assume 91 days) at the forward-forward rate, say, $y_0$.
2.  Invest for the whole period, $(n_1 + 91)$ days, at $y_2$, the current going rate for deposits of that longer maturity.

On a simple interest basis the equation of value thus produced is,

$$\left(1+\frac{y_0}{100}\cdot\frac{91}{365}\right)\times\left(1+\frac{y_1}{100}\cdot\frac{n_1}{365}\right)=\left(1+\frac{y_2}{100}\cdot\frac{(91+n_1)}{365}\right)$$

Let us look at a practical example where $n_1 = 62$ days and $y_1 = 5.25\%$, and $y_2 = 6.00\%$. This produces a value for $y_0$ equal to,

$$100\times\left(\frac{1+0.06\times153/365}{1+0.0525\times62/365}-1\right)\times\frac{365}{91}=6.4534\%$$

and the futures price relating to this value of $y_0$ is thus,

$$100 - 6.4534 = 93.5466$$

When performing such calculations in practice it has become customary to use values of LIMEAN (the midway value between LIBOR and LIBID) for $y_1$ and $y_2$, which will produce a corresponding LIMEAN value of $y_0$; and then convert this to a LIBOR equivalent by adding to it $\frac{1}{16}\%$. If this were the case in the above example the LIBOR rate so established would be,

$$6.4534 + 0.0625 = 6.5159$$

and the fair value price of the future would be 93.4841.

Although, taken individually, short-sterling contracts for successive delivery months (March, June, September, December) represent forward-forward values of three-month sterling interest rates, taken in combination they can be used to hedge against or closely replicate longer interest rate exposures.

174

This comes about because of the very nature of interest rates themselves. A longer term interest rate can be considered the result of combining the immediate short-term rate for a short period, with the forward rate at this intermediate point for another short period, followed by the forward rate at this next point for a further period, and so on and so on until maturity is reached. Buying successive short-sterling futures contracts (known as a 'strip') produces an exposure to interest rate risk, equivalent to that of a security whose maturity is at the delivery date of the latest contract in the strip. For example a strip of short-sterling contracts, September 1994, December 1994, March 1995, June 1995, taken out in say August 1994, will provide a close hedge for a security maturing in June 1995.

## Gilt-edged options

As derivative instruments financial futures and options are often classed together, but in practice they serve quite significantly different purposes. Whereas in the case of a futures contract it is mandatory for the seller to deliver bonds or close out his position, an option (as its name suggests) conveys upon its owner the right (but not the obligation) to exercise his option to buy (or sell) a given bond or alternatively let it lapse. It follows, therefore, that the most a purchaser of an option stands to lose if prices of the underlying bond move against him is the price paid for the option, whilst his potential gain is unlimited. This contrasts clearly with the situation in futures where the price movement is theoretically unlimited in either direction.

There are basically two types of options: call options and put options. A *call* option is a contract that enables the buyer to purchase (*call*) a specified entity at a predetermined price (the exercise price) either throughout a given time period (American-type option) or at the end of that period (European-type option). The price that the buyer of the option pays for this right is known as the 'option premium'.

The counterparty to this bargain is the call option seller (or 'writer' as he is often called). This person receives the option premium but stands committed to sell the relevant entity to the buyer at the exercise price at any valid time under the terms of the option. If he already owns the entity in question he is called a 'covered' writer; if he does not he is called an 'uncovered' or (rather more exotically) a 'naked' writer.

A *put* option entitles the buyer of the option to sell (*put*) a specified entity at the predetermined exercise price at any valid time for the option, and the writer of a put option pockets the option premium in return for his obligation to buy the bond at the exercise price if requested.

As with many other markets the traded option market has its own jargon and nomenclature. All options of the same nature (i.e. calls or puts) relating to the same underlying security form what is called an 'option class'; and all options of the same class with the same exercise price and the same expiry date form an 'option series'.

If the price of the physical entity in the market is higher than the exercise price of a call option on it (or if the physical price is lower than the exercise price of a put option) the option in question is termed to be 'in the money'.

If the physical price equals the exercise price the option is said to be 'at the money'.

If the physical price is lower than the exercise price of a call option (or is higher than the exercise price of a put option) the option is considered to be 'out of the money'.

When option prices are being considered, expressions such as 'intrinsic value' and 'time premium' will be encountered. For an option that is in the money the intrinsic value is the absolute value of the difference between the price of the underlying instrument and the exercise price of the option, and for out of the money options the intrinsic value is zero. The time premium is the amount by which the actual option price exceeds the intrinsic value. Fig. 9.1 illustrates these in the case of call option with an exercise price of 96.

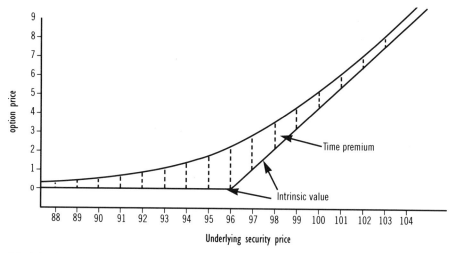

**Fig 9.1**   Call option. Exercise Price 96

The market in gilt-edged options has undergone a lot of change since they were first appeared on 10 January 1985. Originally they took the form of traded options contracts on LTOM (London Traded Options Market) which then operated within the general ambit of the London Stock Exchange. These contracts were based on specific gilts and were similar in structure to LTOM's equity contracts. As a product they never fully captured the imagination of investors and market practitioners and eventually were closed down. But the needs of the market generally for some form of options capability remained and was eventually met in two different ways.

Firstly, the evolution of a 'negotiated options' market in which some investment banks, securities houses and gilt-edged market makers are prepared to write options on gilt-edged and fixed-interest bonds on a bilateral 'over-the-counter' basis with their clients or counterparties of good standing. The minimum size for these instruments is £100,000 nominal of the underlying bond and the maximum period to expiry is two years. Other than that these can be tailored to the specific requirements of the buyer, with virtually complete freedom of choice of underlying bond and exercise price, but they are not normally assignable to third parties. They are thus very flexible but rather illiquid instruments. Historically these were preceeded by a small number of gilt-edged warrant issues made by some of the GEMMs which were not particularly successful. Here the underlying bond was chosen by the issuer, there was a single, fixed, exercise price and the maturity of the warrant was limited to within one year. A particular problem with these warrants was that because of their single exercise price, any significant movement in market price that took place after their issue would take their value well 'into' or 'out of' the money, when what the majority of potential buyers wanted were propositions either 'at the money' or close to it.

The second area of development has been in traded options based on the LIFFE gilt-edged future. This has been rather more sucessful than its predecessors largely because it concentrates activity on a single underlying instrument which is itself a major pool of liquidity in a highly transparent market. But a secondary factor has been the merger between LIFFE and LTOM bringing futures and traded options under the same roof, and promoting their use in parallel. Long gilt futures options (which are American-style options) obviously relate to the same nominal amount (£50,000) of underlying bond as the long-gilt future on which they are based, but unlike the future their unit of price quotation is $\frac{1}{64}$th.

Long gilt futures options are transacted on the floor of LIFFE by an open outcry method, and are settled through the London Clearing House (LCH), which places itself as the central counterparty to both buying and selling (writing) clearing members. This obviates the necessity for the two parties to have any further dealings with each other in respect of that bargain. Business in options on the long-gilt future, like most of LIFFE's non-equity options, is not settled immediately. Instead it is subjected to a daily mark-to-market procedure (similar to that used with futures) which generates positive or negative variation margin flows.

## Exercising or closing out a long gilt futures option

The initiative in exercising a long gilt futures option position lies wholly with the buyer – the seller has no control of whether or when an option is exercised. Since the option is of the American type the buyer can exercise his option at any time during its life by giving notice to his broker/clearing member so as to enable that person to inform LCH of his intentions via the clearing processing system (CPS) by 5.00 p.m. that day (11.30 a.m. on the expiry day, which in the case of the gilt-edged contracts is the last business day of the expiry month). Once such notice has been given, LCH – using a random selection process – chooses a counterparty from the pool of outstanding sellers of that particular option series, and assigns positions in the long gilt futures contract representing the exercise of the option.

If rather than exercise an option the buyer chooses to close out his position by effecting an equal sale in the relevant option series, LCH must be notified so that the positions can be closed out against each other. Without such settlement the two positions would remain independently in the clearing system instead of cancelling each other out. This could easily lead to the (closing) sale being matched by LCH against an exercise of an option by a totally unrelated party, thereby leaving the original buyer with an unwanted open position.

## Option pricing

The pricing of traded options is an area of investment where probability theory comes into its own. This is hardly surprising when one considers that the essential determinants of value are the probability that a given bond will reach or exceed certain price targets within a specified time frame. It is important to realise right from the beginning that the calculation of these probabilities is highly subjective and that the whole business of valuing option premiums is far from precise. However, there are certain limiting boundaries within which option values are constrained which provide a basic framework for price analysis.

It is also worth reiterating at this point the essential difference between European and American type options since they are capable of being valued differently. A European option can only be exercised on its formally stated exercise date. An American option permits its owner to exercise it at any time up to and including its formal exercise date. Of the options associated with the gilt-edged market, most negotiated (OTC) options are European, but the LIFFE option on the long gilt future is American.

## Call options

It is probably most instructive to start by examining a European call option on a zero coupon bond so that there is no incidence of complicating factors

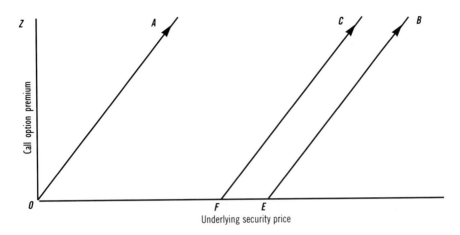

**Fig 9.2**   Call option boundaries

such as accrued interest or dividend payments. Consider Fig. 9.2. In this case
the option premium is plotted against the *y*-axis and the underlying price
against the *x*-axis. The exercise price (*E*) is represented by the point *E* on that
axis.

The first point to make is a rather obvious one. Since nobody in his right
mind should pay more for a call option (irrespective of exercise price) than
the current price of the underlying instrument, the point in the option-
price/underlying-price diagram representing their relationship must always
be below and to the right of the 45° angled line OA.

Secondly, the price of an option can never be negative for this would imply
that the option represented a liability to its owner; and since at worst an
option can always be abandoned this can never be the case.

Next, consider the 45° line EB drawn through the point *E* on the *x*-axis
representing the exercise price. If by any chance the option-price/underlying-
price point were to be to the right of this line, this would imply that it would
be possible to make a riskless profit by selling the underlying instrument,
buying the call option, earning interest on the balance of the cash proceeds
and eventually closing the position by exercising the option. The efficiency
of the market will normally preclude this from happening.

It would thus appear that by combining these three logical considerations
we have established the boundaries of European call option pricing, i.e.
within the parallelogram *AOEB*. But no. This does not take into account that
element of the riskless profit referred to above emanating from the interest on
the cash balance between the current date and exercise. When this is taken

179

into account it establishes the current boundary of valid option pricing will not be the line *EB* but another line, *FC*, parallel and a little way separated from it. As time progresses this gap will narrow, and at expiry *FC* and *EB* will be one and the same.

Mathematically this can be expressed by the inequality,

$$Z_C + v^q \cdot E \geqslant P_0$$

where,

$P_0$ represents the current bond price

$Z_C$ represents the current call option price

$E$ represents the exercise price of the option

$q$ represents the time period until exercise

$v^q$ represents the discounting factor at the riskless rate of interest for the period until exercise.

Let us now expand this analysis to a coupon paying bond and take into account accrued interest and the receipt of dividends, letting:

$a_0$ represent the current gross accrued interest

$a_q$ represent the gross accrued interest at exercise

$d$ represent the present value of any dividends due on the underlying bond in the period to exercise.

This produces the following relationship.

$$Z_C + v^q \cdot (E + a_q) \geqslant (P_0 + a_0) - d$$

$$\text{or } Z_C \geqslant [(P_0 + a_0) - d] - v^q \cdot (E + a_q). \tag{9.4}$$

Put in words this says that a European call option price should always be greater or equal to the current *total* (i.e. including accrued interest) price less the discounted value of any dividend payments due in the period, minus the discounted value of the *total* future exercise price.

If one rewrites the equation as:

$$Z_C \geqslant P_0 - [v^q \cdot (E + a_q) - a_0 + d]$$

this establishes the value on the *x*-axis of the point *F* as the term in square brackets on the right hand side of the equation. If one takes the case of a call option on a 5% bond with an exercise price of 96 and expiry in three months' time, where the initial accrued interest is, say, 0.3125 and that at expiry

180

1.5625, with no dividends due to be received, and where three-month money rates are, say, 6%, then:

$$F = v_q \cdot (E + a_q) + d - a_0$$
$$= 0.985329\ (96 + 1.5625) + 0 - 0.3125$$

$$= 95.82$$

## Black and Scholes model

Having established the boundaries of European call option pricing thus, the next step is to create a model within that framework for pricing more precisely. In the early 1970s a great deal of pioneering work was done by Fischer Black and Myron Scholes and the Black and Scholes model has become an established industry standard in the field of equity options. However, it is open to argument whether the application of the Black and Scholes model to options involving redeemable fixed-income securities is completely valid. The Black and Scholes method is based upon assumptions that the expected price of the underlying instrument at expiry is lognormally distributed about the current price, and that the underlying bond's price volatility is both accurately quantifiable and stable. Unfortunately, there is little hard evidence to support the stability assumption and there are practical difficulties in establishing satisfactory prospective volatility figures simply from analysing historic price movements. In the first instance one can quite easily get radically different volatility figures depending on the retrospective time period chosen for analysis, and, secondly, because the life to maturity of a redeemable bond is reducing day by day these historic figures will tend to reflect the volatility of a bond somewhat longer than that in question. Nevertheless, a number of versions of this method have been adapted for use with fixed-income options and their basic modus operandi is examined below.

Using the notation established earlier in this chapter the basic Black and Scholes valuation of a European call option on non-dividend paying security is:

$$Z_C = P_0 \cdot N(d_1) - v^q \cdot E \cdot N(d_2) \tag{9.5}$$

It will be seen that this is quite similar in structure to our earlier equation defining the line $F_C$ except for the application of factors $N(d_1)$ and $N(d_2)$ to the terms on the right hand side of the equation.

What are these factors and how are they calculated? In its general form, $N(x)$ is the cumulative probability distribution function for a standardised normal variable. $N(x)$ is the probability that such a variable will be in the

181

range $-\infty$ to $x$, i.e. that it will be less than $x$. Tables of standardised normal distribution values are found in most statistical textbooks and algorithms giving close approximations to these values are available for computer use.

The specific values of $d_1$ and $d_2$ to be used in the $N(x)$ function involve the underlying security price, the exercise price, the time to expiry, the riskless rate of interest and the security's volatility. Before going on to the formulae for $d_1$ and $d_2$ we should consider this entity, volatility.

Historic volatility is defined as the standard deviation of the log price relative of a security's past price action expressed in annual terms. Let us look at an example where the hypothetical price action is as shown in Table 9.5.

**Table 9.5** Example of calculation of historic option volatility

| Day No. | Security price = $P$ | Price relative $P(T)/P(T-1) = R$ | Log price relative $LN(R) = X$ | $W =$ X–mean $X$ | $W^2$ |
|---|---|---|---|---|---|
| 1 | 96.000 | | | | |
| 2 | 97.125 | 1.011719 | 0.011651 | 0.010953 | 0.0001199610 |
| 3 | 96.875 | 0.997426 | −0.002577 | −0.003275 | 0.0000107274 |
| 4 | 98.500 | 1.016774 | 0.016635 | 0.015937 | 0.0002539916 |
| 5 | 99.000 | 1.005076 | 0.005063 | 0.004365 | 0.0000190563 |
| 6 | 99.125 | 1.001263 | 0.001262 | 0.000564 | 0.0000003180 |
| 7 | 98.875 | 0.997478 | −0.002525 | −0.003223 | 0.0000103890 |
| 8 | 98.375 | 0.994943 | −0.005070 | −0.005768 | 0.0000332660 |
| 9 | 98.750 | 1.003812 | 0.003805 | 0.003107 | 0.0000096519 |
| 10 | 98.000 | 0.992405 | −0.007624 | −0.008322 | 0.0000692535 |
| 11 | 97.750 | 0.997449 | −0.002554 | −0.003252 | 0.0000105770 |
| 12 | 97.000 | 0.992327 | −0.007702 | −0.008400 | 0.0000705628 |
| 13 | 96.625 | 0.996134 | −0.003873 | −0.004571 | 0.0000208979 |
| 14 | 96.875 | 1.002587 | 0.002584 | 0.001886 | 0.0000035571 |

|  |  | Mean $X$ | 0.0006979 | Total $W^2$ | 0.0006322095 |
|---|---|---|---|---|---|
| | | | | Daily variance | 0.0000526841 |
| | | | | Annual variance | 0.0027395744 |
| | | | Volatility = standard deviation | 0.0523409436 | = 5.23 % |

In this example prices of a security are recorded for 14 days. (There is no particular significance in the number 14, it just suits the construction of this example – in practice volatilities are measured over periods ranging from a few days to over a year.)

Next each day's price, P(T), is divided by that of the previous day, P(T–1), to form what is called the 'price relative', $R$.

The fourth column contains daily figures for $X$ which are the natural logarithm of the corresponding value of $R$. These are known as the 'log price relatives'. These are summed and their arithmetic mean established (in this case by dividing by 13).

The fifth column shows the deviation between each log price relative and their mean, denoted by the symbol $W$; and the sixth column contains this value squared, $W^2$.

The sum of the squares of the deviations is then divided by the number of its constituents minus 1 (in this case $13 - 1 = 12$) to form the variance of the log price relative (0.0000526841). Since this has been computed by considering daily price relatives it is known as the daily variance.

Volatility is defined as the annual standard deviation of the log price relative, and to obtain this it is necessary to multiply the daily variance by, say, 253, the number of trading days in the average year, and then take the square root of the resultant figure. In the example above this comes to 0.05234 or, as expressed in market parlance, 5.23%.

Having had this long look at volatility we are now in a position to consider further the values $d_1$ and $d_2$ to be fed into the $N(x)$ function. These are,

$$d_1 = \frac{\log_e(P_0 / E \cdot v^q)}{u \cdot q^{0.5}} + \frac{u \cdot q^{0.5}}{2}$$

$$d_2 = \frac{\log_e(P_0 / E \cdot v^q)}{u \cdot q^{0.5}} - \frac{u \cdot q^{0.5}}{2}$$

where $u$ denotes the annual volatility e.g. $u = 0.05234$ and where $\log_e$ denotes the natural logarithm of the value concerned,

and when these variables are input to equation (9.5), which for convenience is restated here as,

$$Z_C = P_0 \cdot N(d_1) - v^q \cdot E \cdot N(d_2) \tag{9.5}$$

this establishes the Black and Scholes model price for a European call option on a non-dividend paying security.

This basic price formula can be adapted, given some assumptions and approximations, to provide values for European call options on futures and on dividend paying securities.

For Options on futures the formula is:

$$Z_C = v^q \cdot F_0 \cdot N(d_1) - v^q \cdot E \cdot N(d_2) \tag{9.6}$$

$$\text{where, } d_1 = \frac{\log_e(F_0 / E)}{u \cdot q^{0.5}} + \frac{u \cdot q^{0.5}}{2}$$

$$\text{and, } d_2 = \frac{\log_e(F_0 / E)}{u \cdot q^{0.5}} - \frac{u \cdot q^{0.5}}{2}$$

where $F_0$ denotes the current futures price.

183

For a dividend paying security, such as a gilt, the formula for the price of a European call option takes the form:

$$Z_C = \{(P_0 + a_0) - d\} \cdot N(d_1) - v^q \cdot (E + a_q) \cdot N(d_2) \qquad (9.7)$$

$$\text{where, } d_1 = \frac{\log_e[\{(P_0 + a_0) - d\}/v^q \cdot E]}{u \cdot q^{0.5}} + \frac{u \cdot q^{0.5}}{2}$$

$$\text{and, } d_2 = \frac{\log_e[\{(P_0 + a_0) - d\}/v^q \cdot E]}{u \cdot q^{0.5}} - \frac{u \cdot q^{0.5}}{2}$$

and d is the discounted present value of dividends receivable

but in these cases the volatility to be used should be that relating to the total price of the underlying bond minus the discounted value of the dividends to be received before the option's expiry. Perhaps the best way to appreciate how variations in the parameters used in these models affect option pricing is to look at Fig. 9.3.

In the diagram the curve labelled A relates to a European call option with an exercise price ($E$) of 96, a life to expiry of six months ($q = 1$), a volatility of 12% ($u = 0.12$), and a riskless interest rate of 6% ($v = 1/1.03$).

Curve B shows the effect of halving the volatility to 6% ($u = 0.06$) but keeping all the other parameters unchanged. It can be readily seen that this reduces the value of the option generally but that these differences are minimised when the option is either heavily in the money or heavily out of the money.

Curve C demonstrates the effect of having a longer time period to expiry, in this case one year ($q = 2$) instead of six months as shown in A. This results in substantially increased values of the option across the whole range of prices for the underlying security.

Curve D shows how having a higher value for the riskless rate of interest is relatively small when the option is deep out of the money, but is significant when the option is at the money, and becomes increasingly so as the option progresses to being heavily in the money.

One of the most important entities used when combining options and their underlying security is what is called the option 'delta'. This is the rate of change of the option price with respect to changes in the underlying price. Mathematically this is expressed as:

$$\text{option delta} = \frac{dZ}{dP_0} = N(d_1) \qquad (9.8)$$

184

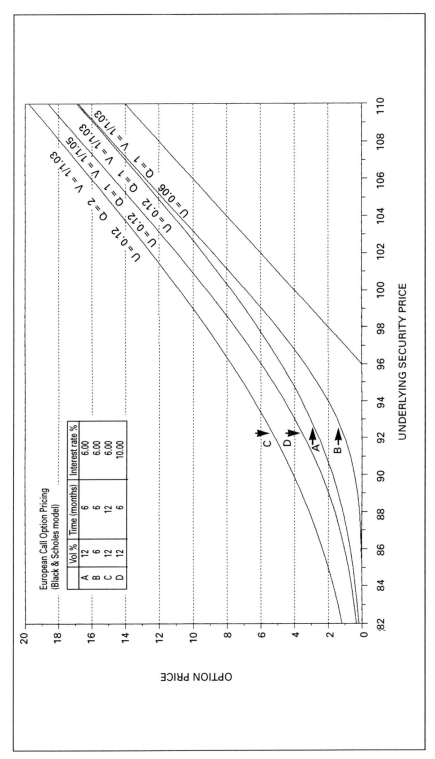

**Fig 9.3** Comparative prices of options with varying characteristics

185

and graphically can be observed as the gradient of the relevant option price curve at that point along its length corresponding to any given underlying price. Its importance springs from the fact that anybody wishing to hedge an exposure in the underlying bond by holding countervailing options, will require the size of the option position to exceed the size of the position in the underlying bond by a factor ('the hedge ratio') equal to the reciprocal of the option delta. Without exception the delta of an option ranges from a minimum of zero (when the option is 'totally' out of the money) to a maximum of one (when the option is 'totally' in the money), and thus this hedge ratio is always greater than or equal to unity.

One of the problems with 'delta hedging' is that the delta is clearly not constant and adjustments to the hedge require to be made whenever there is a significant change in the underlying price. The size of this effect is measured by the rate of change of the delta with respect to the underlying price and is called the option 'gamma'.

Two other sensitivity measures need to be mentioned here also.

'Theta' is the rate of change of the option price with respect to change in the time to expiry.

'Kappa' is the rate of change of the option price with respect to change in volatility.

## Put option pricing

Very similar considerations to those above apply to the pricing of put options. In the case of the riskless arbitrage, this now consists of an initial purchase of both the put option and the underlying instrument, and the closing of the arbitrage is effected by the exercise of the put option. Using the same notation as before it is possible to establish the basic relationship for put options,

$$Z_P \geq v^q \cdot (E + a_q) + d - (P_0 + a_0). \tag{9.9}$$

where $Z_P$ denotes the current put option price.

Once again the fundamental principle that the option price cannot be negative applies, but the other basic pricing boundary is determined by the fact that it would be illogical for the put option price to exceed the exercise price. This leads to a diagrammatic representation of a put option, as shown in Fig. 9.4.

Following very much the same thought processes as before, it is clear that valid put option values must at least fall within the area *ABEX*, and when

186

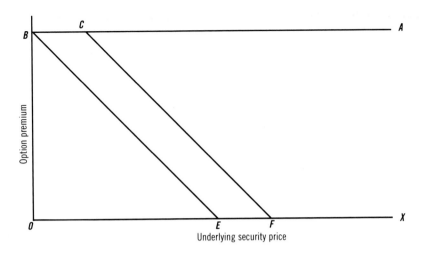

**Fig 9.4** Put option price boundaries

allowance for interest is taken into account they must be further constrained to fall within the area *ACFX*. In which case *F* takes the value:

$$F = v^q \cdot (E + a_q) + d - a_0$$

just as before.

All this leads to establishing the following formulae for European put options. For a European put option on a non-dividend paying security:

$$Z_P = v^q \cdot E \cdot N(-d_2) - P_0 \cdot N(-d_1) \qquad (9.10)$$

$$\text{where, } d_1 = \frac{\log_e(P_0 / E \cdot v^q)}{u \cdot q^{0.5}} + \frac{u \cdot q^{0.5}}{2}$$

$$\text{and, } d_2 = \frac{\log_e(P_0 / E \cdot v^q)}{u \cdot q^{0.5}} - \frac{u \cdot q^{0.5}}{2}$$

For a European put option on a future:

$$Z_P = v^q \cdot E \cdot N(-d_2) - v^q \cdot F_0 \cdot N(-d_1) \qquad (9.11)$$

$$\text{where, } d_1 = \frac{\log_e(F_0 / E)}{u \cdot q^{0.5}} + \frac{u \cdot q^{0.5}}{2}$$

$$\text{and,} \quad d_2 = \frac{\log_e(F_0/E)}{u \cdot q^{0.5}} - \frac{u \cdot q^{0.5}}{2}$$

where $F_0$ denotes the current futures price.
and for a European put option on a dividend paying security:

$$Z_P = v^q \cdot (E + a_q) \cdot N(-d_2) - [(P_0 + a_0) - d] \cdot N(d_1) \tag{9.12}$$

$$\text{where,} \quad d_1 = \frac{\log_e[\{(P_0 + a_0) - d\}/v^q \cdot E]}{u \cdot q^{0.5}} + \frac{u \cdot q^{0.5}}{2}$$

$$\text{and,} \quad d_2 = \frac{\log_e[\{(P_0 + a_0) - d\}/v^q \cdot E]}{u \cdot q^{0.5}} - \frac{u \cdot q^{0.5}}{2}$$

and the same considerations regarding the computation of volatility that were mentioned with regard to European call options apply here also.

## The relationship between put and call option prices

There is a tidy price relationship between the price of a European put option and that of the call option of the same series. This comes about by virtue of the equivalence of two option strategies, the first to hold a portfolio consisting of both the instrument and a put option, and the second to hold the relevant amount of cash plus a call option. That these two strategies are equivalent can be argued thus. If, at expiry, the instrument's price has risen above the exercise price, the owner of the first portfolio can abandon the put option and end up simply holding the bond, whilst the owner of the second portfolio will exercise his call option using his cash to finance the acquisition. Likewise, if the bond price at expiry is below the exercise price the first investor can exercise his put option against his holding, whilst the second will just abandon the call option. In the first instance both portfolios end up holding an equal amount of the underlying instrument, and in the second they end up holding the same amount of cash. They are therefore equivalent and their present values (allowing for receipt of any intervening dividends) must equate. Thus

$$(P_0 + a_0 - d) + Z_P = v^q \cdot (E + a_q) + Z_C$$

i.e.

$$Z_P = Z_C + v^q \cdot (E + a_q) - (P_0 + a_0 - d) \tag{9.13}$$

188

## American options

All the foregoing analysis has been devoted to the valuation of European-type options. The basic formulae for a call option on a non-dividend paying security or a future are also valid for American-type options. The reason for this is that at any time prior to expiry an option will always have some time value, and any holder will therefore do better by selling it rather than exercising it. Accordingly one should not expect an American option to be exercised early and it can therefore be valued as if it were a European option. Sadly, the same logic does not hold for American puts, but the ability of the holder to exercise early has some value (even if undefined) and therefore one can state that the value of an American put will be not less than that of the equivalent European put.

## Option trading strategies

The ability to combine limited liability instruments like traded options with physical security positions, futures, or with other options, opens up a vast new area of potential for investors and market practitioners alike. People venturing into this area for the first time are sometimes confused and uncertain about the results of combining various options. This problem can most often be solved by looking at the potential levels of profit or loss at expiry corresponding to a wide range of prices of the underlying instrument. This is not as difficult as it might seem, since there are only four basic option actions: buy calls, write calls, buy puts and write puts. Each of these has a distinct and different profit profile as shown in Fig. 9.5, and where options are combined the aggregated profit or loss profile quickly unmasks the character of the combined strategy.

Clearly there are a multitude of ways in which options on the same underlying instrument, but with various exercise prices and expiry dates, can be combined. We shall conclude this chapter with an example which illustrates the result of simultaneously buying 96 puts at 2 and writing 96 calls at 1. This is portrayed in Fig. 9.6 in which the profit profiles for both options are shown individually, together with the overall profit of the combined strategy. Ignoring for the moment the costs of financing the cash flow deficit (of 1) and any other expenses, this clearly breaks even if the underlying instrument's price at expiry is 95 and makes a further one-point profit for every point it falls below that level. It can thus be seen that by deploying this strategy combination one has effectively created a synthetic short sale of the instrument in question at a price of 95.

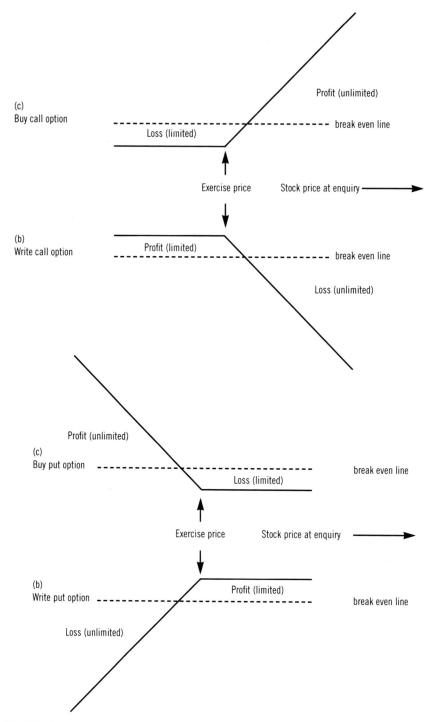

**Fig 9.5** Profit/Loss profiles of four basic options strategies related to the price of the under-lying instrument at expiry

190

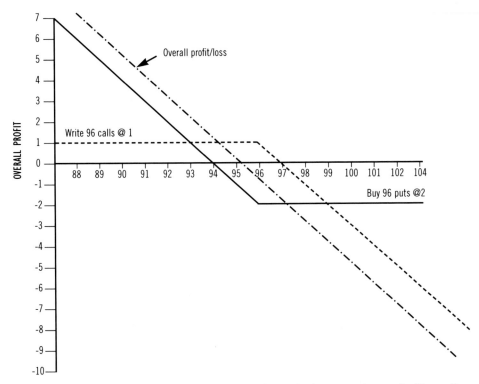

**Fig 9.6** Profit profile of a strategy of simultaneously purchasing put options and selling call options

191

# 10

## Taxation of gilt-edged securities and associated instruments.

### The events of 1995

The year 1995 saw dramatic and far-reaching changes announced regarding the way gilt-edged securities are to be taxed in the future.

In February 1995 the Chancellor of the Exchequer announced details of the formation of an open gilt repo market in the UK (see Chapter 3). In order to enable this market to function a number of taxation arrangements required to be altered and one of these, enabling corporate holders of gilts (whether UK resident or not) to receive interest payments without deduction of tax at source in future (providing they submit to quarterly tax accounting), was particularly radical.

Whilst this did not come as a suprise to the market, a second announcement on 25 May 1995 from the Treasury and the Inland Revenue proposing to tax capital gains on gilts and other bonds as income was totally unexpected. The *raison d'être* for this reform was stated to be the desire to simplify the tax rules for gilts and bonds, and create a regime in which there would be a more consistent tax treatment of different types of bond and investor. It would also be a prerequisite for the development of an official gilt strips market and possibly other subsequent innovations.

This announcement was accompanied by the simultaneous issuance of two consultative documents, 'The Taxation of Gilts and Bonds' from the Inland Revenue, and 'Strips and New Instruments in the Gilt-Edged Market' from the Bank of England. The former called for views on the desirability of proceeding with the proposed tax reform to be submitted by 30 June, and the accompanying foreword implied that the starting date for the new regime would be quite soon after that date. In the event when the Chancellor of the Exchequer announced, on 10 July, that that Government was going to proceed with this reform certain critical changes from the original proposals emerged.

Firstly, the reform will not apply to private investors whose aggregate nominal holdings of bonds is £200,000 or less.

192

Secondly, it will not apply to non-equity shares (including zero-coupon preference shares) and two lower-coupon gilts, Funding $3\frac{1}{2}\%$ 99/04 and Treasury $5\frac{1}{2}\%$ 08/12.

Thirdly, the starting date for the new regime was delayed until 1 April 1996 for companies, and 6 April 1996 for those private investors above the £200,000 nominal threshold.

Additionally it was confirmed that there would be special rules for gilt-edged and bond unit trusts to ensure that they were not disadvantaged, and that corporate bond PEPs would have tax exemption.

Taken together these two reforms have resulted in a major redrawing of the taxation map of the gilt-edged and sterling bond markets. There are now a number of different classes of investor subject to different sets of tax rules, and likewise a variety of tax treatments afforded to varying types of securities. The complexity of the situation is illustrated by the matrix of investor classes and security types contained in Appendix 1 at the end of the book; but to comprehend the situation fully it is necessary to have an understanding of the evolution of gilt and bond taxation over recent years.

Let us start with the taxation changes announced in the 1985 Budget (which became effective in 1986).

*The 1986 tax changes*

The 1986 changes greatly simplified the then taxation environment for gilts. The major fiscal gluepot had always been capital gains tax, where an accumulation of successive pieces of legislation from 1965 onwards had created a veritable tangle of rules for stock identification, indexation, loss offsetting and so on. All this ceased to matter when on 2 July 1986 capital gains tax on gilt-edged bonds and certain other fixed-interest securities (known as 'qualifying' bonds) was abolished.

The key to allowing capital gains tax (CGT) to be abolished was a parallel change to the way income from gilts and similar instruments was to be taxed, which removed the ability of tax-paying investors to convert taxable income into tax-free capital gains. The device by which this was achieved was the introduction on 28 February 1986 of the accrued income scheme (AIS) which has remained in operation ever since. Although this introduced one or two new complexities, taken together the overall effect of these changes was to create an environment where there were no longer any artificial restraints on dealing such as had been previously experienced, and where bond values were free to find their own levels under the basic forces of supply and demand.

Traders in securities such as banks, discount houses, gilt-edged market-makers and others dealers were not affected by these changes as for them both capital gains and interest payments were, and continue to be, treated simply as elements of their overall profit/loss and taxed accordingly

(Schedule D Case I). But for investors in gilts and qualifying corporate bonds it meant that from 2 July 1986 until the beginning of April 1996 virtually the only taxation with which they have needed to concern themselves has been that on income.

*Deep discount legislation*

One uses the word 'virtually' in the sentence above because of the introduction in 1989 of what has become known as 'deep discount' legislation. Broadly speaking, 'deep discount securities' are defined as redeemable securities whose price at the time of issue stands at a discount to par exceeding $\frac{1}{2}\%$ per year of the term to maturity, or 15% in total. In such cases the Inland Revenue considers the capital gain between the issue price and the theoretical price at the time of disposal equivalent to the original issue yield to be income, and will subject this to income tax. A parallel tax treatment is afforded to securities whose redemption value may be expected to rise above their issue price by similar amounts, and these are referred to as 'deep gain securities'.

*Qualifying indexed securities (QIS)*

Left to their own devices index-linked gilts would have fallen into this new category of deep gain securities contrary to the wishes and interests of the authorities and investors alike. A way had to be found to prevent this happening, and this was achieved by yet further legislation creating a category of securities known as 'qualifying indexed securities' which are excluded from the charge on deep gain securities. The main criteria for a security obtaining QIS status currently are:

It must be issued for a definite period which must not be less than five years.

Its redemption value must, if a sterling issue, be determined by reference to the Retail Price Index; or if a non-sterling issue, by reference to a general index of prices published by or on behalf of the government of the territory in whose currency it is denominated.

It must not be convertible into or redeemable in a currency other than that in which it is denominated on issue.

It must bear indexed interest payable at least annually, at a reasonable commercial rate in the light of market conditions at the time of issue.

The index applied for the purpose of indexation of interest and the redemption price must be applied precisely and without restriction under the terms of issue.

Where a 'lagging' index is used the lag must not be longer than eight months.

*Transitional arrangements*

The deep discount, deep gain and qualifying indexed securities provisions all emanate from the Income and Corporation Tax Act 1988 and came into operation in 1989. However, all gilt-edged issues, including index-linked, first issued before that time are excluded from their provisions. The legislation also allows further tranches of gilts to be issued at a deep discount up to the amount already issued at a shallow discount without the new issue or the whole issue being classed as a deep discount security.

An understanding of these events is important not only because of their historical significance but, equally importantly, because a great many UK private investors (all those below the £200,000 aggregate nominal threshold) will continue to be taxed on this basis after 6 April 1996 when the new regime for corporate and larger private investors commences.

We shall now examine how the combination of these historic tax arrangements, and those announced in 1995 and expected to pass into law via the 1996 Finance Act, affect the way dividends, accrued interest and capital gains on gilts and bonds are now to be treated.

## The taxation of dividends

The arrangements to permit gross payment of gilt-edged interest to certain classes of investor made as a prerequisite to the development of the gilt repo market have, in effect, created a two-tier structure for the taxation of dividends.

From 2 January 1996 onwards the following will be eligible to hold gilts (directly or through an intermediary) in a Central Gilt Office (CGO) 'Star' account (so called because such account numbers will be prefixed with a *) from which gilt interest payments will be paid gross:

> Corporate bodies (whether UK resident or not)
> Premiums trust funds of Lloyd's syndicates
> Pensions funds, charities, local authorities and government bodies.

In order that these new arrangements do not result in a huge cash flow disadvantage to the Government, a system of quarterly tax accounting will apply to those benefiting from these facilities (with the exception of non-resident bodies and UK gross funds).

It should be stressed that these gross-paying arrangements specifically exclude individuals whether resident in the UK or elsewhere, and for them most interest payments (dividends) will continue to be paid after deduction at source of the basic rate of income tax in the time honoured way. There are, however, as usual, some significant exceptions to this rule.

Firstly, dividends on War 3½% 1952/after (War Loan) and the Floating Rate Treasury Stock 1999 are always paid gross, (and one would suppose that any further floating rate issues that may be made in future would be treated similarly) whether to residents or non-residents of the UK.

Secondly, the Bank of England maintains a register of holders of gilts who are exempt from tax, pension funds, charities, etc., and dividends related to these holdings can be paid gross. The process of registering an exempt holding is a bit cumbersome, and if a total holding is disposed of and re-acquired later the process has to be repeated. It is not unknown, however, for a tax-exempt fund to acquire and register a series of small holdings of all the gilt-edged bonds it has a reasonable prospect of owning in future, and to retain these permanently for no other purpose than maintaining their places on the 'exempt' register.

The third category is the payment of gross dividends on certain specified gilts to non-residents of the UK upon application. The list of bonds to which this facility is applicable is a little limited. As at end-July 1995 only thirty out of fifty-nine conventional gilts and only four of thirteen index-lined issues carried this facility. However, this ratio is gradually increasing as nearly all new issues since 1988 have been of this type. These bonds are formally designated in the Stock Exchange official list as tax free to non-residents and known in the market and internationally as FOTRA (Free Of Tax to Residents Abroad) bonds.

At that time they comprised the following:

Floating Rate Treasury Stock 1999 (paid gross to allcomers)
Treasury 12$\frac{3}{4}$% 1995
Treasury 15$\frac{1}{4}$% 1996
Exchequer 13$\frac{1}{4}$% 1996
Treasury 13$\frac{1}{4}$% 1997
Treasury 7% Convertible 1997
Treasury 8$\frac{3}{4}$% 1997
Treasury 7$\frac{1}{4}$% 1998
Treasury 6$\frac{3}{4}$% 95/98
Treasury 15$\frac{1}{2}$% 1998
Treasury 9$\frac{1}{2}$% 1999
Treasury 6% 1999
Conversion 9% 2000
Treasury 8% 2000
Treasury 7% 2001
Treasury 8% 2003
Treasury 6$\frac{3}{4}$% 2004
Treasury 8$\frac{1}{2}$% 2005
Treasury 7$\frac{3}{4}$% 2006
Treasury 8% 2002/06
Treasury 8$\frac{1}{2}$% 2007
Treasury 9% 2008
Treasury 6$\frac{1}{4}$% 2010

Conversion 9% 2011
Treasury 9% 2012
Treasury $5\frac{1}{2}$% 2008/12
Treasury 8% 2013
Treasury $7\frac{3}{4}$% 2012/15
Treasury 8% 2015
Treasury $8\frac{3}{4}$% 2017
War $3\frac{1}{2}$% 1952/after (paid gross to allcomers)
Index Linked $4\frac{5}{8}$% 1998
Index Linked $4\frac{3}{8}$% 2004
Index Linked $2\frac{1}{2}$% 2024
Index Linked $4\frac{1}{8}$% 2030

In order for an 'individual' non-resident to obtain payment of dividends on these bonds in gross form, or to be able to claim back tax already deducted at source, he must first make application to the Inspector of Foreign Dividends, Inland Revenue, Lynwood Road, Thames Ditton, Surrey, KT7 0DP. For exemption to be granted it is necessary for the investor to declare that he is a bona fide non-resident of the UK, that he is the beneficial owner of the relevant bond and, prior to 24 May 1995 when the requirement was rescinded, that he had the intention to hold them for at least two, or preferably three successive dividend dates.

There is a second way for an 'individual' non-resident to obtain dividends on FOTRA bonds by use of a so-called 'E' arrangement which allows banks and corporate members of the London Stock Exchange to obtain block exemption from UK income tax for some of their overseas clients. Under this procedure the investor is normally saved the bother of completing the Inland Revenue forms himself, but the arrangement is subject to certain restrictions and excludes, amongst others:

1. Securities held on behalf of a Liechtenstein Anstalt, Foundation, Establishment, Etablissement or Stiftung;
2. holdings forming part of a trust, settlement, or an estate in the course of administration;
3. and cases where a bond is sold specially ex-dividend.

It is also possible for a non-resident to obtain full or partial tax exemption from gilts through the operation of double taxation agreements with some overseas countries. Non-resident investors wishing to make use of such facilities should approach the Inspector of Foreign Dividends in the normal way. Tax exemptions granted under this aegis are not necessarily restricted to FOTRA bonds.

There are, however, some important considerations relating to gross dividends paid abroad under these arrangements. In its strictest sense, the legislation requires the non-resident to be the beneficial owner of the bond in question on the day the dividend is paid. In the past this has normally been some five weeks and two days after going ex-dividend, and this, if rigidly applied, could lock an overseas investor into a holding for that period. The move to shorten the ex-dividend period to seven working days (ten working days in the case of War $3\frac{1}{2}\%$ 1952/after) will greatly alleviate this problem.

One thing which is clear is that when an overseas resident sells bonds in the special ex-dividend form prior to becoming officially ex-dividend, no claim for repayment of tax will be considered, except possibly under certain double taxation arrangements.

## The taxation of accrued interest. The accrued income scheme

As outlined earlier, the whole basis of taxation of income from gilts and qualifying bonds changed radically on 28 February 1986. Hitherto only actual dividend payments received counted as taxable income, but the introduction and operation of the accrued income scheme from that date widened the tax net. Under this scheme the gross accrued interest at the time of sale is considered for the purposes of UK taxation to be a receipt of income and as such becomes chargeable to income tax. As a natural offset to this the accrued interest content of the purchase consideration is treated as negative income allowable against the first interest payment received. The overall result of these arrangements is to make the total taxable income derived from a gilt or bond holding proportional to the time it is held, rather than have it incremented in lumps every time a dividend is paid. The advent of this scheme thereby eliminated, at a stroke, the previously highly advantageous situation whereby income could be converted into capital gain by judicious sales of bonds shortly before they went ex-dividend.

Technically, the tax relating to accrued interest items becomes payable (or, in the case of a purchase, creditable) on the date of the immediately following dividend payment, but in practice may not be settled until perhaps as long as a year later, when the annual tax return is made. This allows a modest cash flow strategy to exist by which taxed investors making sales just before bonds become ex-dividend, and repurchases just afterwards, obtain a temporary cash flow advantage approximating in size to the tax at basic rate on the dividend in question.

Not all investors are subject to tax under this scheme. Clearly it is inappropriate for overseas investors and they are exempted from it. So too are UK individuals whose holdings of all securities within the scheme do not exceed £5,000 nominal value in both their current and previous tax years.

In the Inland Revenue press release accompanying the Chancellor of the Exchequer's 10 July 1995 reform announcement, mention was made of the possibility of simplifying and restricting the application to private investors of the accrued income scheme and the rules for deep discount securities, but at the time of writing (end August 1995) no proposals have yet emerged.

## Taxation of capital gains from gilts and bonds

Under the taxation arrangements commencing in April 1996 (1 April for corporates, 6 April for individuals) capital gains from gilts and bonds will once again be taxed, so ending a ten-year period of capital tax freedom. In fact, for many UK investors gilt-edged gains had been effectively free from capital gains tax since 1968 when the exemption for holdings having been held for over one year was introduced.

The need for this significant change of stance was attributed to the authorities' desire to simplify the tax system, but also because the previous capital gains tax-free environment was seen to present an impediment to the development of a UK gilt strips market and other possible innovations.

The method chosen by the authorities to achieve their ends and overcome this problem was not to reinstate capital gains tax as such, but to deem capital gains derived from gilts and bonds to be items of income and subject them to income tax or corporation tax where applicable.

Although the claim was made that on balance the change would be tax neutral, it was very clear that the big losers under these proposals would be private investors, many of whom had been previously encouraged into gilts (and bonds) by the nature of their capital-gains-tax-free returns. All sorts of personal financial arrangements were suddenly at risk: loan repayment schemes, school fee plans, Lloyd's deposits etc., to say nothing of the general reduction in net rates of return on all below par bonds – the sort most usually held by private investors. These concerns were vigorously aired during the period provided for consultation and, as mentioned at the beginning of this chapter, when the decision to proceed with the reform was made on 10 July 1995, provisions were made to exclude most private investors and certain securities from its scope.

To recapitulate:

1. Private investors whose total aggregate nominal holdings of gilts and bonds do not exceed £200,000 will be outside the scheme. It has not, at the time of writing, been made clear exactly how this criterion for exclusion will be operated, but it is reasonable to expect the Inland Revenue to require the £200,000 threshold not to have been breached at any time in a given tax year for exclusion to apply.

2. Two lower-coupon gilts whose origins date back to the 1950s, Funding 3½% 99/04 and Treasury 5½% 08/12, are excluded from the scope of the scheme largely because of certain assurances given as to their future tax treatment by the then Chancellor of the Exchequer, James Callaghan, in 1965.

3. Also excluded are all non-equity shares. In practice this mainly means preference shares of which one particular subgroup, zero-coupon preference shares, is of special importance to private investors.

4. The element in the return on index-linked gilts due to indexation of the principal repayment will remain tax-free but as before, details of the precise way in which this will be achieved have not emerged at the time of writing. It seems possible that this will follow the method of indexation of capital gains on equities, by which base costs are, for tax computation purposes, uplifted by an amount corresponding to the proportionate change in the RPI between acquisition and disposal, but with one variation. Such indexation of equity base costs is restricted to diminishing taxable capital gains, and cannot be applied to establish an allowable capital loss when in purely money terms no such loss exists. To achieve full protection of real capital values of index-linked gilts by the above method, this latter provision would need not to apply.

Leaving aside all the exclusions from the new regime, let us now examine how it will operate for the two principal classes of investor involved, corporates and personal investors (above the £200,000 aggregate nominal threshold).

For these 'larger' personal investors the capital gain or loss realised at disposal (or redemption) will be considered as income and included in the income tax assessment for the year in which the disposal takes place. In a mechanical sense this is comparable to the application of capital gains tax on equities, but without the benefits of inflation indexation of base costs or the annual capital gains tax allowance to soften the tax blow.

For corporates, tax will be assessed and be payable each year, not only on gains/losses resulting from disposals in each accounting period but also on unrealised gains/losses as valued at the end of each period.

Companies are given a choice as to how such valuations are made.

1. They can opt for a mark-to-market valuation of their gilts and bonds on either a clean or dirty price basis (as long as their treatment of accrued interest and dividend income is consistent with their choice.)

2. They can opt to be taxed on an accruals basis under which successive end-period valuations would lie in some form of smooth price progression between purchase price and redemption value, thus spreading the tax bill more or less evenly along the life of a given bond.

It is probable that the great majority of companies, especially tax-paying investment institutions whose bond market actitivities represent a significant proportion of their business, will choose to be taxed on an accruals basis since this provides a more certain and stable basis for forward financial planning. It also offers them greater flexibility in the management of their bond portfolios. Consider the following example:

A year ago a life office bought a 6% ten-year bond at a price 80.
Under an accruals basis this is about to be valued at the forthcoming year-end at 82 (assuming a straight-line accrual).
But due to a market collapse its current market price is only 75.
If the investment manager keeps the bond in his portfolio over his year-end this will give rise to a taxable 'capital profit' of 2 points. This when taken together with the interest payments on the bond (6 points) will result in a tax charge of

$$(6 + 2) \times 0.25 = 2 \text{ when income tax is levied at } 25\%.$$

If, however, he sells the bond before his year-end he will establish an allowable 'capital loss' of 5 points which can be offset against the interest payments of 6 points, reducing the tax payable to

$$(6 - 5) \times 0.25 = 0.25 \text{ instead.}$$

It is thus clear that there are potential cash-flow advantages to be obtained by funds operating on an accruals basis establishing tax losses when prices fall below accrual-value levels; and by the reverse token it can be seen to be against a fund's interests to make sales when prices rise much above such levels. Whilst the revenue loss from the former possibility is unlikely to be significant within the wider context of the Inland Revenues overall activities, there are negative implications for the liquidity of the market at times of strongly rising prices associated with the latter. Of course this is only speculation. Time alone will tell.

## Taxation of gilt-edged futures and options

The basic intention of the 1996 tax regime is to treat positions in gilt-edged futures and associated options as far as possible in the same way as if they are physical gilts. In its simplest form this means that profits arising from activities in these derivatives will be assessed as to income tax for corporates and 'above threshold' personal investors, but that for 'below threshold' personal investors these instruments are the last remaining investment vehicles totally free of tax.

It also means that the nominal equivalents of long gilt futures and option positions will be taken into account in assessing whether personal investors are above or below the £200,000 threshold, though whether a short position in, say, the long gilt future is considered to add to or subtract from the aggregate nominal total is not at present clear. Nor does it look practical to apply an accruals type valuation system to these instruments, and for tax purposes they will have to be marked to market.

# 11

## Gilt-edged indices and performance measurement

Virtually every securities market in the world has some widely accepted and freely available published indicator or index (many have more than one) by which its aggregate progress can be monitored. In most cases these are products of the media, working in conjunction with the securities market in question. The gilt-edged market is no exception to this rule. There are two main gilt-edged indices, both published by the *Financial Times* newspaper (*FT*) on a daily basis, which have been used by UK investors as domestic bond market yardsticks for many years, and these are considered in the following section. Beyond that there are a number of proprietary indices emanating mostly from major international securities houses which measure the performance of the gilt-edged market in the wider context of global bond markets. These are more frequently used by international investors, and are examined at the end of this chapter.

### *Financial Times* indices

The older of the two indices referred to above is the *Financial Times Government Securities Index*, and comes, so to speak, from the same stable as the *Financial Times Industrial Ordinary Share Index*. Both date from before World War II – the Ordinary Share Index having a base date of 1 July 1935, whilst the Government Securities Index goes back to 15 October 1926. Both of them are geometric averages of prices of a representative selection of bonds or shares in their respective markets.

At 1 September 1994 the eleven constituent members of the *FT* Government Securities Index were:

Treasury $15\frac{1}{4}$% 1996
Exchequer $10\frac{1}{2}$% 1997
Treasury $8\frac{3}{4}$% 1997
Exchequer 12% 1998
Treasury $9\frac{1}{2}$% 1999
Treasury $9\frac{3}{4}$% 2002

Treasury 12½% 2003/05
Treasury 9% 2008
Treasury 5½% 2008/12
War 3½% 1952/after
Consol 2½% 1923/after

It was stated above that the index was a geometric average; by this it is meant that the index figure is found by multiplying together the constituent prices and taking the eleventh root of this product. This process ensures that percentage movements in all bonds, whether they are high-priced or low-priced bonds, are given equal weightings in the averaging process. In this index the relevant prices are clean prices, and the index ignores the incidence of dividends. As such, it is of use only as a broad indicator of changes in market levels, and should not be used for any sophisticated form of performance comparison (discussed later in this chapter). There follows below an analysis of this index, which has a lot in common mathematically with the analysis of price ratios done earlier in Chapter 6.

In this analysis, $q$ represents the *FT* Government Securities Index, formed from bonds whose total prices are $P_1$, $P_2$, ... $P_m$ and whose coupon rates are $g_1$, $g_2$, ... $g_m$, respectively. Using this notation:

$$q = [(P_1 - g_1.t_1) \cdot (P_2 - g_2 \cdot t_2) \ldots (P_m - g_m \cdot t_m)]^{1/m}$$

Taking logarithms of both sides of this equation,

$$m.\log q = \log(P_1 - g_1 \cdot t_1) + \log(P_2 - g_2 \cdot t_2) + \ldots + \log(P_m - g_m \cdot t_m).$$

Differentiating with respect to time, $t$,

$$\frac{m}{q} \cdot \frac{dq}{dt} = \frac{-g_1}{P_1 - g_1 \cdot t_1} + \frac{-g_2}{P_2 - g_2 \cdot t_2} + \ldots + \frac{-g_m}{P_m - g_m \cdot t_m}$$

$$\frac{1}{q} \cdot \frac{dq}{dt} = -\frac{f_1 + f_2 + \ldots + f_m}{m}$$

where $f_1, f_2$ etc. represent the flat yields of the constituents of the index.

If one compares this with a similar analysis for a single bond's clean price, $C$,

$$C = P - gt$$

$$\log C = \log(P - gt)$$

$$\frac{1}{C} \cdot \frac{dC}{dt} = \frac{-g}{P - gt} = -f$$

it can be seen that the geometrically averaged *FT* Government Securities Index acts like a bond with the same flat yield as the arithmetical average of the flat yields of its constituent parts.

It thus follows that the trends shown up by this index will overstate the market's progress if the index's average flat yield is below the 'going market rate', and understate it if the average flat yield exceeds it. If the 'going market rate' is considered to be, say, the average gross redemption yield of the index's constituents (weighted by modified duration) then the size of the bias in this index becomes determined by the difference between its average flat yield and its weighted average gross redemption yield at any particular time.

On 1 September 1994 these values were as in Table 11.1, from which it can be deduced that at that time the index would have had a propensity to understate the performance of the market by about 1% per annum.

**Table 11.1** *Financial Times* Government Securities Index as at 1 September 1994: flat yields and gross redemption yields of its constituents

| Constituent | Flat yield | Gross redemption yield | Modified duration |
|---|---|---|---|
| Treasury 15¼% 1996 | 13.571 | 7.193 | 1.430 |
| Exchequer 10½% 1997 | 9.923 | 7.845 | 2.157 |
| Treasury 8¾% 1997 | 8.586 | 8.034 | 2.594 |
| Exchequer 12% 1998 | 10.687 | 8.454 | 3.244 |
| Treasury 9½% 1999 | 9.146 | 8.406 | 3.503 |
| Treasury 9¾% 2002 | 9.206 | 8.701 | 5.550 |
| Treasury 12½% 03/05 | 10.249 | 8.938 | 5.648 |
| Treasury 9% 2008 | 8.669 | 8.527 | 7.767 |
| Treasury 5½% 08/12 | 7.392 | 8.257 | 10.135 |
| War 3½% 1952/after | 8.390 | 8.390 | 11.666 |
| Consol 2½% 23/after | 8.493 | 8.493 | 11.606 |
| Averages | 9.483 | 8.423* | 5.936 |

*modified duration weighted average.

Like all indices of this sort, the *FT* Government Securities Index suffers from the problem of discontinuities. These normally arise when one of its constituents approaches redemption and has to be replaced with a longer bond. In an index with a relatively small number of constituents, this can cause a non-trivial increase in the 'average life' of the index, and if the flat yields of the outgoing and incoming constituents differ to any great degree this will also affect the time trends outlined above. It can be argued that the effects of these discontinuities are only small and can normally be ignored, but a number of technical analysts around the world have been known to use this index as a basis for making gilt-edged judgements, and they need to be aware of any distortions, large or small, that are encapsulated in the data they are using.

By contrast, the newer set of indices, the *FT* Actuaries Fixed Interest Price Indices, is purposely riddled with discontinuities. These indices were originally designed to act as far as possible like individual bonds, with price indices like total (dirty) prices, and with discontinuities occurring whenever a constituent member went ex-dividend. To compensate for this latter feature, each of these indices has an additional component, the 'ex-dividend adjustment', which is incremented by the appropriate amount on each relevant ex-dividend occasion. Again in contrast to the *FT* Government Securities Index, the *FT* Actuaries Indices take into account the total (dirty) prices of all bonds in the gilt-edged list, and weight them by the nominal amount outstanding. The full details of the methods used for computing both these price indices and the corresponding (gross redemption) yield indices which are published daily in the *Financial Times* can be obtained on request from the *Financial Times*.

In presentation the *FT* Actuaries Fixed Interest Indices, comprising five conventional gilt indices and three index-linked indices all computed on this basis, follow the style shown in Fig. 11.1.

Because of the move to quote all gilt-edged prices clean of accrued interest following the introduction of the accrued interest scheme in 1986, the *FT* Actuaries Fixed Interest Price Indices are nowadays shown as having three parts, a clean price value and a corresponding accrued interest figure, which when added together constitute a total (dirty) price, and the ex-dividend (XD) adjustment for the year to date. These values are shown in the first, fourth and fifth columns of the *Financial Times*' current format. Once again these indices are not best suited for chart purposes, but they are ideal (and were specifically designed) for performance measurement. However, the divided nature of these indices often confuses people when they come to use them. The example that follows has been included to show how they should be used for that purpose.

To compute the performance of any given sector of the market over a specified period, it is necessary to obtain:

(a) the change in the total price index over the period
(b) the income payments received or due in respect of bonds going ex-dividend during the period.

The sum of these two elements should then be divided by the initial total price index.

In each case the total price indices must first be established by adding together the clean price index and the accrued interest on each relevant occasion.

**FT-Actuaries Fixed Interest Indices**

| UK Gilts Price Indices | Fri Mar 31 | Day's change % | Thu Mar 30 | Accrued interest | xd adj yield |
|---|---|---|---|---|---|
| 1 Up to 5 years 24 | 119.61 | -0.17 | 119.81 | 1.78 | 2.89 |
| 2 5–15 years 21 | 140.11 | -0.53 | 140.86 | 1.87 | 3.58 |
| 3 Over 15 years 9 | 156.21 | -0.80 | 157.47 | 1.80 | 4.05 |
| 4 Irredeemables 6 | 180.37 | -0.96 | 182.12 | 3.47 | 1.47 |
| 5 All stocks 60 | 137.10 | -0.46 | 137.73 | 1.86 | 3.41 |

| Index-linked | Fri Mar 31 | Day's change% | Thu Mar 30 | Accrued interest | xd adj yield |
|---|---|---|---|---|---|
| 6 Up to 5 years 2 | 190.47 | +0.06 | 190.35 | -0.0 | 2.57 |
| 7 Over 5 years 11 | 176.02 | -0.13 | 176.24 | 0.82 | 1.28 |
| 8 All stocks 13 | 176.60 | -0.11 | 176.79 | 0.74 | 1.40 |

Yields

| | ....Low coupon yield.... | | | | | ....Medium coupon yield.... | | | | | ....High coupon yield.... | | | | |
|---|---|---|---|---|---|---|---|---|---|---|---|---|---|---|---|
| | Mar 31 | Mar 30 | Yr ago | High | Low | Mar 31 | Mar 30 | Yr ago | High | Low | Mar 31 | Mar 30 | Yr ago | High | Low |
| 5 yrs | 8.43 | 8.33 | 7.10 | 8.95 (20/9*) | 5.57 (19/1*) | 8.48 | 8.39 | 7.33 | 9.01 (20/9*) | 5.82 (19/1*) | 8.51 | 8.62 | 7.45 | 9.16 (20/9*) | 5.91 (19/1*) |
| 15 yrs | 8.46 | 8.36 | 7.59 | 8.89 (20/9*) | 6.30 (20/1*) | 8.54 | 8.44 | 7.70 | 9.05 (20/9*) | 6.39 (20/1*) | 8.65 | 8.75 | 7.97 | 9.25 (20/9*) | 6.63 (20/1*) |
| 20 yrs | 8.43 | 8.34 | 7.68 | 8.81 (20/9*) | 6.41 (20/1*) | 8.54 | 8.44 | 7.70 | 9.05 (20/9*) | 6.42 (20/1*) | 8.60 | 8.70 | 7.90 | 9.09 (20/9*) | 6.65 (20/1*) |
| Irred.† | 8.46 | 8.36 | 7.80 | 8.88 (20/9*) | 6.52 (24/1*) | | | | | | | | | | |

| Index-linked | ....Inflation rate 5%.... | | | | | ....Inflation rate 10%.... | | | | |
|---|---|---|---|---|---|---|---|---|---|---|
| | Mar 31 | Mar 30 | Yr ago | High | Low | Mar 31 | Mar 30 | Yr ago | High | Low |
| Up to 5 yrs | 3.51 | 3.50 | 3.21 | 4.17 (10/1) | 2.13 (4/1*) | 2.10 | 2.08 | 2.29 | 3.01 (11/11*) | 1.19 (16/2*) |
| Over 5 yrs | 3.87 | 3.86 | 3.41 | 3.99 (21/6*) | 2.88 (20/1*) | 3.68 | 3.66 | 3.23 | 3.79 (21/6*) | 2.79 (20/1*) |

Average gross redemption yields are shown above. Coupon Bands: Low: 0% – 7¾%; Medium: 8% – 10¾%; High: 11% and over.   †Flat yield. ytd Year to date.
Base values: UK Gilts Indices 31/12/75 = 100.00 and Index-linked 30/4/82 = 100.00.   *1994 highs and lows.

**Fig 11.1**  FT-Actuaries Fixed Interest Indices format as at 31 March 1995 (Reproduced with kind permission of *Financial Times*)

Let us now measure the gross performance of the All Stocks Index between 31 January 1995 and 31 March 1995.

| | | |
|---|---|---|
| On *31 January* All Stocks Index clean price | = | 136.43 |
| All Stocks Index accrued interest | = | 1.49 |
| so that All Stocks Index total price | = | 137.92 |
| Also on that day All Stocks XD adjustment | = | 1.72 |

Two months later, on *31 March*, the equivalent values were:

| | | |
|---|---|---|
| All Stocks Index clean price | = | 137.10 |
| All Stocks Index accrued interest | = | 1.86 |
| therefore, All Stocks Index total price | = | 138.96 |
| and All Stocks XD adjustment | = | 3.41 |

Thus,

| | | | |
|---|---|---|---|
| (a) the change in the total price index | = | 138.96–137.92 | = 1.04 |
| and (b) the change in the XD adjustment | = | 3.41–1.72 | = 1.69 |
| | | (a) + (b) | = 2.73 |

When we then divide by 31 January total price, 137.92, we get 1.98% as the gross performance of the All Stocks Index over the two months.

The three-part nature of these indices often tempts people to add the three components together and consider the percentage change in this composite figure to be the relevant performance. This is totally incorrect, since in this method the divisor is not the initial price index, but that figure plus the dividends accumulated to date for the year. If the starting date for the period of measurement is the beginning of the year, this latter item will be zero, and arithmetically the result will be accidentally correct, but for all other starting dates it will cause the performance figure to be arithmetically understated.

A further complication occurs when the performance measurement period spans a calendar year end. The XD adjustments run as cumulative totals, and their 'meters' are reset to zero at the beginning of each new year. In such cases, item (b) will have two parts:

(i) relating to the period from the starting date in the earlier year to 31 December of that year, and

(ii) the XD adjustment at the end of the performance period in the later year.

These two elements need to be added together to form the total income relevant to the measurement period.

The essential separation of dividend, accrued interest and capital elements in these indices makes it possible to calculate net of tax performance figures, too. If in the case of the All Stocks Index used earlier, an investor was subject to tax on income under the Accrued Interest Scheme at, say, 25%, and was exempt from capital gains tax, the net performance would be:

$$\frac{(137.10-136.43)+(1-0.25)\{(3.41-1.72)+(1.86-1.49)\}}{137.92}$$

$$= 1.606\% \text{ net of income tax at } 25\%$$

These figures, and others calculated on a comparable basis, can be described as 'simple performance figures', since they just measure simple interest returns, with no allowance made for the compounding of interest (which is an integral part of gilt-edged portfolio management). However, they do provide a series of standard yardsticks against which actual portfolio experience can be compared. For comparisons like this to be meaningful, it is necessary for the actual and comparative portfolio performances to be computed on an exactly similar basis, i.e. capital gain plus income flow added together, and the total divided by the initial capital value.

However, very few gilt-edged funds are totally static. Most will experience new money inflows from time to time (and quite possibly outflows as well) as their investment managers allocate new funds or change their overall asset distributions. It is when new money gets involved with performance calculations that problems start to arise. There are two principal ways of looking at this subject: by (a) money-weighted rates of return (sometimes referred to as the 'internal rate of return'), or (b) time-weighted rates of return.

In the case of a portfolio initially valued at $V_0$ receiving income payments of $D$ after time $t_1$ (measured in half-years), new money for investment of N after time $t_2$, and finally being valued at $V_n$ after time $t_n$, the internal rate of return can be defined as the rate of interest $r\%$ per annum such that

$$V_0\left(1+\frac{r}{200}\right)^{t_n}+D\left(1+\frac{r}{200}\right)^{t_n-t_1}+N\left(1+\frac{r}{200}\right)^{t_n-t_2}=V_n$$

This is a highly satisfactory measure of an individual fund's performance taken in isolation; but it must be realised that the internal rate of return thus

209

produced will be highly dependent upon the fortuitous timing of any new money flows. As such, it does not represent a tool for making performance comparisons between different funds whose new money may become available for investment at different times. For the performance measurement industry, where a great deal of attention is focussed upon league tables of comparative fund performances, this is not sufficient, and the alternative 'time-weighted rate of return' has evolved to meet this requirement.

The essence of time-weighted rates of return is to break the period over which performance is to be measured into segments bordered by the occasions when dividends or new money-flows take place, to compute a succession of simple interest returns for each segment, and to chain-multiply them together to form an overall return. The problem with this method is that to be done properly requires the portfolio to be valued each and every time a dividend is received or an injection of new money is made.

Using the same notation as in the previous example, and designating the portfolio values $V_1$ and $V_2$ at times $t_1$ and $t_2$ respectively,

$$\text{the rate of return between time } t = 0 \text{ and } t_1 = \frac{(V_1 - V_0 + D)}{V_0}$$

$$\text{the rate of return between time } t_1 \text{ and } t_2 = \frac{(V_2 - V_1)}{V_1}$$

$$\text{the rate of return between time } t_2 \text{ and } t_3 = \frac{[V_3 - (V_2 + N)]}{(V_2 + N)}$$

and the time-weighted rate of return ($w$) is defined by the equation

$$\left(1 + \frac{w}{200}\right)^{t_3} = \frac{V_1 + D}{V_0} \times \frac{V_2}{V_1} \times \frac{V_3}{V_2 + N}$$

Both these examples have been deliberately simplified to allow for the incidence of one dividend payment and one new money injection only. In practice, there will tend to be a far greater number of such occurrences and this can become administratively cumbersome. To overcome this, certain systems of computing time-weighted rates of return choose to aggregate dividends and new money inflows, and deem them to be made at average market values and at mean times within certain periods, say, at mid points of months. Whilst this may possibly be acceptable for equity performance measurement, the approximations involved are incompatible with the need for precision in the gilt-edged and fixed interest markets, where margins of over- or under-performance are measured in tenths and hundredths of percentage points.

210

There are sometimes further complications with such systems when a fund manager sells a gilt-edged holding, and does not immediately invest in another bond. In some time-weighted measurement systems, this is treated as an outflow of cash from the fixed interest portfolio rather than a simple timing finesse, and if the subsequent reinvestment takes place in a later accounting period, performance figures can result that do not reflect the profitability or otherwise of that short-term tactical manoeuvre.

Moving away from the area of inter-fund performance comparison to that of monitoring the stewardship of an individual fund's manager, there is a lot to be said for the 'notional' fund approach. With this method, a notional portfolio is selected before the start of the respective period of measurement on the basis that if the fund were not to be actively managed, but were to remain totally passive, the notional portfolio would be the one chosen to meet the fund's needs. As and when new money is invested in the actual portfolio, the notional portfolio is also augmented by a similar cash amount (net of expenses), increasing all its holdings proportionately. The two portfolios – the original and the notional – can thus be compared on a like-for-like basis in cash terms, to see whether the active management of the fund has created added value, over and above that which would have occurred naturally. This method has the additional advantage that it can be adapted without difficulty to take into account interest earned on (a) uninvested cash balances, (b) money reserved for calls on partly-paid bonds, and (c) dividend payments received by portfolios during the measurement period. As such, it is a stringent but fair test of an investment manager's capabilities.

## FT Actuaries Yield Indices

Compared with the price indices the *FT* Actuaries Yield Indices have been rather under-used, and as of July 1995 are under review as regards both content and methodology. To date these indices have been obtained from taking constant term yield values at the five-year, fifteen-year and twenty-year maturity points from three separate yield curves, for low-coupon, medium-coupon and high-coupon bonds respectively. The basic intention has been to keep the numbers of bonds in each of these coupon bands as nearly equal as possible, and from time to time the coupon boundaries of the bands have been adjusted to allow for changes in the composition of the market brought about by redemptions and new issues. As of the end of July 1995 the low-coupon band was defined as 0 to $7\frac{3}{4}\%$, the medium-coupon band 8% to $10\frac{3}{4}\%$ and the high-coupon band 11% and above. This stratification has its roots in the yield structure of the market pre-25 May 1995, on which date the Inland Revenue announced forthcoming changes to the taxation of gilts and bonds. Until then high-coupon gilts

211

had almost always yielded more than lower-coupon gilts of a comparable maturity as a result of capital gains on gilts being tax-free. The move by the Treasury and Inland Revenue to tax (most) gilt-edged capital gains as income after April 1996 caused these valuation divergences to diminish and it is possible that values derived from a single yield curve will suffice in the future.

The yield curves that have provided the basis for these indices over the years are of the form,

$$y(t) = A + B.e^{-Ct} + D.e^{-Ft}$$

Given values for $C$ and $F$, the coefficients $A$, $B$ and $D$ can be obtained using a least squares process as described in Chapter 6, but the method of establishing the combination of values of $C$ and $F$ to minimise the sum of the squares of the differences between the curve values and the yields of the relevant bonds is much more complex. The method used for these curves is the Nelder-Mead Simplex Algorithm under which, starting from a given combination of $C$ and $F$, the algorithm 'searches' systematically until it locates a local minimum. This has normally worked well, but there have been occasions when more than one local minimum has existed causing yield curve values to vary on successive days in a way not consistent with actual yield movements, and so some care should be exercised when using these statistics.

The final yield index relates to the irredeemables, and is found by taking the weighted average of the semi-annually converted yields of irredeemable bonds with the exception of Conversion $3\frac{1}{2}\%$ 1961/after (which is subject to the operation of a sinking fund and therefore on an unrepresentative yield basis). Since the weightings used in this process are the nominal amounts of bonds outstanding this value is highly influenced by the yield of War $3\frac{1}{2}\%$ 1952/after whose nominal issue size of £1,909 million dwarfs the total of £1,166 million for the other four components taken together.

## Proprietary gilt-edged market indices

As mentioned at the beginning of the chapter these indices mainly derive from securities houses whose bond interests are global and where the analytical process used will most often treat the UK gilt-edged market simply as a component of the wider global bond market. Three of the most widely accepted sets of global bond market indices are the:

Merrill Lynch Global Bond Indices
J.P. Morgan Government Bond Indices
Salomon Brothers Government Bond Indices

Clearly one of the prime purposes of producing wide ranging sets of indices of this nature is to allow performance comparisons to be made between various markets, or even market sub-sectors, and this necessitates the usage of a common methodology within each family of indices. Each of the three sets of indices mentioned above are constructed as total return indices, though the criteria used for determining which bonds are eligible for inclusion in the relevant indices, and what weightings should be applied to them, varies from house to house.

Total return indices of this sort are typically constructed by calculating the short-term performance (principal and income combined) of each component over a specified time period, forming the weighted average of these, and then chain-multiplying the previous index value by this weighted average to form the new index figure. Nowadays, the most usual time-period over which performance is measured is one day, though prior to October 1992 the Salomon indices used monthly increments. Cumulative indices of this type are very similar to the performance indices for individual bonds (described earlier in Chapter 6) in so far as they allow for both capital price movements and the receipt and reinvestment of gross income payments. Computation of total return over any intermediate period is relatively straightforward especially when compared with the process required for performing this task using the *FT* Actuaries Fixed Interest Price Indices. It simply requires the end-of-period index to be divided by the start-of-period index, and for the resulting quotient to be expressed either in total return form or as a rate of return % per annum, thus:

$$\text{total return} = \frac{\text{end-of-period index}}{\text{start-of-period index}} - 1$$

$$\text{rate of return \% per annum} = 200 \times \left[ \left\{ \left( \frac{\text{end-of-period index}}{\text{start-of-period index}} \right)^{\frac{1}{\text{time elapsed}}} \right\} - 1 \right]$$

where the time elapsed is measured in half-years.

The shortcoming of these indices is their inability to provide readily net-of-tax rates of return, which are often required for gilts by certain UK domestic investors, and for this purpose the *FT* actuaries indices are probably best.

However for UK gross funds and many international investors this facet of the subject is not critically important and the comprehensive coverage given to bond markets by these indices is impressive. Firstly they cover all the major liquid Government bond markets of the world. Secondly they provide separate indices for different maturity sectors within each market covered (typically, 1-3 years, 3-5 years, 5-7 years, 7-10 years and over 10 years), and thirdly they express these returns in either local currency or US dollar terms.

# 12

## Gilt-edged settlement

### Settlement dates

Gilt-edged bargains are normally settled on the business day following the day of transaction and this assumption will apply unless alternative arrangements are specified at the time of dealing. However, in certain circumstances, it is permissible to deal for forward dates subject to the rules of the London Stock Exchange. These state, *inter alia,*

> Where a member firm is so requested by a non-member, it shall seek to arrange for the settlement of the securities specified ...e.g. Gilts... to be effected up to 10 days (or such longer period as may be agreed with the Exchange) after the date of the transaction if the non-member requires such settlement by reason of:
>
> (i)    a requirement to convert a currency;
> (ii)   a requirement to allow for the transit and execution of any required documents; or
> (iii)  the offsetting of another transaction.

Within the scope of the above the main variations from next-day settlement are,

*(a) 'Cash' (same day) settlement.*   This is sometimes possible but all the necessary documentation must be available within the standard time limits.

*(b) 'Skip' (trade day plus two) settlement.*   Often used to accommodate settlement from clients in different time zones.

*(c) Three business days forward settlement (T+3).*   Mainly used to facilitate reinvestment of proceeds of Eurobonds for which this is currently the standard settlement period.

*(d) Five business days forward settlement (T+5).*   To tie in with the five-day rolling settlement regime for Sterling domestic bonds and UK equities.

215

When dealing other than for normal (next business day) settlement the accrued interest element of the total price will be calculated by reference to the actual settlement date agreed and there may also be an adjustment in the (clean) bargain price to compensate for financing cost differences between short-term money rates and the rate of interest accrual (flat yield) on the bond in question.

## Contingent bargains

Settlement of a purchase may also be effectively deferred for up to ten days, provided that the purchase is financed by the sale proceeds of a gilt-edged security, provided that the purchase costs are within 10% of the sale proceeds, and the bargains were dealt at the same time, for the same investor, with the same market-maker, by the same party, and provided that the 'contingent' (*CN*) condition was applied at the time of dealing. In these circumstances, for the first ten days from settlement day, neither party may deliver bonds until the other is in a position to do likewise. If the condition '*CN NB*' is applied at the time of dealing, then that ten-day period is extended indefinitely.

## Methods of settlement and the role of the Central Gilt Office (CGO)

The methods currently used for settlement have their main origins back in 1979 when the pressures of an ultra-high level of turnover threatened the then existing system with partial collapse owing to the sheer volume of paperwork and to the lack of a sufficiently rigid timetable framework. This experience led to the reform of the physical settlement system but more importantly the creation of a dematerialised computerised book-entry transfer system for major market participants operated by the Central Gilt Office (CGO) of the Bank of England. It is through the CGO that the vast majority of high value gilt-edged transactions are settled, but it should be realised that not all institutions or brokers wish to subscribe to membership of the CGO and that most smaller investors cannot do so. Settlement of a significant proportion of transactions therefore still has to be part-settled outside CGO thus requiring the paper-based physical settlement system to be maintained for the foreseeable future.

CGO members have long included gilt-edged market-makers, inter-dealer brokers, Stock Exchange money brokers, discount houses, settlement banks, custodian banks, institutional investors and nominee companies, but since the advent of the gilt repo market membership has been expanded to cater for investors, domestic or foreign, who wish to receive interest payments without deduction of withholding tax. This can be achieved by eligible persons who have made the necessary declarations through the operation of what is known as a 'Star' account at the CGO. In the case of UK corporate investors it also requires them to submit to quarterly tax accounting.

The CGO allows these members to keep their gilt-edged holdings in book-entry form and transfer bonds between each other electronically without waiting for the underlying transfer to be recorded on the main register maintained by the Bank of England. This method of delivery is complemented by an assured payments system conducted by the settlement banks. This operates so that when, on settlement day, the CGO transfers bonds between two members, the buyer's settlement bank incurs an irrevocable commitment to pay the relevant amount to the seller's settlement bank that same day. To cover the paying settlement bank's risk in giving this commitment it holds a floating charge over securities held in the buyer's CGO account and cash receivable in respect of any sales of securities subsequently transferred out of that member's CGO account.

These arrangements may well be augmented in future by links between CGO and Euroclear and Cedel which would allow international bond investors whose holdings are maintained in either of these systems to hold gilts there also. This could possibly be achieved by creating accounts for Euroclear and Cedel within the CGO and could be expected to enhance the attractiveness of gilts to foreign investors.

Given this background let us now consider the general settlement process. For the moment we will consider only those transactions involving an institutional or private investor. When a bargain is executed the broker/dealer, market-maker or investment house (hereafter referred to as client counterparty) sends a contract note, plus a transfer form in the case of a sale, to the investor, his nominee or the registered holder (or any combination of these). In return, the investor makes payment on the next business day for any bonds he has bought, or, if he has sold, sends back the completed transfer form, together with the relevant certificate, and duly receives payment for the bonds sold.

In principle, therefore, gilt-edged settlement is very simple, but in practice all sorts of contingencies occur, most – if not all – of which are covered in this chapter. First of all, let us review the different types of security to be found in the gilt-edged market.

## Classes of gilt-edged securities

Gilt-edged securities are mainly the UK-registered type. A selection of bonds is available in bearer form with coupons attached, whilst some new bonds exist for the first month or so of their life in allotment letter form – which is effectively bearer, but without coupons, as although interest is earned, no dividends are paid until after they have been changed into registered form. 'Gilt-edged' is a term strictly used to cover only Government securities, but is commonly used to include other first-class securities that are dealt for cash settlement. However, since by far the largest part of the market is in government securities, the rest of this chapter refers solely to them, unless otherwise stated.

*Bearer securities*

Just under one-third of the conventional gilts in issue are currently available in bearer form, but no index-linked issues. The maximum denomination varies from issue to issue between £1,000 and £50,000, whilst the minimum denomination (and therefore the dealing multiple) is either £50 or £100. Such bonds are convertible free of charge from bearer to registered or vice versa, at any time, but settlement may be delayed if sales of either type are made immediately after conversion. Lack of a free market in bearer (due to the limited amount of these bonds available) inhibits demand, but the inconvenience of claiming interest on the coupon, plus the inherent problem of safe custody of a bearer bond, are other limiting factors.

*Registered securities*

Owing to the restricted demand for bearer, gilts are therefore dealt in mainly in the registered form. Holdings are registered at the Bank of England into the name of the purchaser (or his nominee), who subsequently receives a certificate stating that he is in fact the registered holder. Registration can be carried out by the client, his agent or the client's counterparty.

When registered gilts are sold, the registered holder has to sign a transfer form, if a single holder, or seal and sign in accordance with the articles of association, if a corporate body. That transfer form, together with the registered certificate, is forwarded to the client counterparty by a specified time on settlement day. If for any reason the certificate is not available, formalities and deadlines vary according to the circumstances, whilst in some cases settlement may be delayed. Sales by CGO participants are not subject to these settlement delays.

*Allotment letters*

When the Government offers bonds for sale by application or tender, these bonds are not issued in registered form. Successful applicants for these issues receive an 'allotment letter', which is itself a document of title, but in bearer form for a limited period, during which further call money may be due. Whilst still in allotment letter form, delivery is simplified in that no signatures or seal are required; but settlement for bonds sold may be delayed in the case of part sales, sales when bonds bought have not yet been delivered, or when call money or registration is due. At the end of the allotment letter period, these bonds should be registered into the name of the new owner or his nominee. Special registration facilities exist and it is important that they are used if an early sale is probable. Once again CGO participants have special facilities which enable them to avoid most of these delays.

## Settlement procedures

Since CGO participants have special facilities, it follows that when an investor buys, unless the market is short of that particular issue, then the bonds will be delivered on settlement day and must be paid for value that day; for example, if by cheque, this should be drawn on the City branch of a clearing bank. Sale proceeds will similarly be paid for value the date of delivery of the bonds sold.

Because most investors do not have special facilities, it is important that when they buy bonds they are aware of the problems attaching to an early sale, and that when they sell they should already have taken such steps as are possible to avoid (expensive) settlement delays. In this respect, it should be noted that the possible delays mentioned here relate to current procedures on gilts only, and that other erroneously called 'gilt-edged' securities may be subject to different formalities.

A summary of the salient points and problems of settlement is incorporated in the following sections.

### Market-makers settlement

A market-maker is committed to make markets to users of the market generally, and it is one of the fundamental concepts of his trading that he may sell bonds which he does not possess (and which he may not acquire for a considerable time). Conversely, he may purchase bonds (sometimes in large quantities) for which he has no immediate buyer. The consequences which stem from this situation in fact underpin the basic relationship between investor and the market as follows.

In order to take maximum advantage from, or to correct imbalances in, the market place, a market-maker has the choice (subject to availability) of borrowing or depositing money, and borrowing, lending or pledging bonds. He may also deal with other Stock Exchange member firms including, therefore, money brokers, and, under some circumstances, with the Bank of England. Indirectly involved are discount houses, banks and institutional investors. When a market-maker deals with a non-CGO member then a transfer form and certificate (or suitable alternative) pass between them.

Transfer of bonds between CGO members uses the computerised paperless system known as 'book entry transfer' and the facilities provided cover most of the bonds for which the Bank of England acts as registrar. The system permits presentation of a transfer to the CGO where the relevant details are captured within the system and against which bonds up to that amount (and any other already held) can be transferred. Interest payments are made by the Bank of England in the usual way. All necessary information for participants in the system is available on computer screens, with immediate printout facilities, and there are identical back-up systems for both the computer and power sources, and security safeguards to protect confidentiality at a variety of levels.

Once bonds are held within the system they can be transferred:

(a) to any non-CGO member by means of an enfaced transfer form ('enfacement' is a statement on the transfer that the underlying securities are held by the CGO for the new owner), or
(b) to another CGO member by book entry transfer, i.e. by an entry being made on a computer terminal – without the need for transfer forms or certificates.

At the end of each business day information is passed to the registrar concerning the movement of bonds within the CGO system, and the register remains the prime record of legal title. It is also possible for bonds in allotment-letter form to be taken within the CGO system and for ownership to be changed by computerised entry, or to be withdrawn, although the registrar will not be advised of such movements of unregistered securities.

An integral part of this computerised system is an assured payments routine such that irrevocable instructions for guaranteed payments are generated simultaneously with movement of bonds between CGO accounts. The buyer and seller of bonds are thus equally protected. Banks operating the town clearing and Clearing Houses Automated Payment System (CHAPS) systems participate on appointment by a CGO member. A paying bank's position is that, in exchange, there are either bonds held by the CGO for that bank's client or, if sold on, a corresponding irrevocable cash commitment from another settlement bank. The banks are advised by the CGO daily of only the up-to-date net cash position of each client, rather than individual transactions.

This entire concept of computerised transfer is based on the principle of positive acceptance by the taker of both the nominal value of the bonds in question and the cash consideration which have been input by the giver. In the case of non-acceptance, neither bonds nor cash will move within the system.

Movements of bonds into and out of the system which have a cash value of over £100,000 are equally protected by assured payment and there are provisions to protect the banks in the event of the liquidation of a CGO member. Because of the volume of business and the number of his counterparties, a market-maker will need to know as soon as possible, with as much accuracy as possible, the total of all movements of bonds for the day, and he will then need as long a time as possible to deal with the bond/cash adjustments and arrangements. It is for these reasons, and to achieve an orderly settlement, that delivery formalities and deadlines are imposed. From the market-maker's point of view, one of the most important deadlines is that parties to transactions have until 11.15 a.m. to tell each other which bonds they will be delivering that day. It is from this 'call over' that the market-maker projects his bond and cash requirements and commitments.

*Settlement with investors*

The earliest job on settlement day is to contact investors who have sold – firstly in order to arrange collection/receipt of executed transfers and certificates, or other documents, in time to meet the deadlines explained below, and, secondly, in order to advise the market-making departments by 11.15 a.m. of all deliveries that will be made that day. The final time for actual delivery to the market-maker of registered allotment letter or bearer securities is 12.45 p.m.

The client counterparty will require to receive the transfer before that time in order to process even a straightforward delivery (say 12.15 p.m.), earlier for a Stock Exchange certification (11.45 a.m.), as early as 10.45 a.m. for some Bank of England certifications (registered securities), whilst the earliest could be 10.15 a.m. for recently registered allotment letters, although these times could vary slightly either way, depending on how busy the market is.

*Sales*

An executed transfer in respect of registered bonds sold by an investor should, where possible, be accompanied by a certificate for the exact amount. However, this is not always possible, because of the following factors:

1.  The certificate may be for more than the amount of the bond sold, in which case the transfer form can be presented with the larger certificate by the client counterparty to The Stock Exchange, which then forwards details and the certificate to the registrar and certifies on the transfer that it has done so. This certified transfer is then good for delivery. The balance of the bonds due may be held to the order of any member, for a period of up to two months, during which further sale transfers may be certified at The Stock Exchange (i.e. subject only to the deadline of 12.45 p.m. for subsequent delivery to the market-maker). If a 'balance certificate' is requested, this would be issued by the Bank of England in about eight days.
2.  The certificate may be in course of preparation:

(a)   where a certificate has been requested, i.e. as in (1.) above;
(b)   from a recent registration or after a sale certification against part only of a recent registration;
(c)   from recent registration of an allotment letter; or
(d)   a transfer form relating to a recent purchase may not yet have been sent for registration.

'Certification' is a statement on the transfer that the bonds covering the sale have been lodged with the registrar/agent. Under (a) however, although lodgement has to be made by 11.15 a.m. on or after the first day following the request, there may still be a delay in certification, and therefore in delivery also. The above deadlines are critical and, since the client counterparty has to process the transfers before taking them to the Stock Exchange, it follows that he himself will require the documents up to half-an-hour before the times given above, perhaps earlier if the market is very busy, and on this basis the deadlines could vary between 10.15 a.m. and 12.15 p.m.

3.   Bonds sold through one party may have been purchased through another. The basic settlement formalities do not vary, but if the bargains were dealt on different days, there might be a slight further settlement delay when the formalities cannot be completed in time to meet the deadlines.

4.   The certificate may be lost, in which case settlement is delayed until a form of indemnity has been completed and lodged with the Bank of England. The entire procedure, including certification of the executed transfer form, normally delays settlement between two and five days.

5.   Although the foregoing refers to registered securities, it should be mentioned here that there will be a delay in the settlement of allotment letter and bearer bonds in the case of partial sales or sales to different parties where the denominations held cannot be matched to the exact amount sold. Allotment letters will then need to be split by the registrar. To instigate this, the allotment letter should be forwarded to the registrar with a note detailing the required splits, which are then normally available within twenty-four hours.

6.   Bonds purchased may not yet have been delivered by the seller (i.e. the purchase and sale may have been dealt on the same day; the seller may have been short of the bond purchased; or the purchase may have been for deferred settlement). When such purchases are due for settlement, like or part sales can normally be 'made up' (i.e. set off against those purchases, so that no bonds pass). However, the following points should be noted:
(a)   'Making up' is not possible when either bargain is a gilt which has been dealt specially ex-dividend (Sp. *XD*) prior to going officially ex-dividend.

(b) Nor can any cum-dividend bargain be made up with any ordinarily ex-dividend bargain.

(c) Neither is it possible to 'make up' allotment letter bargains if dealt through different market-makers (this also applies equally to bearer transactions). Furthermore, even if the bargains are transacted with the same market-maker, there may be difficulty in making-up when the amounts purchased and sold are not identical. These restrictions may not apply to allotment letters when the bonds are held within the CGO system.

(d) When a bargain cannot be made up under (c) above, the investor may be out of money for one day if the first seller does not deliver the bonds in time for the second seller to send them out against his sale within the normal time limits.

(e) When a bargain cannot be 'made up' under (a) and (b) above, then, after paying for the purchase, settlement of bonds sold specially ex-dividend is delayed:

(i) until the next Stock Exchange business day in all cases;

(ii) until the day after the security is quoted officially ex-dividend, in cases where the special ex-dividend sale cannot be matched exactly with the transfer(s) delivered against the purchase, unless the sale is in excess by an amount which was purchased ordinarily.

In cases where correct 'shapes' might not be available to cover sales of allotment letters or special ex-dividend bargains, the resulting settlement delay could be avoided by asking for splits at the time of dealing for the purchase.

The facility to 'make up' afforded by the market-maker is not mandatory; (c) above cites examples where he does not, or may not, provide the facility, whilst (a) and (b) quote instances where 'make-ups' are forbidden under Stock Exchange rules. If a market-maker should withdraw this facility for any other reason, then the minimum settlement delay would be as in (d) or (e) (i).

*Payment for sales*

When the client counterparty is able to deliver sold gilt-edged bonds to the market-maker, or when the bargain is 'made up', the cash proceeds of the sale can be paid to the investor or his agent, either against delivery of the documents or by independent payment. The payment is made either by cheque drawn on the City branch of a clearing bank or, alternatively, by direct credit to a nominated bank account, either by telegraphic transfer or by using

223

CHAPS. If payment is made by direct credit, the recipient has no control over the paying-in, but, equally, saves the administration cost. When an investor is due both to pay and to receive money on the same day in respect of deals with the same broker, he may choose either to pay and receive in full both ways, or to settle simply the final balance.

*Payment for purchases*

Payment for bonds purchased may also be made as above to the broker's account. Payment can be made by any party, and may similarly be against delivery of documents or by separate payment. In some instances one party to a transaction may insist that settlement takes place by exchanging a banker's draft for the relevant bonds. Such a draft guarantees to the recipient that payment will be honoured, whereas the ordinary methods of payment fail if there are insufficient funds in the account in question.

*Registration of bonds*

When government securities that have been purchased are registered into the name of the buyer or his nominee, special procedures are available. The Bank of England has issued a comprehensive notice (dated August 1979) which sets out the various methods and times of registering transfers and allotment letters, and also quotes the methods and times by which (pending the issue of certificates) sale transfers will be validated – i.e. 'certified' for delivery. If investors wish to handle their own registration, then a detailed knowledge of this document is essential. However, large investors would be well advised to delegate these matters to a professional on the spot.

The following special procedure is intended for use when a sale is anticipated before the certificate would otherwise be in the hands of the seller:

1. A special two-part receipt form is available for registration of registered securities. If lodged with a valid transfer form at the Bank of England before 11.15 a.m., then a receipt is given and a sale transfer against all or part of those bonds (if similarly lodged before 11.15 a.m., from the next day onwards) will be certified for delivery on that day. When registering bonds in this way, care should be taken not to lodge too early in case a sale for same-day settlement should be made (possible up to 11.00 a.m.), in which case –

2. The original purchase deed, without the two-part form, should be presented to the Bank before 11.15 a.m. with the executed sale transfer, for certification and delivery on that day.

3. When allotment letters are presented for registration (the time is normally 3.00 p.m. at the Bank of England) a different 'special' form should be used, but, again, a receipt is issued. In this case, certification

and delivery are not possible on the next Stock Exchange business day, but would be available one day later.

Sale transfers lodged for certification in other circumstances, or with other supporting documents (e.g. probate or power of attorney), will be subject to varying delays, depending on the method and time of lodgement, for both registration and certification. The Bank of England's notice sets out the problems in concise detail. It is sufficient here to illustrate the complexity by pointing out that, for example, a transfer lodged for registration at the Bank, and received in the second postal delivery at about noon, is in fact deemed to have been received one day later than a transfer received after 3.30 p.m. on the same day in the second delivery bag direct from the Stock Exchange.

Certificates arising from special registrations of registered bonds are normally available after eight working days, but quite often take considerably longer when allotment letters are registered. There is frequently a further delay because certificates are despatched by post (except to Stock Exchange members and to others who have made special arrangements).

# 13

## *The sterling bond market: an historical overview*

Back in the early 1960s long before the emergence of 'the global market-place' life was relatively straightforward for most UK investors, both institutional and private. Unless, by chance, they had some way of taking a direct interest in property their main investment options were basically restricted to choosing between UK equities and UK fixed-interest securities. Overseas investment, whilst not prohibited, was severely limited by the need for all such transactions to be carried out via a pool of investment dollars whose rate of exchange traded at a premium (the 'dollar premium') over the commercial rate, and the further requirement that on realisation of such an investment a proportion (25%) of that premium be surrendered to the UK authorities. This and restrictions in other financial walks of life were all part of the panoply of exchange control regulations under which the UK toiled until the incoming Conservative government of Margaret Thatcher abolished them in October 1979.

The prime reason for the existence of these controls was the persistent weakness of sterling during this period which, not suprisingly, also proved to be a major deterrent to inward portfolio investment by foreigners. As a result the development of markets and instruments of investment in these years was, to all intents and purposes, wholly dictated by domestic influences and almost totally insulated from those from abroad.

For the fixed-interest investor in those days there was a varied selection of potential investments from which to choose. In the public sector apart from the prime security of gilts, there was a thriving market in local government securities, and a similar market in issues of the Commonwealth Governments and various public boards. In the corporate sector there was a regular flow of debentures and loan stocks from commercial and industrial companies both large and small, and a steady but rather smaller issuance of preference shares. There were also a number of convertible loan stocks and convertible preference shares which although, in effect, are quasi-equities were traded under the Stock Exchange's fixed interest market rules.

The main point of differentiation between the public sector and corporate sector bonds was that the former were exempt from stamp duty whilst

226

purchases of the latter category were subject to this duty at an *ad valorem* rate (which at various different times ranged from 2% to $\frac{1}{2}$%) up to May 1976, and again for a short period in 1986. As a result fixed-interest investors would tend to 'lock away' their holdings of corporate bonds and use the public sector bonds, gilts in particular, as their vehicles for active trading. In this regard it should be realised that until the Budget of 1965 institutions were not subject to capital gains tax and gilt-edged anomaly switching was a major, if not the major constituent of overall fixed-interest market turnover.

The 1965 Budget, the first of the incoming Labour Government of Harold Wilson following his narrow victory in the previous November, was revolutionary in its impact upon the United Kingdom's securities markets. Apart from introducing a comprehensive capital gains tax regime from which basically only pension funds were exempt, it, or to be precise the Finance Act which followed it, completely changed the basis of corporate taxation replacing the previous profits tax with a new corporation tax. Under the new tax, equity and preference dividends had to be paid out of profits remaining after the deduction of 40% corporation tax, but debenture and loan stock interest was deductible from gross profits before computing this tax. This meant that it was considerably more advantageous for companies to finance themselves by making debt issues than by issuing equities or preference shares; and the resultant shortage of equities distorted the UK capital markets for some years until the situation was alleviated by some corporation tax modifications introduced by the Conservative Government of Edward Heath in the early 1970s.

The advent of corporation tax in 1965 also introduced for the first time the concept of 'franked income'. This is income such as equity or preference share dividends that has been derived from a profit stream that has already borne corporation tax; and where this income itself forms part of a profit stream of another corporation tax paying entity the fact that it has been 'franked' exempts it from being (corporation) taxed for a second time. Franked income therefore became considerably more valuable than unfranked income in the hands of UK insurance companies, investment trusts and other corporate investors but not so in the hands of private investors or exempt pension funds. This influence, coupled with the equity scarcity referred to above, raised the relative valuation of franked income producing securities to a level where, in 1966, wholesale portfolio exchanges were conducted between gross funds selling preference shares and buying debentures and loans, and insurance companies and the like doing precisely the opposite, resulting in gains in yield for both parties after allowing for their respective tax treatments.

In the late 1960s inflation started to accelerate away from the 1%–6% range in which it had fluctuated for most of the previous post-war period. This acceleration continued unabated in the first half of the 1970s culminating in a figure of 26.9% recorded as the year-on-year change in the RPI for August 1975. Although there was a temporary dip in inflation to 7.4% for June 1978 it then rose again to a second peak of 21.9% in May 1980.

As inflation rose so too did nominal yields on fixed interest securities, so much so that issuers of such securities other than the central Government and a handful of local government authorities effectively abandoned the UK fixed interest new issue market. Commonwealth Governments such as Australia and New Zealand found it possible to borrow more cheaply in currencies other than sterling via the developing Euromarkets, whilst UK corporate financing became increasingly a matter of bank borrowing relieved from time to time by the occasional equity rights issue. The principal driving force behind all this was the wholly understandable reluctance of corporate treasurers to commit their companies to paying 'double-figure' nominal coupon rates for twenty or twenty-five years when there was some possibility that rates would revert to more normal levels before that period was over. It has also been argued that the very presence of an avaricious borrower in the form of H.M. Government crowded out potential corporate borrowers from the market during these years, but whilst this influence was undeniably present it was probably only of secondary importance.

The net result of these circumstances was that between the early 1970s and 1982 there was virtually no issuance of corporate debt in the UK. One spark of new life did, however, burst upon the scene towards the end of that period. On 29 July 1980 the so-called 'bulldog' market was born with the issue of £75 million Kingdom of Denmark 13% 2005. This was followed in January 1981 by a rather smaller thirty-five year issue for Iceland (£15 million Iceland $14\frac{1}{2}$% 2016) and thereafter a number of overseas borrowers, some, but not all, sovereign credits, made their way to this new market. In the midst of this foreign borrower activity the long-dated 'corporation' market was reopened in March 1981 by the issuance of £50 million City of Leeds $13\frac{1}{2}$% 2006 – the first local authority issue with a maturity of over twenty years since 1967 – and in April 1981 a £7 million placing of City of Swansea $13\frac{3}{4}$% 2006 followed this.

But it was not until 1982 that the non-gilt sterling bond markets really began to resume new issue activity. In that year long-dated gilt-edged yields fell from over $15\frac{1}{2}$% in January to below 11% as the year came to a close. The first chink of light was the emergence of a £100 million Subordinated Loan Stock for Barclays Bank dated 2002/07. This was issued in February of that year and carried a 16% coupon and was issued at par. In June the Midland Bank followed suit with £100 million 14% 2002/07 yielding 14.21% and in September the first substantial industrial fixed-interest for over ten years appeared in the form of a £100 million placing of $12\frac{1}{4}$% Unsecured Loan

Stock 2012/17 for BOC Group plc. There followed a reasonable flow of new issues; and whilst this could by no means be described as a feast at least the long corporate bond market famine was over.

At about the same time, in the summer of 1982, activity in the Sterling Eurobond market started to develop to sufficient extent that the Bank of England felt it necessary to bring it within arrangements, already applicable to the domestic market, to seek prior consent of the Bank for the timing of new issues. There had been, in February 1982 a £25 million seven-year Eurosterling issue for Reed International – the first time since the abolition of exchange controls that this market had been used by a UK manufacturing company –, three further issues between March and May, and four £30 million issues between June and August. These were all at the shorter end of the market in the five to seven year maturity bracket and would not normally attract the interest of the institutions whose more usual diet would comprise bonds with a twenty year life or longer. Nevertheless, this action on the part of the authorities was an early recognition of the development potential of the Eurosterling bond market.

One factor which at this time kept the domestic and Eurosterling bond markets at arm's length was the fact that main market participants in each of them operated in two distinct camps. The domestic market was almost entirely populated by London Stock Exchange member firms and was subject to Stock Exchange rules, minimum commission scales etc, whereas Eurosterling market activity was mainly the preserve of members of what was then called The Association of International Bond Dealers (AIBD) and is now known as the International Securities Market Association (ISMA). Although it was possible for a Stock Exchange firm to have one foot also in the AIBD camp – few firms took advantage of this (Strauss Turnbull being a notable exception) – foreign or corporate membership of the Stock Exchange was not permissible until the advent of London's 'Big Bang' in 1986. And thus it was that the structural changes brought about by 'Big Bang', enabling wider Exchange membership and permitting the formation, for the first time in the UK, of alliances of banking, market-making and distribution within a single operating entity opened the way for the development of the sterling bond markets as they are today. But before tracing that development further one must note a number of events that took place just prior to 'Big Bang'.

Possibly the most significant of these was the change in the capital gains tax treatment on what are now known as 'qualifying corporate bonds' (QCBs). This occurred in two stages. Firstly it was announced in the Budget of 1984 that QCBs would, with effect from 13 March 1984, be subject to capital gains tax on the same basis as gilts (broadly speaking they would be tax free if held for more than a year); and when capital gains tax on gilts was abolished on 2 July 1986 this was also extended to QCBs. Hand in hand with the 1986 abolition of capital gains tax came the introduction, on 28 February of that year, of the accrued income scheme which included QCBs within its scope. The workings of the accrued income scheme were described in Chapter 10; suffice it to say that under it items chargeable to income tax include interest payments received plus gross accrued interest at the time of sale, minus gross accrued interest at the time of purchase, whilst capital values are now related to 'clean' rather than 'dirty' prices.

As if that was not enough change for one year the 1986 Budget introduced a further complication for the UK domestic corporate bond market by reimposing stamp duty on registered domestic issues at an *ad valorem* rate of $\frac{1}{2}\%$. The reasons for this were not totally clear and it was quickly acknowledged to be counterproductive; but until this action was finally rescinded sometime later that year it gave Eurosterling issues, which were not subject to stamp duty, a conspicuous temporary advantage over their domestic counterparts and opened the eyes of many practitioners to the potential of the Sterling Eurobond market for the first time.

Since then the pattern of new issue activity has shifted steadily in the direction of the Eurosterling market and domestic bond issues, whilst not extinct, are becoming increasingly rare. The principal reasons for this trend have been lower issuing costs for borrowers, greater flexibility in the methods of issuance, wider potential distribution, and the ability to bring issues at short notice as and when windows of opportunity (often swap related) occur. With regard to this last point it should be stated that the queueing arrangements for new issues previously required by the Bank of England were relaxed in 1988.

In the late 1980s this movement towards greater market flexibility coincided with a three year period, 1988-90, when the UK public finances were in substantial surplus and the authorities were engaged in buying-in, rather than issuing, gilts. These conditions proved very favourable for the continuing rehabilitation of the sterling bond market, and the Eurosterling sector was further boosted by the capital flows attracted during the period of the UK's membership of the Exchange Rate Mechanism (ERM) between October 1990 and September 1992.

The pace of legislative change which had been so strong in the mid 1980s slackened thereafter and where change did take place it was usually in the direction of deregulation. In 1988 the maximum size restriction on Eurosterling issues was lifted and a year later the control of borrowing order was eliminated, this latter action opening the way for the establishment of the medium term note (MTN) programmes. However, what may eventually prove to be the most highly significant piece of legislation to affect this market, have been the proposals of the November 1994 Budget to extend the range of eligible investments for general personal equity plans (PEPs) to certain corporate bonds, preference shares and convertible issues. The effect of this liberalisation will be to open up the corporate bond market to a level of potential retail demand not previously experienced. The detailed PEP proposals were announced on 31 March 1995 and came into effect in the summer of 1995 following the passage of the 1995 Finance Act.

In summary they are as follows:

Qualifying PEP bonds must be:

1. Sterling denominated
2. issued at a fixed rate of interest
3. have a minimum life of five years at the time of acquisition
4. must satisfy certain listing requirements.

Qualifying companies must *not* be:

financial companies (e.g. banks, building societies)

and must be:

if corporate or convertible bonds, incorporated in the UK
if preference shares or convertible prefs, incorporated in an E.U. state.

When the initial Budget announcement was made there was considerable doubt whether the scope of this development would include Eurosterling bonds or be restricted to domestic issues. There was considerable relief, therefore, when it was confirmed that Eurosterling issues would be eligible in this regard. It should, however, be noted that gilts, index-linked issues, bull-dogs, and permanent interest bearing shares (PIBS) are specifically *not* eligible for PEP investment.

# 14

## Debentures and loan stocks

### Terminology

First a note is in order regarding the terminology used in this chapter.

As far as possible in this book we have tried to keep to the use of the word 'bond' to describe a fixed interest security as has become general international practice, and to avoid using the word 'stock', which although it is customary in this context in the UK is synonymous with equities in US parlance. The reason for this has been to try and avoid any possible confusion in the minds of those readers not readily conversant with UK conventions.

In this chapter, however, the use of the word 'stock' will become unavoidable because it figures directly in the official titles of the vast majority of the instruments under consideration, for example:

Land Securities plc 10% First Mortgage Debenture Stock 2025, or
B.A.T. Industries plc 12¼% Unsecured Loan Stock 2003/08

and whenever encountered in this chapter 'stock' can be taken to refer to fixed interest securities and not equities.

At the same time it is worth explaining the scope of the following analysis. For the purpose of this book debentures and loan stocks are defined as bonds issued in the UK by companies and other bodies incorporated in the United Kingdom. The scope of this chapter does not extend to those bonds which are convertible into equity which are traded, settled and taxed differently.

### Description and market background

Debenture and loan stocks have been a common source of long-term funding for joint stock companies since the earliest days. Indeed, a number of debentures currently listed on the London Stock Exchange were issued in the last century. In modern times, the size and importance of the domestic debenture and loan stock market has waxed and waned. After a period of strong growth in the 1960s, supply was choked off in 1972 by the high absolute rates of interest which accompanied soaring inflation rates. Few treasurers or finance

232

directors were prepared to issue stocks with ultra high coupons fixed for twenty years or more and, consequently, the following ten years was a period of net redemptions.

Issuance resumed in the 1980s but, as described in the previous chapter, major borrowers have increasingly preferred to use the Eurosterling market because of its greater general flexibility. Nevertheless, the domestic market is not insignificant. It is the only source of long term debt finance for smaller companies, and for most investors it provides the only available pool of securities backed by a charge on assets.

Maturities range from a few weeks to over forty years and a number of perpetual stocks (with no final maturity date) are available. For many years the greatest demand for domestic debentures and loan stocks has come from UK life assurance companies wishing to match their long-term liabilities and bonds have tended to be issued with twenty to thirty year maturities to satisfy this perceived demand. As savings products change, and with pension funds increasing their fixed interest weightings as they become more mature in a lower inflation environment, there are signs that a broader range of maturities is appropriate. This trend may well be enforced by the prospective PEP demand (see Chapter 13) since many intermediaries appear to feel more comfortable with stocks in the five to fifteen year maturity bracket. Another trend is the gradual disappearance of double-dated stocks and stocks with sinking funds. Once common, many stocks with such features issued in the 1960s and 1970s have been falling due for repayment, but the strong investor preference for bullet maturities without call features has restricted their replacement. The remaining double-dated stocks are most commonly callable at par by the issuer on three month's notice at any time within the two dates.

## Status and security

### (a) Debentures

In law, a debenture is a document which creates or acknowledges a debt due from a company and is usually given under seal. However, the London Stock Exchange listing requirements limit the use of the term 'debenture' to secured debt securities. An unsecured issue will fail to meet the listing criteria if it is described as an issue of debentures; instead it must be called a 'loan note' or an 'unsecured loan stock'. In this book we shall follow Stock Exchange practice whereby debentures refer to secured debt.

Debt can be secured in one of two ways; by means of a floating charge or by way of a fixed charge (or, sometimes, a combination of the two). In essence a floating charge gives creditors a general charge over all the borrower's assets, whereas a fixed charge gives investors a more precise charge over certain specific assets. The nature of such charges and the powers and abilities of the two types of charge holders to enforce their rights are governed by the Insolvency Act 1986. This is of necessity a detailed and complex subject, and it is beyond the scope of this book to delve into all the various practicalities of, and differences between, these two types of charge. Suffice it to say that the secured debt of an issuer will, all other things being equal, normally be regarded as safer than the equivalent unsecured debt, and accordingly can be expected to offer a lower yield.

Most debenture issues involve substantial documentation. The listing particulars are required to contain detail of, amongst other things, the covenants and events of default contained in the trust deed. With such issues it is common to find covenants which require the maintenance of a minimum capital cover which is defined as the ratio of the value of the pledged assets to the size of the secured debt. Rather less common are minimum income cover covenants which are intended to control the relationship between total interest cost and profits before tax and debt servicing. Additionally, the issuer may covenant to limit the issuance of any prior ranking stock. For the investor these covenants provide additional reassurance regarding the security of the bond over and above the creditworthiness of the issuer. In the event of the company failing to meet its obligations, secured debt holders can exercise their claim on the secured assets to enforce the security and recover the face value of their bond together with any arrears of accrued interest.

The nature of secured debt does not sit comfortably with the system of credit rating assessment which is pivotal to considerations of unsecured debt. This is because in the case of secured debt it is the quality and value of the pledged assets which are of primary importance to the investor, rather than the overall credit standing of the issuer. Indeed it is possible to envisage circumstances where holders of secured debt in an ailing company could stand to benefit, by being repaid at par, in the event of that company's failure. Also the nature, quality and liquidity of secured assets varies tremendously from one issue to another.

Many trust deeds incorporate a facility for issuers to substitute secured assets to the satisfaction of the trustees but without the necessity of notifying bondholders, and this further exacerbates the problem of making formal ratings. Knowledge regarding substitutions of assets is, however, important for investors and notification of significant substitutions and the submission of an annual report of charged assets have increasingly been required, particularly on more recent debenture issues.

The debenture market is dominated by UK property and hotel groups, breweries and investment trusts. These issuers all have suitable assets upon which loans may be charged. Historically, the finest terms (and hence the lowest yields) have been assigned to investment trust debentures where the underlying assets, being predominantly listed securities, are both liquid and easily valued. Capital cover (the ratio of value of the secured assets to the nominal size of the debt) can be extremely large, particularly in cases of old issues where the value of underlying assets has grown over the years while the nominal amount of the debt has remained static.

Brewery debentures have traditionally enjoyed good demand and trade on fine terms, reflecting the high quality nature of the cash flows and security of principal afforded by that industry. However, implementation of the recommendations of the monopoly and mergers commission report on the UK brewery industry in 1990 has effectively split the roles of brewing and distribution; and thereby hampered the prospects for any significant issuance from this sector in recent years. Property groups have long accessed the debenture market for financing their various needs, and all sectors of the property market from blue chip 'investment' groups through traditional development companies to the more aggressive trading orientated companies can be found in the debenture market.

To sum up, debentures are highly covenanted issues, secured on assets of such quality as to be highly acceptable to most investors; in the event of default, holders have strong legal protection under law and will rank ahead of ordinary unsecured creditors. Debentures are unrated and generally trade on lower yields than their equivalent unsecured debt to reflect the lower risk of loss on default.

*(b)  Unsecured loan stocks*

These stocks are unsecured obligations of the issuer and bondholders have no charge over any of the issuer's assets, relying on guarantees from the issuer (or additionally from other bodies connected with the issuer such as a parent company) for the timely payment of interest and principal. However, in contrast to most unsecured Eurosterling bonds, these unsecured domestic stocks often carry strong covenants and pledges which protect bondholders' interests.

In contrast to debentures, some domestic unsecured loan stocks carry credit ratings from either Standard & Poor's or Moody's, particularly those issues guaranteed by companies with strong overseas interests and/or recognition. In addition, some UK corporates with little or no overseas connections, are increasingly being assigned ratings by the UK based agency IBCA. The assignment of ratings to such stocks has broadened the investor base and further facilitates the assessment of value of individual issues.

The unsecured loan market is not dominated by any one particular sector and is composed of issues from a broad spectrum of UK based companies. In addition to corporate loan stocks, various local government bodies such as city and metropolitan authorities (collectively known as corporation and county stocks in the Stock Exchange Daily Official List) and certain public boards have outstanding issues. In the past these local government issues were considered closer to the gilt-edged market than the corporate bond market – one reason for this being that they, like gilts, were never ever subject to stamp duty whilst debentures and loans used to suffer that impost – but more latterly have tended to be traded together with corporate debt. For a long time, and until quite recently, local authority issues disappeared from the scene as cheaper funding was made available to them via the Public Works Loan Board (PWLB), but the emergence of four new issues from local authorities in the period September 1993 – March 1995 is evidence that the domestic market remains an important source of long term funds for this sector.

The advantages of the Eurosterling market to issuers has caused the domestic market's importance to dwindle significantly in recent years. However, certain types of bodies, such as local authorities, are unable to make Eurobond issues and the domestic market remains their only route for funding through the debt capital markets. In addition, housing associations and higher education establishments, whose appeal lies mainly with UK based institutions, also use the domestic market for raising funds. The financing needs of these three sectors are set to grow substantially over the coming years as public sector support is reduced and replaced with private sector finance.

As well as new issues for cash, loan stocks have frequently been issued as part of the consideration in takeover bids. For example, B.A.T. Industries $12\frac{1}{4}\%$ Unsecured Loan Stock 2003/08 was issued to the ordinary shareholders of Eagle Star Holdings plc and Hambro Life Assurance plc (subsequently Allied Dunbar) in the course of their acquisition.

In the future, the proposals to allow corporate loan stocks of UK based issuers to be eligible for inclusion in PEPs may enable the domestic loan stock market to be revived as some smaller companies, lacking access to the Eurosterling market through lack of international recognition, take advantage of the greater domestic demand expected as a result of the new proposals. This may present many new opportunities for private investors as relatively well-known companies come to use the domestic loan stock market as an additional means of raising finance.

## Form and denomination

With few exceptions, debenture and loan stocks exist in registered form and are commonly transferrable in multiples of £1. By definition, all listed debenture and loan stocks are listed on the London Stock Exchange. Unlisted stocks which may previously have traded under Stock Exchange rule 4.2(a) will after 29 September 1995 have to be traded off market.

Coupons are usually payable semi-annually in arrears. However, some issues, such as LCC 3% Consolidated Stock 1920 or after, or the more recently issued University of Lancaster $9\frac{3}{4}\%$ First Mortgage Debenture Stock 2025, make their coupon payments on a quarterly basis.

## Dealing arrangements

Prices of debentures and loans are quoted as a percentage of their principal amount. The more active, or liquid, bonds trade on a $\frac{3}{8}\%$ to $\frac{1}{2}\%$ price spread i.e. the price at which an investor can sell stock is $\frac{3}{8}\%$ to $\frac{1}{2}\%$ lower than the price at which he can buy stock. However, some very liquid bonds (such as Allied Domecq $9\frac{3}{4}\%$ 2019 and Land Securities 10% 2025) may trade on a narrower $\frac{1}{4}\%$ spread in sizes up to £2.5 million nominal. Conversely, some of the more illiquid issues tend to trade on a $\frac{3}{4}\%$ to 1% spread, and others (particularly those issues where little remains outstanding and/or where their life to maturity is very short) on a negotiated basis only. Special prices may be quoted for very small amounts, but generally the smaller denominations of debentures and loans compared to Eurobonds allow much greater flexibility in investing broken cash values, and modest amounts may often be traded without a price penalty.

## Price conventions, accrued interest and ex-dividend arrangements

As with gilt-edged stocks and bulldogs, prices of debentures and loans are quoted 'clean' i.e. exclusive of gross accrued interest, so that the total price paid by a buyer will have two component parts, (a) the quoted price and (b) the gross accrued interest. This latter quantity is the amount of interest that has accrued between the last interest payment date (or in the case of a new issue, the issue payment date) and the transaction's settlement date as explained in Chapter 4. The calendar convention used for debentures and loans is that of the actual number of days between the relevant dates and a 365-day year.

As with gilts, debentures and loans have an ex-dividend period prior to the payment date. However, unlike gilts, the date on which bonds go ex-dividend in relation to the coupon payment date can vary significantly. It is also possible to deal 'special ex-dividend' up to seven calendar days before the official ex-dividend date. In this special ex-dividend period, trades may occur in either cum-dividend or ex-dividend form but, unless otherwise specified, prices are considered to be in cum-dividend form. In contrast to the gilt market, special cum-dividend trades may be agreed at any time before the actual interest payment date, even though the stock is officially ex-dividend. Trades in unlisted securities are assumed to be cum-dividend unless otherwise specified since no official ex-dividend date is prescribed.

## Stamp duty and levies

In contrast to preference shares and convertibles, no stamp duty is payable on transfers of most straight debentures and loans, but each contract for a consideration in excess of £10,000 is subject to a levy (currently £1) to fund the Panel for Takeovers and Mergers.

## Commission

A stockbroker acting as an investor's agent may charge a client commission for carrying out transactions in debentures and loans in accordance with individual client agreements.

## Settlement

Unless otherwise agreed at the time of dealing, settlement of the vast majority of debentures and loans occurs through the Talisman system five business days after the trade date. Most UK based stockbrokers will be familiar with this system from their experience of settling UK equity bargains. The loan stocks of public boards (e.g. Port of London Authority) and local authorities are normally traded for settlement on the business day following the transaction. Settlement of trades transacted in the few stocks which trade outside Talisman is agreed at the time of dealing for a day convenient for both parties. These bonds are listed in Appendix I at the end of this chapter.

## Custody

No custodial facilities are required for registered stock, although the introduction of a new dematerialised settlement system, CREST, in 1996, may encourage investors, especially active investors, to arrange holding facilities with a stockbroker in the future. However, one of the advantages of registering the stock directly in the beneficial owner's name is that the listing agreement provides for the stockholder to receive copies of the annual report and accounts and the interim statement, which will not be the case with bonds held in nominee accounts.

Since debenture and loan stockholders do not have the right to vote in general meetings, there is no additional disadvantage to holding stock in a nominee name or personal equity plan in this regard.

## New issues procedures

Under the traditional issuing procedure, a lead manager is appointed and takes responsibility for negotiating the terms (e.g. coupon, maturity etc.), conditions (e.g. definition of events of default etc.) and price of the new issue. This manager will normally undertake to underwrite the whole issue. In addition to the underwriter, the issuer may choose to appoint a sponsor and/or stockbroker who will normally be responsible for distributing the new issue. If not appointed, the underwriter will undertake both functions. Conversely, the responsibility for both underwriting and distributing may be shared between several firms.

Most domestic new issues are announced early in the day and subsequently placed/sold to investors following a Stock Exchange announcement. It has been standard practice to price the new issue by reference to a yield margin over that of a specified gilt at a given time, most usually 3.00 p.m., on the day of issue. This allows potential investors to examine the terms of the issue on a comparative basis against gilts as soon as the issue is announced whilst the absolute price is not determined until later in the day. At that point a further Stock Exchange announcement detailing the result of the fixing is made.

For smaller issues (under £50 million) or those of a specialist nature which may necessitate a substantial element of pre-placing, the bonds might well be placed on a fixed price basis without going through the above process. Payment for new issues is usually required within a few days of the original placing.

## Partly-paid issues

The more usual form is for new issues in this market to be made fully-paid, but from time to time partly-paid issues occur where an initial down payment is made at the time of issue followed by the balance in instalments at a later date or dates. For example, if a stock is issued in partly-paid form with an issue price of £98.60, it may have, say, £20 as the initial down payment, with, say, two further calls of £40 and £38.60 due for payment two and four months respectively later on.

The decision whether to issue in fully-paid or partly-paid form will depend upon a variety of factors affecting both the issuer and investor. It may suit the issuer not to receive the full proceeds of the issue at the outset, particularly if the issue is funding a project with staggered cash flow requirements; and the timing and size of the calls can be tailored to fit these accordingly. From an investor's point of view, partly paid issues can offer the opportunity to lever-age their exposure to the fixed interest market by purchasing additional stock with the unused call monies. In a rising market this can prove very advanta-geous. But this strategy carries significant risks. Apart from the additional risk derived from simply holding the larger investment, there is the very real possibility that others too will be adopting the same leveraging strategy, and that as the calls become due for payment there will be an excess of sellers in the market. In some circumstances it may be difficult to exit from the strategy without loss.

Another way in which investors benefit from partly-paid issues arises in a negative yield curve environment, when short-term interest rates are higher than the yield on the (longer-dated) new issue. This means that the overall return to an investor, part of whose money will be residing temporarily in the money market, will be marginally higher than the redemption yield of the bond as conventionally calculated. Of course the obverse is also true, so that when money rates are lower than a partly-paid new issue's yield that yield will overstate the bond's attractions.

In cases of partly-paid stocks the first coupon payment will be non-standard to reflect the partly-paid nature of the bond in the period concerned. This topic has previously been examined within a gilt-edged context in Chapter 4 and exactly the same principles apply to debentures and loans. Essentially, the gross interest paid on its first coupon date will reflect the number of days for which the stock has accrued weighted by the proportion of issue price paid for each part of the period since the issue. The following example illustrates this.

*Example: calculation of first coupon amount on a partly-paid domestic bond*
Let us assume a bond is issued with a coupon of 9% and an issue price of 98.60 for value on the 10 May, but with payments spread as follows,

| | | |
|---|---|---|
| At issue: | 20.00 | on 10 May |
| First call: | 40.00 | on 14 June |
| Second call: | 38.60 | on 15 August |
| | ___ | |
| Issue price | 98.60 | |

For the first 35 days between 10 May and 14 June the bond is £20 paid and earns accrued interest at 20/98.60 of the full coupon rate, i.e.

$$9.0 \times 35 \times (20/98.60)/365 = 0.175053$$

For the next 62 days between 14 June and 15 August the bond is £60 paid and earns accrued interest at 60/98.60 of the full coupon rate, i.e.

$$9.0 \times 62 \times (60/98.60)/365 = 0.930284$$

For the last 46 days between 15 August and the first coupon payment date, 30 September, the stock is fully paid and earns accrued interest at the full coupon rate, i.e.

$$9.0 \times 46 \times (98.60/98.60)/365 = 1.134246$$

Adding these three elements together we obtain the value of the first coupon payment as,

$$0.175053 + 0.930284 + 1.134246 = 2.239583$$

The first coupon is normally rounded to four decimal places and in this case would be declared as £2.2396 per £100 nominal of stock. This first coupon compares with an amount of £3.5260 (143/365 x 9) which would have been payable if the stock had been issued in fully paid form.

Market convention has developed slightly different ways of calculating accrued interest and first coupons on domestic bonds as opposed to Euro-sterling bonds. In the former case, as seen above, the accrued element for any period is the annual coupon multiplied by the proportion of year elapsed (on an actual/365 day basis) multiplied by the proportion paid of the *issue price* of the bond. With Eurosterling bonds, the accrued element for any period is the annual coupon multiplied by the proportion of year elapsed (on 30/360 day basis) multiplied by the proportion paid of the nominal *value* of the bond.

It is worth noting that some partly paid bonds may be issued with only one call and this may be due for payment on the first coupon date. This has been the case with the recent local authority issues by Salford, Leicester, Dudley and Newport.

## Yields

The two main criteria for valuing debentures and loans are a bond's flat and redemption yields (see Chapter 5).

The flat yield, which is a measure of the annual income return obtainable from a bond, is obtained in the normal way by dividing the coupon rate by a bond's clean price and multiplying the result by 100.

Of greater importance is the redemption yield which takes into account both the annual income obtained from a bond and the eventual gain or loss at maturity.

The calendar conventions used in calculating yields in this market are exactly the same as those used for gilts – the actual number of days between relevant dates and a 365-day year – sometimes referred to as 'Actual/365'. Since the vast majority of issues pay coupons semi-annually, redemption yields are calculated and quoted on a semi-annual basis – again just like gilts. For those few issues that make interest payments quarterly, their gross redemption yields can be converted to semi-annual equivalents by using the following formula:

$$\text{Semi-annual yield} = \left\{ \left( 1 + \frac{\text{Quarterly yield}}{400} \right)^2 - 1 \right\} \times 200$$

Whilst a debenture or loan's gross redemption yield is a perfectly acceptable measure of its absolute value, most investors will wish to compare this yield with those of similarly dated gilts and, perhaps, other sterling fixed-interest instruments in order to assess the issue's value relative to the market. As yields on these issues and gilts are both quoted on a semi-annual compounding basis, direct comparisons between them can be made. This difference in yield – the 'yield margin over gilts' or 'yield spread' – is an indicator of the risk premium associated with a particular issue and reflects, amongst other things, such factors as the higher risk of default and the lesser liquidity of the bond. As a general rule, the higher the perceived risk and/or the worse the liquidity, the greater should be the spread. Thus a debenture stock will normally trade on a narrower spread than an unsecured loan issued by the same borrower. Likewise, a strongly covenanted loan will tend to trade on a narrower spread than a similar credit with weak covenants since the risk of credit deterioration in the future is reduced. Yet, in reality, it makes very little difference whether a debenture is five times covered or one hundred times covered, as long as the lower level of cover is more than adequate.

In the case of debentures trading at a substantial discount to par, capital cover will generally be of paramount importance, since a default triggering a repayment at par would actually generate a capital gain rather than a loss. In very much the same way a low-priced unsecured loan could benefit from a breach of a particularly tight borrowing covenant.

By contrast, investors in bonds with coupons above, or close to, the prevailing market rate will be more concerned with the ability of the issuer to meet its interest payment obligations and should concentrate on income cover.

Tax-paying investors will need to make their individual assessments of either absolute or relative value on the basis of net, rather than gross, redemption yields. These are particularly important for UK resident individuals, especially higher-rate tax payers. Calculations of this nature should be made on the basis of an individual's anticipated marginal rates of tax on income and capital and the particular tax regime under which he falls.

## Taxation

Debentures and loan stocks pay interest net of UK basic rate tax (currently 25%). There is no facility for obtaining gross payment. However, certain classes of investor, such as tax-exempt charities, pension funds and individuals whose total income is below the starting point for basic rate tax, should subsequently be able to reclaim all or part of the tax deducted.

Debentures and loans come within the scope of the new (1996) taxation arrangements for gilts and bonds.

This means that for UK corporate investors and personal investors whose aggregated gilt-edged and other bond holdings exceed £200,000 nominal, capital gains on debentures and loans are treated as income items and are taxed accordingly (see Chapter 10).

For personal investors at or below the £200,000 nominal threshold, debentures and loans (with a few exceptions) fall into the accrued income scheme, and as qualifying corporate bonds (QCBs) are free from capital gains tax. The main provisions of the accrued income scheme treat as taxable income not only interest or dividend payments received, but also accrued interest at the time of sale less accrued interest at the time of purchase. The effect of this is to ensure that the income assessable to tax is directly proportional to the period of time the investment concerned is held.

The below threshold personal investor will also have to contend with deep discount provisions. To prevent abuse of the asymmetry between the taxation of income and the taxation of capital, certain bonds are designated deep discount securities. Broadly speaking, bonds issued at a discount to par of greater than 15% or by more than $\frac{1}{2}$% multiplied by the number of years to maturity will be so classified, and most bonds issued with low or zero coupons will fall into this category. Tax treatment is basically designed to prevent income being rolled up in the form of capital gain over the life of the bond to the benefit of an income tax payer and the detriment of the Inland Revenue. Its central provision is that the part of the price movement of a deep discount bond that is attributable to its remaining on its original gross redemption yield as time progresses is deemed to be an item of income and is taxed accordingly at the time of disposal. Any price movement over and above that level is considered to be a capital gain and, for this category of investor, will be free of capital gains tax if the deep discount bond is also a qualifying corporate bond.

These deep discount provisions do not apply to UK corporate investors and above threshold personal investors since under the 1996 tax arrangements all capital gains derived from their holdings of gilts and bonds are taxed as income in any case.

NOTE: The comments on taxation above are of a general nature based on our understanding of current UK law and Inland Revenue practice. They relate only to the position of persons who are the absolute beneficial owners and may not apply to certain classes of persons such as traders and market-makers. Any person who is in doubt as to his/her personal tax position should consult a professional adviser.

## Appendix I: Debenture and loan stocks which settle outside the Talisman system

Anglian Water plc 5$\frac{1}{8}$% Index-Linked Stock 2008
Home Housing Association Ltd 0% Loan Stock 2019
Home Housing Association Ltd 0% Loan Stock 2027
Home Housing Association Ltd 8$\frac{3}{4}$% Guaranteed Loan Stock 2037
The Housing Finance Corporation Ltd 0% Debenture Stock 2012

The Housing Finance Corporation Ltd 5% Debenture Stock 2027
The Housing Finance Corporation Ltd 7% Debenture Stock 2009
The Housing Finance Corporation Ltd 8⅝% Debenture Stock 2023
The Housing Finance Corporation Ltd 11½% Debenture Stock 2016
The Housing Finance Corporation Ltd 5.65% Index-Linked Debenture Stock 2020
Nationwide Building Society 3⅞% Index-Linked Stock 2021
Nationwide Building Society 4¼% Index-Linked Stock 2024
Quebec Central Railway 4% First Mortgage Debenture Stock undated
Raglan Estates 10¼% – 11¼% Stepped Debenture Stock 2012
St Lawrence & Ottawa Railway Co. 4% First Mortgage Bonds 2880
Savoy Theatre Ltd 4% First Mortgage Debenture Stock undated
Toronto Grey & Bruce Railway Co. 4% First Mortgage Bonds 2883

## Appendix II: Summary of the more common covenants and clauses on domestic issues

*(i) Guarantee.* A guarantee is a promise by one company to meet the obligations of another company (usually related to the former). It is common for a parent company to guarantee the debt of a finance subsidiary, or for operating subsidiaries to guarantee the obligations of a non-operating holding company.

Guarantees often give rise to a contingent liability on the guarantor's balance sheet. If this is not acceptable to the guarantor, guarantees can be modified or replaced by support agreements or keepwell agreements. These commonly acknowledge the obligations of the issuer and covenant that ownership of the issuer by, for example its parent, will be maintained. In this form the agreement is indirect and this avoids the problems of it being a strict contingent liability.

*(ii) Limitation on secured and unsecured borrowings.* Borrowing limits generally consist of two sections; the outer borrowing limit and the inner borrowing limit. The outer borrowing limit restricts the total borrowings of the issuer and its subsidiaries to a set percentage of an appropriate base (generally the adjusted share capital plus reserves). The inner borrowing limit restricts the secured debt of the issuer, sometimes including the total debt of its subsidiaries, to a set percentage of the relevant base. These limits vary widely depending on specific circumstances, but ordinarily might be set in the 150% – 175% and 30% – 50% ranges for the outer and inner limits respectively.

Investors should note that the level of protection that these covenants can provide is heavily dependent upon the definitions of the borrowings to be included and the base to which the limit refers. Accordingly, two issues both having an outer borrowing limit of, say, 150% may not necessarily afford the same level of protection if the definitions of the borrowings and base are different in each case, for example, the inclusion or not of goodwill.

*(iii) Negative pledge.*    A negative pledge is a guarantee given by the issuer of an unsecured bond that it will not give security for certain other issues unless it provides matching security for the issue in question. In some cases, the pledge may be modified to allow the restricted issue of secured borrowings – say 30% of gross assets – and has some characteristics in common with an inner borrowing limit.

*(iv) Limitation on disposal of assets. 'Tickler' clause.*    This covenant restricts the issuer's ability to dispose of its assets. While affording the bondholder some protection, most covenants contain a fair degree of flexibility for the issuer to conduct business without undue hindrance. Generally, such limits are set with regard to a given percentage of the existing asset base being disposed of within a specified rolling time period. These limits are very often set at 30% of assets within any rolling five year period – often referred to as the '30% five year rule'.

Some issues also include a 'new owner' clause under the asset disposal heading. Usually defining a new owner as any person or body which acquires control of the issuer, such provisions are designed to prevent asset stripping by a predator to the detriment of existing bondholders.

*(v) 'Spens' clause.*    Although the vast majority of sterling debentures and loans have only a single redemption date, many of them (and some long-dated Eurosterling issues) have provision under which they may, in certain circumstances, be called by the issuer prior to redemption. Originally these clauses were used to determine the price at which a debenture or loan stock would become repayable in the event of a voluntary winding-up. Normally this would be the higher of (i) par, and (ii) the average market price over the three months prior to the notice of the resolution to wind up being served. These clauses were almost invariably included in investment trust debentures where the probability of such an event, perhaps for unitisation, was higher than elsewhere. In the past few years, however, this type of clause has developed to give the issuer the right to call the issue at other times. Clearly the price at which this option may be exercised needs to be defined so as to afford the bondholder protection against reinvestment risk. Often the exercise price is set as the higher of (i) par and (ii) the price at which the issue will have a gross redemption yield equal to that of the corresponding benchmark gilt.

Since most of these bonds nearly always trade on a higher yield than gilts such a call is likely to result in a, sometimes substantial, capital gain for the bondholder and be a correspondingly expensive exercise for the issuer. But they do provide the issuer with a mechanism for forcing redemption and subsequent cancellation of all (but not part of) the outstanding issue; and this can be valuable if, for example, the issue has been subject to a substantial reduction in size, and become an administrative problem, or if the existing covenants are proving onerous.

*(vi) Change of business clause.*   It is not unusual for some debentures and loans to have covenants which provide for repayment in the event of there being a fundamental change in the nature of the issuer's business.

*(vii) Further stock issuance restrictions.*   Another type of clause that is frequently encountered is that which prevents the income cover of a bond being diluted by the issuance of further bonds. This can be achieved by stipulating that the gross interest on the total of the existing and prospective new bonds must be covered a specified number of times (typically three times) by, say, the average of the net profits before tax of the past three years. Additionally, it is common to find provisions which insist that any further bonds to be issued do not have earlier maturites than the issue in question.

*(viii) First mortgage debentures – substitution or withdrawal of assets.* With first mortgage debentures it is often necessary for practical purposes to vary the assets upon which these bonds are secured. The terms under which this can be done are normally defined by substitution of assets clauses, which generally require the value of the new assets to be at least equal to those being withdrawn, and for the income cover to be maintained. Similar clauses may also exist to limit the extent that assets can be withdrawn from the debenture holders' charge over them. Additionally, provisions are often laid down for regular valuations of the secured assets or whenever demanded by the trustee to the issue.

*(ix) Miscellaneous.*   Finally there are a number of other miscellaneous items which need to be specified and about which investors should be cognisant. These include defining the powers of an issuer to buy back bonds (and generally insist that bonds repurchased must be cancelled), and the terms under which covenants themselves can be altered. This normally requires a special resolution of bondholders to be passed by at least a 75% majority at a general meeting.

# 15

## *Eurosterling bonds*

Eurocurrency markets evolved in the late 1950s in response to the imposition of various exchange controls around the world and the first Eurobond (which was denominated in US dollars) was issued in 1963. Since then, Eurocurrency markets have expanded rapidly and eurobonds now account for approximately 8% of the total world bond market.

In the UK, non-government bond issuance is nowadays dominated by Eurosterling issues with over 450 fixed rate bonds outstanding, representing an aggregate nominal value of in excess of £63,000 million. Over 88% of new non-government issuance in 1994 was in Eurosterling form, dwarfing other markets, and the total stock outstanding represents approximately 85% of the non-government sterling bond market. About 35% of all sterling bonds, including gilts, is accounted for by Eurosterling bonds compared with 5% for domestic corporate bonds. The overwhelming majority of Eurosterling bonds are listed on one of two exchanges: the London Stock Exchange and the Luxembourg Stock Exchange.

### Status and security

With minor exceptions, Eurosterling bonds are unsecured obligations of the issuer. Many such issues carry a negative pledge whereby the issuer undertakes not to pledge assets at the expense of bondholders' interests. However, many of these pledges need careful examination in order to ascertain fully the precise level of protection afforded to unsecured bondholders. In cases where the issuer is a subsidiary of a larger company, parent company guarantees may exist which will serve to improve the quality of the bond.

In addition to negative pledges and guarantees, corporate unsecured Eurosterling issues may sometimes carry additional covenants giving bondholders protection against a future deterioration in the credit quality of the issuer. These covenants are most prevalent on bonds which were issued with an original maturity of longer than ten years.

The recent developments in rules governing the adequacy of a bank's capital base have increased the issuance of subordinated debt by financial entities such as banks, building societies and, to a lesser extent, insurance companies. In broad terms, subordinated debt ranks behind the issuer's senior debt (such as ordinary deposits) and can count towards a bank or building society's capital base. Many different terms and conditions apply to these subordinated issues and investors need to be cognisant of the precise level of subordination when considering a purchase.

Many issues nowadays carry credit ratings from one or more of the major rating agencies – Moody's, Standard & Poor's, IBCA and Fitch. Investment grade bonds are generally split into ten grades with ratings ranging from the highest, AAA, (colloquially referred to as 'triple A'), where capacity to pay interest and repay principal is extremely strong to the lowest, BBB–, (referred to as 'triple B minus'), where the issuer's capacity is regarded simply as adequate. Ratings continue on down below this level but such bonds are not considered investment grade. The assignment of ratings to many of the outstanding issues has increased the acceptability of Eurosterling bonds both internationally and domestically and broadened the investor base of the market.

## Form and denomination

Eurosterling bonds exist mainly in bearer form. In practice, they are held either in computerised accounts within one of the two main Eurobond clearing houses (Euroclear and CEDEL) or in physical bearer form where the bonds are represented by certificates with detachable coupons. Given the practical problems associated with physical bearer bonds, it is not suprising that the vast majority of Eurosterling bonds are held in book-entry form within accounts at Euroclear and CEDEL.

At the time of issue most bonds are initally represented by a single global note which is subsequently exchangeable for definitive bonds of the relevant denominations two or three months after the issue date. Denominations of £1,000, £5,000, £10,000 and £100,000 are commonly available in numbered form. One of the things that investors in this field need to be aware of is the minimum denomination available for any specific bond, as only exact multiples of this minimum can be purchased and/or subsequently sold.

More recently, a number of Eurosterling issues have been made which have an option under which investors may elect to hold their bonds in registered form. Just as with ordinary shares and domestic debentures and loan stocks this requires a registrar to be responsible for the upkeep of the register and through whom transfers are effected in the normal way. But such activities are the exception rather than the rule and, unless specified to the contrary, dealings in Eurosterling bonds occur on the basis of the bonds being in bearer form.

Coupons on Eurosterling bonds are generally paid annually but there are

248

also a small number of bonds which make semi-annual payments and investors should be clear into which of these two categories their (prospective) investment falls.

## Dealing arrangements

Prices of Eurosterling bonds are quoted as a percentage of their principal amount. In normal circumstances the more active and thus, the more liquid, bonds trade on a price spread of between $\frac{3}{8}$% to $\frac{1}{2}$%. i.e. the price at which an investor can sell bonds will tend to be $\frac{3}{8}$% to $\frac{1}{2}$% lower than the price at which he can buy bonds. However, some very liquid bonds and new issues still in the primary market may trade on a narrower $\frac{1}{8}$% to $\frac{1}{4}$% spread. Conversely, some of the more illiquid issues tend to trade on a $\frac{3}{4}$% to 1% spread and others on a negotiated basis only. These comments, however, relate basically to professional transactions in normal market size. Away from those circumstances bid-offer spreads can be expected to widen. In particular investors should not be surprised to find wider spreads quoted for small trades.

## Price conventions and accrued interest

Prices of Eurosterling bonds are quoted 'clean', i.e. exclusive of gross accrued interest. This is the convention used for gilts, domestic debentures and loans, bulldogs and PIBs, but not for preference shares. This means that the total price paid by a buyer of a Eurosterling bond will have two components, (a) the quoted market price, and (b) the gross accrued interest. This latter quantity is the amount of interest that has accrued on the bond between the date of the last coupon payment (or in the case of a new issue, the issue payment date) and the transaction's settlement date.

The question of accrued interest and how it should be computed has already been discussed in some length in Chapter 4 but that analysis related to gilt-edged securities and others following their conventions. Eurosterling bonds do not use the same calendar convention as gilts, they use the ISMA convention under which the year is considered to have 360 days split into twelve equal 30-day months.

The following example illustrates.

On 19 January 1995, a buyer pays 96.25 for £125,000 nominal of XYZ plc 8% bonds due 30 June 2005 for settlement on the 22 January. The bonds last paid a coupon on 30 June 1994.

First let us establish the number of days accrued interest concerned.

Under ISMA convention this is taken to be 6 whole months of 30 days each and 22 days in January, i.e. 202 days,

and the resulting accrued interest = $202/360 \times 8 = 4.48888$.

The total price is formed thus:

$$
\begin{array}{lll}
\text{Quoted price} & = & 96.25000 \\
+ \text{ Gross accrued interest} & = & 4.48888 \\
\hline
\text{Total market price} & = & 100.73888
\end{array}
$$

## Stamp duty and other transaction expenses

Eurosterling bond transactions attract neither levies nor stamp duty. However, a stockbroker acting as an investor's agent is quite likely to charge a client commission in accordance with individual client agreements.

## Ex-dividend arrangements

There are no ex-dividend periods for Eurosterling bonds. The bonds continue to accrue cum-dividend until the coupon payment date.

## Settlement

Eurosterling bond trades, unless otherwise specified, are effected for sterling settlement three business days after the date of the transaction. However, the international nature of the market taken together with the propensity of different countries to have public holidays on different days sometimes interferes with this seemingly straightforward arrangement. In such cases all parties involved should agree the settlement details at the time of dealing.

Eurosterling bond trades transacted with a market-maker such as Merrill Lynch Gilts Ltd will normally settle through one of the two clearing houses, Euroclear or CEDEL. Each counterparty concerned must have access to an account at one or either of these houses so that the bonds may be transferred between their respective accounts. Settlement of trades between Euroclear and CEDEL is also possible, being effected via an electronic 'bridge'. Delivery of stock to a buyer is normally made on a basis of 'Delivery versus Payment' (DVP) – whereby stock is transferred to the buyer's account only when payment has been received in the equivalent account of the seller.

## Custody

Only those investors, traders and custodians with significant volumes of Eurobond business can justify the relatively high cost of opening and maintaining a Euroclear or CEDEL account in their own name. Consequently, many investors find that it is more cost-effective to conduct their Eurobond activites through a bank offering specialist settlement and custodial facilities. The main UK clearing banks, among others, all offer such services, receiving instructions to settle transactions and maintain custody accounts.

## New issues procedures

Under the traditional issuing procedure, a lead manager is appointed by the issuer and takes responsibility for negotiating the terms (e.g. coupon, maturity etc.), conditions (e.g. covenants etc.) and price of the new issue. Unless the 'lead' wishes to assume all the risk of the issue (and hence retain all the fees), he will undertake to assemble a syndicate of other banks and issuing houses to share in the underwriting and distribution of the issue.

Under primary market convention, all Eurosterling issues are now issued using the fixed price re-offer system whereby all firms in the syndicate undertake to offer the new bonds to potential investors at the same price for a given period of time. Upon notification from the lead manager that the syndicate is 'broken', ex-members of the syndicate are free to price the bonds as they wish as dictated by the balance of supply and demand. This system ensures an orderly start to a new issue's life and gives all investors an equal opportunity to buy bonds at a common price.

Most new issues are announced and sold some time before the bonds are due for payment. This 'primary' market has a duration which may vary from two to six weeks depending on circumstances. Because of the speed with which many new issues are often brought, a full offer prospectus may well not be available at the time of the launch, and the primary market period provides a breathing space for the necessary documentation to be prepared and distributed. Obviously bargains transacted during this period are not for normal settlement after three business days, and care should be taken to confirm the actual settlement date between both parties at the time of dealing. Mention should also be made of the fact that bargains struck during this period are technically 'as and when issued' bargains and that there is always the risk, albeit a very remote risk, of the issue being cancelled between 'announcement' day and the date on which payment is due. Should this happen all bargains previously transacted become null and void.

New issue activity has grown from £500 million in 1980, the first full year after the removal of foreign exchange controls in 1979, to a peak of £20,600 million in 1993, before easing back in 1994. In the early 1980s, the Eurosterling market was small and insignificant. Since then, however, uninterrupted growth has transformed it into the dominant market for non-gilt fixed interest securities.

Fixed interest issues account for roughly 75% of total Eurosterling issuance, the balance being floating rate notes (FRNs), mortgage-backed securities and convertibles. While the Eurosterling market has been growing, the domestic bond market (debentures and unsecured loan stocks) has shrunk to an estimated 15% of the total amount of non-gilt bonds in issue. The reason for this lies in the relative advantages offered by the Eurosterling market to both issuers and investors alike. For issuers the advantages include, greater flexibility in the timing of an issue, a wider investor base (leading to greater demand and thus lower yields) and lower new issue costs. From the international investors' point of view, the anonymity afforded by the bearer form of Eurosterling bonds and the opportunity to receive gross payments of interest has greater appeal than that of registered bonds paying interest net of withholding tax.

The wider investor base also enhances the liquidity of the secondary market, thus attracting more investors who are able to deal in larger size and on tighter dealing spreads. As a result, the Eurosterling bond market is now over six times the size of the domestic bond market which is now only really used by issuers able and willing to pledge assets of specific appeal to UK based investors, and by smaller companies which lack international recognition.

Over 75% of outstanding Eurosterling fixed rate bonds will mature within the next 10 years. This is largely a reflection of the need to appeal to the international investor whose preference is for shorter maturity paper. Notwithstanding this requirement, longer dated securities have increased their share of the market over the past few years. Issuance of bonds with maturities in excess of ten years has been particularly noticeable during periods when the yield curve has been inverted, i.e. when longer-dated yields have been lower than their shorter-dated counterparts.

The range of issuers in the Eurosterling bond market is very broad. Their names include European Union member states, domestic and overseas corporates, banks (both domestic and overseas), building societies and insurance companies. There are plenty of recognisable names with which UK investors should feel comfortable, as well as opportunities for investing in less familiar credits.

## Yields and assessment of value

In common with all other forms of fixed interest investment the two main criteria for making value judgements are a bond's flat and redemption yields. The flat yield of a Eurosterling bond can be ascertained in the normal way by dividing the coupon by the clean market price and multiplying the result by 100. This yield gives an indication of the income return that the bond will generate on an annual basis. (See Chapter 5.) Of far more importance however is the redemption yield (once again see Chapter 5) which takes into account both the annual income obtained from a bond and the eventual gain or loss at maturity. Unlike gilts and other domestic bonds, yields on Eurosterling bonds are calculated on a 30-day month, 360-day year basis under ISMA convention. As the vast majority of issues pay coupons annually, such redemption yields are quoted as annual yields. This means that they are not directly comparable with yields on gilts and domestic bonds which are expressed on a semi-annual basis; however it is possible to convert annual yields to semi-annual yields using the formula,

$$\text{Semi-annual yield} = \left\{ \left( 1 + \frac{\text{Annual yield}}{100} \right)^{1/2} - 1 \right\} \times 200$$

(There are marginal inexactitudes in using this expression where there are differences in the two yield calculation methodologies, but for most practical purposes it will suffice.)

Having ascertained a Eurosterling bond's basic value by calculating its redemption yield, it then becomes necessary to see how that bond is valued in relation to other comparable fixed income securities. The prime yardstick for making such comparisons are the yields of current coupon 'benchmark' gilt-edged issues with maturities as close to that of the Eurosterling bond as possible. The difference between the bond's yield and that of the chosen gilt is usually referred to as the 'yield spread' or 'the margin over gilts' and is normally expressed in terms of basis points (one hundredths of one per cent).

The following example illustrates these relationships.

Imagine a ten-year Eurosterling bond giving a gross yield 9.31% on an ISMA annual yield.

This yield translates to a gross semi-annual equivalent yield of,

$$\left\{ \left( 1 + \frac{9.31}{100} \right)^{1/2} - 1 \right\} \times 200 = 9.10\%$$

If the ten-year benchmark gilt is yielding 8.55% then the bond's 'yield spread' is (9.10% – 8.55%) = 0.55% or 55 basis points.

When this figure increases, spreads are said to be 'widening' and this indicates that the bond is underperforming the benchmark gilt. If on the other hand this figure decreases then spreads are said to be 'narrowing' or 'coming in' and the bond will be the better performing instrument.

Yield spreads can thus be seen to be a fundamental valuation tool for use in assessing Eurosterling bonds' values. They provide a measurment in yield terms of the premiums being offered to investors to compensate for the extra risk involved in investing in these bonds as opposed to 'risk-free' gilts. Making judgements of when these spreads are too narrow or too wide is the very essence of investment in this market.

## Taxation

Interest on Eurosterling bonds is paid to holders of bonds recorded by Euroclear/Cedel or upon presentation of the relevant coupon to a specified paying agent. Interest may be paid free of withholding tax where:

either the agent through whom the payment is made is not in the UK;

or, if the agent through whom the payment is made is in the UK, it is proved that the beneficial owner is a non-resident for UK tax purposes or that the bonds are held within Euroclear or CEDEL.

In all other cases, payments of interest are made net of withholding tax, currently 25% for UK issuers. All investors in Eurosterling bonds who are resident in the UK for tax purposes and use the facilities of an agent for custody and coupon payments will receive interest net of withholding tax.

The only UK based investors able to receive interest gross are those who hold their bonds directly in a Euroclear or Cedel account in their own name. But that, of course, does not exempt them from tax. They will still be required to declare that interest to the Inland Revenue, but it does provide a cash flow advantage by delaying any resultant tax payments.

Eurosterling bonds come within the scope of the new (1996) taxation arrangements for gilts and bonds.

This means that for UK corporate investors and personal investors whose aggregated gilt-edged and other bond holdings exceed £200,000 nominal, capital gains on Eurosterling bonds are treated as income items and are taxed accordingly (see Chapter 10).

For personal investors at or below the £200,000 nominal threshold Eurosterling bonds (with a few exceptions) fall into the accrued income scheme, and as qualifying corporate bonds (QCBs) are free from capital gains tax. The main provisions of the accrued income scheme treat as taxable income not only interest or dividend payments received, but also accrued interest at the time of sale less accrued interest at the time of purchase. The effect of this is to ensure that the income assessable to tax is directly proportional to the period of time the investment concerned is held. Bonds which do not fall into the AIS include some long-dated callable subordinated issues where provision is made for the coupon rate to be reset in the event of the issuer eventually choosing not to exercise his option to call the bonds. It is the fact that the coupon rate is capable of variation that disqualifies such bonds from the accrued income scheme, and some issuers have overcome this problem by arranging for a bond exchange to take place in such an event.

The below threshold personal investor will also have to contend with deep discount provisions. To prevent abuse of the asymmetry between the taxation of income and the taxation of capital, certain bonds are designated deep discount securities. Broadly speaking, bonds issued at a discount to par of greater than 15% or by more than $\frac{1}{2}$% multiplied by the number of years to maturity will be so classified, and most bonds issued with low or zero coupons will fall into this category. Tax treatment is basically designed to prevent income being rolled up in the form of capital gain over the life of the bond to the benefit of an income tax payer and the detriment of the Inland Revenue. Its central provision is that the part of the price movement of a deep discount bond that is attributable to its remaining on its original gross redemption yield as time progresses is deemed to be an item of income and is taxed accordingly at the time of disposal. Any price movement over and above that level is considered to be a capital gain and, for this category of investor, will be free of capital gains tax if the deep discount bond is also a qualifying corporate bond.

These deep discount provisions do not apply to UK corporate investors and above threshold personal investors since under the 1996 tax arrangements all capital gains derived from their holdings of gilts and bonds are taxed as income in any case.

*Note:* The comments on taxation above are of a general nature based on our understanding of current UK law and Inland Revenue practice. They relate only to the position of persons who are the absolute beneficial owners and may not apply to certain classes of persons such as traders and market-makers. Any person who is in doubt as to his/her personal tax position should consult a professional adviser.

# 16

## *Bulldog bonds*

The City of London has a long history of raising sterling loans for overseas companies and foreign government bodies. Indeed, the Toronto Grey & Bruce Railway Company 4% First Mortgage bonds still hold the record for a sterling maturity. Issued in 1884, they are redeemable at par on 14 June 2883. The imposition of exchange controls in 1939, however, closed the sterling domestic market for forty years to overseas borrowers other than members of the old Sterling Area. The effect of this was to limit the market in such bonds to a number of Commonwealth governments and agencies of which the prime credits were Australia and New Zealand.

With the passing of sterling's role as a reserve currency and the consequent demise of the Sterling Area this market gradually withered away, and for a long time through the 1970s there was no overseas issuing activity of any significance on the London Stock Exchange. But then in July 1980, following the removal of UK foreign exchange controls the previous October, the Kingdom of Denmark came to the London market to raise £75 million. This issue was quickly dubbed a 'bulldog bond' and that name attached itself to succeeding issues and the new market that grew up around them. They are more formally classified in the Stock Exchange Daily Official List as 'Sterling Issues by Overseas Borrowers' and it is on issues in this category that the main emphasis of this chapter will be focussed. We will, however, also include in the scope of this chapter two Guaranteed Export Finance Corporation (GEFCO) stocks which, despite being classified under their own heading at the end of the 'British Funds' section, are regarded as bulldogs by market convention.

In the year after the Denmark issue ten further bulldog issues followed in quick succession. These came from a variety of credits ranging from Iceland and the International Bank for Reconstruction and Development (World Bank) to Inco and Mexico. Over the next five years, issuance continued but the pace slowed as the Eurosterling bond market gained favour in the eyes of both issuers and investors alike. Most of the characteristics of bulldogs were replicated and available in the Eurosterling market (with the exception of the ability to hold bonds in registered form) with the added benefits of greater liquidity and a wider investor base. Issuance of bulldogs picked up a little in the late 1980s after a lull in 1987, with various issues from EIB, GEFCO and Portugal but this was not sustained. In April 1991 the Government of Gibraltar came to the market to raise £50 million through the issue of $11\frac{7}{8}\%$ bonds due in 2005, but since then there have been no further issues.

Nevertheless, with over £4 billion of long-dated stock still outstanding, both existing and prospective holders can enjoy the benefits of issues which yield a premium to gilts and to their equivalent Eurosterling counterparts.

All bulldog bonds are listed on the London Stock Exchange and, with one exception, make interest payments semi-annually in arrears. The exception is the set of issues from GEFCO which pay annually in arrears.

## Status and security

Other than two bonds mentioned below, bulldog bonds are unsecured obligations of the issuer. As such, they carry relatively few pledges and covenants. In general terms, the majority of unsecured issues carry negative pledges (with varying degrees of investor protection) and events of default can include cross default and change of business/status clauses. The two secured bulldog bonds are both Canadian issues. Holders of Transcanada Pipelines $16\frac{1}{2}\%$ 2007 have a first mortgage over certain of the issuer's assets, while City of Montreal's 3% perpetual issue is secured by way of a first charge on property within the City limits.

Many bulldogs carry credit ratings from one or both of the major rating agencies, Moody's Investor Services and Standard & Poor's. Investment grade bonds are generally split into ten ratings ranging from the highest, AAA (referred to as triple A), where capacity to pay interest and repay principal is extremely strong, to the lowest, BBB– (referred to as triple B minus), where the issuer's capacity is regarded simply as adequate. Ratings continue down from this level for bonds considered to be below investment grade. The assignment of ratings to a good many of the outstanding bulldog issues has encouraged a broadening of the investor base and has greatly facilitated the assessment of individual issues.

In Table 16.1 we show, *inter alia*, these ratings where applicable as at April 1995.

## Form and denomination

With the exception of Inco $15\frac{3}{4}\%$ 2006, all bulldog bonds exist in registered form with denominations ranging from one penny to £20 (again see Table 16.1). Over half of these issues are also available in bearer form in denominations ranging from £1,000 to £100,000 but most commonly £5,000. Such bearer stock is held either in computerised accounts within one of the two main Eurobond clearing houses (Euroclear and CEDEL) or in physical bearer

**Table 16.1**  Bulldog issues outstanding April 1995

| Sterling issues by overseas borrowers | | | | | Coupon % | Coupon dates | Redemption date |
|---|---|---|---|---|---|---|---|
| Issue date | Amount issued £m | Amount o/s £m | Credit rating[1] Moody's/S&P | Issuer | | | |
| Oct 1984 | 50 | 50 | Aaa/AAA | African Development Bank | $11\frac{1}{8}$% | 4 Jan/4 July | 04.01.2010 |
| Aug 1984 | 30 | 30 | A2/A | American Brands Inc. | $12\frac{1}{2}$% | 15 April/15 Oct | 15.10.2009 |
| Feb 1986 | 50 | 29 | Ba1/– | American Medical International Inc | $9\frac{7}{8}$% | 15 Jan/15 July | 15.07.2011 |
| Feb 1984 | 100 | 98.5 | Aaa/AAA | Asian Development Bank | $10\frac{1}{4}$% | 24 March/24 Sep | 24.03.2009 |
| July 1982 | 100 | 13.709 | Aa2/AA | Commonwealth of Australia | $13\frac{1}{2}$% | 28 Jan/28 July | 28.07.2010 |
| Aug 1985 | 100 | 16.491 | Aa2/AA | Commonwealth of Australia | $9\frac{1}{2}$% | 14 April/14 Oct | 14.10.2012 |
| Oct 1983 | 100 | 13.106 | –/AA | Commonwealth of Australia | $11\frac{3}{8}$% | 26 April/26 Oct | 26.10.2015 |
| Sep 1985 | 75 | 75 | Baa3/– | Bank of Greece | $10\frac{3}{8}$% | 6 March/6 Sep | 06.09.2010 |
| Dec 1990 | 30 | 27.05 | N.R. | Govt. of Barbados | $13\frac{1}{2}$% | 1 Jan/1 July | 01.07.2015 |
| June 1983 | 50 | 0.13264 | Aaa/– | Caisse Francaise de Development (formerly known as C.C.C.E.) | $12\frac{1}{4}$% | 12 Jan/12 July | 12.07.2013 |
| Dec 1981 | 30 | 30 | N.R. | Caisse Nationale des Autoroutes | 16% | 15 June/15 Dec | 15.12.2006 |
| Aug 1983 | 30 | 0.047805 | –/BBB+ | Cigna Overseas Finance NV | 13% | 28 Feb/28 Aug | 28.08.2008 |
| April 1982 | 50 | 50 | –/AAA | Credit Foncier de France | $14\frac{3}{4}$% | 31 March/30 Sep | 31.03.2007 |
| June 1985 | 100 | 100 | Aaa/AAA | Credit Foncier de France | $10\frac{1}{4}$% | 18 Feb/18 Aug | 18.08.2011-14 |
| July 1980 | 75 | 40.125 | –/AA+ | Kingdom of Denmark | 13% | 30 June/31 Dec | 31.12.2005 |
| June 1984 | 35 | 5.85 | –/A | Eaton Finance NV | $12\frac{1}{2}$% | 12 June/12 Dec | 12.06.2014 |
| Aug 1982 | 75 | 1.103 | N.R. | Electricité de France | $12\frac{1}{2}$% | 28 Feb/28 Aug | 28.08.2008 |
| May 1984 | 75 | 0.945 | N.R. | Electricité de France | $11\frac{3}{4}$% | 17 May/17 Nov | 17.05.2009-12 |
| June 1986/Nov 1989 | 185 | 161.5 | Aaa/AAA | European Investment Bank | 9% | 16 Jan/16 July | 16.07.2001 |
| Oct 1982 | 75 | 67.0 | Aaa/AAA | European Investment Bank | 11% | 23 March/23 Sep | 23.09.2002 |
| Sep 1984/Dec 1989/ Dec 1990 | 400 | 361.387 | Aaa/AAA | European Investment Bank | $10\frac{3}{8}$% | 22 May/22 Nov | 22.11.2004 |
| Nov 1988/Feb 1989/ June 1989/Sep 1989 | 500 | 461 | Aaa/AAA | European Investment Bank | $9\frac{1}{2}$% | 9 June/9 Dec | 09.12.2009 |
| March 1984 | 50 | 50 | –/AA– | Republic of Finland | $11\frac{1}{2}$% | 15 April/15 Oct | 15.04.2009 |
| April 1991 | 50 | $50^0$ | N.R. | Govt. of Gibraltar | $11\frac{7}{8}$% | 1 May/1 Nov | 01.05.2005 |
| May 1990 | 250 | 250 | N.R. | Guaranteed Export Finance Corporation plc | $12\frac{7}{8}$% | 29 Sep | 29.09.2002 |
| Aug 1989 | 250 | 250 | N.R. | Guaranteed Export Finance Corporation plc | $9\frac{3}{4}$% | 7 Jan | 07.01.2010 |
| May 1981 | 40 | 40 | –/A+ | Hydro-Quebec | 15% | 31 May/30 Nov | 31.05.2011 |
| Sep 1982 | 50 | 50 | –/A+ | Hydro-Quebec | $12\frac{3}{4}$% | 13 March/13 Sep | 13.09.2015 |
| Dec 1980/May 1983 | 30 | 30 | A2/– | Republic of Iceland | $14\frac{1}{4}$% | 31 Jan/31 July | 31.01.2016 |
| July 1981 | 25 | 22.728 | –/BBB– | Inco Ltd | $15\frac{3}{4}$% | 15 Jan/15 July | 15.07.2006 |

| CGO/ Talisman | Coupon gross/net | Reg. min. denom. | Bearer option | Reg'd – Bearer exchange fee | Notes |
|---|---|---|---|---|---|
| CGO | Gross | 1 penny | £5,000/£50,000 | At cost | Loan Stock |
| Talisman | Net | £1 | No | – | Unsecured Loan Stock |
| Talisman | Net | £1 | No | – | Unsecured Loan Stock |
| CGO | Gross | 1 penny | £5,000 | At cost | Loan Stock |
| CGO | Net | 1 penny | No | – | Loan Stock |
| CGO | Net | 1 penny | £5,000 | At cost | Loan Stock |
| CGO | Net | 1 penny | £5,000 | At cost | Loan Stock |
| Talisman | Net | £1 | £10,000 | At cost | Loan Stock |
| CGO | Net | £1 | £5,000 | At cost | Loan Stock |
| CGO | Net | £20 | £5,000 | 25p per bond (min £5) +VAT | Guaranteed Loan Stock. Unconditional guarantee as to interest and principal by Republic of France |
| Talisman | Net | £1 | £5,000 | 15p per bond (min £5) + VAT | Guaranteed Loan Stock. Unconditional guarantee as to interest and principal by Republic of France |
| Talisman | Net | £1 | No | – | Unsecured Loan Stock. Unconditional guarantee as to interest and principal by Cigna Corporation. London & European Register |
| CGO | Net | £20 | £5,000 | 15p per bond (min £5) + VAT | Guaranteed Loan Stock. Unconditional guarantee as to interest and principal by Republic of France |
| CGO | Net | £20 | £5,000 | 20p per bond (min £5) + VAT | Guaranteed Loan Stock. Unconditional guarantee as to interest and principal by Republic of France. Stock is redeemed in equal instalments on 18 August of each of the years 2011, 2012, 2013 & 2014 |
| Talisman | Net | 1 penny | No | n/a | Loan Stock |
| Talisman | Net | £1 | £5,000 | 20p per bond (min £10) + VAT | Unsecured Loan Stock. Unconditional guarantee as to interest and principal by Eaton Corporation |
| CGO | Net | £20 | £5,000 | 15p per bond (min £5) + VAT | Guaranteed Loan Stock. Unconditional guarantee as to interest and principal by Republic of France |
| CGO | Net | £20 | £5,000 | At cost | Guaranteed Loan Stock. Unconditional guarantee as to interest and principal by Republic of France. Stock is redeemed in equal instalments on 17 May of each of the years 2009, 2010, 2011 & 2012 |
| CGO | Gross | 1 penny | £5,000 | Free of charge | Loan Stock |
| CGO | Gross | 1 penny | £5,000 | Free of charge | Loan Stock |
| CGO | Gross | 1 penny | £5,000 | Free of charge | Loan Stock |
| CGO | Gross | 1 penny | £5,000 | Free of charge | Loan Stock |
| CGO | Net | £1 | £5,000 | At cost | Loan Stock |
| CGO | Net | £1 | No | – | In the event of Issuer ceasing to be a Crown Colony, Issuer must either a) call the stock at the higher of par or a price which equates to level yields with the Cv 9.5% 2005 gilt or b) increase coupon to sum of 7.5% and the prevailing GRY on the Cv 9.5% 2005 gilt. Stock does not fall within Accrued Income Scheme because it is deemed to be a variable rate security |
| CGO | Net | 1 penny | £10,000/£100,000 | At cost | Guaranteed Loan Stock. Unconditional guarantee as to interest and principal by The Secretary of State for Trade & Industry of Her Britannic Majesty's Government |
| CGO | Net | 1 penny | £5,000/£100,000 | At cost | Guaranteed Loan Stock. Unconditional guarantee as to interest and principal by The Secretary of State for Trade & Industry of Her Britannic Majesty's Goverment |
| CGO | Net | £1 | No | – | Loan Stock. Guaranteed by Province of Quebec |
| CGO | Net | £1 | No | – | Loan Stock. Guaranteed by Province of Quebec |
| Talisman | Net | 1 penny | No | – | Loan Stock |
| – | – | n/a | £1,000/£10,000 | – | Exists only in bearer form. US$ principal repayment option at £1 = $1.98; interest payable at investor's option in US$ at spot rate prevailing on second business prior to payment *(continued over)* |

259

**Table 16.1** (continued)

| | | | | | | | |
|---|---|---|---|---|---|---|---|
| Nov 1982 | 75 | 72.75 | –/AAA | Inter-American Development Bank | 12½% | 8 Jan/8 July | 08.01.2003 |
| Dec 1984/Mar 1986 | 175 | 174 | –/AAA | Inter-American Development Bank | 9¾% | 15 May/15 Nov | 15.05.2015 |
| Oct 1983/Aug 1984/ April 1989 | 235 | 235 | –/AAA | International Bank for Reconstruction & Development[2] | 11½% | 9 May/9 Nov | 09.11.2003 |
| July 1985 | 100 | 100 | Aaa/AAA | International Bank for Reconstruction & Development[2] | 9½% | 24 March/24 Sep | 24.09.2010 |
| Oct 1983 | 50 | 28.6205 | Aa2/– | Ireland | 12½% | 12 April/12 Oct | 12.10.2008 |
| April 1985 | 75 | 72.9 | A1/– | Malaysia | 10¾% | 31 Jan/31 July | 31.07.2009 |
| Oct 1888 | 1.44 | 0.396127 | N.R. | City of Montreal | 3% | 1 May/1 Nov | undated |
| April 1983 | 100 | 97.5 | Aa2/AA | New Zealand | 11¼% | 4 May/4 Nov | 04.05.2008 |
| July 1984 | 100 | 100 | Aa2/AA | New Zealand | 11½% | 25 March/25 Sep | 25.09.2014 |
| April 1984 | 60 | 60 | –/A– | Province of Nova Scotia | 11¾% | 18 April/18 Oct | 18.04.2019 |
| Oct 1981 | 30 | 30 | –/A– | Province of Nova Scotia | 16¾% | 30 April/31 Oct | 31.10.2011 |
| April 1981 | 50 | 50 | N.R. | Petroleos Mexicanos[3] | 14½% | 31 March/30 Sep | 31.03.2006 |
| May 1986/Oct 1988 | 150 | 150 | A1/AA– | Republic of Portugal | 9% | 20 May/20 Nov | 20.05.2016 |
| Feb 1984 | 50 | 50 | –/A+ | Province de Quebec | 12¼% | 15 March/15 Sep | 15.03.2020 |
| Feb 1985 | 60 | 60 | Aa2/AA | Kingdom of Spain | 11¾% | 24 March/24 Sep | 24.03.2010 |
| Jan 1983 | 50 | 49.9997 | –/AA+ | Kingdom of Sweden | 13½% | 22 Jan/22 July | 22.01.2010 |
| Oct 1984 | 100 | 100 | –/AA+ | Kingdom of Sweden | 11% | 15 Jan/15 July | 15.07.2012 |
| Nov 1985 | 100 | 100 | Aa3/AA+ | Kingdom of Sweden | 9¾% | 15 March/15 Sep | 15.09.2014 |
| May 1982 | 25 | 25 | A2/– | Transcanada Pipelines Ltd | 16½% | 1 March/1 Sep | 01.09.2007 |
| May 1984 | 50 | 30.202 | N.R. | Republic of Trinidad & Tobago | 12¼% | 23 May/23 Nov | 23.05.2009 |
| Sept 1981 | 50 | 48.65 | N.R. | United Mexican States | 16½% | 1 March/1 Sep | 01.09.2008 |
| TOTALS | 4746.4 | 4009.7 | | | | | |

[0]The issuer is believed to have bought back but not cancelled in excess of £40 million.
[1]Ratings applicable on 7 April 1995.
[2]Commonly referred to as World Bank.
[3]Commonly referred to as Pemex.

*Notes:*
CGO/Talisman – indicates whether the registered form of the stock is deliverable through either the Central Gilts Office for settlement the next business day or the Talisman system for settlement three business days later.
The bearer form will normally settle through CEDEL or EUROCLEAR three business days after the trade date.
Coupon gross/net – indicates whether the registered stock pays its coupon gross or net of UK withholding tax (currently 25%).
Bearer option – indicates whether stock is available in bearer form and the size of the bearer denominations.

form where the stock is represented by documents with detachable coupons. Given the practical problems associated with physical bearer bonds, it is not surprising that the vast majority of bearer bulldog bonds are held in book-entry form within accounts at Euroclear and CEDEL.

Investors will need to be aware of the minimum denomination available for any specific bond in the form required as only exact multiples of this minimum can be purchased and/or subsequently sold. Unless specified to the contrary, dealings in bulldogs occur on the basis of their being in registered form.

Where bulldogs exist in both registered and bearer form, registered bonds may be exchanged for bearer bonds in integral amounts and vice versa. A certificate will be issued for any remaining balance. Application forms for such exchanges are available from the registrar who will normally make a charge for the exchange. This cost varies from 15p to 25p per £5,000 nominal

| | | | | | |
|---|---|---|---|---|---|
| CGO | Gross | 1 penny | No | – | Loan Stock |
| CGO | Gross | 1 penny | No | – | Loan Stock |
| CGO | Gross | 1 penny | No | – | Loan Stock |
| CGO | Gross | 1 penny | £5,000 | At cost | Loan Stock |
| CGO | Net | 1 penny | £5,000 | At cost | Loan Stock |
| Talisman | Net | 1 penny | £5,000 | At cost | Loan Stock |
| Talisman | Net | £1 | No | – | Permanent Debenture Stock. Subject to Stamp Duty. London & Montreal register. Min. Holding £10 |
| CGO | Net | 1 penny | £5,000 | At cost | Loan Stock |
| CGO | Net | 1 penny | £5,000 | At cost | Loan Stock |
| CGO | Net | £1 | No | – | Loan Stock |
| CGO | Net | £1 | No | – | Loan Stock |
| Talisman | Net | £1 | No | – | Loan Stock |
| CGO | Net | £1 | £5,000 | At cost | Loan Stock |
| CGO | Net | £1 | No | – | Loan Stock |
| CGO | Net | 1 penny | £5,000 | At cost | Loan Stock |
| CGO | Net | 1 penny | £1,000/£10,000 | At cost | Loan Stock |
| CGO | Net | 1 penny | £1,000 | At cost | Loan Stock |
| CGO | Net | 1 penny | £10,000 | At cost | Loan Stock |
| Talisman | Net | £1 | No | – | First Mortgage pipeline bonds |
| Talisman | Net | 1 penny | £5,000 | At cost | Loan Stock. Investor has the right to redeem the stock at par on the 23 May in 1999 and 2004 |
| Talisman | Net | 1 penny | £1,000/£10,000 | At cost | Loan Stock. Investor has the right to redeem the stock at par on the September payment date in each of the years 1988 to 2007 inclusive |

(subject to VAT and normally with a minimum charge of £5) with the exception of the European Investment Bank's issues which are exchanged free of charge. Exchanges normally take between three and six days to complete after receipt of the application and accompanying certificate or physical bearer bonds.

## Diminished marketability of certain issues

The competitive pressures from the Eurosterling bond market have not been the bulldog market's only problem. Another has been an internal one – the practice of a number of issuers of buying back their bonds from the market for cancellation. As a result of this, a considerable number of issues have little of their original stock outstanding. These actions, coupled with the threat of further repurchases, have reduced liquidity significantly as market-makers are understandably reluctant to make close two-way prices in size in issues that have been, or may in future be, affected in this way. Table 16.2 lists the main issues to have suffered from this phenomenon.

**Table 16.2**  Bulldog issues which have been subject to significant reduction in issue size

| Amount issued £m | Amount outstanding £m (early 1995) | Issue | % remaining |
|---|---|---|---|
| 50 | 29.000 | American Medical International $9\frac{7}{8}$% 2011 | 58.0% |
| 100 | 13.709 | Commonwealth of Australia $13\frac{1}{2}$% 2010 | 13.7% |
| 100 | 16.491 | Commonwealth of Australia $9\frac{1}{2}$% 2012 | 16.5% |
| 100 | 13.106 | Commonwealth of Australia $11\frac{3}{8}$% 2015 | 13.1% |
| 50 | 0.133 | Caisse Francaise de Development $12\frac{1}{4}$% 2013 | 0.3% |
| 30 | 0.048 | Cigna Overseas Finance NV 13% 2008 | 0.2% |
| 75 | 40.125 | Kingdom of Denmark 13% 2005 | 53.5% |
| 35 | 5.850 | Eaton Finance NV $12\frac{1}{2}$% 2014 | 16.7% |
| 75 | 1.103 | Electricité de France $12\frac{1}{2}$% 2008 | 1.5% |
| 75 | 0.945 | Electricité de France $11\frac{3}{4}$% 2009/12 | 1.3% |
| 50 | 28.621 | Ireland $12\frac{1}{2}$% 2008 | 57.2% |
| 1.44 | 0.396 | City of Montreal 3% undated | 27.5% |
| 50 | 30.202 | Republic of Trinidad & Tobago $12\frac{1}{4}$% 2009 | 60.4% |

## Dealing arrangements

Prices of bulldog bonds are quoted as a percentage of their principal amount. The more active, or liquid, bonds tend to trade on a $\frac{3}{8}$% to $\frac{1}{2}$% price spread i.e. the price at which an investor can sell stock is $\frac{3}{8}$% to $\frac{1}{2}$% lower than the price at which he can buy stock. However, some very liquid bonds (such as European Investment Bank $9\frac{1}{2}$% 2009) may trade on a narrower $\frac{1}{4}$% spread. Conversely, some of the more illiquid issues tend to trade on a $\frac{3}{4}$% to 1% spread and others (particularly those issues where little of the original issue remains outstanding) on a negotiated basis only.

## Price conventions, accrued interest and ex-dividend arrangements

As with gilts and domestic debentures and loans, prices of bulldogs are quoted 'clean' i.e. exclusive of gross accrued interest, so that the total price paid by a buyer will have two component parts, (a) the quoted price and (b) the gross accrued interest. This latter quantity is the amount of interest that has accrued between the last interest payment date (or in the case of a new issue, the issue payment date) and the transaction's settlement date as explained in Chapter 4. The calendar convention used for bulldogs is that of the actual number of days between the relevant dates and a 365-day year for registered securities, and the ISMA convention of thirty-day months and a 360-day year for bearer.

Bulldog bonds in registered form have an ex-dividend period prior to the payment date. The date on which most registered bulldog bonds go ex-dividend is approximately one month before the relevant payment date. It is also possible to deal 'special ex-dividend' up to seven calendar days before the ex-dividend date. In this special ex-dividend period, trades may occur in either cum-dividend or ex-dividend form but, unless otherwise specified, prices are considered to be in the cum-dividend form. Bulldog bonds in bearer form do not have an ex-dividend period, but continue to accrue cum-dividend until the coupon payment date.

## Stamp Duty and levies

None of the bulldog bonds considered in this book are subject to stamp duty or the Panel for Takeovers and Mergers levy (with the exception of City of Montreal 3% perpetual).

## Commission

A stockbroker acting as an investor's agent may charge a client commission for carrying out transactions in bulldogs in accordance with individual client agreements.

## Settlement

*(i) Registered Bulldogs.* Settlement of bulldog transactions depends upon the form (either registered or bearer) and, if registered, whether the securities are held at the Central Gilts Office (CGO). Individuals and stockbrokers without accounts at the CGO will effect transfers in the usual way with the Bank of England's Registrar Department. The majority of trades occur in registered form and, where the stock is held at the CGO, for settlement the following business day. Registered bonds held outside the CGO are settled through the Talisman system five business days after the trade date. Most UK based stockbrokers will be familiar with this system from their experience in settling UK equity bargains.

*(ii) Bearer Bulldogs.* Trades in bearer form settle three business days later, normally through one of the two recognised clearing systems, Euroclear and CEDEL. However, this apparently straightforward arrangement can be upset when public holidays fall on different days in the UK and Europe. It is good practice to be specific about settlement arrangements at the time of dealing, especially so close to public holidays. Settlement of trades between Euroclear and CEDEL are also possible, being effected via an electronic 'bridge' between these two systems. Delivery of stock to a buyer is normally made on a DVP basis – delivery versus payment – whereby stock is

transferred to the buyer's account only when payment has been received in the seller's account.

## Custody

No custodial facilities are required for registered stock (although the introduction of a new dematerialised settlement system, CREST, in 1996 may make it advantageous for investors, especially active investors, to arrange holding facilities at a stockbroker in the future).

Custodial facilities for bearer stock are required. Given the practical problems associated with physical bearer bonds, most bearer stock is held in book-entry form within accounts at Euroclear and CEDEL. However, only those investors, traders and custodians with significant Eurobond business can justify the relatively high cost of opening and maintaining an account in either of these systems in their own name. Consequently, many investors find that it is more cost effective to use the services of a bank offering settlement and custodial facilities for Eurobonds. Most UK clearing banks offer such services, receiving instructions to settle transactions and maintain custody accounts. Brokers having settlement/custodial arrangements for other markets with such banks will be unlikely to find difficulty in establishing the necessary facilities.

## New issue procedures

Under the traditional issuing procedure, a lead manager is appointed and takes responsibility for negotiating the terms (e.g. coupon, maturity etc.) conditions (e.g. definition of events of default etc.) and price of the new issue. This manager will normally undertake to underwrite the whole issue. In addition to the underwriter, the issuer may choose to appoint a sponsor and/or stockbroker who will normally be responsible for distributing the new issue. However, the underwriter may undertake both functions.

Most new bulldog issues are announced early in the day and subsequently placed/sold to investors. It has become standard practice to price the new issue by reference to a yield margin over that of a specified gilt at a given time, say, 3.00pm on the day of issue. This allows potential investors to examine the terms of the issue on a comparative basis against gilts as soon as the issue is announced whilst the absolute price is not determined until later in the day when a further Stock Exchange announcement is then made detailing the result of the fixing. Payment for a new issue is usually required within approximately five days of the original placing.

## Yields and assessment of value

The two main criteria for valuing bulldog bonds are a bond's flat and redemption yields (see Chapter 5).

The flat yield, which is a measure of the annual income return obtainable from a bond, is obtained in the normal way by dividing the coupon rate by a bond's clean price and multiplying the result by 100.

Of greater importance is the redemption yield which takes into account both the annual income obtained from a bond and the eventual gain or loss at maturity.

The calendar conventions used in calculating yields in the bulldog market are exactly the same as those used for gilts – the actual number of days between relevant dates and a 365-day year – sometimes referred to as 'actual/365'.

With the exception of the two GEFCO issues, bulldog issues make interest payments semi-annually. Bulldog redemption yields are thus quoted on a semi-annual basis and are calculated as described in Chapter 5. Yields on the two GEFCO issues, which pay interest annually, are semi-annualised using the following equation,

$$\text{Semi-annual yield} = \left\{ \left( 1 + \frac{\text{Annual yield}}{100} \right)^{1/2} - 1 \right\} \times 200$$

Although bulldogs in bearer form have their accrued interest calculated on a 30-day month and 360-day year basis and therefore should, logically, have their redemption yields calculated with respect to ISMA convention, market practice is to calculate redemption yields on the bearer form in the same way as registered but take into account the different value of the accrued interest.

Whilst a bulldog bond's gross redemption yield is a perfectly acceptable measure of its absolute value, most investors will wish to compare this yield with those of similarly dated gilts and, perhaps, other sterling fixed interest instruments to assess the bulldog's value relative to the market. As yields on bulldogs and gilts are both quoted on a semi-annual compounding basis, direct comparisons between them can be made. This difference in yield – the 'yield margin over gilts' – is an indicator of the risk premium associated with a particular issue and reflects, amongst other things, such factors as relative credit standings and liquidity. Assessing when this margin is likely to widen or narrow is one of the keys to successful investment in this market.

## Taxation

### (i) Registered Stock

The supranational issues listed below pay their semi-annual coupon gross (i.e. without deduction of withholding tax) to holders named on the register irrespective of the nature of the holder.

African Development Bank 11⅛% 2010
Asian Development Bank 10¼% 2009
European Investment Bank 9% 2001
European Investment Bank 11% 2002
European Investment Bank 10⅜% 2004
European Investment Bank 9½% 2009
Inter-American Development Bank 12½% 2003
Inter-American Development Bank 9¾% 2015
World Bank 11½% 2003
World Bank 9½% 2010

The gross paying facility of the registered form of supranational bulldog issues listed above gives cash flow advantages to all investors, irrespective of their tax status. Non-taxpayers are relieved of the task of reclaiming tax and receive their full entitlement on the interest payment date, while tax paying investors have their liability to tax delayed. (However, it should be noted that the registrar of these issues supplies the Inland Revenue with the names and addresses of those to whom gross interest has been paid.)

All other issues (excluding Inco 15¾% 2006 which does not exist in registered form) make interest payments net of UK basic rate tax (currently 25%) unless it is proved to the satisfaction of the Inspector of Foreign Dividends (IFD) that the investor is a non-resident of the UK. In other words, all non-supranational bulldog issues are 'FOTRA' stocks as described in Chapter 10.

Alternatively, overseas investors who are resident in a country which is party to an agreement with the UK may make a claim to recover tax deducted at source under the relevant double taxation agreement.

*(ii) Bearer stock*

Interest on bearer bulldogs is paid to those holders recorded by Euroclear/CEDEL or upon presentation of the relevant coupon to a specified paying agent. Interest may be paid free of withholding tax where:

(a) either the person/agency through whom the payment is made is not located in the UK, or
(b) if the person/agency through whom the payment is made is located in the UK, it is proved that the beneficial owner is a non-resident for UK tax purposes, or that the bonds are held within Euroclear or CEDEL.

In all other cases, payments of interest are made net of basic rate tax, currently 25% for UK issuers. All holders of bearer bulldog bonds who are resident in the UK for tax purposes and use the facilities of an agent for custody and coupon payments will receive interest net of withholding tax.

Only those UK based investors who directly hold their bonds in a Euroclear or Cedel account in their own name are able to receive interest gross. Such interest will, of course, still be subject to UK tax, but there will be a cash flow advantage derived from any such tax payment being delayed.

Bulldog bonds in general (whether registered or bearer) come within the scope of the new (1996) taxation arrangements for gilts and bonds.

This means that for UK corporate investors and personal investors whose aggregated gilt-edged and other bond holdings exceed £200,000 nominal, capital gains on bulldogs are treated as income items and are taxed accordingly (see Chapter 10).

For personal investors at or below the £200,000 nominal threshold, bulldogs (with two exceptions) fall into the accrued income scheme, but because bulldogs are qualifying corporate bonds (QCBs) their capital gains are tax-free. The main provisions of the accrued income scheme treat as taxable income not only interest or dividend payments received, but also accrued interest at the time of sale less accrued interest at the time of purchase. The effect of this is to ensure that the income assessable to tax is directly proportional to the period of time the investment concerned is held. The exceptions are the Government of Gibralter issue, which is classed as a variable rate security on account of certain conditions attached to the bond which provide for an increase in the bond's coupon in the event of Gibralter ceasing to be a Crown colony, and Inco $15\frac{3}{4}$% 2006 as a consequence of holders of this bond having the option to receive the redemption proceeds in US dollars at a fixed exchange rate of $1.98 to £1.

*Note:* The comments on taxation above are of a general nature based on our understanding of current UK law and Inland Revenue practice. They relate only to the position of persons who are the absolute beneficial owners and may not apply to certain classes of persons such as traders and market-makers. Any person who is in doubt as to his/her personal tax position should consult his/her professional advisers.

# 17

## *Preference shares*

Strictly speaking preference shares are not part of the corporate bond market because they are shares in a company rather than instruments of debt. However they are an integral part of the fixed income investment scene and no comprehensive work of reference on this subject would be complete if it did not cover them.

The essential point about preference shares is their status relative to debt instruments and ordinary shares. They rank after all creditors, including bond holders, but before ordinary shareholders in the case of a corporate winding-up and the same order of priority applies to the payment of dividends.

Preference shares have long been a traditional form of corporate capital, and in the past many major companies have issued such shares. 'Prefs' as they are colloquially known in the marketplace, may be either irredeemable (thus forming part of the issuer's permanent share capital), or redeemable (provided that they comply with the law relating to the reduction of capital which normally requires court sanction in order to protect creditors' interests), and many of those currently listed originated as long ago as the last century. We shall restrict our analysis to those preference shares which are domestic, registered securities of UK resident companies.

Preference shares are generally transferable in multiples of one share. The great majority of them have a par value of £1, but there are exceptions to this, with par values ranging from 1p to £10.

Prefs can be either cumulative, or non-cumulative. The difference between these being that in the event of any dividend(s) on a cumulative share being passed, all arrears must subsequently be made good before any distributions can be made to ordinary shareholders, whilst no equivalent obligation applies to passed dividends on non-cumulative shares.

The overwhelming majority of shares pay a fixed dividend, normally at the annual rate implied by their coupon. However, not everything is straightforward. Prior to 1973, when the basis of corporation tax was changed to an imputation system, preference shares were all designated with gross coupon rates in exactly the same way as bonds. As a necessary consequence of the new system which allowed preference and ordinary share dividends to be paid net of advance corporation tax at a rate (until 1993) equal to the basic rate of income tax, all existing gross coupon rates were netted down at the then prevailing basic rate of 30%, so that, for example, a former 8% (gross) coupon rate automatically became a 5.6% net coupon rate. Many companies altered the titles of their shares to take this change into account, but regrettably some companies did not, so generating a degree of confusion which has persisted ever since. For example the so-called BP 8% preference share is really a 5.6% net pref., and, since the associated tax credit is currently (1994/95) only 20%, it nowadays only 'grosses up' to a mere 7%.

Happily, however, UK prefs issued since 1973 have been designated with net coupon rates, but it is not always immediately obvious whether the coupon rate of a particular share is gross or net. If in doubt reference can be made to the Stock Exchange Daily Official List which carries these details.

Preference share dividends are usually payable semi-annually, on predetermined dates, at half the annual coupon rate. Just like equities dividends they are declared by the relevant company's Board of Directors and are payable out of post-tax profits. Directors will not lightly pass a preference dividend, since, as was mentioned earlier, no dividends may be paid on ordinary shares so long as non-cumulative preference dividends are unpaid or cumulative preference dividends are in arrears. It is not always realised, however, that even if a company has the cash resources, the Board may, on occasions, be prevented by law from paying a dividend if the company lacks the necessary distributable reserves.

As owners of that particular section of a company's share capital preference shareholders' rights and interests are governed by the company's Articles of Association. These almost invariably impose limits on a company's power to borrow, and restrict the issuance of prior-ranking shares. As mentioned earlier, preference shareholders rank ahead of ordinary shareholders both as to dividends and as to capital in a winding-up, up to prescribed limits. In the case of a winding-up preference shares are most commonly entitled to repayment at par plus accrued interest, but this is not always so. In some cases preference shares may be entitled to more than par, and in other cases the amount may be determined by a reference formula, say, to the average market price over a recent past period. Where more than one class of preference share is in issue, first preference shares generally rank before second preference shares and so on and so forth. Unless preference share dividends are in arrears preference shareholders rarely have the right to vote at general meetings, except on matters that directly affect their class rights.

The market in preference shares is pretty fragmented. In volume terms the market is currently dominated by business in the ten irredeemable issues shown in Table 17.1, all of which are in the financial sector.

**Table 17.1** Leading preference shares in issue as at May 1995

| Size of issue | Company | Net coupon rate | Dividend payment dates | |
|---|---|---|---|---|
| £100m | Bank of Scotland | $9\frac{1}{4}$% | 31 May | 30 Nov. |
| £100m | Bank of Scotland | $9\frac{3}{4}$% | 31 May | 30 Nov. |
| £100m | Commercial Union | $8\frac{3}{8}$% | 31 March | 30 Sep. |
| £100m | Commercial Union | $8\frac{3}{4}$% | 30 June | 31 Dec. |
| £60m | Cooperative Bank | $9\frac{1}{4}$% | 31 May | 30 Nov. |
| £110m | General Accident | $7\frac{7}{8}$% | 1 April | 1 Oct. |
| £140m | General Accident | $8\frac{7}{8}$% | 1 Jan. | 1 July |
| £140m | National Westminster Bank | 9% | 16 April | 16 Oct. |
| £100m | Standard Chartered | $7\frac{3}{8}$% | 1 April | 1 Oct. |
| £125m | Sun Alliance | $7\frac{3}{8}$% | 1 April | 1 Oct. |

These are the most liquid shares and account for a large proportion of total market turnover. Beyond these there are over four hundred smaller issues listed on the London Stock Exchange, representing a wide range of UK commercial and industrial companies where turnover is more spasmodic. There are also about sixty small preference share issues in the investment trust sector and a number of specialist zero-dividend and stepped preference shares of split-capital trusts. In addition a number of unlisted preference shares have traded from time to time under Stock Exchange rule 4.2(a). However following the regulatory changes involved with the abolition of the Unlisted Securities Market (USM) and the creation of the Alternative Investment Market (AIM) this facility ceased on 29 September 1995 and from now on such transactions will have to be off-Exchange.

Historically preference shares were a traditional form of corporate capital but the introduction of Corporation Tax in 1965 (see Chapter 13) made them a tax-inefficient form of leverage and for some years thereafter there was a dearth of new issues. However, in the late 1980s a number of acquisitive companies started raising preference shares as a means of expanding their capital base quickly without issuing equity, or without waiting to accumulate retained earnings. Unfortunately, several of these companies ran into trouble in the recession that followed and subsequently passed dividends, were reconstructed or went into receivership.

But in the past few years the market has gained a new lease of life as a result of the implementation of internationally agreed minimum capital adequacy requirements in the banking and insurance industries. Some major banks, especially those whose capital ratios were under pressure as a result of having to make a high level of provision for bad debts, took the opportunity to buttress their capital ratios by making issues of non-cumulative irredeemable preference shares which count as valuable core capital; and similar considerations have led to comparable issuance by a number of large composite insurance companies. Stimulated by these influences the market saw a total of just under £1,000 million raised between December 1990 and

December 1993. By contrast only one small company came to the market in 1994, but it has to be remembered that 1994 was an extremely poor year for bond markets in general as interest rates and yields rose substantially all round the world.

## Dealing arrangements

Prices of preference shares are quoted in pence per share. The prices of the leading issues (as well as a few smaller issues) are displayed on the Stock Exchange Automated Quotation (SEAQ) system, and $\frac{1}{2}$p (half a point) bid-to-offer price spreads are typical in sizes up to 100,000 shares in normal market conditions. Although it is frequently possible to trade in these leading issues in much larger size, brokers should find no difficulty in executing business in modest size without suffering a price penalty. Investors should be warned, however, that many of the smaller preference shares are held by long term investors and may not be readily available from the market. Many of these issues will have a bid price only. Generally the availability of preference shares for purchase can be ascertained from market-makers' offer lists or from specific offers made by market-makers to brokers and clients who have expressed a particular interest.

## Price conventions and ex-dividend arrangements

Unlike the majority of sterling fixed interest securities, all preference shares are quoted on a 'dirty' price basis which includes the accrued income in the price.

Prices may be cum-dividend, in which case the buyer is entitled to all future dividend payments, including any arrears due but not yet paid. Alternatively, the shares may be quoted ex-dividend (xd), in which case the seller retains the right to receive a dividend already declared but not yet paid. Shares may be declared officially xd at any time prior to a dividend date, provided that date is notified by the company to the Stock Exchange. The period of notice given varies enormously from company to company, but 'prefs' usually go ex-dividend between four and six weeks prior to payment day.

Provided the ex-dividend date is known in advance, preference shares may be traded in both special ex-dividend and cum-dividend form up to ten working days prior to the ex-dividend date. One consequence of the 'dirty' price system is the discontinuity in price that occurs whenever a preference share is quoted ex-dividend for the first time. Typically the ex-dividend price will be lower than the previous cum-dividend price by an amount approximating to the grossed-up dividend payment.

## Dealing expenses

Unlike most other sterling fixed-interest securities preference shares are subject to stamp duty (or in the case of allotment letters or renounceable certificates stamp duty reserve tax) which is levied at an *ad valorem* rate of $\frac{1}{2}\%$ on the purchase consideration. The only exceptions to this are purchases made by charities and in cases of acquisitions of new issues by the original placee or allottee.

Where bargains are transacted through brokers or other intermediaries their commissions or fees can be expected to be charged in accordance with individual agreements. In addition each contract for a consideration in excess of £10,000 is subject to a PTM levy (currently £1), to fund the Panel for Takeovers and Mergers.

## Settlement

Unless otherwise specified at the time of dealing, preference share trades are settled five business days after the date of the transaction. (This settlement period was reduced from ten days on 26 June 1995). At the present time settlement is effected through the London Stock Exchange's Talisman system, which is also used to settle domestic equity and loan stock trades, but the whole process of settlement and registration is due to change with the introduction of CREST, which is expected to take place in the second half of 1996.

In the case of new issues in the form of allotment letters or renounceable certificates, settlement is normally due on the following business day after the trade date.

## New issue procedures

The traditional procedure for a preference share issue was a 'placing'. Under this system a merchant bank would act as adviser and sponsor to the issue, using a broker to distribute the shares to its clients and the marketplace. Increasingly these functions are being combined under one roof by integrated securities houses or investment banks prepared to assume the full underwriting risk of a 'bought' deal. There is also a growing tendency for issuing houses and placing brokers to offer shares to the retail market via private client stockbrokers and fund managers, as well as to financial institutions.

Shares are generally offered at a fixed price, which may well be determined by reference to the yield on a benchmark gilt on the day of issue.

Payment for new issues is normally required within a week or so of the original placing, the actual date being set by the issuing house concerned.

## Yields and assessment of value

### (1) Irredeemable preference shares

It is conventional to calculate yields on irredeemable preference shares based on prices clean of accrued income. This ensures that the resultant (flat) yields are directly comparable with irredeemables in other markets, notably the gilt-edged market (see Chapter 5). Since preference share prices are quoted dirty it is first necessary to deduct the accrued income in order to arrive at the clean price. In order to calculate a gross yield, it is also necessary to 'gross-up' the net coupon to allow for the associated tax credit, currently 20%. Additionally a purchaser should take into account dealing expenses, notably brokerage and transfer stamp duty, to obtain a true buying yield.

Let us look at the following example:

On 22 January a buyer pays $93\frac{1}{2}$p cum-dividend for 10,000 XYZ plc $7\frac{3}{8}\%$ irredeemable preference shares, for settlement on 29 January. The shares pay dividends on 1 April and 1 October.

*Step (i)*   Compute the buying contract total thus:

| | | |
|---|---|---|
| Consideration = 10000 × 93.50p /100 | = | £9,350.00 |
| Add stamp duty = (1/2% × £9,350) | | |
| rounded up to the next multiple of £0.50 = | | £47.00 |
| Brokerage, say, 0.2% (by negotiation) | = | £18.70 |
| PTM levy | = | £1.00 |
| Total cost | = | £9,416.70 |

This represents a 'dirty' price after dealing expenses of 94.167.

*Step (ii)*   Establish the effective grossed-up coupon rate:

Gross coupon rate  =  Net coupon rate/(1 – Rate of tax credit%)
                            =  7.375%/(1 – 20/100)
                            =  9.21875%

*Step (iii)* Next compute the gross accrued income relevant to the settlement day, 29 January.

Between 1 October and 29 January following there are 120 days.
Thus the Gross accrued income  =  9.21875 × 120 / 365
                            =  3.03082

(Note the accrued income calculation has been done using an exact number of days elapsed divided by 365 convention.)

*Step (iv)* Clean price     = Dirty price minus Accrued income
                                  = 94.16700 − 3.03082
                                  = 91.13618

*Step (v)*  Gross flat yield     = Grossed-up coupon rate% × 100 / Clean price
                                  = 9.21875% × 100 / 91.13618
                                  = 10.115%

*(2) Redeemable preference shares*

With redeemable preference shares the flat yield is clearly inappropriate as an evaluation measure as it does not take into account the capital gain or loss that will occur at redemption. The concept of 'redemption yields' and the basis upon which they are calculated have been dealt with in some detail earlier in this book (Chapter 5). Suffice it to say that precisely the same calculative methodology can be applied to redeemable preference shares as to redeemable bonds, and that a redemption yield combines in one figure both the income and capital gain/loss elements of the prospective return available from the share. Since most preference shares make dividend payments twice a year it is the convention to quote redemption yields on a semi-annual basis, which is the same basis as that used for gilts and domestic corporate bonds (but not Eurosterling bonds whose yields are normally calculated and expressed on an annual basis).

Yields, whether they be flat yields on irredeemables or redemption yields on redeemable preference shares, can be used as a measure of value in two different senses, absolute and relative. The absolute level of yield, irrespective of other values in alternative markets, may be of prime importance to some classes of investor whose only priority is maximisation of income, but the main determinant of preference share prices is their relative valuation *vis-à-vis* other comparable fixed interest instruments, in particular, gilts.

Since preference shares are the lowest ranking form of corporate fixed income security, a wide spread over risk-free gilts of similar maturity will generally be appropriate, even in cases of perfectly sound companies. Obviously, the weaker a company is financially, the greater is the risk of it passing a dividend payment, and the wider is the yield spread over gilts that can be expected as compensation. Since it is unusual for domestic preference shares to be assessed by the rating agencies, evaluation of such risk is essentially a matter of individual judgment and opinions often vary. In addition other extraneous factors often occur which may distort values. At times one comes across examples of relatively small long-standing low-coupon shares trading on yields well below those of the more liquid leading issues, and sometimes standing on gross yields below those available on gilts. When this occurs the explanation is often found to lie in the willingness of investors to speculate on the prospect of some form of capital reorganisation, perhaps related to a takeover, which could involve the preference shares being redeemed either at par or at least at a premium to current price levels. Alternatively, there may be some shareholder perks attached to the shares which give them speciality value. A good example of this is the concessionary cross-channel ferry fares available to holders of P&O $5\frac{1}{2}\%$ preference shares.

When comparing yields on preference shares with those offered by gilts or corporate bonds, care must be taken to consider the different tax treatments afforded to preference shares. This has already been mentioned earlier in this chapter but since this factor is pivotal to understanding preference shares it will do no harm to restate the position.

The first point to remember is that preference share dividends are paid, like equity dividends, out of profits net of corporation tax. Since they are normally paid well before the mainstream corporation tax payment for the relevant year is due, the company makes a payment of advance corporation tax (ACT) to the Inland Revenue at the same time as paying net dividends to its preference shareholders. From a UK non-corporate investor's point of view this payment of ACT is treated as a tax credit and thus the 'grossed-up' dividend (net dividend plus tax credit) varies with the prevailing rate of ACT. Historically this rate was the same as the basic rate of income tax, currently 25%, but in the Budget of 1993 the rate of ACT was reduced to 20% whilst basic rate tax remained at 25%.

Next one must remember that preference share dividends represent 'franked income' in the hands of a corporation tax paying holder, and that if such a holder wishes to make gross yield comparisons between prefs and other fixed interest instruments, the net preference share dividends should be 'grossed-up' at the full corporation tax rate of 33% (25% for smaller companies) and not at the 20% ACT rate.

Some people find the concept of 'grossed-up' values difficult to comprehend. A 'grossed-up net' amount is that amount which after deduction of tax at the rate in question produces a given net value. Mathematically it can be expressed thus,

$$\text{Grossed-up value} = \frac{\text{Net value}}{(1 - \text{Tax rate}/100)}$$

## Taxation of income

Preference shareholders receive a net dividend at the fixed (or predetermined) net coupon rate. Thus a holder of 10,000 NatWest 9% preference shares of £1 par value will receive every 16 April and 16 October a payment of £450 (9p × 10,000/2). The voucher accompanying the payment will show not only the dividend, but also the tax credit in respect of tax paid on the underlying profits by the issuing company. The tax credit is an amount which corresponds to the rate of ACT in force when the distribution is made. For the financial year 1995/96 this rate is 20% and applies to the gross amount in question, i.e., the sum of the net dividend and the tax credit itself.

Let us take the above example of a holder of 10,000 NatWest 9% prefs and a rate of ACT of 20% and observe how tax affects differing classes of investor.

The half-yearly dividend paid net was £450.

Using a 20% rate of ACT this grosses up to £450 / (1−20/100) = £562.50.

The tax credit is 20% of this gross amount i.e. £562.50 × .2 = £112.50 which can also be seen to be the difference between the gross and net amounts.

The tax treatment of dividends depends on the status of the recipient.

1. A UK resident individual may set off the tax credit against his liability to income tax, using as the quantum of income under schedule F the dividend grossed up for the tax credit. Since the lower rate of tax on dividend income is currently 20%, a basic rate (25%) taxpayer will have no further tax to pay on the dividend. A higher rate taxpayer, however, will have a further liability. Using the above example, he will be liable to pay tax on the grossed-up value of this dividend (£562.50) at the current rate of 40%, i.e. £225, against which he will be able to offset the £112.50 credit, leaving a further £112.50 to pay. Individuals with incomes below the tax threshold should be able to claim repayment of all or part of the tax credit.
2. Tax-exempt bodies such as charities and pension funds should be able to reclaim the tax credit.
3. Non-resident individuals entitled to claim a proportion of personal reliefs, e.g. Commonwealth or Republic of Ireland citizens or residents of the Isle of Man or the Channel Islands, are entitled to a tax credit. Other non-UK resident recipients of dividends should be eligible for a restricted tax credit under most double tax agreements.
4. For a UK resident company, the dividend received constitutes franked investment income. Since the dividend is paid out of profits which have already been subjected to corporation tax, it will not normally fall to be charged to corporation tax a second time. For a company paying corpo-

276

ration tax at 33%, an alternative bond investment would need to pay a gross coupon of 13.43% in order to generate the same post-tax income as that from a 9% net preference share. Furthermore, there is a cash flow advantage in that the tax credit on franked investment income may be set off against the recipient company's liability to pay ACT on any franked payments of their own made in the same accounting period, and any surplus franked investment income may be carried forward.

Preference shares do not come within the scope of the new (1996) taxation arrangements for gilts and bonds, neither are they included in the accrued income scheme. This means that, unlike gilts and other fixed-interest instruments that are subject to that regime, the accrued income of a preference share will not normally be subject to income tax (unless the holder is assessed as a dealer or trader in securities), but will be considered to be a component part of the total price in any capital gains tax computation.

## Taxation of capital

For capital gains tax purposes, preference shares are treated in exactly the same way as ordinary shares. Gains realised by UK resident individuals are subject to capital gains tax, and losses may be offset against other chargeable gains. The indexation allowance enables the cost price to be inflated by reference to the change in the RPI during the period of ownership (except where this creates or increases the size of an offsetable loss), and the first £6,000 (for 1995/96) of aggregated chargeable gains in a given tax year are tax-free. For companies, corporation tax is chargeable on profits, which include chargeable gains on shares.

*Note:* the comments on taxation above are of a general nature based on our understanding of current UK law and Inland Revenue practice. They relate only to the position of persons who are the absolute beneficial owners and may not apply to certain classes of persons such as traders and market-makers. Any person who is in doubt as to his/her personal tax position should consult his/her professional advisers.

# 18

## *Permanent interest bearing shares (PIBS)*

One of the effects of the general move towards deregulation in financial markets in recent years has been the growing competition between banks and building societies, where both have sought to extend their activities into territory that traditionally was the preserve of the other. Banks have become aggressive mortgage lenders whilst many building societies have, *inter alia*, built retail current account banking operations to complement their savings products. At the same time changes to capital adequacy requirements of lending institutions made the size of such an institution's capital base, and the ability to expand it, an increasingly important consideration. In this regard the playing field was far from level. In contrast to a bank's ability to raise such capital via the equity and bond markets, mutually owned building societies were unable to tap this source for funds and, until 1991, had to rely solely on internally generated surpluses as a means of expanding their core capital. The changes brought about by the 1991 budget redressed this inequality to a considerable extent by empowering building societies to issue a new form of capital called permanent interest bearing shares (PIBS). These, as their name suggests, are irredeemables. In capital adequacy terms they rank equally with a bank's ordinary and irredeemable preference shares and just like them are deeply subordinated.

The Leeds Permanent Building Society was the first to take advantage of this new capability and issued £75 million PIBS in June 1991. These shares carried a coupon rate of $13\frac{5}{8}\%$ per annum, and at the time of issue gave a gross yield of $3\frac{1}{2}\%$ more than the equivalent gilt. These securities were well received by investors and since then the market in sterling PIBS has grown so that there are now a total of eighteen separate issues from fourteen different societies in existence – a total of £905 million in nominal terms. In addition, there is also an Irish Punt issue from First National Building Society.

It is important to understand the exact status of PIBS. PIBS are deferred shares of the issuer and are thus unsecured. In order to count towards a society's core capital base for regulatory purposes they have to be both perpetual and deeply subordinated.

Given the nature of PIBS and the risks attached to holding them, PIBS

278

carry, *inter alia*, certain 'health warnings' which are printed on the reverse of each certificate. These risks are expressed in the general form as follows:

(a) The principal of PIBS is not repayable and PIBS are not withdrawable and accordingly the only way that PIBS may be realised is by the sale at such price and on such terms as may from time to time be available in the market (which may mean that the investor does not recoup his investment) and the proceeds may be subject to brokers' commissions.
(b) In the event of a winding-up or dissolution of a society with issued PIBS, holders' claims will rank behind all other creditors of the society including members holding shares (other than deferred shares) as to both interest and principal.
(c) PIBS are not protected investments for the purposes of payments out of the Building Societies Investor Protection Fund.
(d) Interest in respect of PIBS shall not be payable where to make payment would result in the society's capital falling below prescribed levels, if the directors of the society resolve that such interest should not be paid, or where the society has not paid interest in respect of deposits or shares (other than deferred shares); and
(e) If the society does not make an interest payment in respect of PIBS in accordance with paragraph (d) above such interest will be cancelled.

Although all sterling denominated PIBS have no provision for repayment (and are thus perpetual), two issues made by the Halifax Building Society are callable at the issuer's option. The Halifax 12% issue is callable at an adjusted redemption price up until 30 January 2022 and thereafter at par. The Halifax $8\frac{3}{4}$% issue is callable at an adjusted redemption price up until 14 September 2023 and thereafter at par.

The adjusted redemption price in each case is defined as the price of the PIBS at which the gross redemption yield (calculated on the basis of the PIBS being redeemed at par on 30 January 2022 for the 12% issue and 14 September 2023 for the $8\frac{3}{4}$% issue) would be equal to the gross redemption yield prevailing on the then appropriate benchmark gilt. At present, the 12% issue is trading above par and whilst that situation persists yields on this issue should be calculated on the basis of redemption at par on 30 January 2022 in order to reflect the likelihood of these shares being called at that time.

Investors should also be aware that, upon the issuer transferring its business to another building society, the outstanding PIBS become the obligation of the combined society without alteration of any terms and conditions. However, if the issuer transfers its business to a bank, the outstanding PIBS will be treated as perpetual subordinated debt, paying the same rate of interest as the original PIBS.

PIBS have no covenants. However, the building society industry in general and the specific issuers all benefit from regulation by the Building Society Commission (BSC). This regulator monitors the general health of individual societies and will help and advise any society which is under pressure even to the extent, if necessary, of facilitating a merger with another stronger society. Although PIBS have no covenants, the BSC specifically advises societies to limit the issuance of PIBS to less than 50% of free reserves, thus attempting to ensure adequate capital cover for investors in the event of a wind-up.

It can thus be seen that PIBS, although sharing many characteristics with other forms of sterling bonds, also carry similar characteristics to bank non-cumulative irredeemable preference shares. This places PIBS among the highest risk, and therefore the highest yielding categories of sterling fixed income securities.

All sterling denominated PIBS are listed on the London Stock Exchange. PIBS exist only in registered form and transfers are made in the same way as domestic loan and debenture stocks. Upon the registrar receiving notification of a transfer, a PIBS certificate is sent to the new registered holder, usually within one month. This certificate shows, *inter alia*, the stock details (such as coupon and dividend dates) and the amount of stock held. However, this certificate does not constitute ownership. Lost or damaged certificates may be replaced by the society concerned, usually at no cost. Joint ownership is generally permitted (e.g. joint registration in husband's and wife's names) but some societies may decline to register a transfer to more than four persons jointly.

PIBS vary in denomination from £1,000 to £50,000 (see Table 18.1 for details). Investors will need to be aware of the denomination available for each PIBS as only exact multiples of this amount can be purchased and/or subsequently sold. With the exception of the floating rate PIBS from the First National and Cheshire societies, shares are issued with a fixed coupon which is payable in equal half-yearly installments (i.e. semi-annually) in arrears. Interest is paid net of UK withholding tax (currently 25%), with the exception of the First National $11\frac{3}{4}\%$ issue which is paid net of Irish withholding tax (currently 27%).

## Dealing arrangements

Prices of PIBS are quoted as a percentage of their nominal amount. The majority of PIBS trade on a $\frac{1}{2}\% - \frac{3}{4}\%$ price spread i.e. the price at which an investor can sell shares is $\frac{1}{2}\% - \frac{3}{4}\%$ lower than the price at which he can buy shares. However, this spread may vary according to a variety of factors such as issue size, transaction size or the existence of (or rumours about) changes concerning the issuer, the PIBS market or the building society industry in general.

**Table 18.1** Building society sterling PIBS issues (in order of original issuance)

| Building society | Coupon | Issue size (£m) | Pay dates | Minimum denomination (£) | MOODY's rating[1] | Issue margin bp | Benchmark gilt | Date |
|---|---|---|---|---|---|---|---|---|
| Halifax (originally Leeds) | 13⅝% | 75 | 10 June/10 Dec | 50,000 | Baa1 | 350 | TY9 08 | June 91 |
| Bradford & Bingley | 13% | 60 | 7 April/7 Oct | 10,000 | Baa2 | 360 | TY9 08 | Oct 91 |
| Bristol & West (2 tranches) | 13⅜% | 75 | 7 May/7 Nov | 1,000 | Ba3 | 385/370 | TY9 08 | Nov 91/Dec 91 |
| Britannia (2 tranches) | 13% | 110 | 31 Jan/31 July | 1,000 | Baa3 | 360/280 | TY9 08 | Jan 92/Oct 92 |
| Halifax | 12% | 100 | 1 March/1 Sep | 50,000 | A1 (S&P A+) | 275 | TY9 08 | Jan 92 |
| Skipton | 12⅞% | 25 | 31 Jan/31 July | 1,000 | nr | 375 | TY9 08 | March 92 |
| Leeds & Holbeck | 13⅜% | 25 | 31 Jan/31 July | 1,000 | nr | 370 | TY9 08 | April 92 |
| Coventry | 12⅛% | 40 | 1 March/1 Sep | 1,000 | nr | 325 | TY9 08 | June 92 |
| Northern Rock (originally North of England) | 12⅝% | 20 | 30 June/31 Dec | 1,000 | nr | 350 | TY9 08 | June 92 |
| Bradford & Bingley | 11⅝% | 50 | 20 Jan/20 July | 10,000 | Baa2 | 260 | TY9 08 | July 92 |
| Newcastle | 12⅝% | 10 | 15 March/15 Sep | 1,000 | nr | 360 | TY9 08 | Sept 92 |
| First National | 11¾% | 20 | 11 May/11 Nov | 10,000 | nr | 330 | TY9 08 | May 93 |
| Newcastle | 10¾% | 10 | 22 June/22 Dec | 1,000 | nr | 240 | TY9 08 | June 93 |
| Halifax | 8¾% | 100 | 1 March/1 Sep | 50,000 | A1 (S&P A+) | 150 | TY8T17 | Sep 93 |
| Birmingham & Midshires | 9⅜% | 50 | 1 March/1 Sep | 1,000 | Ba1 | 280 | TY8T17 | Dec 93 |
| First National | FLOAT | 25 | 18 March/18 Sep | 1,000 | nr | n/a | n/a | March 94 |
| Cheshire | FLOAT | 10 | 28 March/28 Sep | 1,000 | nr | n/a | n/a | March 94 |

[1]Ratings as prevailing at 13 February 1995

## Price conventions and accrued interest

As with gilts and domestic debentures and loans, prices of PIBS are quoted 'clean' i.e. exclusive of gross accrued interest, so that the total price paid by a buyer will have two component parts, (a) the quoted price and (b) the gross accrued interest. This latter quantity is the amount of interest that has accrued on the shares between the date of the last dividend payment date (or in the case of a new issue, the issue payment date) and the transaction's settlement date as outlined in Chapter 4. The calendar convention used in the calculation of accrued interest on PIBS is that of the actual number of days and a 365-day year.

## Stamp duty

Stamp duty is not payable on any existing PIBS issues. However, in the past, societies, whilst waiting for the necessary alteration of their rules to permit the issuance of PIBS, have accelerated matters by making new issues of subordinated loan stocks which are mandatorily convertible into PIBS. Should this practice reoccur stamp duty is likely to apply to such issues.

## Commission and other transaction expenses

A stockbroker acting as an investor's agent may charge a client commission for carrying out transactions in PIBS in accordance with individual client agreements . The scope of the PTM levy (to fund the Panel for Takeovers and Mergers) does not extend to PIBS.

## Ex-dividend arrangements

Similarly to gilts, PIBS have an ex-dividend period prior to their dividend payment dates. Dividends are paid by sterling cheques through the post to holders appearing on the register at the close of business on the fifteenth day before the dividend is due. The actual ex-dividend dates, which are always the first business day of a week, are linked to this record date by a pre-deter-mined Stock Exchange calendar and are normally about three and a half weeks before the relevant dividend date.

It is also possible to deal 'special ex-dividend' during the seven days immediately before the ex-dividend date. Transactions in this special ex-divi-dend period can be in either cum-dividend or ex-dividend form but are normally taken to be cum-dividend unless otherwise specified.

## Settlement

PIBS trades, unless otherwise specified, are currently effected for settlement in sterling for delivery five business days after the date of the transaction.

Settlement of PIBS transactions takes place through the London Stock Exchange's Talisman system with which UK based stockbrokers will be familiar from their experience in settling UK equity and domestic loan stock bargains.

## New issue procedures

Under the traditional issuing procedure, a manager is appointed and takes responsibility for negotiating the terms (e.g. coupon, price etc.) of the new issue. This manager will normally undertake to underwrite the whole issue. In addition to the underwriter, the issuer may also choose to appoint a sponsor and/or stockbroker who will normally be responsible for distributing the new shares. If not, the underwriter will undertake both functions.

Most new PIBS issues are announced early in the day and subsequently placed/sold to investors following the official Stock Exchange announcement. New PIBS issues are normally priced by reference to a yield margin over a specified gilt (currently Treasury $8\frac{3}{4}$% 2017) at a given time, say 3.00 p.m., on the day of issue. This means that whilst potential investors are able to examine the terms of the issue on a comparative basis against gilts as soon as the issue is announced, the exact price is not struck until later in the afternoon when a further Stock Exchange announcement is made detailing the result of the fixing (i.e. the coupon rate, the issue price etc.). Payment for the new issue is usually required within about five days of the placing.

The initial placement of new PIBS has varied. Some issues, particularly those with relatively high minimum denominations (e.g. £50,000) have mainly been placed with the large domestic institutions, while others have been largely distributed to the retail sector via stockbrokers.

In 1991, the first year that PIBS were allowed, new issuance totalled £210 million. This increased to £480 million in the following year but declined in 1993 to £180 million. The total outstanding currently stands at £905 million nominal although this figure includes the two floating rate issues made in 1994.

## Yields and assessment of value

The current or flat yield of a PIBS issue can be ascertained in the normal way by dividing the coupon by the clean market price and multiplying the result by 100. This yield gives an indication of the income return that the bond will generate on an annual basis. (See Chapter 5).

Unlike the majority of sterling fixed income securities, PIBS have no maturity date and thus a redemption yield (or yield to maturity) has no meaning. However, as already noted, the two Halifax issues are callable and it is meaningful in these circumstances to quote a so-called 'yield to worst' case. Where the issues are trading below par, the yield quoted is the simple current

283

yield but, if above par, a redemption yield is calculated on the worst case assumption of the issue being called at par, and this will take into account the resulting capital loss.

Having calculated a PIBS's yield the next step in making value assessments is to compare this return with those available on other PIBS and other classes of fixed income instruments, in particular, gilts. The most commonly used criterion of relative value is the gross yield margin over what is currently the longest-dated gilt, Treasury $8\frac{3}{4}\%$ 2017. In principle the benchmark comparator gilt ought to be an irredeemable but although six undated gilts still exist their marketability is nowadays diminished and the accuracy of their pricing is not always totally reliable.

In general, yields on PIBS follow the pattern of increasing return for diminishing creditworthiness and size. Hence the Halifax, regarded as the highest quality society in the sector, tends to yield the least. Creditworthiness is assessed by reference to all the usual criteria, including the level of bad debt provisions and the perceived risks associated with diversification away from the core mortgage/deposit business. In some cases this information is encapsulated in a credit rating (half of the 14 issuers of sterling PIBS carry ratings from Moody's and the Halifax Building Society is also rated by S&P) but in others no formal ratings exist and it is left to the individual to make his own assessment.

Investors should also be aware that prices of PIBS have considerable potential to fluctuate both upwards and downwards. Just because they are Building Society instruments they should not be confused with savings products (sometimes also carrying the word 'shares' in their description) from the same or similar stables. It is important to realise that PIBS are just like other irredeemable fixed-interest investments and have high modified durations. (See Chapter 5). For example a PIBS standing on a 11% gross yield basis will have a propensity to fluctuate by over 9% of its value for a change in its yield of 1%, compared to about 4% for a five-year bond and 1% for a one-year bond. Clearly this can be an added attraction if long-dated yields are expected to fall, but conversely can represent a potential danger for high income seekers who all too often cannot afford to suffer the capital depreciation that would be brought about by a rise in long-term yields. It is perhaps because the PIBS market is still relatively new when compared to other more traditional forms of fixed interest instrument that one feels it necessary to sound this caveat, and concerns that the characteristics of PIBS might not be properly understood by retail investors have been partly responsible for some of the issues carrying minimum denominations of as high as £50,000.

Finally there is one further area where PIBS may have speculative attractions in no way related to their yields. In recent mergers and takeovers involving Building Societies it has become normal for members of societies being acquired to be offered benefits in cash or shares as part of the arrangements enabling such deals to proceed. PIBS holders count as members of societies in this regard and may stand to benefit if their society is subject to such activity.

## Taxation

PIBS pay dividends net of UK basic rate tax (currently 25%). For example, the semi-annual dividend due on each Halifax $8\frac{3}{4}$% PIBS of £50,000 denomination every 1 March and 1 September is £2187.50 (£50,000 × 8.75%/2). The issuer will withhold 25% of this amount i.e. £546.87, and pay a net dividend of £1640.63 to the beneficial shareholder.

Certain classes of UK taxpayer, such as tax exempt investors or investors whose income is below the tax threshold, may be able to reclaim all or part of any tax deducted. However, the rules allowing certain UK individual investors to receive building society interest gross on certification that such investors are unlikely to pay any income tax for the year in which the interest is due, do not apply to PIBS.

PIBS come within the scope of the new (1996) taxation arrangements for gilts and bonds.

This means that for UK corporate investors and personal investors whose aggregated gilt-edged and other bond holdings exceed £200,000 nominal, capital gains on PIBS are treated as income items and are taxed accordingly (see Chapter 10).

For personal investors at or below the £200,000 nominal threshold PIBS fall into the accrued income scheme, but because PIBS are qualifying corporate bonds (QCBs) capital gains are tax-free. The main provisions of the accrued income scheme treat as taxable income not only interest or dividend payments received, but also accrued interest at the time of sale less accrued interest at the time of purchase. The effect of this is to ensure that the income assessable to tax is directly proportional to the period of time the investment concerned is held.

(The above notes on taxation apply to all fixed rate sterling PIBS with the exception of the First National issue. This issue has a different tax treatment, since the First National is a non-UK based building society.)

*Note:* The comments on taxation above are of a general nature based on our understanding of current UK law and Inland Revenue practice. They relate only to the position of persons who are the absolute beneficial owners and may not apply to certain classes of persons such as traders and market-makers. Any person who is in doubt as to his/her personal tax position should consult his/her professional advisers.

# APPENDICES

# Appendix to Chapter 10

| UK Gilt and Bond Tax Matrix | Traders in securities (Dealers) | Corporates (other than Life Funds) | Life Funds | Pension Funds | Individuals above £200,000 nom. threshold | Individuals at/below £200,000 nom. threshold | Dedicated Gilt and Bond Unit Trusts | General Unit or Investment Trusts |
|---|---|---|---|---|---|---|---|---|
| Conventional Gilts (quoted clean) | Schedule D Case I | Corp. Tax on Divs / Corp. Tax on Gains (annually) | C.T. @ 25% on Divs / C.T. @ 25% on Gains (annually) | Divs exempt / Gains exempt | Inc. Tax on Divs / Inc. Tax on Gains (at disposal) | Acc. Income Scheme / Gains free of CGT | Acc. Income Scheme / Gains free of CGT | Corp. Tax on Divs / Corp. Tax on Gains (annually) |
| Funding 3½% 99/04 Treasury 5½% 08.12 (quoted clean) | Schedule D Case I | Acc. Income Scheme / Gains free of CGT | Acc. Income Scheme / Gains free of CGT | Divs exempt / Gains exempt | Acc. Income Scheme / Gains free of CGT | Acc. Income Scheme / Gains free of CGT | Acc. Income Scheme / Gains free of CGT | Acc. Income Scheme / Gains free of CGT |
| Index-linked Gilts (quoted clean) | Schedule D Case I | Corp. Tax on Divs / Special treatment (details awaited) | C.T. @ 25% on Divs / Special treatment (details awaited) | Divs exempt / Gains exempt | Inc. Tax on Divs / Special Treatment (details awaited) | Acc. Income scheme / Gains free of CGT | Acc. Income Scheme / Gains free of CGT | Corp. Tax on Divs / Special treatment (details awaited) |
| Index-linked Bonds (non-gilts) (quoted clean) | Schedule D Case I | Corp. Tax on Divs / Corp. Tax on Gains (annually) | C.T. @ 25% on Divs / C.T. @ 25% on Gains (annually) | Divs exempt / Gains exempt | Inc. Tax on Divs / Inc. Tax on Gains (at disposal) | Acc. Income Scheme / Gains free of CGT | Acc. Income Scheme / Gains free of CGT | Corp. Tax on Divs / Corp. Tax on Gains (annually) |
| Qualifying corporate bonds: Debs/Loans Eurosterling, Bulldogs (quoted clean) | Schedule D Case I | Corp. Tax on Divs / Corp. Tax on Gains (annually) | C.T. @ 25% on Divs / C.T. @ 25% on Gains (annually) | Divs exempt / Gains exempt | Inc. Tax on Divs / Inc. Tax on Gains (at disposal) | Acc. Income Scheme / Gains free of CGT | Acc. Income Scheme / Gains free of CGT | Corp. Tax on Divs / Corp. Tax on Gains (annually) |
| Non-qualifying bonds (quoted clean) | Schedule D Case I | Corp. Tax on Divs / Corp. Tax on Gains (annually) | C.T. @ 25% on Divs / C.T. @ 25% on Gains (annually) | Divs exempt / Gains exempt | Inc. Tax on Divs / Inc. Tax on Gains (at disposal) | Acc. Income Scheme / CGT on Gains with indexation | Acc. Income Scheme / CGT on Gains with indexation | Corp. Tax on Divs / Corp. Tax on Gains (annually) |

| Instrument | Tax Schedule | | | | | | | |
|---|---|---|---|---|---|---|---|---|
| Zero-coupon bonds | Schedule D Case I | Divs N/A<br>Corp. Tax on Gains (annually) | Divs N/A<br>C.T. @ 25% on Gains (annually) | Divs N/A<br>Gains exempt | Divs N/A<br>Inc. Tax on Gains (at disposal) | Divs N/A<br>Deep Discount rules | Divs N/A<br>Deep Discount rules | Divs N/A<br>Corp. Tax on Gains (annually) |
| PIBS (quoted clean) | Schedule D Case I | Corp. Tax on Divs<br>Corp. Tax on Gains (annually) | C.T. @ 25% on Divs<br>C.T. @ 25% on Gains (annually) | Divs exempt<br>Gains exempt | Inc. Tax on Divs<br>Inc. Tax on Gains (at disposal) | Acc. Income Scheme<br>Gains free of CGT | Acc. Income Scheme<br>Gains free of CGT | Corp. Tax on Divs<br>Corp. Tax on Gains (annually) |
| Preference shares (quoted dirty) | Schedule D Case I | Franked Income<br>Corp. Tax on Gains with indexation | Franked Income<br>C.T. @ 25% on Gains with indexation | Divs exempt<br>Gains exempt | Inc. Tax on Divs<br>CGT on Gains with indexation | Inc. Tax on Divs<br>CGT on Gains with indexation | Inc. Tax on DivS<br>Gains free of CGT | Franked Income<br>Gains free of CGT |
| Zero-coupon preference shares | Schedule D Case I | Divs N/A<br>Corp. Tax on Gains with indexation | Divs N/A<br>C.T. @ 25% on Gains with indexation | Divs N/A<br>Gains exempt | Divs N/A<br>CGT on Gains with indexation | Divs N/A<br>CGT on Gains with indexation | Divs N/A<br>Gains free of CGT | Divs N/A<br>Gains free of CGT |
| Convertibles (domestic quoted dirty euros quoted clean) | Schedule D Case I | Corp. Tax on Divs<br>Corp. Tax on Gains with indexation | C.T. @ 25% on Divs<br>C.T. @ 25% on Gains with indexation | Divs exempt<br>Gains exempt | Acc. Income Scheme<br>CGT on Gains with indexation | Acc. Income Scheme<br>CGT on Gains with indexation | Acc. Income Scheme<br>Gains free of CGT | Acc. Income Scheme<br>Gains free of CGT |

N.B. This table was compiled in July 1995 and reflects the proposals made at that time. It may require amendment in the light of actual subsequent legislation.

APPLICATION FORMS MUST BE SENT TO THE BANK OF ENGLAND, NEW ISSUES, PO BOX 444, GLOUCESTER, GL1 1NP TO ARRIVE NOT LATER THAN 10.00 AM ON WEDNESDAY, 25 JANUARY 1995; OR LODGED BY HAND AT THE CENTRAL GILTS OFFICE, BANK OF ENGLAND, BANK BUILDINGS, 19 OLD JEWRY, LONDON NOT LATER THAN 10.00 AM ON WEDNESDAY, 25 JANUARY 1995; OR LODGED BY HAND AT ANY OF THE BRANCHES OR AGENCIES OF THE BANK OF ENGLAND NOT LATER THAN 3.30 PM ON TUESDAY, 24 JANUARY 1995.

ISSUE OF £2,000,000,000

# 8% TREASURY STOCK 2015

### INTEREST PAYABLE HALF-YEARLY ON 7 JUNE AND 7 DECEMBER
### FOR AUCTION ON A BID PRICE BASIS ON 25 JANUARY 1995

PAYABLE IN FULL WITH APPLICATION

| | |
|---|---|
| With a competitive bid | Price bid |
| With a non-competitive bid | £100 per £100 nominal of Stock |

*This Stock will, on issue, be an investment falling within Part II of the First Schedule to the Trustee Investments Act 1961. Application has been made to the London Stock Exchange for the Stock to be admitted to the Official List on 26 January 1995.*

1.  THE GOVERNOR AND COMPANY OF THE BANK OF ENGLAND invite bids for the above Stock.

2.  The principal of and interest on the Stock will be a charge on the National Loans Fund, with recourse to the Consolidated Fund of the United Kingdom.

3.  The Stock will be repaid at par on 7 December 2015.

4.  The Stock will be registered at the Bank of England or at the Bank of Ireland, Belfast, and will be transferable, in multiples of one penny, by instrument in writing in accordance with the Stock Transfer Act 1963. Stock registered at the Bank of England held for the account of members of the Central Gilts Office (CGO) Service will also be transferable, in multiples of one penny, by exempt transfer in accordance with the Stock Transfer Act 1982 and the relevant subordinate legislation. Transfers will be free of stamp duty.

5.  Interest will be payable half-yearly on 7 June and 7 December. Income tax will be deducted from payments of more than £5 per annum. Interest warrants will be transmitted by post. Interest will accrue from Thursday, 26 January 1995 and the first interest payment will be made on 7 June 1995 at the rate of £2.8932 per £100 nominal of Stock.

6.  The Stock may be held on the National Savings Stock Register.

7.  The Stock and the interest payable thereon will be exempt from all United Kingdom taxation, present or future, so long as it is shown that the Stock is in the beneficial ownership of persons who are neither domiciled nor ordinarily resident in the United Kingdom of Great Britain and Northern Ireland.

8.  Further, the interest payable on the Stock will be exempt from United Kingdom income tax, present or future, so long as it is shown that the Stock is in the beneficial ownership of persons who are not ordinarily resident in the United Kingdom of Great Britain and Northern Ireland.

9.  For the purposes of the preceding paragraphs, persons are not ordinarily resident in the United Kingdom if they are regarded as not ordinarily resident for the purposes of United Kingdom income tax.

10.  Applications for exemption from United Kingdom income tax should be made in such form as may be required by the Commissioners of Inland Revenue. The appropriate forms may be obtained from the Inspector of Foreign Dividends, Inland Revenue, Lynwood Road, Thames Ditton, Surrey, KT7 0DP.

11.  These exemptions will not entitle a person to claim repayment of tax deducted from interest unless the claim to such repayment is made within the time limit provided for such claims under income tax law; under the provisions of the Taxes Management Act 1970, Section 43 (1), no such claim will be outside this time limit if it is made within six years from the date on which the interest is payable. In addition, these exemptions will not apply so as to exclude the interest from any computation for taxation purposes of the profits of any trade or business carried on in the United Kingdom. Moreover, the allowance of the exemptions is subject to the provisions of any law, present or future, of the United Kingdom directed to preventing avoidance of taxation by persons domiciled, resident or ordinarily resident in the United Kingdom, and, in particular, the interest will not be exempt from income tax where, under any such provision, it falls to be treated for the purpose of the Income Tax Acts as income of any person resident or ordinarily resident in the United Kingdom.

**Method of Application**

12.  Bids may be made on either a competitive or a non-competitive basis, as set out below, and must be submitted on the application form published with the prospectus. Each application form must comprise either one competitive bid or one non-competitive bid. Gilt-edged market makers may make competitive bids by telephone to the Bank of England not later than 10.00 am on Wednesday, 25 January 1995.

13. Application forms must be sent to the Bank of England, New Issues, PO Box 444, Gloucester, GL1 1NP to arrive not later than **10.00 AM ON WEDNESDAY, 25 JANUARY 1995**; or lodged by hand at the Central Gilts Office, Bank of England, Bank Buildings, 19 Old Jewry, London not later than **10.00 AM ON WEDNESDAY, 25 JANUARY 1995**; or lodged by hand at any of the Branches or Agencies of the Bank of England not later than **3.30 PM ON TUESDAY, 24 JANUARY 1995**. Bids will not be revocable between 10.00 am on Wednesday, 25 January 1995 and 10.00 am on Monday, 30 January 1995.

14. **COMPETITIVE BIDS**

(i) Each competitive bid must be for one amount and at one price expressed as a multiple of 1/32nd of £1 and must be for a minimum of £500,000 nominal of Stock and for a multiple of Stock as follows:-

| *Amount of Stock applied for* | *Multiple* |
|---|---|
| **£500,000-£1,000,000** | **£100,000** |
| **£1,000,000 or greater** | **£1,000,000** |

(ii) Unless the applicant is a member of the CGO Service, a separate cheque representing **PAYMENT IN FULL AT THE PRICE BID** must accompany each competitive bid. Cheques must be drawn on a branch or office, situated within the Town Clearing area, of a settlement member of CHAPS and Town Clearing Company Limited.

(iii) The Bank of England reserves the right to reject any competitive bid or part of any competitive bid. Competitive bids will be ranked in descending order of price and Stock will be sold to applicants whose competitive bids are at or above the lowest price at which the Bank of England decides that any competitive bid should be accepted (the lowest accepted price). **APPLICANTS WHOSE COMPETITIVE BIDS ARE ACCEPTED WILL PURCHASE STOCK AT THE PRICES WHICH THEY BID**: competitive bids which are accepted and which are made at prices above the lowest accepted price will be satisfied in full; competitive bids which are accepted and which are made at the lowest accepted price may be satisfied in full or in part only.

15. **NON-COMPETITIVE BIDS**

(i) A non-competitive bid must be for not less than £1,000 nominal and not more than £500,000 nominal of Stock, and must be for a multiple of £1,000 nominal of Stock.

(ii) Only one non-competitive bid may be submitted for the benefit of any one person, and each non-competitive application form may comprise only one non-competitive bid. Multiple applications or suspected multiple applications are liable to be rejected.

(iii) Unless the applicant is a member of the CGO Service, a separate cheque representing **PAYMENT AT THE RATE OF £100 FOR EVERY £100 NOMINAL OF STOCK APPLIED FOR** must accompany each non-competitive bid; cheques must be drawn on a bank in, and be payable in, the United Kingdom, the Channel Islands or the Isle of Man.

(iv) The Bank of England reserves the right to reject any non-competitive bid. Non-competitive bids which are accepted will be accepted in full **AT A PRICE (the non-competitive sale price) EQUAL TO THE AVERAGE OF THE PRICES AT WHICH COMPETITIVE BIDS HAVE BEEN ACCEPTED, the average being weighted by reference to the amount accepted at each price and ROUNDED DOWN TO THE NEAREST MULTIPLE OF 1/32ND OF £1.**

(v) If the non-competitive sale price is less than £100 per £100 nominal of Stock, the balance of the amount paid will be refunded by cheque despatched by post at the risk of the applicant.

(vi) If the non-competitive sale price is greater than £100 per £100 nominal of Stock, applicants whose non-competitive bids are accepted may be required to make a further payment equal to the non-competitive sale price less £100 for every £100 nominal of Stock allocated to them. An applicant from whom a further payment is required will be notified by letter by the Bank of England of the amount of Stock allocated to him and of the further payment due, but such notification will confer no right on the applicant to transfer the amount of Stock so allocated. The despatch of allotment letters to applicants from whom a further payment is required will be delayed until such further payment has been made.

16. The Bank of England may sell less than the full amount of the Stock on offer at the auction.

17. The Stock will be initially issued at a price such that it will not be a deep discount security for the purposes of Schedule 4 to the Income and Corporation Taxes Act 1988. Further issues of the Stock may be at a deep discount (broadly, a discount exceeding ½% per annum) and in certain circumstances this could result in all of the Stock being treated thereafter as a deep discount security. However, it is the intention of Her Majesty's Treasury that further issues of the Stock will be conducted so as to prevent any of such Stock being treated as a deep discount security for United Kingdom tax purposes. Provided the Stock is neither a deep discount security, nor treated as a deep discount security, any discount to the nominal value at which the Stock is issued will not represent taxable income for the purposes of the relevant provisions.

18. Allotment letters in respect of the Stock sold, being the only form in which the Stock (other than amounts held in the CGO Service for the account of members) may be transferred prior to registration, will be despatched by post at the risk of the applicant, but the despatch of any allotment letter, and the refund of any excess amount paid, may at the discretion of the Bank of England be withheld until the applicant's cheque has been paid. In the event of such withholding, the applicant will be notified by letter by the Bank of England of the acceptance of his application and of the amount of Stock allocated to him, subject in each case to the payment of his cheque, but such notification will confer no right on the applicant to transfer the Stock so allocated.

291

19. No sale will be made of a less amount than £1,000 nominal of Stock. If an application is satisfied in part only, the excess amount paid will, when refunded, be remitted by cheque despatched by post at the risk of the applicant; if an application is rejected the amount paid on application will be returned likewise. Non-payment on presentation of a cheque in respect of any Stock sold will render such Stock liable to forfeiture. Interest at a rate equal to the London Inter-Bank Offered Rate for seven day deposits in sterling ("LIBOR") plus 1% per annum may, however, be charged on the amount payable in respect of any Stock for which payment is accepted after the due date. Such rate will be determined by the Bank of England by reference to market quotations, on the due date for such payment, for LIBOR obtained from such source or sources as the Bank of England shall consider appropriate.

20. Allotment letters may be split into denominations of multiples of £100 on written request to the Bank of England, New Issues, Southgate House, Southgate Street, Gloucester, GL1 1UW received not later than 9 February 1995. Such requests must be signed and must be accompanied by the allotment letters. Allotment letters, accompanied by a completed registration form, may be lodged for registration forthwith and in any case must be lodged for registration not later than 13 February 1995; in the case of Stock held for the account of members of the CGO Service registration of Stock will be effected under separate arrangements.

21. Subject to the provisions governing membership of the CGO Service, a member of that Service may, by completing Section C of the application form, request that any Stock sold to him be credited direct to his account in the CGO on Thursday, 26 January 1995 by means of a member-to-member delivery from an account in the name of the Governor and Company of the Bank of England, Number 2 Account. Failure to accept such delivery by the deadline for member-to-member deliveries under the rules of the CGO Service on 26 January 1995 shall for the purposes of this prospectus constitute default in due payment of the amount payable in respect of the relevant Stock. A member of the CGO Service may also, subject to the provisions governing membership of that Service, surrender an allotment letter to the CGO for cancellation and for the Stock comprised therein to be credited to the member's account. The member who is shown by the accounts of the CGO as being entitled to any Stock shall, to the exclusion of all persons previously entitled to such Stock and any person claiming any entitlement thereto, both be treated as entitled to such Stock as if that member were the holder of an allotment letter and be liable for the payment of any amount due in respect of such Stock.

22. Application forms and copies of this prospectus may be obtained by post from the Bank of England, New Issues, Southgate House, Southgate Street, Gloucester, GL1 1UW; at the Central Gilts Office, Bank of England, 1 Bank Buildings, Princes Street, London, EC2R 8EU or at any of the Branches or Agencies of the Bank of England; at the Bank of Ireland, Moyne Buildings, 1st Floor, 20 Callender Street, Belfast, BT1 5BN; or at any office of the London Stock Exchange.

*Government Statement*
Attention is drawn to the statement issued by Her Majesty's Treasury on 29 May 1985 which explained that, in the interest of the orderly conduct of fiscal policy, neither Her Majesty's Government nor the Bank of England or their respective servants or agents undertake to disclose tax changes decided on but not yet announced, even where they may specifically affect the terms on which, or the conditions under which, this Stock is issued or sold by or on behalf of the Government or the Bank; that no responsibility can therefore be accepted for any omission to make such disclosure; and that such omission shall neither render any transaction liable to be set aside nor give rise to any claim for compensation.


BANK OF ENGLAND
LONDON

17 January 1995

PARTICULARS OF AN ISSUE OF £400,000,000

# VARIABLE RATE TREASURY STOCK, 1981

### INTEREST PAYABLE HALF-YEARLY ON 17th MAY AND 17th NOVEMBER

1. *An Order in Council has been made and laid before Parliament to amend the Trustee Investments Act 1961. The intention is that this Order shall take effect on 9th June 1977 from which date this Stock would be an investment falling within Part II of the First Schedule to that Act. Application has been made to the Council of The Stock Exchange for the Stock to be admitted to the Official List.*

2. The whole of the Stock will be issued to the Bank of England on 27th May 1977.

3. The principal of and interest on the Stock will be a charge on the National Loans Fund, with recourse to the Consolidated Fund of the United Kingdom.

4. Subject to the provisions of paragraphs 11 to 13 of this notice, the Stock will be repaid at par on 17th November 1981.

5. The Stock will be registered at the Bank of England or at the Bank of Ireland, Belfast, and will be transferable, in multiples of one new penny, by instrument in writing in accordance with the Stock Transfer Act 1963. Transfers will be free of stamp duty.

### INTEREST

6. Interest will be payable half-yearly on 17th May and 17th November. Income tax will be deducted from payments of more than £5 per annum. Interest warrants will be transmitted by post.

7. The rate of interest will be variable. Each half-yearly payment will be at a rate per £100 of Stock equal to half of the sum of an indicator rate and a fixed margin of $\frac{1}{2}$. The indicator rate will be the daily average over a reference period of Treasury Bill Rate the calculation and period of effectiveness of which is described in the Annex.

8. The reference period for the calculation of the indicator rate for each interest payment except the first will be from the ex-dividend date for the preceding interest payment up to the relative ex-dividend date. The ex-dividend date is the last day on which transfers can be lodged at the Bank of England for registration entitling the new holders to receive the next interest payment.

9. The first interest payment will be made on 17th November 1977 at the rate per £100 of Stock of 174/365ths of the sum of the indicator rate and the margin. The reference period for this payment will be the 137 days from 27th May 1977 up to 11th October 1977, the first ex-dividend date.

10. The rate for each interest payment, expressed as a percentage in pounds sterling to two places of decimals rounded, will be announced by the Bank of England on the business day immediately preceding the relative ex-dividend date.

### CONVERSION TO FIXED RATE AND OPTIONAL REDEMPTION

11. If there should be a change in the arrangements for or relating to the issue of Treasury bills which in the opinion of the Bank of England would or could be detrimental to the interests of stockholders, the rate of interest will cease to be variable and will become fixed. Her Majesty's Treasury shall publish, not later than five business days after the change, a notice in the London

Gazette specifying the date on which the change is deemed to have taken place. The fixed rate will take effect from the date of the change and will be the sum of the margin and an indicator rate, for the calculation of which the reference period will be from the ex-dividend date for the preceding interest payment up to the date of the change.

12.   In the event of such a change, stockholders will have the right to require Her Majesty's Treasury to redeem their Stock at par and a notice setting out the administrative arrangements will be sent to stockholders by the Bank of England at the appropriate time. Where stockholders exercise this right repayment will be effected within three months from the date of publication of the notice in the London Gazette, and any interest which has accrued will be payable at the same time.

13.   If stockholders together holding 80 per cent or more in nominal value of the Stock outstanding require Her Majesty's Treasury to redeem their Stock, Her Majesty's Treasury will have the right to redeem the remaining Stock at par within six months of the date on which the fixed rate took effect subject to their giving notice of their intention in the London Gazette.

GENERAL

14.   Copies of this notice may be obtained at the Bank of England, New Issues, Watling Street, London, EC4M 9AA, or at any of the branches of the Bank of England; at the Bank of Ireland, P.O. Box 13, Donegall Place, Belfast, BT1 5BX; from Messrs. Mullens & Co., 15 Moorgate, London, EC2R 6AN; or at any office of The Stock Exchange in the United Kingdom.


BANK OF ENGLAND
LONDON
27th May 1977.


ANNEX

CALCULATION OF TREASURY BILL RATE

Treasury bills are negotiable obligations of Her Majesty's Treasury, are charged on the National Loans Fund and are issued under the Treasury Bills Act 1877 and the National Loans Act 1968. They are offered for sale by tender by the Bank of England in accordance with the Treasury Bill Regulations 1968.

Under present practice, tenders are received at the Bank of England for 91-day Treasury bills on the last business day of each week, for bills to be issued in the following week. Tenders must be made by or through a London Banker, Discount House or Broker. Tenders are expressed as a price per £100 nominal value of bills and are accepted in descending order of price (i.e. ascending order of discount) until the total of tenders which are to be accepted in whole or in part is equal to or exceeds the amount of bills to be allotted. If the total of tenders at the lowest accepted price exceeds the remaining amount of bills to be allotted, allotments at that price are made *pro rata* to such tenders.

91-day Treasury bills are due and payable in full at the Bank of England 91 days after issue, except that, if the due date is not a business day (e.g. a Bank Holiday), they are payable on the first business day thereafter.

Treasury Bill Rate is the average rate of discount on 91-day Treasury bills allotted pursuant to tenders, weighted by the nominal value of bills allotted at each price and expressed as an annual percentage rate of discount calculated to four places of decimals rounded. If allotments are made of bills payable more than 91 days after issue (i.e. because the 91st day after issue will not be a business day), the discount on such bills is converted, for the purpose of calculating Treasury Bill Rate, to a discount for 91 days by dividing it by the number of days to the date on which the bills are payable and multiplying by 91.

Treasury Bill Rate is announced by the Bank of England on the afternoon on which allotments of Treasury bills pursuant to tenders are made. The Rate so announced takes effect on the next business day.

APPLICATION FORMS MUST BE SENT TO THE BANK OF ENGLAND, NEW ISSUES, PO BOX 444, GLOUCESTER, GL1 1NP TO ARRIVE NOT LATER THAN 10.00 AM ON WEDNESDAY, 30 MARCH 1994; OR LODGED BY HAND AT THE CENTRAL GILTS OFFICE, BANK OF ENGLAND, BANK BUILDINGS, 19 OLD JEWRY, LONDON NOT LATER THAN 10.00 AM ON WEDNESDAY, 30 MARCH 1994; OR LODGED BY HAND AT ANY OF THE BRANCHES OR AGENCIES OF THE BANK OF ENGLAND NOT LATER THAN 3.30 PM ON TUESDAY, 29 MARCH 1994.

## BID PRICE AUCTION FOR £2,500,000,000

# FLOATING RATE TREASURY STOCK 1999

## INTEREST PAYABLE QUARTERLY AT LIBID LESS ⅛%
## AT A MINIMUM PRICE OF £99.50 PER £100 NOMINAL OF STOCK

### PAYABLE IN FULL WITH APPLICATION

*This Stock will, on issue, be an investment falling within Part II of the First Schedule to the Trustee Investments Act 1961. Application has been made to the London Stock Exchange for the Stock to be admitted to the Official List on 31 March 1994.*

1.  THE GOVERNOR AND COMPANY OF THE BANK OF ENGLAND invite bids for the above Stock.

2.  The principal of and interest on the Stock will be a charge on the National Loans Fund, with recourse to the Consolidated Fund of the United Kingdom.

3.  The Stock will be repaid at par on the interest payment date (as defined in paragraph 10 below) falling in March 1999.

4.  Applications must be for not less than £50,000 nominal of Stock.

5.  The Stock will be registered at the Bank of England or at the Bank of Ireland, Belfast, and will be transferable by instrument in writing in accordance with the Stock Transfer Act 1963. Stock registered at the Bank of England held for the account of members of the Central Gilts Office (CGO) Service will also be transferable by exempt transfer in accordance with the Stock Transfer Act 1982 and the relevant subordinate legislation. Transfers will be free of stamp duty.

**Interest**

6.  Interest will be payable quarterly in accordance with paragraph 10 below. Interest warrants will be transmitted by post.

7.  Pursuant to a direction of Her Majesty's Treasury under Section 50 of the Income and Corporation Taxes Act 1988, interest on the Stock will be paid without deduction for or on account of United Kingdom income tax. However, the interest has a United Kingdom source and therefore may be chargeable to United Kingdom tax by direct assessment.

8.  The Stock will be issued by Her Majesty's Treasury with the conditions that:

(a)  so long as Stock is in the beneficial ownership of persons who are not ordinarily resident in the United Kingdom, the interest thereon shall be exempt from income tax; and

(b)  so long as Stock is in the beneficial ownership of persons who are neither domiciled nor ordinarily resident in the United Kingdom, neither the capital thereof nor the interest thereon shall be liable to any taxation present or future.

For these purposes, persons are not ordinarily resident in the United Kingdom if they are regarded as not ordinarily resident for the purposes of United Kingdom income tax.

These exemptions will not apply so as to exclude the interest from any computation for taxation purposes of the profits of any trade or business carried on in the United Kingdom. Moreover, the availability of these exemptions is subject to the provisions of any law, present or future, of the United Kingdom directed to preventing avoidance of taxation by persons domiciled, resident or ordinarily resident in the United Kingdom, and, in particular, the interest will not be exempt from income tax where, under any such provision, it falls to be treated for the purpose of the Income Tax Acts as income of any person resident or ordinarily resident in the United Kingdom.

9.  In addition, the Inland Revenue has confirmed that, on the basis of a long-standing published concession, interest on the Stock will not be charged to United Kingdom tax in the hands of a stockholder who is not at any time in the relevant tax year resident in the United Kingdom, except where such stockholder:

(a)  is chargeable under Section 78 of the Taxes Management Act 1970 in the name of a trustee or other representative mentioned in Section 72 of that Act or in the name of an agent or branch in the United Kingdom having the management or control of the interest; or

(b)  seeks to claim relief in respect of taxed income from United Kingdom sources; or

(c)  is chargeable to corporation tax on the income of a United Kingdom branch or agency to which the interest is attributable; or

(d)  is chargeable to income tax on the profits of a trade carried on in the United Kingdom to which the interest is attributable.

**Interest Payment Dates**

10. Interest will accrue from 31 March 1994 (the issue date) and such interest will be payable on 9 June 1994 and on each date thereafter which (except as stated below) falls three months after the preceding interest payment date (each such date being an "interest payment date"). If any interest payment date would otherwise fall on a day which is not a business day (as defined below) it shall be postponed to the next business day unless it would thereby fall in the next calendar month, in which event that interest payment date shall be the immediately preceding business day and each subsequent interest payment date shall be the last business day of the third month after the month in which the preceding interest payment date fell. In this prospectus the period from (and including) one interest payment date (or the issue date) to (but excluding) the next (or first) interest payment date is called an "interest period" and "business day" means a day (other than Saturday or Sunday) on which banks are open for business in London.

**Rate of Interest**

11. The rate of interest per annum payable in respect of the Stock for each interest period shall be 1/8% below the rate per annum determined by the Bank of England to be the arithmetic mean (rounded if necessary to the nearest fifth decimal place) of the rates at which three month deposits in sterling are bid as at 11.00 am on each interest determination date (as described in paragraph 14 below) by the twenty reference banks referred to in paragraph 12 below, provided that (i) if sixteen or more such quotations are so available, the five highest (or, if there are more than five such highest rates, only five of such rates) and the five lowest (or, if there are more than five such lowest rates, only five of such rates) shall be disregarded by the Bank of England for the purposes of determining such arithmetic mean; (ii) if fewer than sixteen but more than eight such quotations are available, the two highest (or, if there are more than two such highest rates, only two of such rates) and the two lowest (or, if there are more than two such lowest rates, only two of such rates) shall be disregarded by the Bank of England for the purposes of determining such arithmetic mean; (iii) if fewer than nine such quotations are available, the Bank of England shall request quotations of the rates at which three month deposits in sterling are bid at 11.00 am on the interest determination date by such other banks as the Bank of England shall select, if practicable consulting Her Majesty's Treasury, so that (ii) above may be applied. If the rate of interest cannot be determined in accordance with the foregoing provisions the rate of interest shall be that established on the last preceding interest determination date.

12. For the purposes of paragraph 11 above the reference banks shall be the twenty authorised institutions, within the meaning of the Banking Act 1987, which, disregarding any excluded institutions referred to below, had outstanding as at the 31 December immediately preceding the relevant interest determination date the largest sterling eligible liabilities as determined by the Bank of England. For this purpose there shall be excluded any institution which is a wholly-owned subsidiary of another institution if that other institution itself is, or will by reason of such exclusion be, a reference bank.

**Publication of Rate of Interest per annum and Coupon Amounts**

13. The Bank of England will, as soon as practicable after 11.00 am on each interest determination date, determine the rate of interest per annum and calculate the amount of interest payable per £100 nominal of Stock (the "interest amount") for the relevant interest period, and will publish both figures. The interest amount shall be calculated by applying the rate of interest per annum per £100 nominal of Stock, multiplying such product by the actual number of days in the interest period concerned divided by 365 and rounding the resulting figure to the nearest fourth decimal place. The Bank of England's determination of the rate of interest and the interest amount shall be final and binding upon all parties.

14. The rate of interest for the first interest period will be set on Wednesday, 23 March 1994 as described in paragraph 11 above. Thereafter the interest determination date will be the first business day of each interest period.

**Method of Application**

15. Bids must be submitted on the application form published with the prospectus. Application forms must be sent to the Bank of England, New Issues, PO Box 444, Gloucester, GL1 1NP to arrive not later than **10.00 AM ON WEDNESDAY, 30 MARCH 1994**; or lodged by hand at the Central Gilts Office, Bank of England, Bank Buildings, 19 Old Jewry, London not later than **10.00 AM ON WEDNESDAY, 30 MARCH 1994**; or lodged by hand at any of the Branches or Agencies of the Bank of England not later than **3.30 PM ON TUESDAY, 29 MARCH 1994.** Gilt-edged market makers may bid by telephone to the Bank of England not later than 10.00 am on Wednesday, 30 March 1994. Bids will not be revocable between 10.00 am on Wednesday, 30 March 1994 and 10.00 am on Tuesday, 5 April 1994.

16. Each bid must be for one amount and for a minimum of £50,000 nominal of Stock and for a multiple of Stock as follows:-

| Amount of Stock applied for | Multiple |
| --- | --- |
| **£50,000-£1,000,000** | **£50,000** |
| **£1,000,000 or greater** | **£1,000,000** |

17. The minimum price, below which bids will not be accepted, is £99.50 per £100 nominal of Stock. Bids must be made at the minimum price or at higher prices which are multiples of one penny. Bids lodged without a price being stated will be deemed to have been made at the minimum price.

18. Unless the applicant is a member of the CGO Service, a separate cheque representing **PAYMENT IN FULL AT THE PRICE BID** must accompany each bid. Cheques must be drawn on a branch or office, situated within the Town Clearing area, of a settlement member of CHAPS and Town Clearing Company Limited.

19. The Bank of England reserves the right to reject any bid or part of any bid. Bids will be ranked in descending order of price and Stock will be sold to applicants whose bids are at or above the lowest price at which the Bank of England

decides that any bids should be accepted (the lowest accepted price), which will be not less than the minimum price. **APPLICANTS WHOSE BIDS ARE ACCEPTED WILL PURCHASE STOCK AT THE PRICES AT WHICH THEY BID**: bids which are accepted and which are made at prices above the lowest accepted price will be satisfied in full; bids which are accepted and which are made at the lowest accepted price may be satisfied in full or in part only.

20. The Bank of England may sell to applicants less than the full amount of the Stock.

21. The Stock will be initially issued at a price and on terms such that it will not be a deep discount security for the purposes of Schedule 4 to the Income and Corporation Taxes Act 1988 or a deep gain security for the purposes of Schedule 11 to the Finance Act 1989. Further issues of the Stock may be at a deep discount (broadly, a discount exceeding ½% per annum) and in certain circumstances this could result in all of the Stock being treated thereafter as such a security. However, it is the intention of Her Majesty's Treasury that further issues of Stock will be conducted so as to prevent any of the Stock being treated as a deep discount security or a deep gain security for United Kingdom tax purposes. Provided the Stock is neither a deep discount security nor a deep gain security and is not treated as such, any discount to the nominal value at which the Stock is issued will not represent taxable income for the purposes of the relevant provisions.

22. Letters of allotment in respect of the Stock sold, being the only form in which the Stock (other than amounts held in the CGO Service for the account of members) may be transferred prior to registration, will be despatched by post at the risk of the applicant, but the despatch of any letter of allotment, and the refund of any excess amount paid, may at the discretion of the Bank of England be withheld until the applicant's cheque has been paid. In the event of such withholding, the applicant will be notified by letter by the Bank of England of the acceptance of his application and of the amount of Stock allocated to him, subject in each case to the payment of his cheque, but such notification will confer no right on the applicant to transfer the Stock so allocated.

23. No sale will be made of a less amount than £50,000 nominal of Stock. If an application is satisfied in part only, the excess amount paid will, when refunded, be remitted by cheque despatched by post at the risk of the applicant; if an application is rejected the amount paid on application will be returned likewise. Non-payment on presentation of a cheque in respect of any Stock sold will render such Stock liable to forfeiture. Interest at a rate equal to the London Inter-Bank Offered Rate for seven day deposits in sterling ("LIBOR") plus 1% per annum may, however, be charged on the amount payable in respect of any Stock for which payment is accepted after the due date. Such rate will be determined by the Bank of England by reference to market quotations, on the due date for such payment, for LIBOR obtained from such source or sources as the Bank of England shall consider appropriate.

24. Letters of allotment may be split into denominations of multiples of £50,000 on written request to the Bank of England, New Issues, Southgate House, Southgate Street, Gloucester, GL1 1UW received not later than 6 April 1994. Such requests must be signed and must be accompanied by the letters of allotment. Letters of allotment, accompanied by a completed registration form, may be lodged for registration forthwith and in any case must be lodged for registration not later than 8 April 1994; in the case of Stock held for the account of members of the CGO Service registration of Stock will be effected under separate arrangements.

25. Subject to the provisions governing membership of the CGO Service, a member of that Service may, by completing Section B of the application form, request that any Stock sold to him be credited direct to his account in the CGO on Thursday, 31 March 1994 by means of a member-to-member delivery from an account in the name of the Governor and Company of the Bank of England, Number 2 Account. Failure to accept such delivery by the deadline for member-to-member deliveries under the rules of the CGO Service on 31 March 1994 shall for the purposes of this prospectus constitute default in due payment of the amount payable in respect of the relevant Stock. A member of the CGO Service may also, subject to the provisions governing membership of that Service, surrender a letter of allotment to the CGO for cancellation and for the Stock comprised therein to be credited to the member's account. The member who is shown by the accounts of the CGO as being entitled to any Stock shall, to the exclusion of all persons previously entitled to such Stock and any person claiming any entitlement thereto, both be treated as entitled to such Stock as if that member were the holder of a letter of allotment and be liable for the payment of any amount due in respect of such Stock.

26. Application forms and copies of the prospectus may be obtained by post from the Bank of England, New Issues, Southgate House, Southgate Street, Gloucester, GL1 1UW; at the Central Gilts Office, Bank of England, 1 Bank Buildings, Princes Street, London, EC2R 8EU or at any of the Branches or Agencies of the Bank of England; at the Bank of Ireland, Moyne Buildings, 1st Floor, 20 Callender Street, Belfast, BT1 5BN; or at any office of the London Stock Exchange in the United Kingdom.

*Government Statement*

Attention is drawn to the statement issued by Her Majesty's Treasury on 29 May 1985 which explained that, in the interest of the orderly conduct of fiscal policy, neither Her Majesty's Government nor the Bank of England or their respective servants or agents undertake to disclose tax changes decided on but not yet announced, even where they may specifically affect the terms on which, or the conditions under which, this Stock is issued or sold by or on behalf of the Government or the Bank; that no responsibility can therefore be accepted for any omission to make such disclosure; and that such omission shall neither render any transaction liable to be set aside nor give rise to any claim for compensation.

BANK OF ENGLAND
LONDON

22 March 1994

APPLICATION FORMS MUST BE SENT TO THE BANK OF ENGLAND, NEW ISSUES, PO BOX 444, GLOUCESTER, GL1 1NP TO ARRIVE NOT LATER THAN 10.00 AM ON WEDNESDAY, 25 MAY 1994; OR LODGED BY HAND AT THE CENTRAL GILTS OFFICE, BANK OF ENGLAND, BANK BUILDINGS, 19 OLD JEWRY, LONDON NOT LATER THAN 10.00 AM ON WEDNESDAY, 25 MAY 1994; OR LODGED BY HAND AT ANY OF THE BRANCHES OR AGENCIES OF THE BANK OF ENGLAND NOT LATER THAN 3.30 PM ON TUESDAY, 24 MAY 1994.

## ISSUE OF £2,000,000,000

# 7% TREASURY CONVERTIBLE STOCK 1997

## INTEREST PAYABLE HALF-YEARLY ON 6 FEBRUARY AND 6 AUGUST
## FOR AUCTION ON A BID PRICE BASIS ON 25 MAY 1994

### PAYABLE IN FULL WITH APPLICATION

| | |
|---|---|
| *With a competitive bid* | *Price bid* |
| *With a non-competitive bid* | *£100 per £100 nominal of Stock* |

*This Stock will, on issue, be an investment falling within Part II of the First Schedule to the Trustee Investments Act 1961. Application has been made to the London Stock Exchange for the Stock to be admitted to the Official List on 26 May 1994.*

1.  THE GOVERNOR AND COMPANY OF THE BANK OF ENGLAND invite bids for the above Stock.

2.  The principal of and interest on the Stock will be a charge on the National Loans Fund, with recourse to the Consolidated Fund of the United Kingdom.

3.  The Stock will be registered at the Bank of England or at the Bank of Ireland, Belfast, and will be transferable, in multiples of one penny, by instrument in writing in accordance with the Stock Transfer Act 1963. Stock registered at the Bank of England held for the account of members of the Central Gilts Office (CGO) Service will also be transferable, in multiples of one penny, by exempt transfer in accordance with the Stock Transfer Act 1982 and the relevant subordinate legislation. Transfers will be free of stamp duty.

4.  Interest will be payable half-yearly on 6 February and 6 August. Income tax will be deducted from payments of more than £5 per annum. Interest warrants will be transmitted by post. Interest will accrue from Thursday, 26 May 1994 and the first interest payment will be made as on 6 August 1994 at the rate of £1.3809 per £100 nominal of Stock.

5.  The Stock may be held on the National Savings Stock Register.

6.  Holdings of 7% Treasury Convertible Stock 1997 may, at the option of holders, be converted in whole or in part into 9% Treasury Stock 2012, as on the following dates and at the indicated rates:-

| Date of conversion | Nominal amount of 9% Treasury Stock 2012 per £100 nominal of 7% Treasury Convertible Stock 1997 |
|---|---|
| 6 August 1994 | £89 |
| 6 February 1995 | £88 |
| 6 August 1995 | £87 |
| 6 February 1996 | £86 |

7.  Amounts of 9% Treasury Stock 2012 issued in order to meet the exercise of the above options to convert will rank equally in all respects with Stock already issued and will be subject to the provisions of the prospectus dated 7 February 1992. Notices setting out the administrative arrangements for the exercise of the options to convert and forms of acceptance for completion will be issued to holders at the appropriate times.

8.  Her Majesty's Treasury has directed that Section 471 of the Income and Corporation Taxes Act 1988 (which relates to the treatment for taxation purposes of financial concerns whose business consists wholly or partly in dealing in securities) shall apply to exchanges of securities made in pursuance of the conversion offer.

9.  Holdings of 7% Treasury Convertible Stock 1997 in respect of which options to convert have not been exercised will be repaid at par on 6 August 1997.

10.  7% Treasury Convertible Stock 1997 and the interest payable thereon will be exempt from all United Kingdom taxation, present or future, so long as it is shown that the Stock is in the beneficial ownership of persons who are neither domiciled nor ordinarily resident in the United Kingdom of Great Britain and Northern Ireland.

11.  Further, the interest payable on 7% Treasury Convertible Stock 1997 will be exempt from United Kingdom income tax, present or future, so long as it is shown that the Stock is in the beneficial ownership of persons who are not ordinarily resident in the United Kingdom of Great Britain and Northern Ireland.

12.  For the purposes of the preceding paragraphs, persons are not ordinarily resident in the United Kingdom if they are regarded as not ordinarily resident for the purposes of United Kingdom income tax.

13. Applications for exemption from United Kingdom income tax should be made in such form as may be required by the Commissioners of Inland Revenue. The appropriate forms may be obtained from the Inspector of Foreign Dividends, Inland Revenue, Lynwood Road, Thames Ditton, Surrey, KT7 0DP.

14. These exemptions will not entitle a person to claim repayment of tax deducted from interest unless the claim to such repayment is made within the time limit provided for such claims under income tax law; under the provisions of the Taxes Management Act 1970, Section 43 (1), no such claim will be outside this time limit if it is made within six years from the date on which the interest is payable. In addition, these exemptions will not apply so as to exclude the interest from any computation for taxation purposes of the profits of any trade or business carried on in the United Kingdom. Moreover, the allowance of the exemptions is subject to the provisions of any law, present or future, of the United Kingdom directed to preventing avoidance of taxation by persons domiciled, resident or ordinarily resident in the United Kingdom, and, in particular, the interest will not be exempt from income tax where, under any such provision, it falls to be treated for the purpose of the Income Tax Acts as income of any person resident or ordinarily resident in the United Kingdom.

15. The issue price of 7% Treasury Convertible Stock 1997 is such that it will not be a deep discount security for the purposes of Schedule 4 to the Income and Corporation Taxes Act 1988 or a deep gain security for the purposes of Schedule 11 to the Finance Act 1989. In certain circumstances further issues of such Stock could result in all of the Stock, whenever issued, being subject to one of these special regimes. However, it is the intention of Her Majesty's Treasury that further issues of the Stock will be conducted so as to prevent either of these regimes applying. Some or all of the 9% Treasury Stock 2012 issued to meet the exercise of options in paragraph 6 could in certain circumstances fall to be treated as a deep discount security for the purposes of Schedule 4 to the Income and Corporation Taxes Act 1988. However, it is the intention of Her Majesty's Treasury that further issues of 9% Treasury Stock 2012 and 7% Treasury Convertible Stock 1997 will be conducted so as to prevent any 9% Treasury Stock 2012 falling to be treated as a deep discount security for United Kingdom tax purposes. Provided that 7% Treasury Convertible Stock 1997 is not, and does not fall to be treated as, a deep discount or a deep gain security and 9% Treasury Stock 2012 is not, and does not fall to be treated as, a deep discount security, neither any difference between the price at which 7% Treasury Convertible Stock 1997 is issued and the proceeds of redemption of the Stock (if options to convert are not exercised) or of any 9% Treasury Stock 2012 into which it is converted nor any discount to the nominal value at which such 9% Treasury Stock 2012 is issued will represent taxable income for the purposes of the relevant provisions.

**Method of Application**

16. Bids may be made on either a competitive or a non-competitive basis, as set out below, and must be submitted on the application form published with the prospectus. Each application form must comprise either one competitive bid or one non-competitive bid. Gilt-edged market makers may make competitive bids by telephone to the Bank of England not later than 10.00 am on Wednesday, 25 May 1994.

17. Application forms must be sent to the Bank of England, New Issues, PO Box 444, Gloucester, GL1 1NP to arrive not later than **10.00 AM ON WEDNESDAY, 25 MAY 1994**; or lodged by hand at the Central Gilts Office, Bank of England, Bank Buildings, 19 Old Jewry, London not later than **10.00 AM ON WEDNESDAY, 25 MAY 1994**; or lodged by hand at any of the Branches or Agencies of the Bank of England not later than **3.30 PM ON TUESDAY, 24 MAY 1994.** Bids will not be revocable between 10.00 am on Wednesday, 25 May 1994 and 10.00 am on Tuesday, 31 May 1994.

18. **COMPETITIVE BIDS**

(i) Each competitive bid must be for one amount and at one price expressed as a multiple of 1/32nd of £1 and must be for a minimum of £500,000 nominal of Stock and for a multiple of Stock as follows:-

| Amount of Stock applied for | Multiple |
|---|---|
| £500,000-£1,000,000 | £100,000 |
| £1,000,000 or greater | £1,000,000 |

(ii) Unless the applicant is a member of the CGO Service, a separate cheque representing **PAYMENT IN FULL AT THE PRICE BID** must accompany each competitive bid. Cheques must be drawn on a branch or office, situated within the Town Clearing area, of a settlement member of CHAPS and Town Clearing Company Limited.

(iii) The Bank of England reserves the right to reject any competitive bid or part of any competitive bid. Competitive bids will be ranked in descending order of price and Stock will be sold to applicants whose competitive bids are at or above the lowest price at which the Bank of England decides that any competitive bid should be accepted (the lowest accepted price). **APPLICANTS WHOSE COMPETITIVE BIDS ARE ACCEPTED WILL PURCHASE STOCK AT THE PRICES WHICH THEY BID**: competitive bids which are accepted and which are made at prices above the lowest accepted price will be satisfied in full; competitive bids which are accepted and which are made at the lowest accepted price may be satisfied in full or in part only.

19. **NON-COMPETITIVE BIDS**

(i) A non-competitive bid must be for not less than £1,000 nominal and not more than £500,000 nominal of Stock, and must be for a multiple of £1,000 nominal of Stock.

(ii) Only one non-competitive bid may be submitted for the benefit of any one person. Multiple applications or suspected multiple applications are liable to be rejected.

(iii) Unless the applicant is a member of the CGO Service, a separate cheque representing **PAYMENT AT THE RATE OF £100 FOR EVERY £100 NOMINAL OF STOCK APPLIED FOR** must accompany each non-competitive bid; cheques must be drawn on a bank in, and be payable in, the United Kingdom, the Channel Islands or the Isle of Man.

(iv) The Bank of England reserves the right to reject any non-competitive bid. Non-competitive bids which are accepted will be accepted in full **AT A PRICE (the non-competitive sale price) EQUAL TO THE AVERAGE OF THE PRICES AT WHICH COMPETITIVE BIDS HAVE BEEN ACCEPTED, the average being weighted by reference to the amount accepted at each price and ROUNDED DOWN TO THE NEAREST MULTIPLE OF 1/32ND OF £1.**

(v) If the non-competitive sale price is less than £100 per £100 nominal of Stock, the balance of the amount paid will be refunded by cheque despatched by post at the risk of the applicant.

(vi) If the non-competitive sale price is greater than £100 per £100 nominal of Stock, applicants whose non-competitive bids are accepted may be required to make a further payment equal to the non-competitive sale price less £100 for every £100 nominal of Stock allocated to them. An applicant from whom a further payment is required will be notified by letter by the Bank of England of the amount of Stock allocated to him and of the further payment due, but such notification will confer no right on the applicant to transfer the amount of Stock so allocated. The despatch of allotment letters to applicants from whom a further payment is required will be delayed until such further payment has been made.

20. The Bank of England may sell less than the full amount of the Stock on offer at the auction.

21. Letters of allotment in respect of the Stock sold, being the only form in which the Stock (other than amounts held in the CGO Service for the account of members) may be transferred prior to registration, will be despatched by post at the risk of the applicant, but the despatch of any letter of allotment, and the refund of any excess amount paid, may at the discretion of the Bank of England be withheld until the applicant's cheque has been paid. In the event of such withholding, the applicant will be notified by letter by the Bank of England of the acceptance of his application and of the amount of Stock allocated to him, subject in each case to the payment of his cheque, but such notification will confer no right on the applicant to transfer the Stock so allocated.

22. No sale will be made of a less amount than £1,000 nominal of Stock. If an application is satisfied in part only, the excess amount paid will, when refunded, be remitted by cheque despatched by post at the risk of the applicant; if an application is rejected the amount paid on application will be returned likewise. Non-payment on presentation of a cheque in respect of any Stock sold will render such Stock liable to forfeiture. Interest at a rate equal to the London Inter-Bank Offered Rate for seven day deposits in sterling ("LIBOR") plus 1% per annum may, however, be charged on the amount payable in respect of any Stock for which payment is accepted after the due date. Such rate will be determined by the Bank of England by reference to market quotations, on the due date for such payment, for LIBOR obtained from such source or sources as the Bank of England shall consider appropriate.

23. Letters of allotment may be split into denominations of multiples of £100 on written request to the Bank of England, New Issues, Southgate House, Southgate Street, Gloucester, GL1 1UW received not later than 9 June 1994. Such requests must be signed and must be accompanied by the letters of allotment. Letters of allotment, accompanied by a completed registration form, may be lodged for registration forthwith and in any case must be lodged for registration not later than 13 June 1994; in the case of Stock held for the account of members of the CGO Service registration of Stock will be effected under separate arrangements.

24. Subject to the provisions governing membership of the CGO Service, a member of that Service may, by completing Section C of the application form, request that any Stock sold to him be credited direct to his account in the CGO on Thursday, 26 May 1994 by means of a member-to-member delivery from an account in the name of the Governor and Company of the Bank of England, Number 2 Account. Failure to accept such delivery by the deadline for member-to-member deliveries under the rules of the CGO Service on 26 May 1994 shall for the purposes of this prospectus constitute default in due payment of the amount payable in respect of the relevant Stock. A member of the CGO Service may also, subject to the provisions governing membership of that Service, surrender a letter of allotment to the CGO for cancellation and for the Stock comprised therein to be credited to the member's account. The member who is shown by the accounts of the CGO as being entitled to any Stock shall, to the exclusion of all persons previously entitled to such Stock and any person claiming any entitlement thereto, both be treated as entitled to such Stock as if that member were the holder of a letter of allotment and be liable for the payment of any amount due in respect of such Stock.

25. Application forms and copies of this prospectus may be obtained by post from the Bank of England, New Issues, Southgate House, Southgate Street, Gloucester, GL1 1UW; at the Central Gilts Office, Bank of England, 1 Bank Buildings, Princes Street, London, EC2R 8EU or at any of the Branches or Agencies of the Bank of England; at the Bank of Ireland, Moyne Buildings, 1st Floor, 20 Callender Street, Belfast, BT1 5BN; or at any office of the London Stock Exchange in the United Kingdom.

*Government Statement*
Attention is drawn to the statement issued by Her Majesty's Treasury on 29 May 1985 which explained that, in the interest of the orderly conduct of fiscal policy, neither Her Majesty's Government nor the Bank of England or their respective servants or agents undertake to disclose tax changes decided on but not yet announced, even where they may specifically affect the terms on which, or the conditions under which, 7% Treasury Convertible Stock 1997 and 9% Treasury Sock 2012 are issued or sold by or on behalf of the Government or the Bank; that no responsibility can therefore be accepted for any omission to make such disclosure; and that such omission shall neither render any transaction liable to be set aside nor give rise to any claim for compensation.

BANK OF ENGLAND
LONDON

17 May 1994

THIS NOTICE DOES NOT CONSTITUTE AN OFFER FOR SALE AND THE STOCK DESCRIBED BELOW IS NOT AVAILABLE FOR PURCHASE DIRECT FROM THE BANK OF ENGLAND. OFFICIAL DEALINGS IN THE STOCK ON THE INTERNATIONAL STOCK EXCHANGE ARE EXPECTED TO COMMENCE ON TUESDAY 16TH JUNE 1992.

PARTICULARS OF AN ISSUE OF £500,000,000

# 4⅛ per cent INDEX-LINKED TREASURY STOCK, 2030

INTEREST PAYABLE HALF-YEARLY ON 22ND JANUARY AND 22ND JULY

*This Stock is an investment falling within Part II of the First Schedule to the Trustee Investments Act 1961. Application has been made to the Council of The International Stock Exchange for the Stock to be admitted to the Official List on 16th June 1992.*

1.   The whole of the Stock has been issued to the Bank of England on 12th June 1992 at a price of £100.00 per cent.

2.   The principal of and interest on the Stock will be a charge on the National Loans Fund, with recourse to the Consolidated Fund of the United Kingdom.

3.   The Stock will be registered at the Bank of England or at the Bank of Ireland, Belfast, and will be transferable, in multiples of one penny, by instrument in writing in accordance with the Stock Transfer Act 1963. Stock registered at the Bank of England held for the account of members of the Central Gilts Office (CGO) Service will also be transferable, in multiples of one penny, by exempt transfer in accordance with the Stock Transfer Act 1982 and the relevant subordinate legislation. Transfers will be free of stamp duty.

4.   The Stock and the interest payable thereon will be exempt from all United Kingdom taxation, present or future, so long as it is shown that the Stock is in the beneficial ownership of persons who are neither domiciled nor ordinarily resident in the United Kingdom of Great Britain and Northern Ireland.

5.   Further, the interest payable on the Stock will be exempt from United Kingdom income tax, present or future, so long as it is shown that the Stock is in the beneficial ownership of persons who are not ordinarily resident in the United Kingdom of Great Britain and Northern Ireland.

6.   For the purposes of the preceding paragraphs, persons are not ordinarily resident in the United Kingdom if they are regarded as not ordinarily resident for the purposes of United Kingdom income tax.

7.   Applications for exemption from United Kingdom income tax should, in the case of interest on stock, be made in such form as may be required by the Commissioners of Inland Revenue. The appropriate forms may be obtained from the Inspector of Foreign Dividends, Inland Revenue, Lynwood Road, Thames Ditton, Surrey, KT7 0DP.

8.   These exemptions will not entitle a person to claim repayment of tax deducted from interest unless the claim to such repayment is made within the time limit provided for such claims under income tax law; under the provisions of the Taxes Management Act 1970, Section 43 (1), no such claim will be outside this time limit if it is made within six years from the date on which the interest is payable. In addition, these exemptions will not apply so as to exclude the interest from any computation for taxation purposes of the profits of any trade or business carried on in the United Kingdom. Moreover, the allowance of the exemptions is subject to the provisions of any law, present or future, of the United Kingdom directed to preventing avoidance of taxation by persons domiciled, resident or ordinarily resident in the United Kingdom, and, in particular, the interest will not be exempt from income tax where, under any such provision, it falls to be treated for the purpose of the Income Tax Acts as income of any person resident or ordinarily resident in the United Kingdom.

9.   If not previously redeemed under the provisions of paragraph 17, the Stock will be repaid on 22nd July 2030. The value of the principal on repayment will be related, subject to the terms of this notice, to the movement, during the life of the Stock, of the United Kingdom General Index of Retail Prices (for all items) published by the Central Statistical Office of the Chancellor of the Exchequer, or any Index which may replace that Index for the purposes of this notice, such movement being indicated by the Index figure issued monthly and subsequently published in the London, Edinburgh and Belfast Gazettes.

10.  For the purposes of this notice, the Index figure applicable to any month will be the Index figure issued seven months prior to the relevant month and relating to the month before that prior month; "month" means calendar month, and the Index ratio applicable to any month will be equal to the Index figure applicable to that month divided by the Index figure applicable to June 1992.

11.  The amount due on repayment, per £100 nominal of Stock, will be £100 multiplied by the Index ratio applicable to the month in which repayment takes place. This amount, expressed in pounds sterling to four

301

places of decimals rounded to the nearest figure below, will be announced by the Bank of England not later than the business day immediately preceding the date of the penultimate interest payment.

12. Interest will be payable half-yearly on 22nd January and 22nd July. Income tax will be deducted from payments of more than £5 per annum. Interest warrants will be transmitted by post. The first interest payment will be made on 22nd January 1993 at the rate of £2.6102 per £100 nominal of Stock.

13. Each subsequent half-yearly interest payment will be at a rate, per £100 nominal of Stock, of £2.0625 multiplied by the Index ratio applicable to the month in which the payment falls due.

14. The rate of interest for each interest payment other than the first, expressed as a percentage in pounds sterling to four places of decimals rounded to the nearest figure below, will be announced by the Bank of England not later than the business day immediately preceding the date of the previous interest payment.

15. If the Index is revised to a new base after the Stock is issued, it will be necessary, for the purposes of the preceding paragraphs, to calculate and use a notional Index figure in substitution for the Index figure applicable to the month in which repayment takes place and/or an interest payment falls due ("the month of payment"). This notional Index figure will be calculated by multiplying the actual Index figure applicable to the month of payment by the Index figure on the old base for the month on which the revised Index is based and dividing the product by the new base figure for the same month. This procedure will be used for each occasion on which a revision is made during the life of the Stock.

16. If the Index is not published for a month for which it is relevant for the purposes of this notice, the Bank of England will nominate a substitute Index figure which shall be an Index figure applicable to the month of payment published as a substitute figure by the Central Statistical Office of the Chancellor of the Exchequer, and such substitute Index figure shall be used for all purposes for which the actual Index figure would have been relevant. The calculation by the Bank of England of the amounts of principal and/or interest payable on the basis of a substitute Index figure shall be conclusive and binding upon all stockholders.

17. If any change should be made to the coverage or the basic calculation of the Index which, in the opinion of the Bank of England, constitutes a fundamental change in the Index which would be materially detrimental to the interests of stockholders, Her Majesty's Treasury will publish a notice in the London, Edinburgh and Belfast Gazettes immediately following the announcement by the relevant Government Department of the change, informing stockholders and offering them the right to require Her Majesty's Treasury to redeem their stock. For the purposes of this paragraph, repayment to stockholders who exercise this right will be effected, on a date to be chosen by Her Majesty's Treasury, not later than seven months from the last month of publication of the old Index. The amount of principal due on repayment and of any interest which has accrued will be calculated on the basis of the Index ratio applicable to the month in which repayment takes place. A notice setting out the administrative arrangements will be sent to stockholders at their registered address by the Bank of England at the appropriate time.

18. The terms of issue of this Stock are such that it will fall within the definition of a qualifying indexed security in paragraph 2 of Schedule 11 to the Finance Act 1989 and the Inland Revenue has confirmed that it will treat it as such. The Stock will therefore not be a deep gain security for the purposes of that schedule. Further issues of this Stock may be made in circumstances such that the Stock then issued does not constitute a qualifying indexed security and in certain cases this could result in all of the Stock issued under this notice being treated thereafter as a deep gain security. However, it is the intention of Her Majesty's Treasury that further issues of Stock under this notice will be conducted so as to prevent any of the Stock being treated as a deep gain security for United Kingdom tax purposes. Provided the Stock is neither a deep gain security nor treated as a deep gain security, any difference between the price at which the Stock is issued and the amount paid on repayment of the Stock will not constitute income for the purposes of Schedule 11 to the Finance Act 1989.

19. Copies of this notice may be obtained by post from the Bank of England, New Issues, Southgate House, Southgate Street, Gloucester, GL1 1UW; at the Central Gilts Office, Bank of England, 1 Bank Buildings, Princes Street, London, EC2R 8EU or at any of the Branches or Agencies of the Bank of England; at the Bank of Ireland, Moyne Buildings, 1st Floor, 20 Callender Street, Belfast, BT1 5BN; or at any office of The International Stock Exchange in the United Kingdom.

*Government Statement*
Attention is drawn to the statement issued by Her Majesty's Treasury on 29th May 1985 which explained that, in the interest of the orderly conduct of fiscal policy, neither Her Majesty's Government nor the Bank of England or their respective servants or agents undertake to disclose tax changes decided on but not yet announced, even where they may specifically affect the terms on which, or the conditions under which, this Stock is issued or sold by or on behalf of the Government or the Bank; that no responsibility can therefore be accepted for any omission to make such disclosure; and that such omission shall neither render any transaction liable to be set aside nor give rise to any claim for compensation.

BANK OF ENGLAND
LONDON

12th June 1992